ReFocus: The Films of Pablo Larraín

ReFocus: The International Directors Series

Series Editors: Robert Singer, Stefanie Van de Peer, and Gary D. Rhodes

Editorial Board: Lizelle Bisschoff, Stephanie Hemelryck Donald, Anna Misiak, and Des O'Rawe

ReFocus is a series of contemporary methodological and theoretical approaches to the interdisciplinary analyses and interpretations of international film directors, from the celebrated to the ignored, in direct relationship to their respective culture—its myths, values, and historical precepts—and the broader parameters of international film history and theory. The series provides a forum for introducing a broad spectrum of directors, working in and establishing movements, trends, cycles, and genres including those historical, currently popular, or emergent, and in need of critical assessment or reassessment. It ignores no director who created a historical space—either in or outside of the studio system—beginning with the origins of cinema and up to the present. *ReFocus* brings these film directors to a new audience of scholars and general readers of Film Studies.

Titles in the series include:

ReFocus: The Films of Susanne Bier
Edited by Missy Molloy, Mimi Nielsen, and Meryl Shriver-Rice

ReFocus: The Films of Francis Veber
Keith Corson

ReFocus: The Films of Jia Zhangke
Maureen Turim and Ying Xiao

ReFocus: The Films of Xavier Dolan
Edited by Andrée Lafontaine

ReFocus: The Films of Pedro Costa: Producing and Consuming Contemporary Art Cinema
Nuno Barradas Jorge

ReFocus: The Films of Sohrab Shahid Saless: Exile, Displacement and the Stateless Moving Image
Edited by Azadeh Fatehrad

ReFocus: The Films of Pablo Larraín
Edited by Laura Hatry

ReFocus: The Films of Michel Gondry
Edited by Marcelline Block and Jennifer Kirby

edinburghuniversitypress.com/series/refocint

ReFocus:
The Films of Pablo Larraín

Edited by Laura Hatry

EDINBURGH
University Press

Edinburgh University Press is one of the leading university presses in the UK. We publish academic books and journals in our selected subject areas across the humanities and social sciences, combining cutting-edge scholarship with high editorial and production values to produce academic works of lasting importance. For more information visit our website: edinburghuniversitypress.com

© editorial matter and organisation Laura Hatry, 2020, 2022
© the chapters their several authors, 2020, 2022

Edinburgh University Press Ltd
The Tun—Holyrood Road
12 (2f) Jackson's Entry
Edinburgh EH8 8PJ

First published in hardback by Edinburgh University Press 2020

Typeset in 11/13 Ehrhardt MT by
IDSUK (DataConnection) Ltd

A CIP record for this book is available from the British Library

ISBN 978 1 4744 4828 4 (hardback)
ISBN 978 1 4744 4829 1 (paperback)
ISBN 978 1 4744 4830 7 (webready PDF)
ISBN 978 1 4744 4831 4 (epub)

The right of the contributors to be identified as authors of this work has been asserted in accordance with the Copyright, Designs and Patents Act 1988 and the Copyright and Related Rights Regulations 2003 (SI No. 2498).

Contents

List of Figures   vii
Notes on Contributors   ix
Acknowledgments   xii

    An Introduction. Pablo Larraín: Doomed to Repeat It   1
    Laura Hatry

1 A Cracked Gaze: Pablo Larraín's Cultural Context   15
    Arturo Márquez-Gómez

2 The Synecdochic Series of Pablo Larraín: The Castro Cycle of Chilean Complicity in *Fuga*, *Tony Manero*, *Post Mortem*, *No*, *El Club*, and *Neruda*   38
    Amanda Eaton McMenamin

3 "Within the Limits of the Possible": Realist Aesthetics in Pablo Larraín's Dictatorship Trilogy   69
    Berenike Jung

4 When Violence Meets Experimentalism: Unraveling Cinematic Suture in Raúl Ruiz's *Tres Tristes Tigres* and Pablo Larraín's *Post Mortem*   89
    Eduardo Ledesma

5 Gothic Memory and Ghostly Aesthetics: *Post Mortem* as a Horror Film   113
    Rosana Díaz-Zambrana

6 Aestheticization of Politics and the War Machine in *No* by Pablo Larraín   131
    Ignasi Gozalo-Salellas and Xavier Dapena

7	Adaptation and the Use of Documentary Material in *No* Laura Hatry	147
8	The Blurred Image: The Aesthetics of Impunity in Pablo Larraín's *No* and *El Club* Susana Domingo Amestoy	161
9	Reimagining the Left in *Neruda*: Inclusivity and Encounters with Secondary Characters Rachel VanWieren and Victoria L. Garrett	177
10	Surfaces in *Jackie*: Representing Crisis and the Crisis of Representation James Harvey	196
11	"When on Stage, I Am Not There, I Am Not That One" An Interview with Alfredo Castro by Arturo Márquez-Gómez	213
Index		225

Figures

1.1	Alfredo Castro performing Claudio in Larraín's *Fuga*	17
1.2	Evelyn after the whole process of crossdressing and make-up	22
1.3	Alfredo Castro as Raúl Peralta	29
2.1	Mario Cornejo's sly smile upon being informed that he now serves Pinochet's Chile	47
2.2	Raúl Peralta mimes the lines to *Saturday Night Fever*	49
2.3	The abject body of Claudio Leal in the psychiatric ward	59
3.1	*Tony Manero* (2008)	74
3.2	*Post mortem* (2010)	80
3.3	*No* (2012)	81
4.1	Eccentric camera placement	96
4.2	Narrow POV from underside of tank	100
4.3	An emotionless Mario transcribes Allende's autopsy	105
5.1	Mario's body lying on bed	120
5.2	A recurrent cinematic motif of a ghostlike Mario	122
5.3	A disturbing and yet undramatic final shot	126
7.1	Patricio Aylwin in *No*	152
7.2	Remediated material from the No campaign video showing Patricio Aylwin	152
7.3	Patricio Bañados in *No*	153
7.4	Patricio Bañados in the original No campaign video	153
8.1	A blurred image with Fernando and Urrutia's heads missing	166
8.2	Sandokan's gaze, a long take, impunity in jeopardy	172
9.1	A man in drag kisses Neruda inside a brothel	185
9.2	Working-class communist woman Silvia challenges Neruda	187
10.1	Jackie prepares for a campaign event	200

10.2	Remediating archive footage in the camera operator's screen	203
10.3	Remediating archival photography on the surface of the windshield	204
10.4	Restaging the swearing-in of Johnson	206
11.1	Theater company La Memoria performing *La manzana de Adán*	216
11.2	Theater company La Memoria performing *Historia de la sangre*	221

Notes on Contributors

Xavier Dapena is an Assistant Professor of Spanish at Iowa State University and his research explores the forms of politicization on graphic narrative with a Cultural Studies approach. He received an MFA in Audiovisual Production from the University of A Coruña, an MA in Spanish and Spanish American Literature from the University of Colorado at Boulder, and an MA in Hispanic Studies with a Certificate in Cinema Studies from the University of Pennsylvania. He has published several articles in scholarly journals and edited volumes.

Rosana Díaz-Zambrana is Professor of Spanish at Rollins College. She completed her PhD in Comparative Literature at the University of Illinois at Urbana-Champaign. She has co-edited *Cinema paraíso: Representaciones e imágenes audiovisuales en el Caribe hispano* (Isla Negra, 2010) and *Horrofílmico: Aproximaciones al cine de terror en Latinoamérica y el Caribe* (2012). In 2015, she published the anthology, *Terra zombi: El fenómeno transnacional de los muertos vivientes*.

Susana Domingo Amestoy is Assistant Professor at the University of Massachusetts Boston, where she teaches Latin American and Iberian Studies and Cinema Studies. She has published articles on Spanish and Latin American literature and film and is currently working on a book project on the aesthetics of impunity in the films of a new generation of Chilean filmmakers.

Victoria L. Garrett is author of *Performing Everyday Life: Argentine Popular Theater, 1890–1934* (2018) and co-author of *The Improbable Conquest: Letters from the Río de la Plata, 1537–1556* (2015). Her articles on Argentine literature and theater, as well as violence, illness, and disability in contemporary Latin American film, have appeared in several journals and edited volumes.

Ignasi Gozalo-Salellas holds a PhD in Hispanic Studies at the University of Pennsylvania. He is currently Visiting Assistant Professor at the Ohio State University, where he teaches Iberian Visual Cultures. He is also an Affiliated Faculty of the Film Studies Program at the Ohio State University. His research focuses on theories of transmedia discourses and archives. Besides his academic career, he is also a filmmaker with a wide and long experience in television, documentaries, and experimental formats. He is co-author of the book *El síntoma Trump* (Lengua de Trapo, 2019) and is currently working on a manuscript about counter-hegemonic audiovisual works in Spain after Francoism.

James Harvey is a lecturer in Film Studies at the University of Sussex. His research focuses on the politics of contemporary art cinema, artists' film, and documentary. He is the author of *Jacques Rancière and the Politics of Art Cinema* (Edinburgh University Press, 2018) and the editor of *Nationalism in Contemporary Western European Cinema* (2018). He is currently writing the first monograph devoted to the career of British-Ghanaian artist-filmmaker, John Akomfrah.

Laura Hatry earned her PhD from Universidad Autónoma de Madrid in Hispanic Studies. Her research focuses on cinematic adaptations of Latin American literary works, as well as other convergences (and divergences) among the arts. In addition, she holds an MA in Contemporary Art History and Visual Culture from the Reina Sofía Museum in Madrid and a postgraduate certification in Library Science. She also works as a professional translator.

Berenike Jung is a lecturer in Film Studies at King's College London. She previously held a post as teaching fellow at the Institute of Media Studies, University of Tübingen. She received her PhD in Film and Television Studies from the University of Warwick in 2016. Her book, *The Invisibilities of Torture: The Presence of Absence in US and Chilean Cinema and Television* is forthcoming with Edinburgh University Press, and she co-edited the anthology *Beyond the Rhetoric of Pain* with Stella Bruzzi (2019). She is currently working on the role of affect, performativity, voice, and agency in moving image formats such as in GIFs and TikTok.

Eduardo Ledesma is an Associate Professor of Spanish at the University of Illinois at Urbana-Champaign, where he teaches Hispanic and Lusophone literature, film, and new media. After a first career as a Structural Engineer, he received his PhD in Romance Languages and Literatures from Harvard University in 2012. He is the author of *Radical Poetry: Aesthetics, Politics, Technology, and the Ibero-American Avant-Gardes, 1900–2015* (2016). His articles on film, new media, and digital literature have appeared in the *Studies in*

Spanish and Latin American Cinemas, Arizona Journal of Hispanic Cultural Studies, Revista Iberoamericana, Revista Hispánica Moderna, and the *Revista de Estudios Hispánicos*, among other venues. He is currently completing a book titled *Cinemas of Marginality: Experimental, Avant-Garde and Documentary Film in Ibero-America*.

Arturo Márquez-Gómez is an Assistant Professor of Spanish at the University of the South (USA). His research explores contemporary audiovisual and multimedia practices in the Hispanic and Latino world, with a focus on issues related to queerness, gender, and sexuality. He is currently working on a book of interviews with Chilean women filmmakers.

Amanda Eaton McMenamin earned her PhD from Johns Hopkins University and is currently Associate Professor of Spanish at Wilson College in Chambersburg, Pennsylvania. Recent work includes the co-edited volume, *A Cuban Cinema Companion* (2019), in addition to journal articles in *Verbeia* (2016), *Short Story Journal* (2016), and *Ámbitos feministas* (2018). Recent anthology pieces appear in *The Routledge Companion to Food and Literature* (2018), *Making Strangers: Outsiders, Aliens, and Foreigners* (2018), and *Shifting Subjectivities in Contemporary Fiction and Film from Spain* (2018). Forthcoming is a co-edited anthology, *ReFocus: The Films of Carlos Reygadas* (Edinburgh University Press, 2021).

Rachel VanWieren is an Associate Professor of Spanish at National University in Los Angeles. Her research focuses on Chilean literature and film, with a particular interest in fictional portrayals of workers and labor movements. She has published a number of articles on representations in Chilean fiction of Patagonia's colonization and settlement. Her most recent work is "Reconsidering the Patagonian Worker Movements of the 1920s: Francisco Coloane's and Luis Sepúlveda's Rebellious Chilotes" in *A Contracorriente* (2017) and "Sketching Social Mobility in the Gold Rushes of California and Patagonia: Bret Harte and Manuel Rojas" in *Hispanófila* (2015).

Acknowledgments

I am very grateful to the series editors, Robert Singer, Gary D. Rhodes, and Stefanie Van de Peer for their unflagging enthusiasm and wonderful support at every stage of the editorial process. At Edinburgh University Press, my thanks to Richard Strachan, Gillian Leslie, Eddie Clark, and Rebecca Mackenzie, who graciously accompanied me in the production of this book and were always quick to resolve any questions that arose. Of course, without its insightful and conscientious contributors this collection would have never seen the light of day, and I would like to extend my gratitude to all of them for their magnificent work.

Finally, my deepest thanks belong to Heide Hatry, John Wronoski, and Layla Ferrández Melero for their counsel and encouragement during the course of this project.

Laura Hatry

An Introduction. Pablo Larraín: Doomed to Repeat It

Laura Hatry

Although his career began only in 2006, Pablo Larraín is recognized as one of the most prominent filmmakers in contemporary Chilean cinema—in fact, he has forged himself an important niche in not only the Chilean, or Latin American, but even the international film world, created his own cinematic language, and established a focused critical dialogue about Chile's recent past through his work. So far, he has directed the rather neglected *Fuga* (2006), a critically acclaimed dictatorship trilogy—*Tony Manero* (2008), *Post mortem* (2010), and *No* (2012)—and more recently, *El club* (2015), *Neruda* (2016), and *Jackie* (2016).[1] His work presents a harsh portrait of his country's tortured history and its current reality in a direct, honest, sometimes surprising, and often controversial series of films, never retreating in the face of violence or painful truths about the past. Nevertheless, in-depth academic analysis of his work is scant, and no book-length English-language critical anthology has yet focused on his work. The present collection of essays by scholars offering a wide range of historical, critical, and interdisciplinary perspectives will provide a multi-faceted appraisal of all of his films, and of his films overall.

In the 1990s, Chilean cinema enjoyed a resurgence following nearly two decades of suppression and censorship under the Pinochet dictatorship. The slogan chosen for the International Film Festival of Viña del Mar in 1990 was, accordingly, *Reencuentro de Chile con su Cine* (*Chile's Reencounter with its Cinema*). A series of events that strengthened national filmmaking took place in the following years: the creation of the Association of Short Film Directors, the foundation of Cine-Chile, and the creation of the National Council of Culture and the Arts. All these eventually led to the passing, in 2004, of Law No. 19.981 for Audiovisual Promotion, commonly known as the Cinema Law, emphasizing the relationship between cinema and the state, recognizing film as cultural heritage, and asserting its importance for "the preservation of national identity and the development of culture and education."[2] Furthermore, the foundation of the Escuela de Cine de Chile (the Film School of Chile) in 1995 marked a milestone for the country's film industry, giving aspiring young Chilean directors—including students such as Matías Bize and Sebastián Lelio—the opportunity to train for their careers in a formal setting, which launched a broader interest in bringing audiovisual studies to the universities, ultimately giving rise to the *novísimo cine chileno* (Newest Chilean Cinema). Ascanio Cavallo and Gonzalo Maza coined this notion of the *novísimos* in which they include, along with Pablo Larraín, and among others, Matías Bize (*Sábado / Saturday*, 2003), Sebastián Lelio (*La sagrada familia / The Sacred Family*, 2007), Alicia Scherson (*Play*, 2005), Alberto Fuguet (*Se arrienda / For Rent*, 2005), Sebastián Silva (*La nana / The Maid*, 2009), Alejandro Fernández Almendras (*Huacho*, 2009), and José Luis Sepúlveda and Carolina Adriazola (*El pejesapo / The Goosefish*, 2007). These directors are the product of what might be seen as a new institutionality in Chilean film, one in which cinema is understood as a career, whether in public or private educational institutions, and where semiprivate entities such as CinemaChile[3] provide economic support for promotion and distribution. All the previously mentioned changes have contributed to a transnational and experimental vision of cinema that has resulted in a diversity of perspectives and themes. Cavallo and Maza suggest that, on the national level, these directors are intimately connected to the Nuevo Cine Chileno (New Chilean Cinema) from the 1960s, which is also the origin of their accepted generational name, deeply educated in the works of Sergio Bravo, Miguel Littín, Pedro Chaskel, Patricio Guzmán, and particularly Raúl Ruiz: "the most inspired and rebellious generation in the history of our cinema."[4] More globally, Cavallo and Maza argue that the *novísimos* have been powerfully affected by directors like the Dardenne brothers, Béla Tarr, Jim Jarmusch, Aki Kaurismäki, and Apichatpong Weerasethakul.

But even among his contemporaries, and in spite of the experience and influences that unite them, Larraín's intensive focus on and complex approach to an understanding of the recent past is unusual. Whereas most cinematic recounting of the dictatorship consists of documentaries, with some rare exceptions, such as Andrés Wood's much acclaimed *Machuca* (2004) and Ricardo Larraín's early treatment of exile in *La frontera*, from 1991, the historical weight of the Pinochet era pervades Larraín's work even when he has taken pains to keep it well in the background. In this sense, he does share the generational aesthetic concerns of his fellow *novísimos* in "an interest in intimate space as a territory of conflict."[5]

Of course, their intimate space is explored in different ways by different directors, and even the notions of the subject that prevail in their respective works vary enormously. In contrast with the films of the 1990s, the political is rarely if ever an explicit part of the main plot any longer, and these contemporary narratives are, as Carolina Urrutia observes, "projected from a perspective of the individual, the subjective, implying a cinematic worldview in which the political finally pervades all of the possible interstices in the story."[6] Their characters typically express their relationship to history and the present situation, however involved or marginal they may be, through their personal malaise or political indifference. In Urrutia's view, the dictatorship is depicted in Larraín's work in the way it affects his characters' psychology and is artistically represented through the fragment, the ruin, and the marginal. Overt examples of this abound in *Tony Manero* and *Post mortem*: the glass stage made from discarded materials or the humble disco ball made from fragments of mirrors glued to a soccer ball. Larraín's cinematographic gaze has, accordingly, been mediated by his own time and its cultural inclinations, such that, in his imagining of Chile under dictatorship, he focuses on ways of being that, in the midst of authoritarianism, violence, and censorship, serve to develop new languages and artistic approaches to experience.

Born in 1976 to a family associated with Chile's conservative, aristocratic right wing, Larraín did not live the terror of the September 11, 1973 military coup, and though this has not discouraged him from imaginative encounters with those times, he has also been subjected to criticism on account of both his family history and his way of looking at the past. In an interview, he explained how the topic of the dictatorship became a central motif in his work:

> I was never exposed to poverty. So in a way, my life during the dictatorship was comfortable and completely out of danger . . . When I realized what happened in this country, I was 15, 16. I felt that I had missed something, [I wanted to] understand it, not to experience it—not even to tell it, just to expose it.[7]

His vision of the time has been challenging for those who directly experienced its horrors—exile, torture, death—and this is a site of constant critique of Larraín's trilogy. His view of the past is, after all, one that, according to Urrutia, is mediated by "a lens that carries a filter of 20 years of democracy."[8]

After graduating from the University for the Arts, Sciences, and Communication in Santiago, Larraín co-founded, along with his brother Juan de Dios Larraín, the film and advertising production company, Fabula, in 2004. His career as a producer might be less well known than his achievements as a filmmaker, but is certainly worth noting, given that he can reasonably be considered Chile's major current producer. Most significant among his productions are *Gloria* (2013) and *Una mujer fantástica* (*A Fantastic Woman*, 2017), both directed by Sebastián Lelio and both selected as the Chilean submission for the Academy Award for Best Foreign Language Film, and while the first was not nominated, the second was not only nominated but became the first Chilean submission ever to win this Academy Award. Such work demonstrates not only Larraín's abiding commitment to Chilean film, but also his interest in giving voice to risky or daring subjects and his determination to revolutionize the mainstream media: following its critical acclaim, Daniela Vega, the star of *A Fantastic Woman*, was selected as the first openly trans woman to be a presenter at the Oscars.

Larraín's first film, *Fuga*, concerns a Chilean musician, Eliseo (Benjamín Vicuña), who has witnessed the rape and murder of his sister. During the rape, the piano upon which she is lying produces an accidental melody with which Eliseo becomes obsessed, gradually going insane and ending up in a psychiatric hospital. Though the movie initially received some critical applause, notably at the 2007 edition of the International Film Festival of Cartagena, he soon came under criticism, on the one hand unfairly, for his right-wing family background,[9] on the other, for the film itself: "[he was] accused of being overly ambitious, of using techniques from the publicity sector, with nods to classic cinema, and its own excesses made the film implausible."[10] Arturo Márquez-Gómez revisits *Fuga* in his chapter, "A Cracked Gaze: Pablo Larraín's Cultural Context," in which he analyzes how Larraín's vision has been forged by radical and avant-garde artistic projects developed during and after the dictatorship. The so-called *escena de avanzada* (avant-garde scene), a group of artists whose work sought to elude and subvert the semiotics of authoritarianism, erasing homogeneous disciplinary limits and rejecting the prevailing conventions of art, was one of the major art movements in Chile, studied in depth by Nelly Richard. Their work extended beyond the years of the dictatorship and informed the subsequent period of artistic development during the transition to democracy. In this period, artists like Diamela Eltit, Paz Errázuriz, and Pedro Lemebel would depict characters who, like those recreated by Larraín, examine and question the rationality of the national discourse from positions of social marginality. These include, for example, transgender sex workers, psychiatric patients, errant and obsessive madmen, vagabonds, or criminals moved by passion. *Fuga*, *Tony Manero*, and *Post mortem* are also informed by the concerns not only of more mainstream global and national cinema, but also by these dissident artistic explorations. Márquez-Gómez argues that the avant-garde scene, the photography of Paz Errázuriz, the texts and the persona of Pedro Lemebel, and the insightful theatrical techniques pioneered by the theater company La Memoria are crucial to situate and appreciate Larraín's cinematic project in the embattled cultural context of post-dictatorship in Chile. In the case of *Fuga*, the imagery of madness and the space of the asylum is rooted in the photographic monograph *El infarto del alma* by Errázuriz and Eltit, while Claudio (Alfredo Castro) is inspired by Lemebel's *Manifiesto*. And Lemebel's vivid characters and intense descriptions of the city during the curfew are crucial to the depiction of the psycho-cinemapath Raúl (Alfredo Castro) in *Tony Manero*. Finally, Márquez-Gómez contends that Larraín's casting itself provides subversive strategies for sabotaging the normative order imposed by the dictatorship and its neoliberal legacy, aligning Larraín's controversial opus with artistic experiences that critically innervated the cultural field during and after the dictatorship.[11]

To shed more light on the ways Larraín works with his actors, we have included an interview that Márquez-Gómez conducted with Alfredo Castro, who has starred in a great number of roles in Larraín's films. In it, Castro discusses his personal experience working with Larraín, the theatrical innovations of La Memoria, and how Larraín's own conception of acting permeates the films, as well as Castro's personal analysis of certain aspects of Larraín's filmmaking. He is, for example, of the opinion that the trilogy is not comprised of the films traditionally included by the critics, but, instead of *No*, it is rather *El club* that constitutes its finale, specifically noting the divergent language in which *No* has been composed.

Amanda Eaton McMenamin takes up related themes in her chapter discussing Castro's importance in Larraín's films, entitled "The Synecdochic Series of Pablo Larraín: The Castro Cycle of Chilean Complicity in *Fuga* (2006), *Tony Manero* (2008), *Post Mortem* (2010), *No* (2012), *El Club* (2015), and *Neruda* (2016)," in which she argues that the actor as protagonist functions as representative for "the Chilean nation and its positionality of subservience to the hegemonic social, political, and economic forces of northern-born neoliberalism in the region." Like Castro himself, McMenamin contends that the trilogy should be extended to what she calls the *synecdochic series*, that is, instead of replacing *No* with *El club*, adding *Fuga*, *El club*, and *Neruda*. This expanded series is connected through Castro as a central character as well as via cinematic techniques such as *monumental temporality*, and what McMenamin calls "Chile's neoliberal nexus of *high-density capitalism*." In her chapter, she delves into Larraín's character construction and also explains how he created a cinematic cosmos that relies on the denunciation of Chilean complicity with the neoliberal, North American model: here, as always, one should keep in mind that Pinochet's bloody coup was, after all, US-backed. She shows that even *Fuga*, otherwise eccentric though it might seem, supports such a view, as the main character's degeneration—both mentally and physically, as a result of shock treatment—can be seen as representative of the neoliberal decay that has begotten contemporary Chile. Particularly noteworthy is her analysis of what she calls *extreme jump cuts*, "that portray, temporally, the eternal return of Chilean capitulation to US interventionism." In this respect, it is also important to recognize the national specificity of Larraín's cinema: though he lacks a robust national audience, his determination to make Chilean issues the focus of his films and to criticize Chile's involvement in neoliberalism has never waned.

In *Tony Manero*, set in 1978 in Santiago de Chile during the height of Pinochet's dictatorship, clandestine acts of dissidence and solidarity—efforts to overcome daily struggles such as the *ollas comunes* (common pots of food), for example—appear as mere background. While Goyo (Héctor Morales), the film's most politically active character, is literally shit upon, Larraín focuses instead on a marginal and alienated subject, Raúl Peralta, who is obsessed with Tony Manero, the character John Travolta played in the mass pop culture phenomenon, *Saturday Night Fever* (John Badham, 1977), and portrays the larger social sphere as a fragile and treacherous space of encounter. He thereby reveals the monstrous effects that US popular culture, imposed in many ways, but very powerfully through cinema, has had in Chile. Larraín himself remarks concerning *Tony Manero*:

> In 1976 Pinochet hired a few young people who were studying at Chicago University, with all these new capitalist systems that they were learning over there with Milton Friedman, and he put these Chicago boys into the government. So Chile became an open-market economy and, when he did that, a lot of things changed socially. We began to import a lot of stuff, cultural and economic. And that's what the film is about. The Pinochet regime did enormous damage to our folk traditions. Pinochet was very ignorant. He probably never watched cinema in his life. He certainly didn't care about it.[12]

Even though some critics have complained that he does not treat the dictatorship explicitly enough, one could well argue that he actually does engage it quite particularly, only through a different lens. Just as the campaign against the Pinochet regime remained in the background of the narrative in *Tony Manero*, in *Post mortem*, Mario Cornejo's (Alfredo Castro) fictional story, inspired by the assistant coroner during the Allende autopsy in September 1973, the massive pile of bodies in the Santiago morgue—an image seen earlier in Costa-Gavras's 1982 film *Missing*, which was banned in Chile for many years—is the backdrop against which events unfold, rather than their centerpiece. At the precise moment the coup is under way, Mario is in the shower, unaware of the fact that history is being made just outside; the camera, however, with its extra-diegetic consciousness, lets the viewer know what is going on.

The final film in Larraín's unintentional trilogy is *No*, set in 1988 during the plebiscite that ousted Pinochet from power. Now US interests have shifted, and it is the No campaign that is receiving its financial support. Thus, both in the rise of Pinochet and during his fall, it is US hegemony and neoliberalism that set the tone, meaning, of course, that the US has continued to make its problematic influence felt well into Chile's return to democracy, which Larraín reflects by showing how a smart marketing campaign managed to win the referendum, promoting it the same way as it had previously promoted a soft drink.

In her chapter, "'Within the Limits of the Possible': Realist Aesthetics in Pablo Larraín's Dictatorship Trilogy," Berenike Jung provides a comprehensive formal and aesthetic analysis of the dictatorship trilogy. She contends that Larraín's films "reference but also renegotiate key features of realism, establishing cross-connections with previous and transnational cinema movements, and adding supplementary information to specific audience groups." A corporeal metaphor, already central in historical neorealism, plays a crucial role in anchoring the reference of the films to the real: the body reflects the schizophrenia of the system in *Tony Manero*, where social trust and a public sphere have all but disappeared, the previously mentioned pile of bodies in *Post mortem* implying the fungibility of human "stuff"; and in *No*, an aura of authenticity is created by employing historical bodies, as well as the archival "body" of the film within an otherwise fictionalized narrative. These aesthetic strategies are put into context with Chile's historical and contemporary cinematic landscape, including the influence of the global festival circuit and the overwhelming gravitational field of realist tendencies in world cinema.

While Jung focuses on the influence of those realist tendencies, Eduardo Ledesma takes a closer look at *Post mortem* in comparison to Raúl Ruiz's acclaimed *Tres tristes tigres* (*Three Sad Tigers*, 1968), since both films experiment with a thematic and formal violence that has been characteristic of Chilean film since the creation of the Grupo Cine Experimental in the 1950s. This chapter—"When Violence Meets Experimentalism: Unraveling Cinematic Suture in Raúl Ruiz's *Tres Tristes Tigres* (1968) and Pablo Larraín's *Post Mortem* (2010)"—argues that it is the violence itself, perpetrated on the spectator through cinematic suture, that holds the key to both works. The analysis of the respective uses of these experimental techniques aims at demonstrating that they do not serve the same political purpose, and while Ruiz's film subverts realist codes and uses violence as a means of exposing social inequality, Larraín's use of similar techniques can be seen as "minimalist, detached, and even dehistoricizing." Ledesma goes so far as to suggest that while *Tres tristes tigres* seeks social change, *Post mortem* only retraumatizes the viewer, who is left with "a grey and amorphous empty sensation, a state of driftlessness, all expectation banished." His analysis and criticism differ strongly from many others represented here, and, in particular, can be viewed as an adversarial dialogue with James Harvey's position, which sees a democratizing potential in Larraín's political ambivalence and cold minimalism. Ledesma, on the contrary, contends that it does not conduce to a political response, but rather serves "to deaden the senses of the viewing subject, to induce a sense of apathetic hopelessness" and even that "a film like that rather easily slips into the neoliberal mechanism for erasing, forgetting, and distorting the past." He thereby calls into question exactly what most other critics in this volume have argued for and, in fact, what Larraín in general seems to see himself as doing.

Rosana Díaz-Zambrana looks at *Post mortem* from a completely different angle in her chapter, "Gothic Memory and Ghostly Aesthetics: *Post Mortem* as a Horror Film," in which she shows how Larraín has used components of the horror film to deal with the oblivion of the past. She establishes a dialogue with Vania Barraza's assessment about living characters who represent Chile's history in the dictatorship trilogy by showing that the undead occupy an important space as well, since they can be understood as a symbolic debt that Chilean society owes to its own history. She further suggests that Larraín parts company with his contemporaries in choosing to incorporate genres rooted in the commercial culture industry—in this case, the thriller, the Gothic, and body horror—instead of focusing on trauma, as in most other Chilean political drama, within the framework inherited from the New Latin American Cinema of the 1960s. According to Ledesma, *Post mortem* avoids the historical truth, refusing to acknowledge the past and envision a better future, while Díaz-Zambrana—much like Harvey and Barraza, or Mariana Johnson with regard to *Tony Manero*—argues that Larraín consciously uses ellipses to awaken the audience and thereby enables the Gothic memory to trigger "the spectator's active role in reading the negative space and the suggestive implications of the off-screen." From this perspective, *Post mortem* utilizes the haunting phenomenon—the uncanny, the liminal, and the return of the repressed—as a filmic narrative device, but also exploits spatial, symbolic, and visual effects associated with the horror genre film tradition as an alternative means of denouncing the nation's traumatic past.

In their essay, "Aestheticization of Politics and the War Machine in *No* (2012) by Pablo Larraín," Ignasi Gozalo-Salellas and Xavier Dapena analyze *No* within the framework of Walter Benjamin's "aestheticization of politics," from 1930, and Jacques Rancière's response in "Politics of Aesthetics," from 2005. In their analysis of the conflicting positions of the protagonists and the politics as spectacle versus the representation of history, Gozalo-Salellas and Dapena interpret the film as a "war machine"—as proposed by Gilles Deleuze and Félix Guattari—presenting a progressive aestheticization of the political. They also interpret the film as a metalinguistic exercise in "simulacrum" and read the camera as a metaphor for the body politic. That is, Larraín reveals the camera's point of view when the No campaign has its say and hides it when the State, the panoptical authority, is watching. Díaz-Zambrana suggests, similarly, that Mario's surreptitious gaze from the window in *Post mortem* may be seen as a surveillance metaphor for the militarized state. In her chapter, "Adaptation and the Use of Documentary Material in *No*," Laura Hatry analyzes Larraín's adaptation of *No* from the play, *El plebiscito*, by Antonio

Skármeta, through a close reading and textual analysis of the unpublished play, focusing especially on the ideological shift from one work to another. Given the vital importance of archival elements in both the play and the film, this chapter also aims at shedding light on the way in which Larraín incorporates historic, documentary footage, and the real participants in the 1988 referendum into his work. For example, Patricio Bañados and Patricio Aylwin make appearances in *No* in the same clothing they wore in 1988, but without trying to hide their age some twenty-four years later. These shots, appearing as if they had been taken right before the moment the No campaign went on air, are merged with the original footage by means of careful montage. The construction of this spatial–temporal continuity effectively enables Larraín to visually erase the boundaries between fact and fiction, similar to Oliver Stone's *JFK* (1991). Both chapters ponder over the use of advertising language and techniques borrowed from the neoliberal system and the consumer society imported from the US to bring down a regime that had been erected on those very pillars.

Shortly before *No* was released, in 2011, Larraín accepted the job of co-directing (alongside Jonathan Jakubowicz) the HBO Latin America series *Prófugos* (*Fugitives*). The story focuses on a family who convinces their eldest son to become the head of their drug cartel following his father's death. When a planned drug deal—to smuggle liquid cocaine across the Bolivian–Chilean border—goes awry, the son and his three companions are forced to go on the run. As tensions arise among them, Larraín proves that his talent for character construction is equally fitted to the television format as to feature-length films. He maintains a dark atmosphere within a network of corruption, antagonistic interests, and ambitions, where most characters have a mysterious past and are not who they first seem to be: one of the most interesting characters is the mother, who directs the cartel from prison, subverting the typical macho male narco-leader role. Visually, the series also meets Larraín's usual standards, and both the Atacama Desert, at an altitude of four thousand meters, and the freezing Chilean South provide the perfect backdrop. The second season (2013) opens with the spectacular escape of two of the protagonists during which sixty-four other inmates die, leaving the Chilean president with some explaining to do. This scene, in a series seemingly detached from historical events, is in fact inspired by two real-life occurrences: the fire at the San Miguel prison that killed eighty-one inmates in 2010, and the 1986 massacre in the Carandiru Penitentiary in São Paulo, during which 111 prisoners died when military police stormed the prison after riots had broken out.

During this period, Larraín also directed the opera *Katia Kabanova*, by Leoš Janáček, which premiered in 2014. Just as in his cinematographic works, Larraín paid close attention to the audiovisual staging of the piece: together with Cristián Jofré, he produced a hyper-real recreation of the landscape, accomplished mainly through 3D animation, that makes the spectators feel as if they are immersed in freezing Russia. His forays in both television and opera show that Larraín's main concerns are strongly present regardless of the medium in which he is working.

In 2015, Larraín returned to the big screen with *El club*, set in contemporary Chile, and centered on the story of the Catholic Church's cover-up of child abuse in that country, which, horrific in itself, can also be seen as a metaphor for the more general political violence and oppression. Indeed, child abuse is only one of the various crimes on account of which priests have been sent to a sort of retirement home in a quiet coastal area. Father Vidal (Alfredo Castro), who portrays the child abuser, is accompanied by three other priests: one who had ties to the dictatorship, one who was involved with illegal adoptions, and the last of whom does not even remember the crimes he committed. Sister Mónica (Antonia Zegers) is the only woman in the household, and she combines the roles of warden, caretaker, and protector. Within their guilt and denial, the four priests and Sister Mónica live a rather harmonious life—they have taken up the hobby of racing dogs—until a new resident, again accused of child abuse, arrives, followed by the orphan, Sandokan (Roberto Farías), who was the victim of his abuse. The new resident commits suicide, which invokes the arrival of yet another priest, who has been assigned to investigate what happened. In the chapter "The Blurred Image: The Aesthetics of Impunity in Pablo Larraín's *No* and *El Club*," Susana Domingo Amestoy pays special attention to Larraín's use of atmosphere, tone, and texture through filters that simulate old anamorphic lenses and natural lighting. She associates these technical effects with the subject matter and thematic content of the films: a stasis derived from a legacy of impunity, in *No*, for example, the neoliberal foundations and aftermath of the Pinochet regime, or the unpunished crimes of the Catholic Church as depicted in *El club*. Building on Rancière's "distribution of the sensible," Domingo Amestoy shows how Larraín perturbs this very notion by preventing the viewer from enjoying the image as a consumer artifact. Furthermore, as Domingo Amestoy contends, the fogged lens in *El club* serves "to mark the eerie remnants of the past in the present." She also gives a short account of Larraín's national versus international recognition.

In 2016, Larraín released his two biographical dramas, *Neruda* and *Jackie*. In the first, typically reviewed as an anti-biopic, Larraín goes further back in history than in any of his other works to date. In 1946, Gabriel González Videla was elected president with the support of the Chilean Communist Party, but, as soon as he gained power, he turned on his left-wing supporters, criminalized their party, and began an intense persecution against its known members, among them then-Senator Pablo Neruda. The film revolves around Neruda's (Luis Gnecco) escape into exile in 1948, and a major part of the story is focused on the police inspector, Óscar Peluchonneau (Gael García Bernal), who oversees Neruda's persecution.

Adam Feinstein suggests that the film's structure resembles a story by Jorge Luis Borges, citing Larraín's avowed intention: "I realised it could work as a meta-fictional labyrinth. All these characters—Neruda, Óscar the detective, the narrator who narrates himself into the story—are creating each other because they need each other to tell the story."[13] Rachel VanWieren and Victoria L. Garrett dissect the complexity and the multiple layers of *Neruda* in "Reimagining the Left in *Neruda*: Inclusivity and Encounters with Secondary Characters." Through their analysis, they show that, though the film focuses on Cold War-type conflicts between the political left and right, the interactions between key secondary characters and Neruda stress tensions within the left itself and among the historically marginalized. This rereading from a present-day point of view of the Communist Party of Neruda's day bespeaks the importance that contemporary leftist political movements and parties in Chile place on fully incorporating women, sexual minorities, and youth in their agendas, which would not have been central concerns in the late 1940s. Larraín, once again, challenges conventional genre and viewer expectations by moving between biopic, chase film, cat-and-mouse, and road movie, and opting for a "neo-*noir*" style. VanWieren and Garrett argue that "through liberal use of *noir*'s characteristic chiaroscuro and contre-jour lighting, eerie, dramatic, and suspenseful non-diegetic music, and a hard-boiled detective character, this film insistently draws the viewer's attention to its fictional—cinematic as well as literary—nature." Ultimately, the performance of the secondary characters casts the Communist Party's divisive past under a critical light and insinuates the possibility of an inclusive future.

Jackie covers the days in the life of Jacqueline Kennedy between the murder and the funeral of her husband, President John F. Kennedy. She is portrayed by Natalie Portman, who received a well-deserved Oscar nomination for her performance. Like Andy Warhol before him, Pablo Larraín dwells on Jackie's iconicity, operating along the thin line between sincerity and cosmeticism. Like *No*, the film implies that the life of government is a life of performance, with success being contingent upon presenting the most effective façade. The movie takes the interview Theodore H. White conducted for *Life* Magazine only a week after the assassination as its starting point. Through flashbacks, the viewer sees the assassination, its aftermath, and the funeral from Jackie's perspective. As often in Larraín's films, the soundtrack is of crucial importance, and "Mica Levi's orchestral score, with a creamy dissonance of strings, does a lot of work in suggesting both elegiac sadness and post-traumatic stress disorder."[14]

James Harvey's chapter, "Surfaces in *Jackie*: Representing Crisis and the Crisis of Representation," argues that Larraín mobilizes the poetics at the heart of historiography, framing the representation of a real-life event as a negotiation between aesthetic experience and empirical veracity. He draws similarities to themes in Larraín's earlier films, puts them into historical context, and analyzes the dialogue between *Jackie* and Warhol's series of Jackie silkscreens. He further discusses the film's formal style and its subversive potential within the biopic genre. In a similar way to how past and present are intertwined in his earlier films, here:

> two invisible entities—Jackie's personal and America's public memory— are brought to the fore, then, through the employment of disruptive timelines and the unsettling *tableaux vivants* of American colonial history. Jackie's testimony thus becomes a site of temporal coexistence between past and future.

Harvey's conclusions recall McMenamin's analysis of both *Post mortem*, where "Larraín yet again layers the present onto the future past, pointing to the eternal return of Chilean capitulation to the neoliberalism of the Northern Empire," and the *extreme jump cuts* in *Fuga*, where past and present are fused by means of crosscutting. Just as Larraín used categories of modern-day thought in *Neruda* to question certain behaviors of the Communist Party of the past, here he uses the capacity of contemporary digital cinema to mix old media forms with new ones to refine and revise the archival images. Harvey also situates *Jackie*, Larraín's first Hollywood film, within the director's entire cinematographic career, proposing an even larger-scale *de facto* cycle by correlating actors and events in world history, from *Jackie* in the US, to Pinochet's neoliberal coup, to global capitalism in *No*.

At the very least, the diverse perspectives contained in the present volume strongly endorse the aesthetic and philosophical continuity of Larraín's *oeuvre*, his subtle and always critical understanding of the forging and constant reforging of history, particularly through the recognition that secondary or marginal perspectives are irrelevant only when they have been successfully suppressed by its would-be authors, and the all-suffusing proposition that living with the past necessarily means reliving it. Under our present circumstances, both the films and their analysis assume a rather unexpected burden, oddly center stage in their marginality.

NOTES

1. The list contains only his feature films, excluding the ultra-short contribution to *Venezia 70 Future Reloaded* (2013), and his work on the television show *Fugitives*. His (at the time of writing) forthcoming *Ema* (2019) is shot entirely in Chile and focuses on an adoption gone awry, while his *The True American*, an adaptation of Anand Giridharada's 2014 book of the same name, is—as of now—in pre-production.
2. Ministerio de las Culturas, las Artes y el Patrimonio, "Ley 19.981 sobre Fomento Audiovisual" (Santiago de Chile, 2004), 1: <https://www.cultura.gob.cl/wp-content/uploads/2011/10/Ley-19.981-sobre-Fomento-Audiovisual1.pdf> (accessed Febuary 25,

2020). Original Spanish: "la preservación de la identidad nacional y el desarrollo de la cultura y la educación." All translations are mine.
3. CinemaChile is a "public–private agency responsible for the promotion and diffusion of Chilean audiovisual production in the world": <http://www.chiledoc.cl/en/online-cinemachile-org> (accessed Febuary 25, 2020).
4. Ascanio Cavallo and Gonzalo Maza, eds., *El novísimo cine chileno* (Santiago: Uqbar Editores, 2010), 14. Original Spanish: "la generación más inspirada y revoltosa de la historia de nuestro cine."
5. Cavallo and Maza, *El novísimo cine chileno*, 15. Original Spanish: "comparten una preocupación por el espacio íntimo como territorio de conflicto."
6. Carolina Urrutia, *Un cine centrífugo: ficciones chilenas 2005–2010* (Santiago: Cuarto Propio, 2013), 75. Original Spanish: "se proyectan desde una perspectiva del orden de lo individual, de lo subjetivo, proponiendo un cine en donde lo político ya alcanza todos los intersticios posibles en el relato."
7. Larraín qtd. in Manohla Dargis, "Cannes Film Festival: From Chile, Pablo Larraín's *No*," *The New York Times: ArtsBeat*, May 22, 2012: <http://artsbeat.blogs.nytimes.com/2012/05/22/cannes-film-festival-from-chile-pablo-larrains-no/?_r=0> (accessed Febuary 25, 2020). Original Spanish: "nunca estuve expuesto a la pobreza. En cierta manera, mi vida durante la dictadura era cómoda y completamente fuera de peligro . . . Tenía 15, 16 años cuando me di cuenta de lo que sucedía en este país. Sentía que me había perdido algo, [quería] entenderlo, pero no experimentarlo—ni siquiera contarlo, solo exponerlo—."
8. Urrutia, *Un cine centrífugo*, 76. Original Spanish: "desde un objetivo que carga con un filtro de veinte años de democracia."
9. Larraín's father, senator Hernán Larraín, is a member of Chile's conservative party, the Independent Democratic Union, and was appointed Minister of Justice and Human Rights in 2018 under President Sebastián Piñera. Larraín's mother, Magdalena Matte, is also a member of the same party, and was the former Minister of Housing and Urbanism under president Piñera from 2010 to 2014.
10. La Tercera, "De *Fuga* a *No*: la historia del cineasta Pablo Larraín," *La Tercera*, 2012: <https://www.latercera.com/noticia/de-fuga-a-no-la-historia-del-cineasta-pablo-larrain> (accessed February 27, 2020). Original Spanish: "Acusada de ambiciosa, *Fuga* echó mano a recursos propios de la publicidad, le guiñó el ojo a filmes clásicos y su propio exceso la hizo inverosímil."
11. I would like to thank Arturo Márquez-Gómez for his input in this introduction.
12. Larraín qtd. in Demetrios Matheou, *The Faber Book of New South American Cinema* (London: Faber and Faber, 2010), 364–5.
13. Adam Feinstein, "Fast, Loose and Lyrical: Pablo Larraín's Neruda Anti-Biopic," *The Guardian*, April 6, 2017: <https://www.theguardian.com/film/2017/apr/06/neruda-pablo-larrain-biopic> (accessed Febuary 25, 2020).
14. Peter Bradshaw, "Jackie review—Natalie Portman intelligent and poised as JFK's widow," *The Guardian*, January 19, 2017: <https://www.theguardian.com/film/2017/jan/19/jackie-review-natalie-portman-kennedy-assassination> (accessed Febuary 25, 2020).

CHAPTER I

A Cracked Gaze: Pablo Larraín's Cultural Context[1]

Arturo Márquez-Gómez

INTRODUCTION: AN INTENTIONAL INTERTEXTUALITY

An important part of the research that has been done on Pablo Larraín has focused on the analysis of the films that comprise his "unintentional trilogy,"[2] namely *Tony Manero* (2006), *Post mortem* (2008), and *No* (2012). In these films and unlike his contemporaries, the so-called *novísimos* of the Chilean cinema, Larraín actively revisits Chile's recent past, situating the action of his films in various moments of the dictatorship (1973–90) starting with its early days in *Post mortem*, moving to the crisis at the end of the 1970s in *Tony Manero*, and imagining the background of the political campaigns of the 1988 plebiscite in *No*. However, prior to the trilogy, Larraín directed *Fuga* (2006),[3] a commercial film that was quickly pushed aside by academia and coldly received by Chilean critics even though it won the Best First Film Award of the Cartagena Film Festival in Colombia in 2007. Most of the Chilean critics' negative responses were informed by the director's background, an aristocratic right-wing family that had traditionally been seen as supporters of the dictatorship and its legacy. These critics also noted the filmmaker's frequent references to other films and artists. For example, writing on *Fuga*, the now documentarist Maite Alberdi suggested that the film was populated by an "unconscious intertextuality" in which "our senses intuit having seen similar images and characters before."[4] While Alberdi cites Stanley Kubrick's *The Shining* (1980) as an intertext, one could also see references to many other films like Krzysztof Kieślowski's *Bleu* (*Blue*, 1993), Terry Gilliam's *Twelve Monkeys* (1995), and Dario Argento's *Profondo Rosso* (*Deep Red*, 1975). Closer to home, the scenes in the streets of Valparaíso could be easily referencing the classic piece of Chilean cinema

Valparaíso mi amor (*Valparaiso My Love*, 1969) directed by Aldo Francia. Moreover, a cameo of the renowned dramatist Juan Radrigán, author of the play *Hechos consumados* (*Accomplished Facts*, 1981), expands these intertextual references. Far from Alberdi's "unconscious intertextuality," I would argue that the intertextuality in *Fuga* is patent and intentional, even performative in that it seeks to express and develop a cinematographic gaze well aware of a local and international film and art.

In this chapter, I will analyze some of the many artistic frameworks that have informed Pablo Larraín's "cracked gaze," meaning a cinematic perspective impacted by artistic experiences previously forged in the years of the dictatorship and during the transition to democracy in Chile. Critical visions such as those of the photographer Paz Errázuriz, Pedro Lemebel's parodic *locas*,[5] and the innovations of the theater company La Memoria (The Memory)—founded by Alfredo Castro in 1989—constitute important frames of reference for Larraín's imaginary, especially in his early films, *Fuga* and *Tony Manero*.

My point of departure in exploring Larraín's "cracked gaze" is Vania Barraza's characterization of the filmmaker's project as one of postmemory,[6] and therefore mediated by other artistic sources in its imagination of the recent past. In revisiting Larraín's early films like *Fuga* and *Tony Manero* through this idea of the "cracked gaze" one cannot avoid seeing the imprint of Errázuriz's photographic gaze in books like *La manzana de Adán* (*Adam's Apple*, 1990) and *El infarto del alma* (*Soul's Infarct*, 1994), which I see inspiring *Fuga*'s portrayal of the asylum and its inhabitants.[7] Likewise, the obsessions of Raúl Peralta (Alfredo Castro) in *Tony Manero* evoke some of the questions that artists and critics posed in their reflections on the Latin American condition, especially under the siege of the neoliberal dictatorships during the 1970s and 1980s. Pedro Lemebel (1952–2015) developed in his performances and literature characters that mimic and parody foreign pop culture icons. In his early collections of chronicles, Lemebel sought to challenge the ways in which the diverse local "homosexual body" was being dominated and colonized by AIDS, music, and cinema.

These two artistic projects offer a good example of subverting art conventions and borders: Errázuriz blending photography and literature and Lemebel going back and forth between performance and chronicles. Besides being close friends and collaborators on different projects,[8] the photographer and the writer have contributed to create a robust imaginary of social and sexual dissidence, pointing out the fragmented nature of identities as well as of desire as a potent and disturbing drive in authoritarian contexts. From my reading, the overlooked *Fuga* works as an intertextual laboratory where the filmmaker engages with the aforesaid artistic experiences. It is the character of Claudio where one can see the return to the photographic models of Errázuriz, the literature of Lemebel, and the masterly performance of Alfredo Castro.

Figure I.1 Alfredo Castro performing Claudio in Larraín's *Fuga* (2006). Underneath the jacket, Claudio is wearing a white strap, just like the costume worn in the 1990 theater play *La manzana de Adán*.

A decisive aspect that derives from my interview with Alfredo Castro, actor and dramatist, is a confirmation on how vital his presence has been in Larraín's career.[9] I, therefore, consider Castro a third crucial component of Larraín's "cracked gaze." The filmmaker's relationship with the actor extends beyond the movie setting to one of mentorship and education at the Center for Theater Research La Memoria, founded by Castro in 2005. As a sort of actor's studio, the center offered seminars from which Larraín benefited enormously as an artist, especially after the bitter reviews of *Fuga*. I see La Memoria—as Castro refers to both the company and the educational instance—being a *formative* experience in the career of the filmmaker, but also an *informative* space where the director is introduced to new themes, critical concepts, and creative methodologies. As an important cog in Larraín's cinematic machinery, Castro exposed the filmmaker to his theater experience, especially the innovative work of the groundbreaking *La trilogía testimonial de Chile* (*Chile's Testimonial Trilogy*) composed by the plays *La manzana de Adán*, an adaptation of Errázuriz's book, *Historia de la sangre* (*Blood's History*, 1992), and *Los días tuertos* (*The One-Eyed Days*, 1993–4). Because of their use of real testimonies as a dramatic text, these pieces renovated the theater practices in Chile that were still under surveillance and strict censorship in the late 1980s.[10] More importantly, these plays were the result of a collaborative effort of different artists from various disciplines like photography, journalism, psychoanalysis, literature, and theater. The close relationship with members of La Memoria impacted and marked Larraín's cinematographic gaze. La Memoria allowed the director to renew his project, recreate his narrative as a young filmmaker, and knit himself into this established network of artists. Eventually, Larraín's engagement with La Memoria facilitated his particular intervention in the contested artistic terrain on Chile's recent past.

This does not mean that one should leave aside, much less dismiss, Larraín's originality as a filmmaker. On the contrary, reviewing and resituating his filmography in a larger context of artistic practices allows us to think of his films—and Chilean films in general—as immersed within a much broader cultural field. More than close reading sequences of Larraín's films, my analysis shows how the works of Paz Errázuriz, Pedro Lemebel, and Alfredo Castro influence the conception of the marginal characters and decaying *mise-en-scène*.

My argument of the "cracked gaze" in relation to these three artists comes in part from the lucid observations made by Vania Barraza Toledo, who states that postmemory is a conceptual tool for approaching Larraín's trilogy. As a term coined by Marianne Hirsch, it refers to a specific type of memory whose object or source—which is remembered or evoked by the artistic piece—is mediated by "an imaginative investment and creation."[11] Postmemory characterizes the experience of individuals who grew up in a context that was "dominated by narratives that preceded their birth, whose own belated stories are evacuated by the stories of the previous generations shaped by traumatic events that can be neither understood nor recreated."[12] Hirsch extends the use of this term to describe second generations or descendants of people who experienced collective traumas, such as the terror inflicted by the military regime in Chile. As such, postmemory is a useful term for appreciating Larraín's cinematography as well as that of many contemporary artists from the Southern Cone. More importantly, it provides us with the idea of how second generations figure out and elaborate events that they did not experience directly.

The artistic experiences of Errázuriz, Lemebel, and Castro are woven together through friendship, collaboration, and intertextuality. I do not seek to exhaust or reduce an artistic imaginary as rich as Larraín's to these three artists, but rather to situate the filmmaker's early cinema as one emerging from and dialoguing with a preexisting artistic and cultural context.

POSTCARDS FROM THE *OTHER* CHILE: PAZ ERRÁZURIZ'S *ADAM'S APPLE* AND *SOUL'S INFARCT*

The photography of Paz Errázuriz, the winner of the National Award of Plastic Arts 2017, offers multiple views of a hidden Chile. Her photography could be seen as the result of her own exploration of the city, of a gaze that intentionally goes astray in the urban surveilled space and explores it in its "labyrinths of prohibited traffic."[13] Her photographic archive wanders through spaces and faces: circuses in "El circo / The Circus," homes for senior citizens in "Vejez / Old People," childhood in the streets in "La calle / The Street" and skinny boxers in the series "El combate contra el ángel / The Fight Against the Angel."[14] Her photographs find and address exclusion and violence against the forgotten, even signaling their extinction as she demonstrates in her collection *Káweskar, hijos de la mujer sol / Káweskar, Descendants of the Woman of the Sun*.[15] As a whole, her portraits have developed a "visual aesthetic of deterioration"[16] that has been embraced by contemporary artists like Pedro Lemebel and Alfredo Castro. Due to her innovative thematic exploration, Errázuriz's photographs have remained etched in the national imaginary, exposing precariousness and melancholy as well as a disquieting desire. Gonzalo Leiva states that her photography moves away from the stereotypes of Chile's national identity to serve as a Lacanian mirror that deconstructs the illusory nature of its stability and unity. As a diverse journey, her photography takes the spectator to:

> [a] Chile that is buried under traditional representation. The excluded appear with a felt temporal dignity leaving a sweet admonishment of the memory and historical existence of these last generations . . . She is one of the first artists to soundly and systematically propose a reflexive ethics of Chilean society of the new century from an iconographic series.[17]

The ominous effect of her photographs makes it impossible for the viewer to remain indifferent; they bring to the foreground what Chile's economic miracle wants to hide and forget. I believe that this revelatory effect of the photography is central to Larraín's films, especially in the elaboration of the *mise-en-scène* of his three first films—*Fuga*, *Tony Manero*, and *Post mortem*—that highlight the ruinous, claustrophobic marginality of their characters. However, in the process of referencing other works, Larraín strips his characters of the fundamental dissident gesture that we find in books like *La manzana de Adán* and *El infarto del alma*, which respectively portray transvestite subcultures during the dictatorship and residents of an asylum who are in love.

La manzana was conceived between 1982 and 1986, in the middle of the dictatorship, but was not released until September 1990, once censorship was lifted in Chile. It is one of the most important works of the imaginary woven around the figure of the transvestite and the practice of transvestitism, both of which were broadly cited by artists during the dictatorship and the transition to democracy such as the performer Carlos Leppe (*El happening de las gallinas / The Happening of the Hens*, 1974), the filmmaker Gloria Camiruaga (*Casa Particular / Brothel*, 1990), the painter Juan Dávila (*Libertador Simón Bolívar / The Libertator Simón Bolívar*, 1994), and the performance collective, Las Yeguas del Apocalipsis / The

Mares of the Apocalypse, led by Lemebel and the poet and writer Francisco Casas[18] (*La conquista de América / The Conquest of America*, 1989). The cultural critic Nelly Richard, who has studied Chile's artistic culture in the last four decades, states that the artistic imaginary around the transvestite was a recurrent theme due to its subversive potential:

> The convulsion of the transvestite's asymmetrical madness burst into a wry expression of identity which signaled the failings of uniform(ed) and uni-forming genders, dissolving their faces and facades into a doubly gendered caricature that shattered the mold of dichotomous appearances, a mold fixed by rigid systems of national and civil cataloguing and identification.[19]

The narrative that *La manzana* offered almost three decades ago has been seen as one of the first pieces of artistic work addressing sexual diversity in Chile. However, more than portraying a certain identity, the book plays with the fluidity of gender, from the *daylight-official-masculine* to a *nocturnal-unofficial-feminine* body. The book delves into questions of desire, what intimate impulses motivate the daily switching from a masculine attire to the feminine look that deceives their clients.

Besides revealing a hidden social scene from the majority of the audience, *La manzana* combined a quasi-ethnographic methodology in approaching the testimonies and life stories compiled by the journalist and writer Claudia Donoso. I cite part of one of them, which belongs to Pilar:

> We were with Leila in Valparaíso when the coup occurred, and they took all of us to a ship moored in the port. They took us there blindfolded, in a van. For six days, I was left there, piled up with the others, in the hole. The first thing the soldiers did was cut our hair; they pulled it by the roots and afterwards they pissed on us . . . They killed several of us during the coup. They killed Mariliz who was really pretty, just like Liz Taylor. This happened over Christmas. Her body was found in the Mapocho river, full of bayonet holes.[20]

Pilar's testimony opens the book and stands alongside many other voices from the inhabitants of brothels in Talca and Santiago in 1984. The fragment expresses the traumatic memory of multiple *golpes/coups*: the September 1973 military coup that began in the city of Valparaíso under the grasp of the Navy and the many other physical aggressions and blows delivered by the military and police. Allegorically, the damaged national body is connected to the defeated body of the surviving transvestites whose memory of torture has been marginalized from reports such as those of the Rettig and Valech commissions. However, this story of violence and death coexists with a desire anchored in a foreign imaginary, that of Hollywood, which temporarily introduces another scene in the narration of terror. The beauty of Taylor and Monroe—Mariliz— provisionally occlude or coexist with the indecent aggressions to which Pilar and those closest to her have suffered.

It would be impossible to conduct a Barthian "studium" of all of the photographs in this treasured book, but it is worth mentioning the portraits and interviews with the members of the Paredes Sierra family; Mercedes, the mother, and her two sons, Evelyn-Leo and Pilar-Sergio, both transvestites and sex workers. Their story, like a mother–child triangle, was the dramatic backbone of Castro's theater adaptation. Another interesting sequence of photos is the one that traces the portraits of Coral, showing the changes from being a daytime young man to a nighttime woman; as well as the photographs that expose the extensive and studied work of make-up and the use of accessories like the elastic band that Evelyn wears around her neck, an ornament that covers up the signs of the male body.

The gender metamorphosis occurs in private spaces, bedrooms and improvised salons in brothels, but also touches, subtly and timidly, the public space, window frames and doorways that lead to the street. Mirrors, beds, and posters frame Evelyn as she poses as an odalisque or Pilar lying on the bed in a leopard-print dress. Amid the evident signs of ruin—through time, poverty, the dictatorship, and earthquakes—of rundown curtains, chintz bedspreads, and faded wallpaper, the fantasy is kept alive and activated every night by the music and the temporary alteration of the body. The dance room is an impromptu space with tables, chairs, dim lighting, and mirrors. Three photographs of La Sota, a brothel in Talca, show two transvestites dancing animatedly. The flash freezes their gestures, they are laughing, and moving through the night.

La manzana emphasizes the transformation of the surfaces of the body and the socioeconomic conditions that determine these communities. Their testimonies of fantasy and violence are revisited in Larraín's *Tony Manero*. I see these photographs and testimonies function as a prototype for the *mise-en-scène* of *Tony Manero*, especially through all the objects that serve Raúl's fantastic and violent transformation: the suit, the stolen television, the mirror, or even the chintz that serves as a curtain on the main stage. It is not a question of cross-checking Larraín's work with Errázuriz's photos, but there are elusive elements of those portraits that are reproduced in certain sequences or shots in the film.

Similarly, *Fuga*, a film that takes place mainly in an asylum and whose protagonist is a traumatized music composer, evokes Errázuriz's book *El infarto*, composed in collaboration with the Chilean writer Diamela Eltit.[21] The book examines the themes of madness and love through the portrayal of patients in a psychiatric institution outside Chile's capital.

At the beginning of the collection, the couples pose in an orderly fashion in front of Errázuriz's camera; however, as the book continues, the poses become

Figure 1.2 Evelyn after the whole process of crossdressing and make-up. Note the black band that covers the Adam's apple (photograph by Paz Errázuriz, b. Chile 1944, from the collection *La manzana de Adán*, 1990).

progressively more disorganized. The subjects are no longer standing, but lying on the floor, looking at each other and kissing close to the lens, even undressing in front of the photographer. The book also collects some photos of the building's precarious premises, ghostly hallways, and stairways that remind us of the use of the electroshock therapy, the same that is used to "cure" the protagonist of Larraín's film, Eliseo Montalbán (Benjamín Vicuña), of his affective disorder. In *El infarto* there are no testimonies; Eltit accompanies the portraits providing impressions of her first visit to the asylum with some reflections on madness and the psychiatric institution. These reflections are intertwined with fictional texts that resemble the delirious discourse of love, the "mad love" presented as a destabilizing force resisting the rationality and normalization of the psychiatric institution.

Invited by Errázuriz, Eltit narrates the circumstances of her first visit to the hospital, describing it as an urban building that has escaped the city, as a "psychotic fugue."[22] She also describes the noises that she hears during her visit as "music executed with the febrile, continuous movement of the tongue that makes me evoke the sounds of the Berbers."[23] Her visit to the asylum coincides with the hospital's anniversary, which leads her to question what could be celebrated in those conditions of confinement. As the photographer and writer navigate the labyrinthine halls of the facility, they realize how many couples live in the hospital who will happily pose for Errázuriz:

> There are so many couples that I've lost count . . . They are living an extraordinary love story while locked up in the hospital; chronic, indigent, canting, lame, mutilated, with fixed expressions . . . Chileans forgotten by the hand of God, subjected to the rigid charity of the State.[24]

Eltit's observations place the romantic encounters in a more critical sociopolitical background of marginality that challenged the national discourses of the 1990s.

Whether as a visual framework that prefigures the space of the asylum in *Fuga* or a lyrical universe that approaches the marginal subject, *El infarto* offers numerous elements that can be traced in the script of Larraín's first film. The "psychotic fugue" from psychiatric terms could be what inspires the musical genre played by Montalbán. In *Fuga*, madness does not represent any kind of dissidence, but just a result of childhood trauma. The use of the term *fuga* to describe an escape in the midst of the institutional celebration could be read as an analogous moment reported by Eltit. In *Fuga*, however, the person who escapes the scene to enter a different one is Claudio, a character who, because of his fascination with the spectacle world, prefigures Raúl in *Tony Manero*.

THE URGE OF BEING OTHER: PEDRO LEMEBEL'S FRANTIC CHRONICLES

If *El infarto* provided *Fuga* with visual references of the asylum and a poetic approach to madness, Pedro Lemebel's *Manifiesto. Hablo por mi diferencia*

(*Manifesto. I Speak from My Difference*) is at the core of the character of Claudio, a homosexual hospitalized by his family during the dictatorship for his violent behavior and for his communist ideas. This reference to Lemebel has been noticed by various Chilean critics familiar with the irreverent figure of the chronicler and performer who, for his part, has acidly criticized Larraín for his one-dimensional vision of the dictatorship in his chronicle "¿Dónde estabas tú? / Where were you?"[25] One of the elements that stands out within the extensive work of Lemebel is his reflection on what he considers to be a progressive colonization of the *loca*—a supple category where he situates a wide array of dissident sexualities—by foreign models and denominations, such as the English word *gay*. *Manifiesto* is precisely one of the texts that best exemplifies the author's position on identity politics and his troublesome relationship with the Communist Party in Chile. *Manifiesto* also resembles an autobiographical account of what it was like to be a homosexual during the dictatorship, experiencing the twofold censorship of conservative muteness regarding dissident sexualities and silence in connection to the emergency of AIDS.

Lemebel always expressed doubt and confronted the presupposed principles of the democratic discourses forged during the 1990s in Chile: "And I suspect this democratic *cueca* / But don't talk to me about the proletariat / Because being a poor *maricón* is worse / One must be acid to withstand it."[26] In *Manifiesto*, the political struggle is always intertwined with a personal experience of discrimination, one that he suffered inside the same political party that was seeking equality and respect for human rights. Lemebel expresses a deep distrust of institutions, particularly those that sustain and reproduce gender oppression from their hegemonic positions. Politics, a male-dominated sphere, was considered by Lemebel as a camouflaged space of homoeroticism. He criticized and questioned its supposed political inclusiveness proposing his sexuality as a site of political resistance: "I'm not going to change for Marxism / That rebuked me so many times / I don't need to change / I am more subversive than you."[27]

Some of these ideas and powerful verses are cited in a scene in *Fuga* when Claudio covertly enters Eliseo's exclusive room in the asylum. The walls have been transformed into a musical staff where the distressed composer refashions his macabre rhapsody. Claudio enters the room unexpectedly, wearing make-up, dyed hair, and a handkerchief around his neck that resembles the characterization of Castro in the theater adaptation of *La manzana*. The musician rejects Claudio and between blows and slaps, Claudio responds with an armed and poetic speech in which he introduces himself and his damaged biography.

There is no strict parallelism between Lemebel's text and the script of *Fuga*, but on a certain level, Larraín's imagination is writing over a previous text like *Manifiesto* and even the very persona of Pedro Lemebel. If one collates the script of the film and *Manifiesto*, Lemebel's creative universe, concerns, and characters work as a sort of template for Larraín's liminal characters.[28] Likewise, Claudio's costume, the handkerchief on his neck, and his monologue based on Lemebel and Castro's performance connect this character to Errázuriz's transvestites portrayed in *La manzana*.

This relationship to Lemebel's world is even stronger if we consider the ample imaginary of sexual dissidence created by the writer. His first two collections, *La esquina es mi corazón: Crónica urbana* (*The Corner Is My Heart: Urban Chronicles*, 1995) and *Loco afán: Crónicas de sidario* (*Wild Urge: Chronicles from the AIDS Asylum*, 1996), deploy the figure of *la loca* in frantic sexual explorations in the city under the dictatorship. In *La esquina*, the city is a transforming being, subjected to small *coups* and modifications that erase faces and places of sexual dissidence, like parks, theaters, saunas, and cinemas. The chronicle "Baba de caracol en terciopelo negro / Snail's Slime over Black Velvet" pays homage to those rotative cinema shows in which a closeted audience pays little attention to what happens on the screen, but furtively have sex in the velvet seats.[29] The second book of chronicles, *Loco afán*, explores queer subcultures during the dictatorship and under the silent threat of AIDS. The narrators of *Loco afán* critically explore the brothels, the sex work scene, the streets, and the discotheques. Lemebel's queer eye, or in Spanish, "Ojo de loca, no se equivoca," was also extended to an important corpus of icons of popular culture, such as Madonna, Elizabeth Taylor, and of course, John Travolta.

Lemebel's relationship with cinema has been a vast one. He has been the protagonist of two documentaries about his work and life: in 2008, *Pedro Lemebel: Corazón en Fuga* (*Pedro Lemebel: Fleeting Heart*) by Verónica Qüense and *Lemebel* by Joanna Reposi from 2019. His chronicles have also inspired new Chilean filmmakers such as Marialy Rivas (*Young and Wild*, 2012) who adapted the chronicle "La esquina es mi corazón (o los New Kids del bloque) (The Corner Is My Heart (or the New Kids on the Block)" into the short movie *Blocks* (2010). Additionally, the 2013 film, Esteban Larraín's *La pasión de Michelangelo* (*The Passion of Michelangelo*) is partially based on the chronicle "La transfiguración de Miguel Ángel (o 'la fe mueve montañas') / Miguel Angel's Transfiguration (or 'Faith Can Move Mountains')."[30]

Whether as a source of fascination or parody, cinema and foreign popular culture are seen by Lemebel as historical media that have shaped local identities by imposing foreign aesthetics, something that we can also see in Larraín's *Tony Manero*. The chronicle, "La muerte de Madonna / Madonna's Death," narrates the story of a Mapuche transvestite who, during the years of the dictatorship, aspires to resemble the pop diva:

> she deeply fell in love with the *gringa*, she almost went mad mimicking her, imitating her gestures, her laugh, the ways she moves . . . she dyed her hair blonde, almost white. But "the mistery" [AIDS] already debilitated

her hair. The peroxide burnt the roots and the brush after combing was full of hair. She was losing it.[31]

This beaten character applies extreme measures to change her appearance and ends up corroding her own body, exposing the irrational desire that drives her to look like Madonna, but at the same time parodying the icon in her own fictionality. More than shortening the distance between the original and the copy, the Chilean Madonna destroys both the icon and herself. One can see how this character foreshadows *Tony Manero*'s Raúl Peralta and his obsession with John Travolta's character in *Saturday Night Fever* (John Badham, 1977). However, the Chilean Madonna is self-destructive rather than a psychopath, and suffers the rough violence of the police and the immunological complications of the virus "full of bruises in the back, kidneys, face. Big bruises that could not be masked with make-up. With no hair and no teeth, she was not the same Madonna."[32] The streets are a scenario where she can perform this desire in front of potential clients, all while improvising in English: "Mister, lovmi plis [Mister, love me, please]. She knew all the songs, but she did not have any idea of what they were saying . . . Her cherry-like mouth pronounced the 'to you,' the 'me please,' the 'remember loving me' so well."[33]

Similarly, Raúl Peralta, a mature man of blue eyes—like those of General Pinochet, according to his first victim—dyes his gray hair borrowing the dye from Cony (Amparo Noguera), and with Wilma's (Elsa Poblete) money he purchases a suit that covers his scrawny and probably hungry body; he is so hungry that he eats an expired can of tuna. In *Tony Manero*, crossdressing is a "class dressing" in which efforts to look "like the real Tony" are made to "stay alive," out of the claustrophobic marginality. Raúl's metamorphosis idealizes a foreign body, young, virile, covered in Hollywood glitz, a body that crosses borders with the hegemony of English. The close-ups of Raúl's face show how absorbed he is in the film, how closely he is reading it, fantasizing in color and sound, forgetting the tough streets of the surveilled city.

But why Travolta? Why *Tony Manero*, and not Rocky or Madonna herself? In an interview, Larraín explains that the central idea of the film *Tony Manero* came from a photograph:

I'm in Spain, at the Museo Reina Sofía. I find there this big Taschen book of photography. I'm leafing through it, kind of bored. I see this picture of this super-skinny guy in his fifties, sitting on a sofa, smoking, staring out the window. I start thinking, "Who is this man?" He could be a dancer. And a serial killer. I'm thinking about *Saturday Night Fever*, which was released in Chile in 1978. I'm wondering if this could have a political dimension, and: *Tony Manero*.[34]

Just as Castro uses *La manzana* as inspiration for a completely new way of doing theater in the late 1980s, for Larraín, this photograph elicits a series of ideas that, piece by piece, will compose the characters and the context of *Tony Manero*. However, Lemebel and his queer eye also influence Larraín's interest in Travolta as an icon that arouses curiosity among the underground gay community during the years of the dictatorship. In the chronicle "Nalgas lycra, sodoma disco / Lycra Bootie, Disco Sodom," the voice of *la loca* conceives the space of the discotheque as a site of negotiation of identities. The narrator questions the sudden cult of the body and the foreign aesthetics that are imposed through music, fashion, and the incomprehensible English term *gay*. More than a political stance, these identities travel, as goods of consumption, especially through cinema. In this context, the discotheque operates as an identity laboratory where one could observe the local arrangements and/or mismatches between local and foreign cultures:

> [Gay discos] exist in Chile since the seventies and it is only in the eighties when they were turned into an institution that stages the "gay cause" that reproduces the *Travolta model*, only for men. Thus, the homo-dance temples are more successful in bringing the ghetto together than political activism. They imposed a lifestyle and a philosophy of virile camouflage that through fashion homogenized the diversity of local homosexualities.[35]

Thus, more than a space of freedom and self-expression, the "dancing cathedral" produces and reproduces a foreign model within local bodies, invalidating the differences as sites of dissent and resistance, which were crucial for Lemebel as an artist during the years of the authoritarian regime. Another chronicle that enriches this vision of Travolta is "'Biblia rosa y sin estrellas' (La balada del rock homosexual) / 'Pink Bible without Stars' (The Ballad of Homosexual Rock)," in which Lemebel reflects on the ways in which the music industry profits from using figures of sexual dissidence, using crossdressing as a disguise to sell albums. The North American band Village People, for example, is highly criticized by the writer because their "mixture of muscles, chains, moustaches, and military boots brought to an extreme the fabrication of the masculine gay in *yanquilandia*. Navy and police uniforms ejaculating to the rhythm of 'In the Navy.'"[36] This quote expresses the problematic translations of foreign aesthetics showing how, in the context of the dictatorship in Chile, the costumes worn by the band were not viewed positively. How, under such a repression, can one connect with the uniforms and that eager hypermasculinity? Considering this discordance, Lemebel points out how the Travolta model summoned audiences into a more individualistic fascination: "Many local 'queens' preferred the Travolta look, the cute and flounced suit, and dancing to the Bee-Gees and their fairy voices."[37] The suit that Lemebel mocks in his chronicle is a highly codified piece of clothing in the film. Raúl carries it around the city and everyone talks about it, scrutinizing its authenticity. The suit operates as a talisman that Raúl zealously looks after and wears on the day of the contest only after defecating on Goyo's own suit.

Pedro Lemebel's view of Travolta is highly influenced by his political position as part of the Chilean left during the decades of the 1970s and 1980s. With his *ojo de loca* he observed how fictional figures imagined by cinema moved audiences more effectively than if they marched against the oppression. To calibrate the effects of Hollywood's cultural imperialism during a dictatorship is, undoubtedly, a subject of multiple creative edges. I have selected some moments of Lemebel's work in which certain mediations of Larraín's postmemory are visible. However, the construction of the complex character of Raúl Peralta shows a reflection on the subject of the dictatorship different from that proposed by Lemebel. Larraín suppresses the political consciousness of Lemebel's *loca* and replaces it with an alienated subjectivity to create a Cronenbergian subject, one "videodromed" by the spectacle and the mediatic fantasy in the middle of Santiago during the curfew. Larraín also erradicates the homosexual element of Lemebel's furtive character: it seems that Cony is the only one aware of the latent homoerotism that is involved in Raúl's spectacular fantasies.

Both Lemebel and Errázuriz are artists who created a thematic matrix— marginal sexual identities—on which Larraín draws as a model for his early films. Both artists provide a visuality that frames and unframes new perspectives on the subject of the dictatorship, gazes that are undeniably feeding a fragile historical memory updated and convulsed by Larraín's trilogy.

THE "THIRD BODY": ALFREDO CASTRO'S THEATER COMPANY LA MEMORIA

In the text "Lo crudo, la piel, lo cruel / The Raw, the Skin, the Cruel," Alfredo Castro states his perspective on acting:

> as the work of a clairvoyant who must think simultaneously multiple subjects in his own body, in his own psyche, as a subject that suffers from images, an erogenous body made for representation. His job is to materialize the *jouissance* of insanely being and not being in his body, of being him/her and at the same time being another.[38]

These conceptualizations are certainly the result of Castro's vast career in theater, television, and cinema, *Fuga* being his first film. One must consider his skilled performances in films like *Tony Manero* or *El club* as crowning moments of an acting vocation that began at La Memoria, the theater company he founded in 1989. When cast in a leading role in a film, Alfredo Castro has a presence that signals, at least to those familiar with the actor's career, a style of acting reflecting his work forged in the cultural scene of the transition to democracy in Chile. Castro's self-reflective style, taciturn posture, eloquent gesturing, and persuasive body language imprint the films with a signature hallmark that has been recognized internationally, for example by the Fénix Film Award for Best Actor in 2015 for his role in *El club*. Castro is a third element of the "cracked gaze," not only through his performance based on conceptual frameworks, but as mediator of Larraín's postmemory project. Therefore, not only can his influential presence be observed in film settings, but it can also be felt in educational settings, like the Center for Theater Research led by Castro and where Larraín was a student.

In my interview with the actor in May of 2018, besides his willingness to share his experiences as an actor, what stood out was his elaborated and conceptual approach to acting. During his thirty years in theater and cinema, Castro has developed a remarkable vision of what it means to be artistically, psychologically, and culturally an actor. Some of his ideas have been published in the context of the center La Memoria and presented in several international conferences to which he has been invited as a guest. In "Lo crudo," Castro pledges to reinstall in theater and cinema "the bodies of the actors as a place of organic origin of emotions and ideas, actors as 'athletes' of the heart, and representation as a hard physical and spiritual test."[39] As a "triathlete" in theater, television, and especially in cinema, Castro has put these ideas into practice and provided Chilean cinema with some of the most daring and uncanny moments, particularly in his role as Raúl Peralta, who dances alone in his room on an improvised stage.

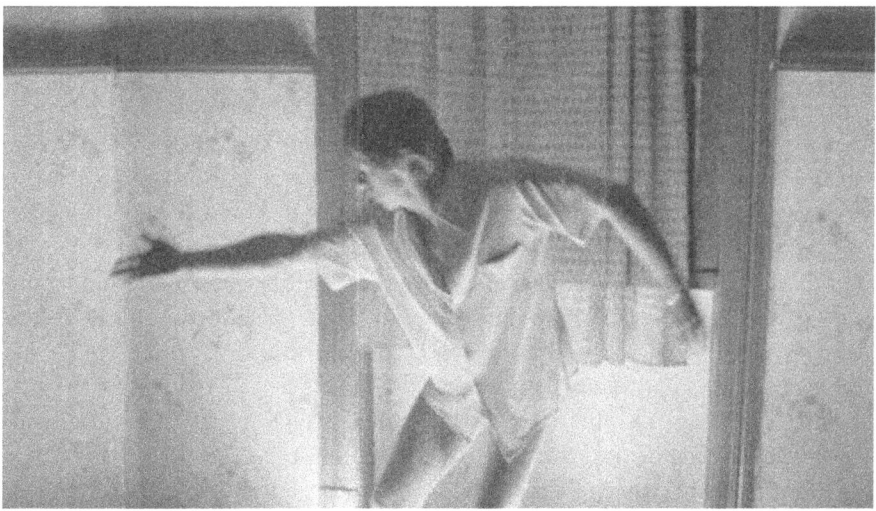

Figure 1.3   Alfredo Castro as Raúl Peralta. The character has built his own glass dance floor in his room (from *Tony Manero*, 2008).

There, blinking white fluorescent lights are placed under the glass bricks illuminating the character from below and creating an eerie and gloomy effect. The light goes out and darkness fills the screen, therefore we are unable to follow the actor's body. Luciferic, this sequence sharply contrasts with the dancing scenes saturated with color in the original *Saturday Night Fever*. The body moves to the sound of "¿Qué clase de hombre eres? / What Kind of Man Are You?" by the Chilean band Frecuencia Mod,[40] half dressed, disheveled, a parody at its best. Castro breathes, but works in silence, his body movements expressing the obedience and submission to Hollywood fantasy and simultaneously disavowing the *cueca* as the national dance proclaimed by the dictator in 1979.

A vital notion in Castro's conceptualization of acting is the idea of the "third body," an entity that mediates both the body and the desires of the performer and the character. This "third body" allows the actor a unique flexibility in developing "all shapes, all sexualities, all possible or desired ideologies, embodying tension, contradiction, and conflict."[41] Because of its litheness, Castro affirms, the third body is also a possible insurgent that transgresses all sorts of oppressions. As a plastic notion, the "third body" offers an enormous range of possibilities, especially for a director like Larraín whose cinematic project is highly mediated by different artistic perspectives. The "third body" as an anomic territory is the breeding ground where characters like the cruel Raúl, the impassible Mario Cornejo, or the perverse padre Vidal[42] can fruitfully emerge in the films. In short: Larraín's imaginations can only happen in the context of a self-reflective and informed performing practice such as Castro's. Reversibly, this conceptual framework is derived from a postmemory imagination such as Larraín's.

Castro's conceptual work stems from the deep influence of Antonin Artaud's *The Theater and Its Double* from 1938 and from his own practice in the theater company La Memoria. Before embarking on their groundbreaking project, *La trilogía testimonial de Chile*, the company staged various pieces mainly based on foreign authors.[43] The innovation of *La trilogía* consisted in the use of testimonies as a dramatic text for their plays. *La manzana de Adán*, a homonymous adaptation of Paz Errázuriz and Claudia Donoso's book, works with the testimonies of the transvestites, focusing on the story of Mercedes Paredes Sierra and her two sons, Leila, and the delusional Mr. Padilla. Beyond the persuasiveness of Errázuriz's photographs, what struck Castro was the poetic world that emerged from the testimonies: "I was deeply moved by them [the photographs and testimonies], I cried, and I said to myself: 'this is our language. This is what we speak.'"[44] The testimonies, according to Castro, reinstituted the magical effectiveness of the theater's discourse, leaving behind the fixity of preexisting texts.

From the experience of *La manzana de Adán* the use of testimony became Castro's main source of inspiration for playwriting. In 1991, in collaboration with Rodrigo Pérez and Francesca Lombardo, Castro began a second project titled *Historia de la sangre*, which was based on the crimes of passion of men and women who had committed murders because of "love." They interviewed inmates and psychiatric patients, and consulted the infamous 1923 crime known as the "crime of water boxes" in which Rosa Faúndez dismembered her partner and spread the body parts across Santiago.

The third play, *Los días tuertos*, was written by Claudia Donoso, who was motivated by Castro to gather and record testimonies from workers in marginal occupations: circus workers, magicians, cemetery workers. Originally a journalist, Donoso started recollecting personal stories in the 1980s as an "archeology that consists in vacuuming biographical waste, there, where lives do not have a certificate of residence in the public scene."[45] Traveling through Chile with Errázuriz or by herself, Donoso gathered neglected voices with a tape recorder, conceived as an "orthopedic organ to vacuum verbal pieces."[46] These recordings were not intended to serve as ethnographic documents, but more as sources to be recuperated and elaborated in a larger artistic work. For example, the testimonies of Mercedes Sierra and her two sons are interwoven into discourses on identity fluidity and negotiations of gender in the practice of crossdressing or trans bodies in *La manzana*. As raw material, the testimonies suffered a symbolic elaboration that connected their particularity to a wider cultural and symbolic order, often represented by the idea of the nation.

The concept of testimony was useful for the members of La Memoria: it helped them to mediate their own artistic searches and the territories of Chile that were unknown to them. Donoso expresses this idea without concealing the fact that fantasy is a drive for these quests:

> My fantasy is to immerse myself in the history of my *inner country*, exploration that *I have groped, from a fault*. In what I experience as a complicated relationship with the idea of writing, *I have needed others and I have dressed in other's clothes*. The fear of writing lies in the difficulty of naming, in the trap and power of the word: the established word and the one that is impossible to install.[47]

I have emphasized some of Donoso's ideas to consider how they also inspire Larraín's project as he began to explore his country's past in the mid-2000s. This difficult task, even for artists who lived and experienced the harsh years of the dictatorship, is a mediated process. While Donoso works with language—always a contested terrain—Larraín does it with moving images that are necessarily fed by other gazes, like the one of Errázuriz. In conclusion, I see *La trilogía* working as a framework of multiple references that precedes Larraín's trilogy, but not only or exclusively in terms of themes, but as a continuous reflection on that inner and conflicted country.

Considering the influence of La Memoria on Larraín's work, it is important to note that Castro conceives an alternative cinematic trilogy from the one that critics have studied; instead of *No*, he suggests *El club* as the third film. Castro's trilogy is composed by films that "are different in the way they were born. They are the result of Pablo's elaboration of the 'Real,' like 'let's do this right now' . . . in these movies, Pablo testifies about himself as an artist."[48] Larraín's own cinematic testimonies are mediated by La Memoria's trilogy, an artistic experience that opened up thematic possibilities by offering a fascinating world of peripheral subjects: queer subcultures, crimes of passion, impoverished populations, and ruined spaces. It also provided Larraín with a methodology of interdisciplinary work (photography, theater, psychoanalysis) and the testimony as a source of creation.

This contact between Castro, La Memoria, and Larraín happened under an educational setting at the Center for Theater Research founded by Castro and other professionals, like the psychoanalyst Francesca Lombardo. The center taught several seminars on dramaturgy, acting, theater direction, and visual narrative, among other subjects. Unfortunately, there is not much information available about the center itself or about how formative this experience was for Larraín, who shared the classroom with two other successful theater directors: Alexandra von Hummel (founder of Teatro La María) and Cristián Plana. As a student in those seminars, I argue, he became familiar with drama techniques and conceptual frameworks, especially those of psychoanalysis, but also with a mode of collaborative work, exchange, and intertextuality that defined La Memoria's theatrical work. Although this influence is evident, one wonders why the director has not communicated more extensively about this enlightening and privileged experience. This lack of communication or recognition is complex, because La Memoria and its members have become a "theater capital" participating actively in Larraín's films. On one hand, former members of La Memoria, like Amparo Noguera and Luis Gnecco are well-known actors on public television, both in telenovelas or series (like Larraín's *Prófugos / Fugitives*, broadcast from 2011 to 2013). This element of popularity can play favorably in attracting national audiences. On the other hand, as professional performers, they have benefited from being introduced to the Chilean proto-film industry. For example, Noguera acted in Rodrigo Sepúlveda's *Aurora* from 2014, and Gnecco performed in Matías Lira's 2015 mini-series and then movie *El bosque de Karadima*, about infamous cases of unpunished pedophiles in Chile.

CONCLUSION

What is enacted in Raúl's somber dance over his fluorescent stage? Who is he dancing for? Is the absurd ineptitude of Mario typing the autopsy of President

Allende an indication of how complex it is to rewrite history through cinema? Can we comprehend the obscure hopes that the hellish community in *El club* has put on Rayo, the grayhound? Can we conceive the abduction of Sandokan (Roberto Farías) by these monstrous priests? Pablo Larraín's cinema will continue raising more questions than answers for the spectator. As a young filmmaker, Larraín has crossed representational boundaries in Chile's cinematic context, proposing polemical images about the nation's recent past. His work, and the work of the *novísimos*, has circulated globally and has radically internationalized Chilean cinema through the film festival circuit and the international recognition they have received. An example is Sebastián Lelio's *Una mujer fantástica* (*A Fantastic Woman*, 2017), which won the Academy Award for Best International Feature Film in 2018.

As director and producer, Larraín has been an ambassador of Chilean cinema and there are healthy signs, *Neruda* for example, that he will keep working that inner country that he started to explore in *Fuga*. As an ambassador, however, he travels with a dense and rich cultural background that, in a country that has been subjected to inclement forces of consensus and oblivion, must be acknowledged.

Thinking through the idea of a "cracked gaze" is to rewind his career as a filmmaker. It is to appreciate how a cinematic gaze is not born in the void, but rather finds its roots in a preexisting cultural context. *Fuga* is a film populated with intertexts where we can appreciate how the "cracked gaze" is being forged in relationship to other artistic projects such as Paz Errázuriz, Pedro Lemebel, and the critical mentorship of Alfredo Castro. My intention, then, has been to first locate and briefly analyze those moments where his gaze has been cracked by the aforementioned artists in order to provide an alternative framework within which to analyze the filmmaker's project.

I did not intend to overlook Larraín's talent and accomplished work as a filmmaker, but rather to consider how his early cinematography is immersed and informed by innovative and critical visions of the subject of the dictatorship. How, in writing about Larraín's films, can we forget about Castro's role as a mentor? How, in considering Larraín's impact, can we overlook previous contributions of women and queer artists that created their own artistic language merging the biographical but never neglecting the political?

Undoubtedly, the "cracked gaze" has transformed over the years in films such as *No*, *El club*, and the transnational productions of 2016, *Neruda* and *Jackie*. Where will Larraín's work go in the future? Will it follow its adventures exploring foreign stories like it did in *Jackie*? Or will it return to the always problematic national archive? One thing is certain, that to comprehend Larraín's journey toward an international arena, one must understand its origins in the Chilean cultural context.

NOTES

1. This chapter was translated by Katherine Goldman.
2. Larry Rohter, "Pablo Larraín and His Unintentional Trilogy," *The New York Times*, January 8, 2013: <https://carpetbagger.blogs.nytimes.com/2013/01/08/pablo-larrain-and-his-unintentional-trilogy> (accessed February 25, 2020).
3. Given that in Spanish the word *fuga* has several meanings—it can be a musical fugue, an escape, or a brief psychotic break—the title of the film leaves much room for interpretation.
4. Maite Alberdi, "Fuga. ¿Qué hay detrás del espectáculo?," *laFuga*, September 1, 2018: <http://www.lafuga.cl/fuga/145> (accessed February 25, 2020). Original Spanish: "nuestros sentidos intuyen haber visto imágenes y personajes similares anteriormente."
5. Defining *la loca*, Melissa González asserts that the noun *loca* describes not only a "crazy woman but also a gender-nonconforming homosexual man" (123). In English, one can find analogous terms like "sissy" or "flaming queen." *Loca* can be derogatory, but has also been re-signified by minorities and amply used by the writer and performer Pedro Lemebel. For more about this definition see Melissa M. González's complete entry: "La Loca," *Transgender Studies Quarterly* 1, no. 1–2 (2014): 123–5.
6. Vania Barraza Toledo, "Reviewing the Present in Pablo Larraín's Historical Cinema," *Iberoamericana* 13, no. 51 (2013): 159–72.
7. Both publications have been re-edited; *Adam's Apple* in 2014 by FAMA Foundation and *Soul's Infarct* in 2017 by Hueders. Both books are available online in their original versions; *Adam's Apple* at the Centro de Documentación de Artes Visuales: <http://centrodedocumentaciondelasartes.cl/g2/cgi-bin/library.cgi> and *Soul's Infarct* at Memoria Chilena: <http://www.memoriachilena.cl/602/w3-article-78829.html> (both accessed Febuary 25, 2020).
8. Errázuriz captured Lemebel in various portraits and photographs of his performances. Some of them have been used by publishers as Lemebel's book covers. In *Arder* (2017), a book of photographs of Lemebel, some of the portraits done by Errázuriz can be seen. Lemebel inspired his chronicle "Reírse en la fila / Laughing in line" in *Adam's Apple*.
9. Alfredo Castro, "'When on Stage, I Am Not There, I Am Not That One.' An Interview with Alfredo Castro," interview by Arturo Márquez-Gómez, May 28, 2018.
10. For a more extended revision on La Memoria's history see Gabriela González Fajardo, "Haciendo memoria: historia de la compañía de teatro La Memoria" (BA thesis, Universidad de Chile, 2010).
11. Marianne Hirsch, *Family Frames: Photography, Narrative, and Postmemory* (Cambridge, MA: Harvard University Press, 1997), 22.
12. Ibid.
13. Nelly Richard, "Underworlds and Flaws of Identity," in *Paz Errázuriz: Photograhy 1983–2002* (Santiago: Paz Errázuriz Körner, 2004), 10.
14. Errázuriz's work can be partially seen at <http://www.pazerrazuriz.com> (accessed Febuary 25, 2020).
15. The book portrays the last descendants of the Káweskar culture in Chilean Patagonia.
16. Nelly Richard, *Poéticas de la disidencia: Paz Errázuriz y Lotty Rosenfeld / Poetics of Dissent: Paz Errázuriz and Lotty Rosenfeld* (Chile's National Pavilion at the Venice Biennale, 2015), 44.
17. Gonzalo Leiva, "Of Melancholies and Metaphors," in *Paz Errázuriz: Photograhy 1983–2002* (Santiago: Paz Errázuriz Körner, 2004), 38.

18. Important research has been conducted on Las Yeguas: the website <http://www.yeguasdelapocalipsis.cl/inicio> (accessed Febuary 25, 2020) includes a very complete account of their work, photographs, and descriptions of their performances.
19. Nelly Richard, *Masculine/Feminine: Practices of Difference(s)*, trans. Silvia R. Tandeciarz and Alice A. Nelson (Durham, NC: Duke University Press, 2004), 43.
20. Paz Errázuriz and Claudia Donoso, *La manzana de Adán*, trans. Gonzalo Donoso Yañez (Santiago: Zona Editorial, 1990), 91.
21. Among her numerous publications are *Lumpérica* (1983), *El cuarto mundo* (1988), and *Jamás el fuego nunca* (2007). Eltit was awarded with the National Prize for Literature in 2018.
22. Paz Errázuriz and Diamela Eltit, *El infarto del alma* (Santiago: Hueders, 2017), 11. Original Spanish: "fuga psicótica."
23. Ibid., 13. Original Spanish: "música ejecutada con el movimiento febril y continuo de la lengua que me hace evocar los sonidos de los berebere."
24. Ibid., 17. Original Spanish: "Hay tantos enamorados que ya pierdo la cuenta . . . Ellos están viviendo una extraordinaria historia de amor encerrados en el hospital; crónicos, indigentes, ladeados, cojos, mutilados, con la mirada fija . . . Chilenos olvidados de la mano de Dios, entregados a la caridad del Estado."
25. Pedro Lemebel, "¿Dónde estabas tú?," Movimiento Generación Ochenta: <http://www.g80.cl/noticias/columna_completa.php?varid=3276> (accessed Febuary 25, 2020). In this chronicle published in his weekly column "Ojo de loca, no se equivoca" in the newspaper *La Nación* on October 19, 2008, Lemebel aggressively confronted and rejected the unidimensional vision of the dictatorship developed by Larraín in *Tony Manero*.
26. Arielle A. Concilio, "Pedro Lemebel and the Translatxrsation: On a Genderqueer Translation Praxis," *Transgender Studies Quarterly* 3 (November 2016): 462–84, p. 473.
27. Ibid., 475.
28. The following is a partial reproduction of the film's dialogue; in parentheses Lemebel's original verses of the English translation by Arielle A. Concilio are quoted:

> *Eliseo:* Get out, I don't know who you are. Get out!
>
> *Claudio:* And you? Who are you going to be? A musician looks like it . . . or are you a mime disguised as a trumpet? Or a closet queer like the boxers, politicians, or the fucking drunks? ("Football is another gay closet / Like boxing, politics, and wine / My manhood was biting back jokes," ibid., 475.) Who the fuck you think you are talking to? You, fucking high-class fairy. [*They start to fight; Claudio continues*] I don't turn the other cheek, no way. ("And I don't turn the other cheek," ibid.) I don't give a shit that you don't know who I am. I do know who I am, and I don't wallow in my own shit like you. ("I need no disguise / Here is my face / I speak from my difference," Ibid., 472) . . .
>
> *E:* You haven't lost anybody . . .
>
> *C:* I've lost more brothers than you've ever dreamed of having. I spent my life screaming like a wild beast, catching knives in the dark. ("And is not fear / The fear of knives slowly stabbing / through the sexual sheets where I romped . . . I have scars of laughter on my back," ibid., 474.) I was born like this, sweetie. With a broken wing and I fell. ("There are so many kids who will be born / With a broken wing / And I want them to fly, comrade," ibid., 476.) So many times, I fell, that they lock me up in here and they screwed me. They screwed me. They screwed me for being a fag. For being a communist. For being wicked and beautiful.

29. Las Yeguas del Apocalipsis frequently parodied cinema stars. In the performance *De la nostalgia* (*Of Nostalgia*, 1991), Lemebel and Casas wore make-up, wigs, and elegant dresses to interrupt the last show of the Normandie Art Cinema. During the credits of Terry Gilliam's *The Adventures of Baron Munchausen* (1988), the Mares dabbed their eyes with eyedrops to create artificial tears and to stage a dramatic farewell to this movie theater, a long stronghold of intellectual openness during the dictatorship. As a melodramatic gesture, they exit the cinema and urinate over two stars drawn on the floor, and then, walking on the red carpet, they say goodbye as queer divas.
30. Currently, director Rodrigo Sepúlveda (*Aurora*, 2014) is filming an adaptation of Lemebel's 2001 novel, *Tengo miedo torero* (translated by Katherine Silver in 2003 as *My Tender Matador*), with Alfredo Castro as the *loca del frente* (queen of the corner).
31. Pedro Lemebel, *Loco afán: Crónicas de sidario* (Santiago: LOM Ediciones, 1996), 33. This one and the following are my translations of Lemebel's texts. Original Spanish: "se enamoró de la gringa, casi se volvió loca imitándola, copiando sus gestos, su risa, su forma de moverse . . . se tiñó el pelo rubio, casi blanco. Pero ya el misterio le había debilitado las mechas. Con el agua oxigenada se le quemaron las raíces y el cepillo quedaba lleno de pelos. Se le caía a mechones."
32. Ibid. Original Spanish: "llena de moretones en la espalda, en los riñones, en la cara. Grandes hematomas que no se podían tapar con maquillaje . . . Sin pelo ni dientes, ya no era la misma Madonna."
33. Ibid., 34. Original Spanish: "Mister, lovmi plis. Ella se sabía todas las canciones, pero no tenía idea lo que decían . . . Su boca de cereza modulaba tan bien los tuyú, los miplís, los rimember lovmi."
34. Pablo Larraín, "The State That I Am In," interview by José Teodoro, *Film Comment*, November/December 2016: <https://www.filmcomment.com/article/pablo-larrain-jackie-neruda-interview> (accessed February 25, 2020).
35. Pedro Lemebel, *Loco afán*, 53. The emphasis is mine. Original Spanish: "aunque la disco gay existe en Chile desde los setenta, y solamente en los ochenta se institucionaliza como escenario de la causa gay que reproduce el modelo Travolta solo para hombres. Así, los templos homo-dance reúnen el ghetto con más éxito que la militancia política, imponiendo estilos de vida que va uniformando, a través de la moda, la diversidad de las homosexualidades locales."
36. Ibid., 100–1. Original Spanish: "Una camionada de músculos, cadenas, bigotes y bototos, que llevaron al extremo la masculinización de lo gay fabricado en yanquilandia. Uniformes de marineros y policías eyaculaban al compás de 'In the Navy.'"
37. Ibid., 101. Original Spanish: "Muchas locas nacionales preferían el look Travolta del trajecito y los vuelos, y bailaban el disco dance de los Bee-Gees por el amariconamiento de las voces."
38. Alfredo Castro, "Lo crudo, la piel, lo cruel," *Cuadernos de Cinema* 23, Mexico: La Internacional Cinematográfica, Iberocine (2018): 18. Translations are mine. Original Spanish: "Comprendo el trabajo actoral como el de un vidente que debe pensar simultáneamente múltiples sujetos en su propio cuerpo, en su propia psiquis, como un sujeto enfermo de imágenes, un cuerpo erógeno hecho para la representación. Su oficio consiste en materializar el goce demencialmente de estar y no estar en su cuerpo, de ser él y ser al mismo tiempo otro."
39. Ibid., 8. Original Spanish: "los cuerpos de los actores como lugar de origen orgánico de las emociones y las ideas, actores como 'atletas' del corazón, y la representación como una dura prueba física y espiritual."
40. The music band Frecuencia Mod, active between the years 1970 to 1986, was a feminine trio that locally reproduced the rhythms and themes of the disco music. Their hits

conform the musical soundtrack of *Tony Manero* with songs like "Gigolo" and "Cállate, ya no me mientas / Hush, Don't Lie to Me Anymore," the song that Raúl sings along the rest of his crew and leads him and Pauli (Paola Lattus) to have sex.
41. Ibid., 9. Original Spanish: "todas las formas, todas las sexualidades, todas las ideologías posibles o deseadas, encarnando así la tensión, la contradicción y el conflicto."
42. This role was awarded the Fénix Film Award for Best Actor in 2015.
43. Among them, Federico García Lorca's *Buster Keaton Goes for a Stroll* from 1928, Jorge Aceituno's *Estación Pajaritos* (*Pajaritos Station*) from 1987 and in 1989, *La tierra no es redonda* (*The Earth Is Not Round*) based on the work of French poet Paul Claudel.
44. Castro, interview.
45. Claudia Donoso, "Un beso con lengua en la huesera," in *Los días tuertos*, ed. Teatro La Memoria, n.d. Original Spanish: "arqueología que consiste en aspirar residuos biográficos allí donde las vidas no cuentan con certificado de residencia en la escena pública."
46. Ibid. Original Spanish: "órgano ortopédico para succionar piezas verbales."
47. The emphasis is mine. Ibid. Original Spanish: "Mi fantasía es sumergirme en la historia de mi país interno, exploración que he realizado a tientas, desde una falla. En lo que experimento como una complicada relación con la idea de escribir, he necesitado de otros y me he vestido con ropa ajena. El miedo de escribir radica en la dificultad de nombrar, en la trampa y el poder de la palabra: de la palabra instalada y de la imposible de instalar."
48. Castro, interview.

CHAPTER 2

The Synecdochic Series of Pablo Larraín: The Castro Cycle of Chilean Complicity in *Fuga*, *Tony Manero*, *Post Mortem*, *No*, *El Club*, and *Neruda*

Amanda Eaton McMenamin

INTRODUCTION: THE SYNECDOCHIC SERIES—
THE CASTRO CYCLE OF CHILEAN COMPLICITY

The president of Chile in 1948, an inane state functionary in 1973, a *Saturday Night Fever* (John Badham, 1977), Tony Manero-obsessed serial killer in 1978, an adman for the Yes campaign in 1988, and a pedophilic priest and an institutionalized man somewhere, sometime in contemporary Chile. What do they all share? Beyond being the protagonists interpreted by actor Alfredo Castro in cineaste Pablo Larraín's feature films set in the Chilean milieu—*Neruda* (2016), *Post mortem* (2010), *Tony Manero* (2008), *No* (2012), and *El club* (2015) and *Fuga* (2006), respectively—these characters all bear markers—interwoven threads—of continuity. These connections, moreover, refer to the way that the Castro protagonists (or antagonists, as the case may be) become representative of the Chilean nation and, most importantly, its problematic relationship to its far-off, yet looming northern neighbor, the indelible United States of America. In this vein, this intervention seeks to fill a scholarly gap in the dialogue about the auteur's films set in Chile, by offering a rereading of Larraín's cinematic corpus that firmly establishes the concatenating connections between what has been considered previously the "dictatorial trilogy"[1]—formed by *Tony Manero*, *Post mortem*, and *No*—the understudied *Fuga*, and the more recent *El club* and *Neruda*, which are yet to be intently focalized by scholarly criticism. I thus contend that a review (re-viewing) of all six features as a series provides an opportunity for a sort of interserial interpretation, in this case, of the central role that star Alfredo Castro plays in each of the works. Castro protagonists become representative—as synecdoche—for the Chilean nation and its positionality of subservience to the hegemonic social, political, and economic forces of northern-born neoliberalism in the region. In other words, beyond the frequently studied denigration of the Pinochet regime apparent in the "dictatorial trilogy,"[2] Larraín equally excoriates Chilean capitulation to US interests and ideologies, throughout what I am calling the entire *synecdochic series*, via the characters that Castro interprets, as well as a complementary set of cinematic techniques that highlight the eternal return, or *monumental temporality*, of what I will term Chile's neoliberal nexus of *high-density capitalism*. I thus propose a filmic frame for the Larraínian cinematic cosmos that is centered on the dogged denunciation of Chilean complicity with North American neoliberalism, which persistently permeates both the Castro characters and their filmic framing in the auteur's *oeuvre*.

In several interviews about his films, Larraín has been quick to denigrate the neoliberalism that continues to infect Chilean society. In a piece for *Sight & Sound*, he clearly criticizes the neoliberal trajectory of his nation while also pointing to the relationship between protagonist Raúl Peralta of *Tony Manero* and the state of Chile:

> With *Tony Manero* I intended to take a harsh look at a society that's incapable of coming face to face with its recent past. A society whose hands are covered in blood, but which tries to look stylish and trendy, dancing under the flashy lights while ignoring the suffering of others. A country that turns its back on itself in exchange for the dream of progress. Raúl represents our irrepressible craving for the modern world while we're sinking into poverty. But attaining this modernity—moving up the social scale—is impossible. The failure to attain the dream becomes a trauma that somehow extends over the whole country. Raúl's actions are also the actions of the system that has taught him to base his expectations on everything that is alien to him—alien to us.[3]

Here we note Larraín's disdain for both neoliberalism in Chile and the foreign, "alien," ideology on which it is based, causing the nation to "turn its back on itself." Raúl, then, as synecdoche for the nation, a part that represents the whole, symbolizes the "trauma" of that failed project that extends over the body politic: the monstrous inequality that plagues the nation under neoliberalism. And from where is this "alien" model derived? The United States, clearly. Larraín proclaims in a recent interview, "It's the country that keeps sticking its nose in my country, man."⁴ What he means by this, as he explains in another interview, is that:

> For me the true change does not date back to '73, the year of the coup. The crucial moment is when Pinochet introduces the Chicago boys, five economists trained in the United States that Pinochet brought to the Ministry of Treasury and Finance, and it is there where the new system begins. In that very moment a great repression was produced.⁵

In these proclamations, Larraín mirrors many of the same denouncements that Naomi Klein makes in her now-classic text, *The Shock Doctrine: The Rise of Disaster Capitalism* (2007), published between Larraín's opera prima, *Fuga*, and his second feature, *Tony Manero*. Therein, Klein provides an analysis of US involvement in Chile leading up to Pinochet, his dictatorship, and the long-lasting repercussions. First, the US intervened in the ideas market in Chile, in order to undermine developmentalism, by selecting the University of Chicago to train the exceptional Chilean students sent abroad to study in the States. The University of Chicago's Economics Department, home to Milton Friedman, preached the "near-complete dismantling of government" in order to allow the market to be completely "free" from influence.⁶

Following, the CIA conspired against democratically elected socialist president Salvador Allende. This fact was revealed during an official Senate investigation that found that over 75 percent of the funding for "opposition research" was coming directly from the CIA.⁷ In the wake of the CIA-backed Pinochet coup, CIA collaborators were involved in the preparation of the economic plan for the Junta, based on Friedman's neoliberal principles.⁸ In addition, the CIA provided training in torture techniques for the Junta, in order to "control subversion."⁹

The result, according to Klein, was the very first experiment in what she terms "disaster capitalism," born as an idea in the United States and deployed in practice in the Chilean state. This "disaster capitalism" represented the powerful combination of three forms of shock enacted on the body politic of the nation, supported by US economic and ideological interests (represented overtly by the Chicago School), as well as political and intelligence interests (represented covertly by the CIA). These were the shock of the coup itself, Friedman's neoliberal economic shock treatment, and the torture techniques, often literally electroshock, deployed to keep the population in a state of shock.¹⁰ Unfortunately, as many scholars continue to note, the neoliberal experiment in Chile holds steadfast in many ways in contemporary society. As Klein describes:

> The radical economic model that took such deep root during dictatorship would prove hardier than the generals who implemented it. Long

after the soldiers returned to their barracks, and Latin Americans were permitted to elect their governments once again, the Chicago School logic remained firmly entrenched.[11]

Larraín echoes these sentiments, stating:

> We have a rightest government that controls practically everything and in addition it is a right that has no need to overshadow anyone, because nothing stands against it. I believe that it is a process of conquest that comes from Pinochet and continues from that moment on.[12]

He then clarifies what characterizes the persistence of this rightest leadership, explaining:

> I believe that the problem is that the right-wing project is what is truly in control around the world, and every other movement that promotes equality is going down. No matter what the government, the rich are getting richer and the poor are getting poorer.[13]

In other words, it is the vastly disequalizing project of neoliberalism that continues, like an impenetrable virus, to infect Chile today. It is Chilean capitulation, "turning its own back" on the populace and selling out to this neoliberal model, steeped in the interests of its far-off, yet looming northern neighbor and those that benefit from this complicity, that Larraín's Castro characters are intended to critique.[14]

Indeed, Alfredo Castro himself seems cognizant of the ways in which the antagonists that he plays call for a national reckoning with the neoliberal past and present of Chile, which he too excoriates. Castro's father belonged to the same Masonic Lodge as Salvador Allende, and in 2009, when he decided to become involved in national politics, he served as cultural consultant to the communist presidential candidate, Jorge Arrate.[15] Castro criticizes "the free market," and he says that actors too "are treated like a product—how much you are worth, what your price is. It's dirty and it bothers me. I'm not for sale."[16] He continues, expressing that state-supported neoliberal practices, from the dictatorship onward, represent where:

> impunity was consecrated, both in the dismantling of the Republican State through the usurpation and privatization of its enterprises, education and health systems, as well as in the cruel and criminal treatment of its victims and all of the abuses against human rights and dignity.[17]

Further, he sees this impunity entrenched in the very fiber of the characters that he interprets in Larraín's films:

> Raúl Peralta becomes a butchering predator to obtain a glass floor where he can dance like Tony Manero (John Travolta's character from the 1977 film *Saturday Night Fever*). Faced with unrequited love, Mario Cornejo in *Post mortem* becomes a murderer as well; both characters act with complete impunity. And in *No*, without committing a crime, Luis Guzmán becomes a fervent adherent of democracy once it triumphs, right after being a fierce defender and collaborator of the dictatorship, at no ethical cost whatsoever.[18]

Larraín has also commented on the symbolism and importance of his Castro characters. He says that Castro "is essential to my work, a driving force for what I want to show on screen,"[19] also claiming, this time specifically regarding *Fuga*, that Castro provides an "emblematic character."[20] In short, the Castro characters act as synecdoche for the nation, most particularly as a jarring critique of Chilean capitulation to neoliberalism and its bulwark, the nation's North American neighbor.[21]

Following Castro and Larraín's own thoughts about the protagonists that Castro portrays, and in examining their developmental arch across the films, not in terms of chronological film release, but rather in terms of historical chronology, there has been an evolution in the *synecdochic series*. Derogation of Chilean capitulation to US influence begins in a sort of blind buffoonery of bureaucratic ineptitude serving US aims and goals in the region with the characters represented by President González Videla in *Neruda* (located in 1948) and state functionary Mario Cornejo in *Post mortem* (located in 1973). Indeed, these two films mark the earliest twentieth-century moments of Larraín's Chilean *oeuvre*: during the rabid pursuit of Pablo Neruda for his communist principles and the Pinochet coup. As Pinochet's dictatorship wears on, what the characters of *Tony Manero* (located in 1978) and *No* (located in 1988) really expose are the intensifying forces of corporatist neoliberalism, or "disaster capitalism," and the commercialization of all aspects of life. While Raúl Peralta, of *Tony Manero*, has one true God, and it is the foreign, Hollywood icon of the film *Saturday Night Fever*, Lucho Guzmán of the Yes campaign in *No*, who desires the continuation of the Pinochet regime, is no different or distinct from his counterpart, René Saavedra (Gael García Bernal), of the No campaign. They both commercialize democracy, and when "No" wins, Lucho calmly goes back to work with René under the same "alien" neoliberal principles that they both fostered in their respective campaigns.

In all actuality, "disaster capitalism" continues in Chilean society long after Pinochet or the return to democracy. The consequences of this become apparent in the abject bodies of the putrid paternal figures that Alfredo Castro occupies in the two films set in contemporary Chile, although Larraín has been quick to discuss their universalism, or what I will term their *monumental temporality*. In *El club*, Father Vidal is a pedophilic priest, but we come to understand that, like the nation of Chile, and inverting his own perverted positionality in relationship to young boys, he represents the abused child of a corrupt, dominant American father, such that, by the end of the film, like his nation, he languishes, broken, under a subjugating paternalism. The costs then seem heightened in the corpse-like body of Claudio Leal in *Fuga*, who is interned in a psych ward and submitted to literal shock treatment; symbolic, in a Kleinian vein, of the neoliberal "shock doctrine" enacted on the body of the nation. This leads to the degeneration of his physical corpus and mental capacities, representative of the contemporary Chilean nation in neoliberal decay.

DUOLOGY OF BUREAUCRATIC BLINDNESS—*NERUDA* (2016, 1948) AND *POST MORTEM* (2010, 1973)

It all begins, in a historically chronological sense, with the presidency of Gabriel González Videla in *Neruda*. Here Castro, through his portrayal of the president, encapsulates the selling out of Chile to US interests. This is highlighted on several brief occasions, given that the president appears in total for only a few minutes of the film. Nonetheless, it is his orders to capture Neruda that drive the entire plot of the film. In essence, bureaucratic blindness is manifested bimodally. González Videla appears in the film as a US lackey, blind to his subservience to US interests. Meanwhile, his visual absence from the film means that we experience his presence as a blind person would: we typically cannot see him, but we sense his omnipresence. In the opening scene of the film, for example, we see Neruda (Luis Gnecco) enter the gentlemen's bathroom in the Senate Hall. He decries, to his fellow senators, that Communist Party members are being incarcerated by "your president, the traitor González Videla, who sold out to the Northern Empire."[22] In this way, the president's looming presence-in-absence, replicating the haunting of the Chilean nation by US interests, is established from the incipit.

Just a few short scenes later, detective Óscar Peluchonneau (Gael García Bernal) is called to the presidential palace to meet with González Videla and receive his marching orders to capture Neruda. As Peluchonneau enters, we listen, in voiceover, as he conveys, "My president has a boss—the president of the United States. When he says that we need to kill our local communists, this trained monkey must obey."[23] Although Peluchonneau may be the antagonist that Neruda writes into existence for his own life story, we note the slippery, metonymic relationship established between the detective, President González Videla of Chile, and President Harry Truman of the United States. Because of the non-specificity of the subject of Peluchonneau's statement, we come to understand that if Truman says that the communists must be extinguished, then trained monkey González Videla blindly parrots the same, and subservient detective Peluchonneau must obediently follow through with these orders. Beyond the frame of Neruda's individual story, then, Chile's antagonist is the United States, but more than this, it is the nation's own capitulation to US interests, as seen through González Videla's subservience to the Northern Empire. As if to highlight this further, the Chilean president only appears once more in the film, all but replaced by the American ambassador (Brian Welsh). For example, when Peluchonneau returns to update the president, he is greeted by the American ambassador at the president's door. The ambassador will not allow him to see the president, and he tells Peluchonneau that *he* is his superior. It is clear that Chile has elected to answer to the United States.

In addition to the persistence of the looming American presence in the film, depicted by the substitution of the American ambassador for the Chilean president in several scenes, a complementary formal technique provides a marker of Chilean subservience to US interests. The film, like *El club* and *No* before it, deploys what I would like to term *extreme jump cuts* that portray, temporally, the eternal return of Chilean capitulation to US interventionism. What is meant by *extreme jump cut* here is a particular strategy where Larraín films a singular conversation, typically between two characters, in which the conversation carries on seamlessly as the setting and time abruptly jump from one moment and space to another. For example, in an early scene of the film, Neruda and Chilean Senate President Arturo Alessandri (Jaime Vadell) discuss González Videla. While their conversation is stitched together seamlessly, without disruption, the visual shots cut rapidly across several venues and timeframes. The discussion begins in one of Alessandri's salons, in the actual Palacio Cousiño in Santiago, where the family is having lunch,[24] then cuts to the palatial stairs of the mansion, then jumps to an empty Senate Hall in the dark of night, and then finally cuts back to Alessandri's lavish mansion, this time in a well-lit, ornate corridor.

The content of the conversation once again highlights the Chilean president's looming presence-in-absence, now extending its reach across space and time through the *extreme jump cuts*. In their discussion, Alessandri chides Neruda for allowing the Communist Party to be tricked by a "three-penny populist"[25] like González Videla. Neruda then scolds Alessandri, facetiously averring that the way to get rid of the communists is not by jail or exile but by killing them all. Alessandri exclaims that Neruda should not repeat that, as some may want to try it. This indeed is the very assault that Pinochet's neoliberal regime enforces on left-leaning Chileans during the long dictatorship, as well as what we have seen Larraín lament as the suffocation of all projects of equality by the right in Chile. In other words, through these *extreme jump cuts*, what is exposed is an eternal present, the continuation of the past in the future, or the future in the past, which is emphasized by the very nature of the cut and then highlighted by the omnipresence-in-absence of González Videla himself. As Gnecco and Larraín describe in the director's commentary to the film:

> And, you know, what I like the most in this scene is that the effect you . . . I mean, this effect of shoot[ing] the scene in very different places. In this scene, because of, you know, of . . . the extension of the scene, it's more present.[26]

The result is an atemporality, more so a *monumental temporality*, in which the present is layered on the past and the future, particularly as it relates to the eternal return of US interventionism and Chilean capitulation to US interests and the neoliberal model.

In another such monumental layering of time, creating an eternal present of Chilean capitulation to neoliberal and US interests, toward the end of the film, one last mention is made of President González Videla, as usual in absentia. This time it is by a dissident "feudal lord who invented capitalism on his land,"[27] as Peluchonneau describes him, and whose land Neruda needs to cross to escape into Argentina. Pedro Domínguez (Marcelo Alonso), the "feudal lord," tells Neruda that he will not help that "faggot president"[28] for anything. He firmly believes that "the state is the enemy of freedom."[29] He continues, paradoxically, that it is more fun to help the communists. Meanwhile, Peluchonneau's voiceover comments, "On his shoulders and soul the future of the Republic is built. The millionaire is always more intelligent than the law of the nation."[30] In this way, González Videla is yet again replaced, not by the American ambassador this time, but by another Chilean who superficially appears to be siding with the left, only to obscure his thinly veiled rightest leanings and intents. It is highly symbolic, then, that Peluchonneau remarks that the capitalist lord Domínguez founds the future of the Republic, in particular, pointing rather directly to Pinochet's neoliberal order, as well as current and past President Sebastián Piñera (2010–14; 2018–), whom Larraín has also excoriated for maintaining the Pinochet model. For example, in a 2013 interview, Larraín decried the same archetype that we see here with Domínguez: "Or the model of social order that Pinochet had, today the country has with eight or 10 owners. One of them is the president of Chile [Piñera]."[31] Yet again, we see present layered on past and past on future, criticizing the monumental extension of Chilean capitulation to the northern neoliberal model.

This same desire to be neoliberal is allegorized in *Post mortem*, set in 1973 in the days directly leading up to and following the Pinochet coup. In this film, Alfredo Castro plays inane state functionary Mario Cornejo, whom Larraín himself calls a "regular person," "but [who] carries this country on his shoulders, and for me that's a symbol of the situation."[32] In other words, yet again the Castro character becomes synecdoche for the Chilean nation. Further, the dancer with whom Mario is obsessed in the film, Nancy Puelma

(Antonia Zegers), is described by Larraín as "represent[ing] the new world ... that will import stuff, that will try to be from a First World country."[33] In other words, Nancy represents neoliberalism. When Mario sleeps with Nancy and his grunts are transposed onto, or coincide with her facial expressions, it represents the symbolic consummation of neoliberal, "disaster capitalism" (Nancy) and the Chilean nation (Mario) that takes place simultaneously with Pinochet's coup. In fact, not only does Mario continuously suggest that they marry, but he does his best to persuade Nancy by taking her to a trendy Chinese restaurant and demonstrating his economic prowess. Suddenly, though, within the first fifteen minutes of the film, the scene cuts to a shot of a woman's autopsy; Dr. Castillo (Jaime Vadell) announces that the corpse is "Nancy Puelma Olivares,"[34] and she has died of starvation. Mario calmly records the doctor's autopsy notes, then helps lift her dead weight off the table.

It is only in the film's denouement that we will learn that Mario has essentially murdered Nancy and her boyfriend, Víctor (Marcelo Alonso), by trapping them in Nancy's family's shed after her house was ransacked during the coup (Nancy's family were stalwart supporters of Allende). In an incredibly long take that extends over time and ends up being the final scene of the film, we watch as Mario piles up furniture in front of the shed door. Mario (Chile), no longer needs Nancy (foreign neoliberalism), because neoliberal desire has infected the nation; Mario becomes the homegrown model of "disaster capitalism" incarnate. For, let us not forget, neoliberalism in practice was born in Chile, following US/Friedmanian ideology, only later to be replicated in its home as a Chilean copy.

Let us also not forget that Mario's embodiment of neoliberalism only becomes possible via the Pinochet coup and its politics of "disaster capitalism," which were free to be imposed amid the great shock reverberating through the Chilean populace. In *Post mortem*, Larraín conveys that sense of shock through the formal techniques he deploys, in particular his use of audiovisual silences and an immobile camera. For example, the film opens to an impossible-point-of-view shot from the undercarriage of a tank, rolling through the streets of Santiago. The camera, persistently jostled, provides the sensation of hypermobility, while the scraping of metal against pavement screeches in our ears. This shot, which occupies the first forty seconds of the film, jarring the audience, then stands in stark contrast with the majority of the rest of the film, characterized by a fixed camera, lack of sustained dialogue, and overall acoustic silence. In this sense, I agree with Amit Thakkar's assessment of silence in the film; he states that "the lack of non-diegetic sound (a feature of the entire film) accentuate[s] the viewer's sensation of being a stunned, powerless bystander."[35] In fact, following the establishing tank shot, there is not a single word uttered until four minutes into the film, and the camera, hyperstatic, at times leaves our antagonist, Mario, behind, remaining in rooms after he leaves. In other words, the film replicates the state of shock rippling through the nation in the wake of the coup, represented by the tank shot, followed directly by neoliberal "shock doctrine" and the tremors of torture and disappearance that the Junta would perpetrate, represented by the camera, shocked into staticity, and the stunned silence of the characters.

We might also think of the silences that plague the soundtrack as a form of acoustic blindness, which is paired with visual absence in the film's diegesis, replicating Mario's blindness, as a bureaucratic lackey, in following along with the new status quo of the incipient neoliberal regime under the Pinochet dictatorship and its "disaster capitalism." In the most emblematic of these instances, the coup itself occurs while Mario is in the shower, unaware of what is happening outside. In this scene, a montage of visual and audio silences emphasizes his blindness to what is occurring. The camera cuts back and forth between contrasting audio and spatial regimes, one being the interior of Mario's bathroom, where we only hear the shower water running and the sound of Mario brushing his teeth. The contrasting shot peers through Mario's bathroom window from the exterior, where we hear the sounds of the coup (tanks rolling, glass breaking, people yelling, and mortars going off) but still are visually blind to the violence by the persistent focalization of Mario through the bathroom window. In this sense, Robert Wells's assessment of the representation of the coup is apt: "That is all that is seen of the coup in *Post mortem*, which, again, suggests that, in fact, it has yet to really be *seen*."[36] In other words, the visual regime here replicates the blindness with which Mario faces the realities of the coup and instead capitulates to it, as highlighted by his coy smile and affirming response when Captain Montes (Marcial Tagle) congratulates him for now serving the Chilean army. Since Larraín himself avers, "He [Mario] is the camera, a point of view . . . I think

Figure 2.1 Mario Cornejo's sly smile upon being informed that he now serves Pinochet's Chile in *Post mortem* (2010).

that it's important because that's how we see the situation. Our point of view is his behavior and I believe that they're very close,"[37] the Chilean viewership is implicated directly in that blindness and capitulation to the foreign-cum-domestic forces of "disaster capitalism."

Nonetheless, the culminating moment of excoriation in the film seems to arrive when, in the final shot, almost six minutes in length, the staticity of the camera recapitulates one last time Mario's perspective. Fixed on the ever-mounting pile of household goods that Mario is stacking up in front of the shed where Nancy and Víctor are hiding, sealing them in to die, the viewer is intensely implicated in the act. Our behavior (view) mimics Mario's, and the metaphor of heaping up stuff to the hilt is a rather translucent comparison to the piling up of misery under the regime of accumulation heralded by the Pinochet Junta and its "disaster capitalism." It is the rubbish heap of the future past set to starve the country, the future ruins of yesterday, yet again layering future on past as present. When there finally appears to be no way out through the mound of stuff—the symbolic confines of "disaster capitalism" for Chile—the screen cuts to black, and the film's title, *Post mortem*, appears. What comes after death? Not life. Neoliberalism.

DUOLOGY OF CAPITALIST CAPITULATION—*TONY MANERO* (2008, 1978) AND *NO* (2012, 1988)

It is precisely this neoliberal project—Chilean capitulation to the "disaster capitalist" construct—that Larraín critiques with greatest translucence in his films set at the apogee (*Tony Manero*) and denouement (*No*) of Pinochet's regime. I concur with Juan Poblete when he claims that "*Tony Manero* is one of the most radical Latin American film explorations of the deep social violence involved in the continental implantation of neoliberalism."[38] I also agree with Wolfgang Bongers, who asserts that Raúl Peralta, the Tony Manero-obsessed serial killer that Alfredo Castro plays, is "not only a product of the criminal regime, but also of perverted consumer anxiety, of the individualistic capitalist ideology, that considers others an obstacle for personal success."[39] Although criticism of *Tony Manero* has thus heartily expressed the critique of neoliberalism apparent in the film, Raúl's synecdochic relationship to the Chilean nation is yet to be thoroughly commented on. We will recall that Larraín himself bemoaned that "Raúl represents our irrepressible craving for the modern world while we're sinking into poverty . . . Raúl's actions are also the actions of the system that has taught him to base his expectations on everything that is alien to him—to us."[40] This capitulation to exterior, foreign, or "alien" interests, namely the neoliberal ideology of the Northern Empire, is highlighted when Raúl's girlfriend,

Figure 2.2 Raúl Peralta mimes the lines to *Saturday Night Fever* in *Tony Manero* (2008).

Cony (Amparo Noguera), chides him for his obsession with Tony Manero, even though she willingly follows him and dances in his *Saturday Night Fever* troupe. She bitingly snaps, "You are so stupid. He is [Tony Manero is] just another gringo,"[41] adding that Raúl is not American, he is like the other members of the ensemble, and he belongs with them. To this, Raúl symbolically retorts, "Not me, not anymore,"[42] after which the film cuts almost directly to Raúl seated in the theater, viewing *Saturday Night Fever* and parroting the film's lines in English.

It is not for naught that Raúl barely speaks, and when he does, it is often in this imitative English. This, plus his obsession with the American disco idol, renders clear that there is a model that Raúl seeks to reflect, which is the highly individualistic, consumer-obsessed neoliberalism of the Unitedstatesian variety.[43] In such a sense, Larraín lucidly denigrates Chilean complicity with this model through Raúl's synecdochic relation to the nation.

This relationship is again highlighted through Raúl's obsession with the glass floor that he seeks to construct in order to better replicate Tony's performance in *Saturday Night Fever*. When he frequents a flooring shop, the clerk (Marcial Tagle) explains that what he needs are "high-density" glass blocks;[44] the English terminology is used. It is rather symbolic that he steals the "high-density" sample from the store and also goes on to murder the Romanian dump vendor (Marcelo Alonso) for his glass blocks. Within the context of the film, I would like to term this the kill-or-be-killed world of *high-density capitalism*, what Klein has otherwise called "corporatist capitalism," which rises out of "disaster capitalism," and whose "main characteristics are huge transfers of public wealth to private hands, often accompanied by exploding debt, an ever-widening chasm between the dazzling rich and the disposable poor."[45] In other words, *high-density capitalism* steals from the poor to make the rich richer; it concerns itself not with life, but with death, with the unfair stamping out of competition to the benefit of the corporation in question. In this vein, Raúl is synecdoche for the nation incorporated under *high-density capitalism*. He is ready to ruthlessly rob others: he steals almost everything he acquires in the film, typically murdering his victims in the process in order to exterminate all forms of solidarity, such as the way in which he abandons his dancing troupe to Pinochet's DINA (Dirección de Inteligencia Nacional) police or the mounting death toll of the victims who stand in his way. He is also prepared to partake in unfair competition, for example, ensuring that the younger Goyo (Héctor Morales) cannot win the Tony Manero contest in which they are both entered by shitting on his white suit.

We might also argue that such *high-density capitalism* is apparent in the filmic form that *Tony Manero* sets to screen. As Christian Gundermann reminds us, "Decades of neoliberalism have produced an unstoppable acceleration . . . bringing with them the effects that Paul Virilio has theorized as dromology and dromocracia (in the sense of 'tyranny of velocity'),"[46] adding that this has been accompanied by "the retraction of space, coproduct of acceleration."[47] The condensation of space paired with accelerated time, or the spatiotemporal "high-density" experience of neoliberalism, seems to manifest itself in the movements of the handheld camera, which restlessly jostles in its furious chase of Raúl as he runs, often aimlessly, through the streets of Santiago. It mimics what Geoffrey Kantaris has described as a similar technique deployed in the Argentine film, *Pizza, birra, faso* (Bruno Stagnaro, Adrián Caetano, 1997), released a little over a decade before *Tony Manero*: "The camera is hyper-mobile to the point of disorientation, showing frantically edited snippets of city bustle, either filmed from some fast-moving mode of transport or jerkily hand-held, twisting this way and that as if time itself had gone into overdrive."[48] In short, the velocity with which the camera chases after Raúl becomes symbolic of time in "overdrive," or the "tyranny of velocity" that *high-density capitalism* fosters. Further, when the unsteady camera catches up with him, there are frequently moments of intense close-up, in which Raúl's face occupies almost the entirety of the frame, condensing its spatiality into an emblematic representation of "high-density" neoliberal experience. Encapsulating this spatiotemporal compression that Raúl participates in and represents, Larraín asserts, "Apparently Raúl Peralta was one step ahead of his country, because his absurd yearning—to be 'modern'—is shared by all of Chile today."[49] In this way, Larraín yet again layers the present onto the future past, pointing to the eternal return of Chilean capitulation to the neoliberalism of the Northern Empire.

It is precisely this iterative neoliberal submission in Chile that Larraín also seeks to critique in *No*. Some critics have complained that the film trivializes the No campaign and aligns it too readily with commercialism.[50] However, this is precisely Larraín's point; the film translucently depicts how the neoliberal lines of Pinochet's regime were used to defeat him in the 1988 plebiscite. Even more crucially, the film alludes to the idea that the country has never been able to shake neoliberalism; this "alien" ideology has been completely coopted by the democratic future of the nation: Larraín's present. He proclaims in an interview following the release of *No*:

> The return to democracy and to the left in 1988 did more than conserve the Pinochet model, it strengthened it. The grand-scale triumph of 'No' secretly implied the small-scale triumph of 'Yes.' We kept Pinochet's Constitution and his economic model, equality remained an abstraction . . . It's [now] like living in a mall. Everything is sold and everything is bought.[51]

But this persistence of Pinochet's "disaster capitalism" in the Chilean present is oft veiled. As Juan Poblete avers:

> the hegemonic Chilean culture of the postdicatorship has, in its effort to push for consensus, simultaneously exaggerated its novelty and its degree of rupture with the authoritarian past and hidden the non-new— the significant degrees of continuity of the legal structures created by the dictatorship and the post-dictatorial governments' policies.[52]

As an example, Larraín reveals:

> Piñera [the then-president of Chile] watches *No* and says that the movie was too entrenched in marketing, such that he did not really like it . . . It's based on marketing because from there it seemed an interesting way to see the allegory. He [Piñera] was a rich person in '88. Now he is a billionaire. What did he not understand?[53]

In fact, Piñera exploited *the very same* marketing strategies used in the 1988 No campaign in his successful presidential run of 2010, right down to borrowed lyrics from the No campaign theme song "Chile, la alegría ya viene" [Chile, happiness is coming], and his rainbow-themed star insignia, a reminder of the No emblem.[54]

In many ways, as in *Neruda*, where the Castro character, President González Videla, is connected, through the film's *monumental temporality*, with the past and future president Piñera—himself an encapsulation of the continuation of

Chilean capitulation to neoliberal values—so does the Castro adman, Lucho Guzmán, in *No*, layer the commercial and neoliberal past of the Pinochet era onto the future past (present) of the post-dictatorship, notably including Piñera's neoliberal Chile. Although several critics have commented on the buying and selling of democracy under neoliberalism that is apparent in the film, none has adequately elaborated on Guzmán's symbolic and synecdochic positionality.[55] In fact, critics typically claim that this emblematic space is occupied by the adman's partner and film's protagonist, René Saavedra (Gael García Bernal).[56] In fact, when we closely examine the presentations of protagonist (René) and antagonist (Lucho), we come to understand that they are two sides of the same neoliberal coin. This is apparent from the opening scene of the film, where Lucho and René meet with clients for whom they are creating an ad campaign. Together they watch the Free Cola commercial that they have put together. As René presses play, he symbolically states, "Today, Chile thinks about its future,"[57] and the camera pans over to Lucho before focalizing the television screen within the filmic frame. Indeed, Chile's future is neoliberal, whether René's "No" or Lucho's "Yes" wins. After the commercial presentation, as the camera pans back out, one of the customers asks what a mime is doing in the piece. René responds, "This is very, very, very original. In America, perhaps, there is something similar, but we have to have confidence in our product."[58] Lucho adds, "This is everything that our youth needs."[59] There is no real difference between the two admen; both commodify freedom as adherents to the neoliberal project, here overtly emblematized by the Free Cola product.

In fact, Lucho and René are mere copies of one another, as are their Yes and No campaigns. In the director's commentary to the film, Larraín answers his character's question as to why a mime was included in the Free Cola commercial. He explains, "Since there was no sort of culture during the dictatorship, then the mime would represent like a lot of things . . . the mime's a metaphor of the culture."[60] In other words, what culture exists in Chile under Pinochet's *high-density capitalism* is a simulacrum, indeed the very example of a simulacrum, a copy (mime) of American consumerism that is more real than the original itself. René alludes to this when he says that perhaps in America there is something similar, but "we have a product that is distinct from the competition."[61] Although born of American economic ideologues, it is in Chile where the "disaster capitalism" of the Chicago School is put into practice, and only later does an evolved copy come home to roost in the United States. The complex relationship between Lucho and René, which Gael García Bernal calls "incestuous,"[62] in the director's commentary to the film, repeatedly represents the deep imbrication between Chile and the United States in relation to the neoliberal model and its copies. In one of their iterative wars of words over the campaigns, Lucho goads René, saying, "Did you see it? Because there's a change in the conceptual strategy. Did you like it?"[63] René responds, erupting, "It's bad. It's really bad. It's awful, Lucho. It's shit piled on shit piled on shit. It's the copy of the copy of the copy of the copy of the copy. Everything is all mixed up."[64] Ironically, René had already been chided in the same way by his estranged wife, Véronica (Antonia Zegers), a radical leftist, for creating a campaign that is "the copy of the copy of the copy of copy of the copy of the copy."[65] Quite symbolically, directly following Lucho and René's corrosive *tête-à-tête*, they enter their agency side by side, warmly greeting their clients for the day. The two are clearly no different; they are "all mixed up," copies of one another, both aligned with the neoliberal commodification of all aspects of life.

In addition to the fact that Lucho, synecdoche for Chile, simply goes back to work at his ad agency after the plebiscite, now under the democratic project of the Concertación rather than the Pinochet regime, it is highly symbolic that the opening scene, in which Lucho and René introduce the Free Cola commercial, is recapitulated with the exact same pitch in the final frames of the film, this time referencing a media stunt for the soap opera, *Bellas y audaces* (*The Beautiful and the Bold*). In the director's commentary, Larraín says of this scene:

> What has actually changed? That's what this scene shows . . . A lot of things remain, and he [René] says the same line . . . You know, it's amazing, at the beginning of the scene Alfredo [Castro] would say, well he [René] is the one who created the "No" campaign. So he uses it in his favor. So, it's just, you know, so dirty, and they don't care as long as they sell.[66]

In other words, this scene is meant to establish the eternal return of neoliberalism, layered over past, future, and present in Chile. This *monumental temporality* is, as in Larraín's other films, firmly established via several key formal techniques. The scene in question here, which introduces Free Cola at the incipit, the No campaign midway through the film, and the commercial for *Bellas y audaces* in the denouement, we might term the *extreme sequence*. If sequence in film typically refers to shots or scenes linked together by a common theme or image, this sequence becomes exaggerated, or extreme, in its word-for-word repetition of René and Lucho's pitch. Further, the careful placement of this *extreme sequence*, not only as filmic bookends but also internal to the diegesis, provides the audience with a sense of the never-ending nature of the neoliberal present, already past and destined to be future, as Chile consistently buys into its model. It ardently emphasizes Larraín's aforementioned desire for us to question, "What has actually changed?"

The *extreme sequence* is not the only cinematic technique that conveys this *monumental temporality* of neoliberalism in the film, its eternal return in Chile. As in *Neruda*, the film is populated by *extreme jump cuts*, where a singular conversation is stitched seamlessly across disparate shots, where the effect is that the conversation appears extended over space and time, highly indicative of the colonization of time (its "tyranny of velocity") and spatial compression perpetrated by the neoliberal order of things. For example, toward the beginning of the film, when No campaign leader José Tomás Urrutia (Luis Gnecco) calls on René to request that he join them, their singular conversation carries on as the scenes cut rapidly in space and time. Their discussion begins, lit by blinding daylight pouring through the windows of the ad agency; it continues onto the street outside the agency, equally illuminated by the sun's rays; it passes down the streets of Santiago, as dusk begins to fall; it tarries on in a dimly lit bar, with the blackness of night obscuring the avenue outside; and it finally ends at a restaurant brightly lit by the morning sun. In the director's commentary, Larraín says of this strategy, "It gives the sensation that the time is passing really quick and they just have been talking [about] this for a while."[67] García Bernal quickly adds, "And you really get this feeling that it was a long conversation, it was a lot of talking and brainstorming, and at the same time, for some reason, just the narrative gets going quickly. It's like a turbo, turbo narrative."[68] It is not for naught that neoliberalism has also been termed "turbo-capitalism," perhaps first by Edward Luttwak in his 1998 book by the same name.[69] It is also not for naught that this scene between René and the organizer of the No campaign is followed by yet another *extreme jump cut* conversation between René and Lucho, who will become the director of the Yes campaign, as if yet again to emphasize the continuities—rather than differences—between the two campaigns in their capitulation to northern neoliberal ideals.

There is one other formal technique applied in *No* that emulates the *monumental temporality* of neoliberalism, or *high-density capitalism*, and this occurs when we view the present (2012) faces of the people who took part in the No campaign, juxtaposed with their younger visages in the original spots from 1988. If a match on action is typically "a cut between two shots of the same action taken from two different positions in order to achieve the illusion of simultaneity,"[70] then these could be termed *extreme matches on action*, because the shots span almost twenty-five years in time, condensed spatially into the same locations as the "original" shots, with the use of the television screen within the filmic frame to "achieve the illusion of simultaneity" between the disparate moments of filming. The most symbolic of these *extreme matches on action* occurs when the film *No* recapitulates the original "No" spot with future (now past) president of the Chilean Republic, Patricio Aylwin. Larraín's camera focuses on René, shaking hands with an elderly Aylwin within the diegesis of *No* in 2012, then shows a second camera filming Aylwin, building a bridge to the 1988 spot and panning over to a television screen on which a younger Aylwin is addressing Chile in the No campaign. He is arguing for democracy, but, as we will remember, Aylwin is the first president following Pinochet after the success of "No" in the plebiscite. Given the already remarked continuation of the neoliberal framework of the dictatorship into the subsequent democracy, with these *extreme match on action* shots, Larraín again pointedly asks us to consider what has changed, and if it is democracy or neoliberalism that continues to reign in Chile.[71]

DUOLOGY OF PUTRID PATERNALISM, ABIDING ABJECTION—*EL CLUB* (2015) AND *FUGA* (2006)

In Larraín's two films set sometime, somewhere in contemporary Chile, *El club* and *Fuga*, he provides us with a perverse response to his own musings about the fate of democracy and neoliberalism. It would appear that neoliberalism continues to infect the nation, and the costs are visibly apparent in the abject, broken bodies of the perverted, paternal figures that Castro plays in these films. Further, it is perhaps in these two films that the *monumental temporality* of the eternal neoliberal return is most lucidly perceived. Regarding *El club*, Larraín explains in an interview, "this movie is a little bit out of sync and not tied to a specific epoch, although there are dramatic elements that I think are very contemporary and speak about the world today."[72] In other words, while the film bespeaks contemporaneity, it also represents what has already been and what will be in Chile; it imitates the persistent capitulation to neoliberalism that Larraín has excoriated throughout his *oeuvre*. In order to achieve this sense of *monumental temporality*, Larraín makes use of yet another formal technique, which are day-for-night filters, having the effect of constructing a filmic frame "where time seems most definitely suspended."[73] This suspension of time reminds us of an aspect of the spatiotemporality of neoliberalism, which is, as Colombian director Víctor Gaviria has described, that:

> time has been paralysed in a consumable present, in the imminence of consumption. The present in which the product lives sealed in its empty packaging, which at any moment will be eaten, consumed, and then will become a piece of junk in the rubbish heap.[74]

And yet, while this suspension of time—a *monumental temporality* in which spatiality is compressed and the future and past are layered on the present—replicates the neoliberal regime, the grainy, gray-washed image that the day-for-night filters produce is also, as Larraín describes, "a silent protest against all those ultra high-definition images in HD. Nowadays there's an obsession with definition and resolution. People are happy to say they are filming in 4K! No, in 8K! No, in 100K! Please. What rubbish."[75] In this way, Larraín constructs a cinematic frame that at once replicates Chilean capitulation to *high-density capitalism* but also symbolically eschews its high-definition imagery, which points to an obsession with the density of the image, an image destined to be chucked in the "rubbish heap" upon the lightning-fast (tyranny-of-velocity), next evolution in HD.

Larraín also constructs (in order to criticize) this *monumental temporality* of Chilean capitulation to the neoliberal order through the now-familiar technique of the *extreme jump cut*. Perhaps one of the most symbolic of such scenes occurs during an exchange between Father Silva (Jaime Vadell) and Father Ortega (Alejandro Goic). As the setting changes, their unitary discussion, rapidly colonizing space with the velocity of the symbolic weight of neoliberalism, passes from the garden of the priests' little yellow house to different points across the beach, while the day-for-night filters continue to imbue a sense of hazy temporal monumentality. Father Silva and Father Ortega discuss Father García (Marcelo Alonso), and Silva reminds Ortega that García is a Jesuit, a member of the New Church under Pope Francis. Silva has heard Father García speak before, wherein the Jesuit expressed his desire to do away with poverty. Father Silva chides, "if there are no more poor, there are no more saints, and that would be very serious."[76] He continues, in bleak tenor, "This García came to sell us out. The Church washes its hands of us and we are left as the scapegoats."[77] It is quite symbolic that the discussion revolves around economic interests: Silva scoffs at the project of economic equality that he identifies with Father García, while he remains entrenched in the *high-density capitalism* fostered by the Pinochet regime, for which he was a military chaplain. It is thus intensely ironic that Father Silva reproaches Father García for "selling out," for he and his defrocked colleagues are the ones who long ago "sold out" to the "disaster capitalist" model, in which the Catholic Church was and still is imbricated. As a literal marker of their wholesale "sell-out," the priests, led by Castro's character, Father Vidal, train a *galgo* for racing, on which they lasciviously wager. While Sister Mónica (Antonia Zegers) calls the money a blessing, what becomes clear is that the insatiable desires of neoliberal greed have been seamlessly married to the Church.

Lest we believe that the New Church, as opposed to the Old, is washed clean of its ties to neoliberalism (as Silva bemoans, by "washing its hands" of the criminal, excommunicated priests), it is precisely in its drive for cleansing that it replicates the "disaster capitalism" model. As Joseba García Martín explains, "The strategy of closing the homes for penitence operates as a response to the necessity [for the Church] to position itself within the institution of the pluralistic market in which, the core as much as appearances, need to be transparent, clean."[78] This recalls "disaster capitalism's" need for purity, as Klein reminds us that "the Chicago School strain of capitalism does indeed have something in common with other dangerous ideologies: the signature desire for unattainable purity, for a clean slate on which to build a reengineered model society."[79] In this obsession with purity, a clean image, the Church buys into the *high-density*, turbo-information platform of neoliberal mass media, which commercializes and sensationalizes all aspects of life.

Larraín asserts:

> today the Church has only one fear, and it is mass media. Such that the whistleblower becomes so famous that the Pope himself wants to comment. What people are saying about the clergy is more important to them than what they themselves are doing.[80]

Perhaps it is for this reason, understanding the neoliberal politics of denouncement that have the ability to tarnish a clean image, that Sandokan (Roberto Farías), when visiting the cloister to expose Father Lazcano (José Soza) for the sexual abuse that he suffered as a child, pornifies his story in graphic detail. He meticulously describes how Father Lazcano used to ejaculate on his face. He cries that his mouth used to hurt, because it was not big enough for the girth of the priest's penis, and that he subsequently vomited the semen that he had swallowed. Although she refers specifically to Sandokan in *Acceso* (2014), the play also starring Roberto Farías as Sandokan, upon which *El club* is based, María Lorena Saavedra González's comments remain an apt description of the character's relationship to neoliberal, *high-density capitalism* in the film. She avers, "The body of Sandokan is bearer of the recycled culture and identity of late modernity, which is identifiable as the complete economic transformation of human affect and desire on the verge of neoliberal model in crisis."[81] In other words, his abject, broken character becomes emblematic of neoliberal degeneration within the cultural logic of *high-density capitalism* and Chilean capitulation to its corrosive cosmology.

What is more, Sandokan becomes the symbolic son of Chile: spiritual son of the criminal priests who have abused his small body in exchange for their own pleasure. While Father Lazcano is identified as the perpetrator, Father García is quick to also denounce Castro's character, Father Vidal, noting the congruency between the two men. García tells Vidal, "Did you know that you and Father Matías Lazcano had things in common? That you were both excommunicated from the Church for penetrating little boys?"[82] Father Vidal finally confesses:

> I asked *that* boy to sleep with me, in my bed. To embrace, to pray. To ... sleep face to face, so that I breathed in his breath. Such that he knew that my head was twice as big as his and that he needed me to survive.[83]

That boy could easily have been Sandokan, who represents in synecdoche the congregate of abused little boys in Chile. In this way, Father Vidal becomes highly symbolic—synecdochic himself—of bad paternalism, representative of US interventionism (also bad paternalism) in Chile under the same "disaster"-cum-*high-density capitalism* that infects the Church and these cloistered criminal priests. The abject symbiosis between symbolic son and perverted father/Father is only heightened as the movie climaxes. In a series of parallel actions, we cut back and forth between Sandokan being attacked by townspeople and Vidal being assaulted by tourists, visually recapitulating their mutual imbrication. Then, when Sandokan becomes the newest intern in the Fathers' cloister, it is Vidal who renames him Tomás. Tomás is a highly symbolic, biblical name, meaning twin or double. Vidal and Sandokan, not unlike René and Lucho, are two sides of the same coin representing the abject, degenerate(d) body of Chile, replicating the parasitic relationship between the US and Chile. Most strikingly, then, in the end, it is Father Vidal who has been broken by the whirlwind of *high-density* forces around him. After his precious *galgo*, symbolic of his wholesale submission to neoliberal stratification and greed, is killed, he languishes in the tiny house's chapel, curled up in the fetal position. His perverted psychology, emotional wounds, and physically broken body represent the flagellated body politic of Chile, flailing and wailing in the wake of its persistent capitulation to the drives of toxic neoliberalism, under the thumb of the bad paternalism of the United States.

Bad paternalism and abject bodies also plague *Fuga*, Larraín's first feature, which has been criticized for lacking any connection to the contemporary Chile in which it takes place.[84] Such criticism misses the *monumental temporality* of eternal neoliberal return that also imbues this film. What we could call *extreme crosscutting* or *extreme parallel action* populates the majority of the film, crossing between scenes with Chilean composer Eliseo Montalbán (Benjamín Vicuña) and Argentine musician Ricardo Coppa (Gastón Pauls). What makes the cuts *extreme* is that, if the point of parallel action is to suggest to the viewer that the scenes, although in different locales, take place at the same time, the crosscutting in *Fuga* layers past (Eliseo) and present (Ricardo) on top of one another. In this way, Larraín yet again achieves *monumental temporality*, layering the future past on the present, replicating the eternal return of *high-density capitalism*. In this same vein, within these *extreme cross cuts*, Ricardo is attempting to reproduce (copy) Eliseo's masterpiece, *Rapsodia macabra*. He is the simulacratic Argentine copy of the Chilean copy of the American copy, which reminds us of the Argentine adman in *No*, who tells Pinochet's advisors, "Do you know what I have heard all of my Argentine compatriots say? That we want a Pinochet,"[85] as well as the plethora of neoliberal copies of "disaster capitalism" that invade the Southern Cone in the second half of the twentieth century.

This reading draws even greater force when we remember that Eliseo's *Rapsodia macabra* is a death-dealing expression of his trauma surrounding the rape and murder of his sister by his right-wing, extremely wealthy politician father,[86] yet another iteration of bad paternalism imbricated in Chile's "disaster capitalist" model. In this sense, both Eliseo and Ricardo are seeking an outlet for the shock and trauma that they have experienced under perverted, incestuous paternalism, which is represented by Eliseo's father, who willfully capitulates—like the Pinochet regime or the Piñera presidency in Chile, or the Videla regime or the Menem presidency in Argentina (just to name a few of the iterations)—to the neoliberal doctrines of the Northern Empire.

It is highly symbolic, then, that Eliseo's father, Aníbal Montalbán (Willy Semler), sends his son to the state-run psych ward, where he will be subjected to literal shock treatment, emblematic of the "shock doctrine" of "disaster capitalism" inflicted on the country at large. At the facility, Eliseo meets Castro's character, Claudio Leal, who becomes even more symptomatic of the nation deteriorating under this "shock doctrine." He too receives shock therapy and, having been there much longer, has become an abject shell of a person. Looking more like a zombie than a human, Claudio's teeth are rotted, and his skin is diseased, white, and paper thin.

From the moment that he meets Eliseo, he calls him "*mijo*" [my son].[87] In fact, when Eliseo's father comes to visit the ward to see his son's progress, Claudio approaches him and informs him, "I'm your biggest fan."[88] Claudio, shocked, over-medicated, and broken under the rule of law of the psych ward, turns to the very man who has organized the facility and tells him how much he admires him, in fact wants to be him, even calling Aníbal's child (Eliseo) his own. Claudio lucidly represents the willful capitulation of the shattered

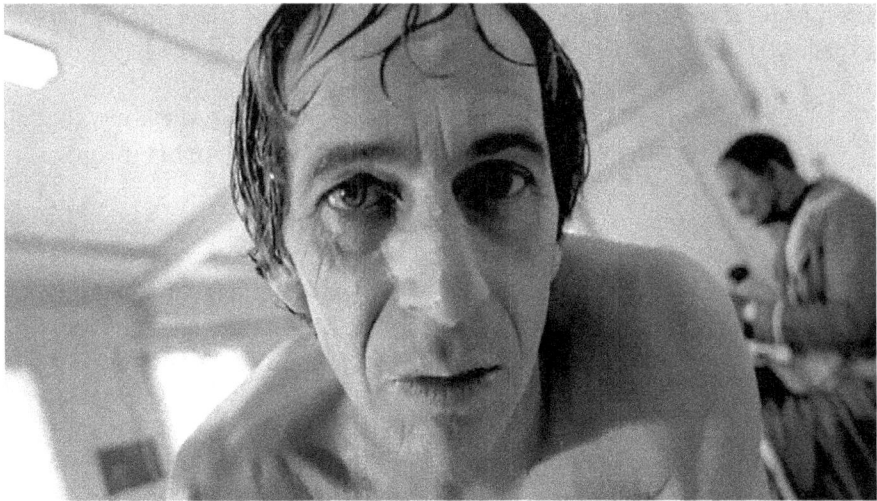

Figure 2.3   The abject body of Claudio Leal in the psychiatric ward in *Fuga* (2006).

Chilean nation to the right-wing "disaster capitalist" model and its participation in its very own degeneration and suffering.

However, not only does Claudio desire to father Eliseo, he also desires him, thus recapitulating the same perverted paternal relationship expressed through the characters of Sandokan and Father Vidal in *El club*. In a symbolic scene, when Claudio clandestinely sneaks into Eliseo's room to see him, he asks him what he is going to become, "a mime disguised as a trumpeter? Or a queer on the inside like all of the boxers and politicians or priests . . .?"[89] The options all refer back—and forward, as is the case—to the mime in *No*, the politicians and bureaucrats throughout Larraín's *oeuvre*, and the Fathers in *El club*, all symbols of capitulation to the "disaster-capitalist," *high-density*, neoliberal model. Eliseo, the son of Chile, like Sandokan, as son of his fathers (Aníbal and Claudio), seems ensnared, with no other options than these. While Claudio desires to be like the father, he also desires his son, such that he and Eliseo become two sides of the same neoliberal coin of capitulation and resultant abjection, just like Vidal and Sandokan. Through these relationships, the *monumental temporality* of "disaster capitalism" continues in its repressively iterative, unending cycle in Chile.

CONCLUSION: A NEW DUOLOGY—DARING TO DEMARCATE AMERICAN ACCOUNTABILITY

Where does Larraín go when he leaves Chile in his films? Incidentally to the United States, with *Jackie* (2016) and *The True American* (at the time of writing in pre-production). Yet there are important connections to be inferred with his thus far six feature films set in Chile. In an interview about *Jackie*, Larraín explains:

> It's at the White House that the decision to support the coup that devastated my country was made, and then later, to support the ousting of Pinochet. It's the White House that pushed the Chileans in power to declare communism illegal, at the end of the 40s, which led to Neruda's flight that I recount in my last film. I'm talking about Chile, but it's the entire world that has been influenced by this place. This is why it can become, in a second, a hell, a paradise, or limbo. It's a labyrinth, a danger zone through which one cannot pass without being affected, sometimes in painful ways. Facing this abyss can be frightening. If I had ever before considered making a film that took place inside the White House, with Jackie Kennedy as the main character, that would have paralyzed me. It was hard but the result is unique, I think. There will never be a *Jackie 2*![90]

In lieu of paralysis, however, throughout his *synecdochic series*, Larraín frankly faces the fear and pain induced in his country by the dominant forces of the White House and its state-supported "shock doctrine" of "disaster capitalism." He does so, moreover, with the assistance of the very same actor that helped to found his directorial career, having met Castro at his Centro de Investigación Teatral [Center for Theater Research] where Larraín went to study film direction.

But Larraín does more than just this; he also faces this fear and pain by moving his critique to the center of the Empire itself. In *Jackie*, for example, only fifteen minutes into the film, we watch as Jackie Kennedy (Natalie Portman) sits in front of her mirror on Air Force One and practices a welcome speech in Spanish (translated here):

> I am happy to be in the great state of Texas. To be with you all, and to experience the noble Spanish heritage, which has achieved so much in Dallas. This heritage began 100 years before Massachusetts, my husband's state, was colonized. It is a heritage that remains alive and long-lasting.[91]

This cuts deeply at US imperialism in the Americas, reminding the nation that a large part of its body politic was usurped from and remains culturally contingent with the Other Americas. Further, although there may never be a *Jackie 2*, *The True American* would seem to follow seamlessly in its wake. Based on the book of the same name by Anand Giridharadas (2014),[92] in which an Air Force officer of Bangladeshi descent is shot by an American terrorist bent on killing Muslims in the aftermath of 9/11, it questions what it means to be a "true" "American" from the underside. Further, it provides Larraín with the opportunity to begin to draw direct connections across his cinematic corpus between September 11 in Chile and in the United States. Returning to Klein in *The Shock Doctrine*, it is as if Larraín cinematically renders visible the process by which for decades:

> Friedman and his followers had methodically exploited moments of shock in other countries—foreign equivalents of 9/11, starting with Pinochet's coup on September 11, 1973. What happened on September 11, 2001, is that an ideology hatched in American universities and fortified in Washington institutions finally had its chance to come home.[93]

In other words, since, as Klein asserts, the Friedmanian corporatist model of neoliberalism is erected on crisis and disaster; the chaos induced by the events of September 11, 2001 facilitated the "shock doctrine's" homecoming to the United States. In this way, Pablo Larraín invites us *all* to a reckoning. Whether facing Chilean capitulation to, or our own imbrication in, the Northern Empire of neoliberalism, we are all called to face the fear and pain that it induces, lest for one more moment we move yet closer to the total impoverishment, the utter abjection, of the global body politic.

NOTES

1. Pablo Larraín qtd. in José Teodoro, "The State That I Am In," *Film Comment* 52, no. 6 (2016): 42. Herein, Larraín establishes *Tony Manero*, *Post mortem*, and *No* as an unintentional trilogy: "While we're making it [*No*], it occurs to me that we have some kind of trilogy. I never planned it."
2. Scholars have repeatedly likened the Alfredo Castro characters in Larraín's films to symbolic representations of Pinochet. Most notably, the following sources equate Raúl Peralta of *Tony Manero* to the dictator: Martha P. Nochimson, "Tony Manero," *Cineaste* 34, no. 4 (2009): 47; Vania Barraza Toledo, "Reviewing the Present in Pablo Larraín's Historical Cinema," *Iberoamericana* 13, no. 51 (2013): 166; Nike Jung, "History, Fiction and the Politics of Corporeality in the Dictatorship Trilogy of Pablo Larraín," in *History, Memory and Film*, eds. J. Carlsten and F. McGarry (Basingstoke: Palgrave Macmillan, 2015), 122; Emmanuel Larraz, "*Tony Manero* (2008) ou la violence *high density*," *L'Ordinaire des Amériques* (2015): para. 5: <https://journals.openedition.org/orda/2422> (accessed February 25, 2020); Wesley Costa de Moraes, "*Tony Manero*, *Post mortem* y *No*: La estética de lo masculino en la trilogía de Pablo Larraín," *Letras Hispanas* 11 (2015): 123; Robert Wells, "Trauma, Male Fantasies, and Cultural Capital in the Films of Pablo Larraín," *Journal of Latin American Cultural Studies* 26, no. 4 (2017): 509; Maria M. Delgado, "'The Capacity to Create Mystery': An Interview with Pablo Larraín," in *A Companion to Latin American Cinema*, eds. Maria M. Delgado, Stephen M. Hart, and Randal Johnson (Chichester: Wiley-Blackwell, 2017), 459; Amit Thakkar, "The Perpetrating Victim: An Allegorical Reading of Pablo Larraín's *Tony Manero* (2008)," *Journal of Latin American Cultural Studies* 26, vol. 4 (2017): 524. In addition, a few scholars have noted that Castro's characters in the "dictatorial trilogy" seem to be connected through their embodiment of the dictatorship: Carolina Urrutia, "*Post mortem* y *Tony Manero*: Memoria centrífuga de un pasado político," *Cinémas d'Amérique Latine* 19 (2011): 73; Wolfgang Bongers, "La estética del (an)archivo en el cine de Pablo Larraín," *A Contracorriente* 12, no. 1 (2014): 200; Wells, "Trauma, Male Fantasies, and Cultural Capital," 511, 515. In contrast, this intervention seeks to highlight the connections between the Castro characters throughout the director's entire cinematic corpus, looking beyond connections to Pinochet—which are veritable, to be sure—and expanding into harsh critique of Chilean capitulation to neoliberalism and the Northern Empire.
3. Pablo Larraín, "Fear and Oblivion," *Sight & Sound* 19, no. 5 (2009): 47.
4. Larraín qtd. in Teodoro, "The State That I Am In," 45.
5. Pablo Larraín qtd. in Roger Alan Koza, "Bailando por una pesadilla: Pablo Larraín habla sobre *Tony Manero*," *Con los ojos abiertos*, April 2, 2009, sec. "¿Cómo ves tu película?": <http://www.conlosojosabiertos.com/bafici-2009-cn-entrevistas-2> (accessed February 25, 2020). All translations from Spanish to English and from French to English have been made by the author of this chapter. Original Spanish: "Porque para mí el verdadero cambio no fecha en el 73, el año del golpe. El momento esencial es cuando Pinochet

introduce a los *chicago boys*, cinco economistas formados en EE.UU. que Pinochet los llevó al Ministerio de Hacienda y Economía, y es ahí en donde empieza este nuevo sistema. En ese mismo momento se produjo una gran represión."

6. Naomi Klein, *The Shock Doctrine: The Rise of Disaster Capitalism* (New York: Metropolitan Books/Henry Holt, 2007), 60.
7. Ibid., 70.
8. Ibid., 71.
9. Ibid., 92.
10. Ibid., 71.
11. Ibid., 125.
12. Pablo Larraín qtd. in Rodrigo González, "Me interesa mostrar la basura que se esconde bajo la alfombra," *La Tercera*, November 21, 2010, sec. "¿Ve autoritarismo aún en el chileno común y corriente?": <https://www.pressreader.com/chile/la-tercera/20101121/282518654895127> (accessed March 16, 2020). Original Spanish: "Tenemos un gobierno de derecha que controla prácticamente todo y además es una derecha que no necesita opacar a nadie, porque no tiene nada en contra. Creo que ese es un proceso de conquista que viene desde Pinochet en adelante."
13. Violet Lucca, "Projecting and Excavating the Past: An Interview with Pablo Larraín," *Film Comment*, April 19, 2012, sec. "You've been very critical of the Right": <https://www.filmcomment.com/blog/projecting-the-past-an-interview-with-pablo-larrain> (accessed February 25, 2020).
14. In this sense, I concur with Joanna Page's analysis of contemporary Chilean cineastes when she claims that, although "today's filmmakers are accused of failing to take up a critical position with regard to the neoliberal policies that have so thoroughly restructured Chilean society since the 1973 coup," it is more apt to understand their positionality as "construct[ing] a possible—and perhaps more authentic—mode of critique in an age in which 'there is no longer an outside to capitalism.'" ("Neoliberalism and the Politics of Affect and Self-Authorship in Contemporary Chilean Cinema," in *A Companion to Latin American Cinema*, eds. Maria M. Delgado, Stephen M. Hart, and Randal Johnson [Chichester: Wiley-Blackwell, 2017], 269–70). This is particularly so for Larraín, who maintains, "I don't intend to divorce myself from politics because I don't believe this is possible" (Larraín qtd. in Teodoro, "The State That I Am In," 45).
15. Leah Kemp, "Stardom in Spanish America," in *A Companion to Latin American Cinema*, eds. Maria M. Delgado, Stephen M. Hart, and Randal Johnson (Chichester: Wiley Blackwell, 2017), 41.
16. Alfredo Castro qtd. in Carola Solari, "El delirio y la cautela," *Revista Caras*, November 21, 2003, 178. Original Spanish: "El contenido de *Mano de obra* tiene que ver con lo que está pasando: el libre mercado, lo que me sucede en la televisión donde somos tratados como un producto, cuánto vales, cuál es tu precio. Eso es sucio y me molesta. Yo no estoy a la venta."
17. Alfredo Castro qtd. in Jessica Kiang, "The Club," in *El club*, dir. Pablo Larraín (Chicago, IL: Music Box Films, 2016), DVD, 11.
18. Ibid.
19. Larraín qtd. in González, "Me interesa mostrar la basura," sec. "¿Cuánto le debe su cine al Teatro La Memoria, de Alfredo Castro?": <https://www.pressreader.com/chile/la-tercera/20101121/282518654895127> (accessed March 16, 2020). Original Spanish: "Es esencial en mi trabajo, un conductor de lo que yo quiero poner en pantalla."
20. Ángela Precht, "La intriga de *Fuga*," *Angelita Action* (blog), January 6, 2005, sec. "¿Y cómo fue trabajar con Alfredo Castro . . .?": <http://angelita.action.at/la-intriga-de-

emfugaem> (accessed February 25, 2020). Original Spanish: "Alfredo tiene un personaje emblemático dentro de la película."
21. Here a note is necessary about the national specificity of Larraín's cinema. It is true that hundreds of neighborhood cinemas have closed, while US and Australian multiplexes have been opened to stream Hollywood hits in Chile (Page, "Neoliberalism and the Politics of Affect," 273). It is further true that, while Larraín's films have garnered acclaim on international film circuits, his biggest hit in Chile, *No*, still only boasted an audience of 209,000, while the other two films of the trilogy had even lower numbers: 86,000 for *Tony Manero* and 20,500 for *Post mortem* (Barraza Toledo, "Reviewing the Present," 160). Even Larraín himself notes, "Persiste un problema con la audiencia. La cantidad de gente que va a ver cine chileno se ha estabilizado en los últimos diez años, pero la cantidad de películas ha aumentado. Y esto es delicado. Por ejemplo, una película como *El cielo, la tierra y la lluvia*, de José Luis Torres Leiva, la vieron 732 personas, siendo una película preciosa. Un delirio, un absurdo" [A problem with the audience persists. The number of people that go to see Chilean cinema has been stabilized in the last ten years, but the number of films has increased. And this is a delicate subject. For example, a film like *El cielo, la tierra y la lluvia*, by José Luis Torres Leiva, was seen by just 732 people, although being a gem of a film. A delirium, an absurdity] (qtd. in Koza, "Bailando por una pesadilla," sec. "Es posible que . . ."). Although lacking a robust national audience, Larraín is intent on focalizing the Chilean nation and criticizing its imbrication in the transnational nexus of neoliberalism in his films.
22. *Neruda*, dir. Pablo Larraín (2016; Culver City, CA: Sony Pictures Home Entertainment, Inc., 2017), DVD. Original Spanish: "su presidente, el traidor González Videla, quien se vendió al imperio del Norte."
23. Ibid. Original Spanish: "Mi presidente tiene un jefe—el presidente de los Estados Unidos. Cuando él dice que tenemos que matar a nuestros comunistas criollos, este similor gavillero tiene que obedecer."
24. Ibid. In the director's commentary, Larraín explains that the scenes in Alessandri's home are filmed in the Palacio Cousiño and that when Neruda first begins his discussion with Alessandri, the family is lunching.
25. Ibid. Original Spanish: "Un populista de puerto," which would also suggest that President González Videla's ties run through the "port" and abroad to the United States. His anti-communist ideology is imported.
26. Ibid.
27. Ibid. Original Spanish: "un señor feudal que inventó el capitalismo en su tierra."
28. Ibid. Original Spanish: "maricón de presidente."
29. Ibid. Original Spanish: "el estado es enemigo de la libertad."
30. Ibid. Original Spanish: "Sobre sus hombros y su alma se construye el futuro de la República. El millonario es siempre más inteligente que la ley de la nación."
31. Pablo Larraín qtd. in Andrew Chernin, "Entendiendo a Pablo Larraín," *La Tercera*, January 20, 2013, para. 22: <http://www2.latercera.com/noticia/entendiendo-a-pablo-larrain> (accessed February 27, 2020). Original Spanish: "O el modelo que tenía Pinochet del orden social, que hoy tiene al país con ocho o 10 dueños. Uno de ellos es el Presidente de Chile [Piñera]."
32. Larraín qtd. in Lucca, "Projecting and Excavating the Past," sec. "The film and Mario's character."
33. Ibid., sec. "I wanted to ask you about Nancy."
34. *Post mortem*, dir. Pablo Larraín (2010; New York: Kino Lorber, Inc., 2012), DVD.

35. Amit Thakkar, "Unclaimed Experience and the Implicated Subject in Pablo Larraín's *Post Mortem*," in *Scars and Wounds*, eds. Nick Hodgin and Amit Thakkar (Basingstoke: Palgrave Macmillan, 2017), 260.
36. Wells, "Trauma, Male Fantasies, and Cultural Capital," 511.
37. Lucca, "Projecting and Excavating the Past," sec. "That archeological impulse . . ."
38. Juan Poblete, "The Memory of the National and the National as Memory," *Latin American Perspectives* 42, no. 3 (2015): 101.
39. Bongers, "La estética del (an)archivo," 200. Original Spanish: "no solo es producto del régimen criminal, sino también de la ansiedad consumista pervertida, de la ideología mercantil individualista, que considera al otro un obstáculo para el éxito personal."
40. Larraín, "Fear and Oblivion," 47. In fact, Raúl's very obsession with Tony Manero of *Saturday Night Fever* represents, according to Tzvi Tal, "una visión melancólica del mundo cultural que la globalización neoliberal destruyó, donde las salas de cine que proyectaban películas con claro contenido político-social fueron reemplazadas por los multiplex que exhiben los productos de los monopolios mediáticos" [a melancholic vision of the cultural world that neoliberal globalization has destroyed, where the movie theatres that used to show films with clear sociopolitical content were replaced by multiplexes that only show the products of media monopolies] ("Memoria y muerte: La dictadura de Pinochet en las películas de Pablo Larraín: *Tony Manero* [2007] y *Post mortem* [2010]," *Nuevo mundo / Mundos nuevos* [2012]: para 18: <https://journals.openedition.org/nuevomundo/62884, accessed February 25, 2020). It is for this reason, in large part, that Castro himself refused to see *Saturday Night Fever* when it debuted in Chile in 1978, averring that it was "una basura que tapaba todo lo horroroso que estaba pasando" [a piece of garbage that pulled the wool over our eyes to all the horrors that were occurring] (qtd. in Oscar Contardo, "Alfredo Castro: 'Aún no he visto *Tony Manero*,'" *El Mercurio* [Santiago, Chile], July 6, 2008, E9).
41. *Tony Manero*, dir. Pablo Larraín (2008; New York: Kino Lorber, Inc., 2010), DVD. Original Spanish: "Es más tonto usted. Es otro gringo."
42. Ibid. Original Spanish: "Yo no po, ya no más."
43. Here "Unitedstatesian" sardonically plays off the Spanish term denominating Americans from the United States—*estadounidenses*—a specificity that counters the imperial drive of the United States to declare itself the sole proprietor of the American identity, overwriting the Other Americas.
44. Larraín, dir., *Tony Manero*.
45. Klein, *The Shock Doctrine*, 15.
46. Christian Gundermann, "*La libertad* entre los escombros de la globalización," *Ciberletras* 13 (2005): sec. 2, para. 18: <http://www.lehman.edu/faculty/guinazu/ciberletras/v13/gunderman.htm> (accessed February 25, 2020). Original Spanish: "Las décadas neoliberales han producido una aceleración implacable . . . conllevando todos los efectos que Paul Virilio ha teorizado bajo los términos dromología y dromocracia (en el sentido de 'tiranía de la velocidad')."
47. Gundermann, "*La libertad*," sec. 2, para. 18. Original Spanish: "la retracción del espacio, coproducto de la aceleración."
48. Geoffrey Kantaris, "The Young and the Damned: Street Visions in Latin American Cinema," in *Contemporary Latin American Cultural Studies*, eds. Stephen Hart and Robert Young (London, UK: Arnold Publishing, 2003), 183.
49. Larraín, "Fear and Oblivion," 47.
50. For example, Robert Wells provides an apt example in "Trauma, Male Fantasies, and Cultural Capital," 514: "Richard, for example, critiques *No* for 'over-aestheticizing' the

matter, and for focusing too much on the US-style advertising that apparently drove the 'NO' campaign and coincided with Pinochet's own political and economic designs."
51. Pablo Larraín qtd. in Nicolas Azalbert, "Santiago 88, post memoriam," *Cahiers du cinéma* 687 (2013): 45. Original French: "Le retour de la démocratie et de la gauche au pouvoir en 1988 n'a pas fait que conserver le modèle de Pinochet, il l'a rendu plus fort. Le grand triomphe du 'non' impliquait secrètement un petit triomphe du 'oui.' Nous avons gardé la Constitution de Pinochet et son modèle économique, l'égalité est restée une abstraction . . . C'est [maintenant] comme vivre dans un centre commercial. Tout se vend et tout s'achète."
52. Poblete, "The Memory of the National," 96.
53. Chernin, "Entendiendo a Pablo Larraín," para. 23. Original Spanish: "El mismo Piñera ve *No* y dice que la película estaba demasiado basada en el marketing, así es que no le gustó mucho . . . Está basada en el marketing porque desde ese lugar nos pareció interesante ver la alegoría. Él era una persona rica [en] el 88. Hoy es billonario. ¿Qué no entendió?"
54. Paula T. Cronovich, "'No' and *No*: The Campaign of 1988 and Pablo Larraín's Film," *Radical History Review* 124 (2016): 165–76.
55. See, for example, Maria M. Delgado, "The Capacity to Create Memory," 459. Therein, she asserts, "Politics—and indeed democracy—becomes another product to be bought and sold if the price is right."
56. See Vania Barraza Toledo, "Reviewing the Present," 169. She explains, "Examined from a contemporary viewpoint the campaign jingle announces an empty dream, and analyzed from a socio-economic perspective, the protagonist [René Saavedra] therefore incarnates the neoliberal model introduced during the dictatorship and maintained by democratic governments in Chile."
57. *No*, dir. Pablo Larraín (2012; Culver City, CA: Sony Pictures Classics, 2013), DVD. Original Spanish: "Hoy Chile piensa en su futuro."
58. Ibid. Original Spanish: "Esto es muy, muy, muy original. En América, quizás, hay algo parecido, pero hay que confiar en nuestro producto."
59. Ibid. Original Spanish: "Esto es todo lo que nuestra juventud necesita."
60. Ibid.
61. Ibid. Original Spanish: "Tenemos un producto distinto a la competencia."
62. Ibid.
63. Ibid. Original Spanish: "¿La viste? Porque hay un cambio en la estrategia conceptual. ¿Te gustó?"
64. Ibid. Original Spanish: "Es mala. Es bien mala. Es malísima, Lucho. Es mierda sobre mierda sobre mierda. Es la copia de la copia de la copia de la copia de la copia. Está todo mezclado."
65. Ibid. Original Spanish: "La copia de la copia de la copia de la copia de la copia de la copia."
66. Ibid.
67. Ibid.
68. Ibid.
69. Edward Luttwak, *Turbo-Capitalism: Winners and Losers in the Global Economy* (New York: Harper Perennial, 2000), 4.
70. Tatjana Pavlović, *100 Years of Spanish Cinema* (Singapore: Utopia Press, 2009), 229.
71. I would also concur with Caetlin Benson-Allot, in "An Illusion Appropriate to the Conditions *No*," when she suggests that "Larraín exploits the U-matic's slightly blurred images to critique the blurred principles of the campaign, its capitulation to the empty promises of 1980s advertising" (*Film Quarterly* 66, no. 3 [2013]: 61).
72. Larraín qtd. in Delgado, "The Capacity to Create Mystery," 461.
73. Mar Diestro-Dópido, "Sins of the Fathers," *Sight & Sound* 26, no. 4 (2016): 30.

74. Víctor Gaviria, "¿Por qué hago cine?," *Revista de Estudios Colombianos* 33–4 (2009): 4.
75. Larraín qtd. in Diestro-Dópido, "Sins of the Fathers," 30.
76. *El club*, dir. Pablo Larraín (2015; Chicago, IL: Music Box Films, 2016), DVD. Original Spanish: "si se acaban los pobres, se nos acabarían los santos, y eso sería gravísimo."
77. Ibid. Original Spanish: "Este García vino a vendernos. La Iglesia se lava las manos y nosotros quedamos como unos chivos expiatorios."
78. Joseba García Martín, "El Club," *Papeles del CEIC* 2 (2016): 5. Original Spanish: "La estrategia de cerrar las casas de penitencia funciona como respuesta a la necesidad de posicionarse dentro del plantel de mercado plural en el que, tanto lo planteado como lo aparente, debe ser transparente, limpio."
79. Klein, *The Shock Doctrine*, 20.
80. Pablo Larraín qtd. in "Trampa perversa y vergonzosa," *Humanitas* 20, no. 78 (2015): 331. Original Spanish: "hoy en día la Iglesia solo tenga un miedo, y que sean los medios de comunicación. Que el portavoz del nuncio [sic] sea más famoso a veces que el mismo Papa quiere decir algo. A los miembros de la curia les importa más lo que se dice de ellos que lo que ellos mismos hacen."
81. María Lorena Saavedra González, "*Acceso*: Un cuerpo cargado de historia y cultura," *Telondefondo: Revista de Teoría y Crítica Teatral* 21 (2015): 137. Original Spanish: "El cuerpo de Sandokan es portador de una cultura e identidad reciclada de la modernidad tardía, la cual es reconocible como la perfecta transformación económica de los afectos y los deseos de los seres humanos al borde de un modelo neoliberal en crisis."
82. Larraín, dir., *El club*. Original Spanish: "¿Usted sabía que el padre Matías Lazcano y usted tenían cosas en común? ¿Qué ambos fueron excomulgados de la Iglesia por penetrar a niños menores de edad?"
83. Ibid. Original Spanish: "le pedí a *ese* niño que durmiera conmigo, en mi cama. Que nos abrazamos, que rezamos. Que . . . dormimos cara a cara, que yo respiré su aliento. Que él sabía que yo tenía el cerebro dos veces más grande que él y que me usaba para sobrevivir" (emphasis mine).
84. For example, see Joachim Lepastier, "Larraín, L'ironie reine," *Cahiers du cinéma* 730 (2017): 22. Herein, he asserts, "On ne peut pas dire qu'on voie grand-chose du Chili d'aujourd'hui dans *Fuga* ou *El Club*, presque un cas d'école sur l'esquive du présent." [One cannot say that one sees a whole lot of present-day Chile in *Fuga* or *El club*, they are almost a textbook example of the evasion of the present.]
85. Larraín, dir., *No*. Original Spanish: "¿Sabéis lo que les he escuchado por la parte de mis compatriotas argentinos? Queremos un Pinochet."
86. In this sense, I concur with Robert Wells's reading of the film, identifying Eliseo's father as the rapist and murderer of his beloved sister, although I want to argue that the bad paternalism that he models reaches beyond Pinochet. Wells states: "Eliseo's last words clarify the matter regarding his sister. In mentioning his father while thinking about swimming, Eliseo identifies the father as her rapist and murderer—precisely because he is incapable of fully doing so, since the trauma has been repressed for so long. What is more, in recurring to the father, Larraín symbolically implicates Chile's greater father figure, Pinochet, as the author and repressor of violent crimes as well" ("Trauma, Male Fantasies, and Cultural Capital," 508).
87. *Fuga*, dir. Pablo Larraín (2006; Las Vegas, NV: Laguna Productions, Inc., 2008), DVD.
88. Ibid. Original Spanish: "Yo soy su ídola."
89. Ibid. Original Spanish: "¿ . . . un mimo disfrazado de trompeta? ¿O una marica de fondo como todos los boxeadores y los políticos o los curas . . . ?"
90. Cyril Béghin, "Les Yeux de Jackie: Entretien avec Pablo Larraín," *Cahiers du cinéma* 730 (2017): 18. Original French: "C'est à la Maison-Blanche qu'a été prise la décision

de soutenir le coup d'État qui a dévasté mon pays, puis plus tard, de soutenir l'éviction de Pinochet. C'est la Maison-Blanche qui a poussé les dirigeants chiliens à déclarer le communisme illégal, à la fin des années 40, ce qui a conduit à la fuite de Neruda que je raconte dans mon précédent film. Je parle du Chili, mais c'est le monde entier qui a été influencé à partir de cet endroit. Voilà pourquoi il peut devenir, en une seconde, un enfer, un paradis ou des limbes. C'est un labyrinthe, une zone dangereuse où on ne peut pas passer sans être affecté, parfois de manière douloureuse. Faire face à ce gouffre peut faire peur. Si j'avais jamais réfléchi à la réalisation d'un film se déroulant à l'intérieur de la Maison-Blanche, avec Jackie Kennedy en personnage principal, ça m'aurait paralysé. Mais j'ai été précipité dans ce projet, et dans ce lieu. Ça a été dur mais le résultat est unique, je crois. Il n'y aura jamais un *Jackie 2*!"

91. *Jackie*, dir. Pablo Larraín (2016; Beverly Hills, CA: Twentieth Century Fox Home Entertainment, LLC, 2016), DVD. Original Spanish: "Estoy muy contenta de estar en el gran estado de Texas. A estar con ustedes, y experimentar de la noble tradición española, que tanto ha conseguido en Dallas. Esta tradición comenzó 100 años antes de que se colonizó Massachusetts, el estado de mi marido. Todo es una tradición que se mantiene viva y rigorosa."
92. Anand Giridharadas, *The True American: Murder and Mercy in Texas* (New York: W. W. Norton, 2014).
93. Klein, *The Shock Doctrine*, 12.

CHAPTER 3

"Within the Limits of the Possible": Realist Aesthetics in Larraín's Dictatorship Trilogy

Berenike Jung

This chapter discusses the contributing reasons for and possible meanings of the realist aesthetic forms in Pablo Larraín's "dictatorship trilogy": *Tony Manero* (2008), *Post mortem* (2010), and *No* (2012). This aesthetic would appear to adapt particularly well to these films' project of creating conditions of belief in the historical truth of their cinematic worlds as well as to their subject matter revolving around Chile's dictatorship past. Close readings, in particular of the role of long takes and the use of a corporeal metaphor, demonstrate how these films reference but also renegotiate key features of realism, establishing cross-connections with previous and transnational cinema movements, and adding supplementary information to specific audience groups. The key question that follows is whether and to what extent, by activating the aesthetic approaches associated with these movements, the films also renegotiate their political-ethical proclivities. The textual analysis will be complemented by contextualizing the films within Chile's particular cinema and memory landscape as well as by considering the influence and limitations posed by industrial parameters. These formal parameters notwithstanding, the films' evocation and modification of a realist aesthetic enable a political critique aimed at both past and present conditions.

WHY REALISM HERE AND WHY NOW?

Following scholars from André Bazin onwards, film critic A. O. Scott suggests discussing the versatile "realist impulse less as a style or genre than as an ethic that finds expression in various places at critical times."[1] Therefore, the question to be resolved in this chapter is which factors encourage the emergence of this aesthetic at this specific historical and cultural moment?

Larraín's trilogy was the first in the recent past to depict the Chilean dictatorship in fiction cinema. While the national past continued to dominate in documentary, Chilean narrative film had all but avoided the topic, except for a brief spike in the early 1990s, immediately after the return to democracy. The reasons given for this schism between fiction and documentary range from real and internalized censorship, the historical experience of mediatic betrayal and collaboration,[2] the discrepancy in economic risk, lack of infrastructure and state support, to a perceived lack of audience: since 1999, the home audience for Chilean films has settled at 6 percent of total spectatorship, or about 1 million, even though production has considerably increased. Only around 10 percent of films shown in Chile are not from the US; if more than a dozen Chilean films come out in a given year, these will compete among themselves.[3]

THE FESTIVAL CIRCUIT, OR "CHILEAN CINEMA DOES NOT APPEAR WHEN IT WANTS TO BUT WHENEVER IT CAN"[4]

Given this pressure on narrative cinema to choose a "sellable" topic, international film festivals increasingly function as producers and (potentially international) distributors, wielding influence and creating streamlined aesthetic expectations in their own right, geared toward a particular kind of global cinephile audience. The spread of the festival circuit has coincided with the resurgence, or in some cases emergence, of several "small national cinemas"; and changes in the festival landscape, often concomitant with changes in national funding policies, particularly affect these cinemas.[5] For lack of alternative forms of funding, filmmakers often employ strategies to render their films globally accessible, and to appeal to particular to audiences at global film festivals. These audiences, in turn, seem to have adapted and been trained to expect certain standards and particular aesthetic shapes.

As a result, the festival circuit can have an effect of creating films "made to order."[6] International co-production or funding is seen to erase cultural specificity. In the case of Chile, María Peirano suggests that the influence of international festivals results in a "Chilean-cosmopolitan aesthetic," including the strategic use of national identity, made to appeal to a specific set of the transnational film community who share a "global cinephilia."[7] Thus, the international film festival scene offers a space for, but also promotes and sustains universalized ideas of "world cinema," the national, as well as a preferred aesthetic.[8] One should bear in mind the evidently problematic implications of "world cinema" or "small nations" (which I use here, following the cited authors) as they necessarily lump together a vast array of different films and styles as non-Hollywood cinema, itself an imaginary monolith.[9]

The precise ways in which funding procedures and requirements—whether foreign or national—impact the type of film proposed and selected for (national or international) funding, is difficult to measure. What *can* be empirically demonstrated, however, is that an internationalized circuit of dissemination has become the established routine in Chile: films are first screened abroad at international festivals and only then (if at all) exhibited and potentially distributed in Chile.[10]

CROSSOVER APPEAL

Yet there also exist particularities to the Chilean cinema landscape that invite a realist aesthetic. Italian neorealism had a profound influence on Latin American filmmakers, reflected in Chilean social documentary of the 1950s and 1960s to revolutionary cinema, including the celebrated Nuevo Cine Chileno (New Chilean Cinema) of the 1960s and 1970s,[11] which in turn remains an important reference point for contemporary film and national (media) history.[12] The aesthetics perceivable in contemporary production that seem to echo these cinematic trends have led some Chilean academics to propose that we are presented with a *novísimo cine chileno* (Newest Chilean cinema); other scholars, such as Verónica Cortínez and Manfred Engelbert, dismiss this notion as a marketing ploy.[13] Accordingly, contemporary Chilean cinema's realism operates within a paradigm that is familiar to global cinephile festival audiences, but its realist style could also appeal specifically to its home audience, once the hurdles of the festival circuits are successfully jumped (and distribution secured).[14] The allure of realism can then be considered as both historically grown and transculturally nourished, and perhaps also as a counter to the pull of international festivals toward what María Soledad Montañez and David Martin-Jones called "auto-erasure" and de-culturalization.[15] These films are layered and complex enough to attract at least two constituencies, a transnational audience that shares a particular type of cinephilia, and the national home audience. And the realist mode in particular offers a sense of ambiguity and a transnational pull that might appeal to filmmakers, "in a post-national era, when attempting to produce a 'crossover' that will successfully address a national audience as well as one beyond geographical boundaries and maximize profits."[16]

In general, contemporary Latin American cinema is characterized by an aesthetic and stylistic multiplicity or hybridity,[17] which makes it accessible for Néstor García Canclíni's "glocal" publics: citizens global in consumption but local in "languages, memory, and national sensibility."[18] While not homogeneous, such interpretative communities share some common frameworks of jokes, references, stereotypes, "everyday games of hide-and-seek that only 'natives' play, unwritten rules of behavior, jokes understood from half a word, a sense of complicity."[19] Juan Poblete, coined the term "supplementarity" to describe the way in which such narratives extend beyond the surface, adding further subordinated information and *double entendres*.[20]

This formal hybridity of Latin American cinema also resonates with the definitions of art cinema as an "impure" or "ambiguous" form. Art Cinema has historically been closely associated both with specific realist movements and with modernist tropes, as well as its prominence at the international festival scene:[21] "Realist conventions [have been part of] the tradition of international art cinema ... [and] central to the creation of the 'global literacy' of an incipient 'cosmopolitan citizenship.'"[22] Beyond the tastes and growing influence of cinephile transnational audiences, something about the aesthetic thrust of an "impure" realism seems to lend itself particularly to the topic of what is hidden or invisible about the national past: "Realism's claim to make visible what otherwise goes unseen meshes with art cinema's attempt to represent the forbidden or unspeakable."[23]

This notion of impurity, as well as audience-specific paratextual information and aesthetic supplementarity, will enhance the analysis of the trilogy.

ETHICS OF REALISM

For Bazin, Italian neorealism is a "styleless style" that allows reality in all its ambiguity to present itself.[24] As a cinematic mode, it realizes cinema's ultimate potential, producing the image without (or with minimal) intervention. But Bazin also found neorealism's aesthetics inextricably interwoven with its political agenda: "Neorealism has a canonical status in Bazin's thought *because* it is more than a style; it directly engages social history."[25] At the end of World War II, neorealism sought to enable a different kind of emotional engagement, and also to contribute to a distinctively national cinema. In his 1952 proclamations on what distinguishes neorealism from "the American cinema," Cesare Zavattini advocates a cinematic style that looks directly and *for extended duration* "on the real things, exactly as they are," that the responsibility of cinema is to help audiences arrive at "a moral discovery," and that this practice of cinema would create emotions that are "more effective, morally stronger, more useful."[26]

Discussing the renewal of realist commitments in "world cinema," Lúcia Nagib and Tiago de Luca also focus on the question of political and ethical intent. Nagib defines this realism by its reliance on exclusive, not simulated profilmic events, real physical activity, and "real-time" shots. Her "ethics of realism" hinges on indexicality: "what Rancière termed 'the inherent honesty of the film medium'... that is to say, the film's indexical property."[27] For her, world cinema's new realism is informed by a political ethics: "To choose reality instead of simulation is a moral question."[28] Not unlike Bazin's focus on how the long take and the deep focus shot capture an element of uncontrollable chance inherent in reality, Nagib also emphasizes the reliance on non-simulated profilmic events, real physical activity, and "real-time" shots, while de Luca explores the "hyperbolic" dimension of the long take and the close-up, their effect on the viewing experience and the type of aesthetic gaze they provoke.[29]

However, because no cinematic technique carries an intrinsic, fixed meaning, it is possible, as Karl Schoonover reminds us, to "appropriate a logic of the image" while rejecting the political, humanist project from which it emerged.[30] Schoonover is critical of the monolithic understandings of neorealist aesthetics as a political act: certain stylistic commonalities may suggest shared concerns but may also hide different agendas. Schoonover also emphasizes how neorealist cinema's appeal to a broadened international audience and its encouragement of a "benevolent receptivity" raises ethical questions. The parallel of a consciously transnational address back then and now is appealing. Moreover, in his influential essay, David Bordwell defines art cinema as an aesthetic practice that resonates with the idea of realism as an ethic.[31] The question to examine then, is whether the shared aesthetic choices and transnational address of these films expand to a shared ethical or political dimension.

TONY MANERO

In *Manero*, protagonist Raúl Peralta (Alfredo Castro) wants to win a Chilean television look-alike contest, specifically the round calling for the star of *Saturday Night Fever* (John Badham, 1977), John Travolta's Tony Manero. This central titular quest can be read as an allegory of the Chilean nation at that point in its history. Just as the protagonist mimics his Hollywood idol, Chile was emulating the glittery appearance of another nation: the United States. What Carlos Flores defined as Chile's "mania of the copy," a sociocultural tic,[32] is certainly not an exclusively Chilean obsession, but it lends itself easily to the interpretation of Raúl rejecting his national identity. In one scene, Raúl's lover tells him he is Chilean and he responds, using *Chilenismos*: "No, not me ... not any more" ("Yo no po ... yo, no más"). Raúl's delusion is that he does not want to be "the Chilean Tony Manero," he wants to *be* Tony Manero, not only a different person or nationality, but an entirely fictional character. The additional sly joke is that Raúl does not really resemble Travolta/Manero.

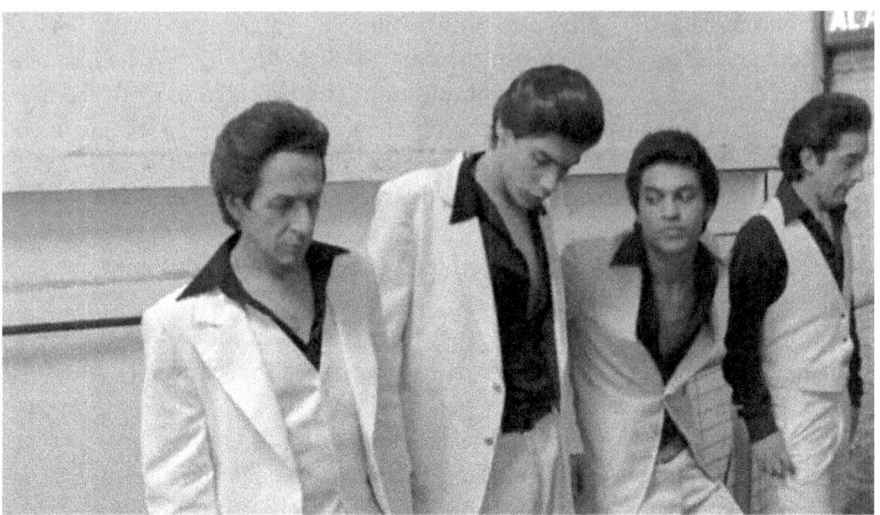

Figure 3.1 *Tony Manero* (2008).

Thomas Elsaesser and Warren Buckland suggest that "[t]he line between the criminal (the extreme embodiment of the system itself, which takes the system at its word) and the resister/contester of the system ... becomes a fine one indeed."[33] As the extreme embodiment of this system, Raúl is walking this very same line: he is a psychopathic criminal, and yet he has internalized the promises of neoliberal capitalism to the point of delusion. Raúl murders an old woman to steal her television set, and he murders a projectionist to steal the film reels of *Saturday Night Fever*. His desire to be free to choose his identity is completely self-centered. As Carolina Urrutia argues, it is this very absence of any larger social or political inclination or a socially inclusive vision, precisely his indifference to politics, that makes his character political.[34] For Urrutia, Raúl represents the unrepresentable of the era. Psychopathic because he lives in a psychopathic moment, Raúl is both result and representation of the military dictatorship, which appears mainly as a "major, monstrous presence"[35] or perhaps, rather, a present absence: "Ostensibly apolitical, Raúl is a true creature of totalitarianism; oppressive circumstances enable him to brutalize and exploit others with apparent impunity, his own crimes fading into the background in a society that is itself institutionally homicidal."[36] The dictatorial state obfuscates what Judith Butler identified as the precariousness of all human life and that we are all bound to and dependent on each other, precisely through our vulnerable, irrevocably material bodies.[37] This fact is negated by the dictatorship, which installs a mercantile calculation in the social body that whatever benefits another is taken from me. In this insane world, Raúl is presented as the logical culmination of the system: under the circumstances, his Darwinian survival instinct and selective schizophrenia seem a rational response. Raúl escapes into the dream world of cinema from a society in which public space and social bonds have been dissolved. His obsession also resonates with Butler's notion of the relationship between grief and unacknowledged lives. Butler argues that a life must first be perceived as living in order to be worthy of grief. In *Manero*, the old lady whom Raúl killed and stole from will not be grieved for. Raúl does not grieve for the members of his dancing troupe, who are taken by the secret police DINA while he is hiding, and who will be imprisoned, hurt, or killed. Most likely, if Raúl died, no one would grieve for him, and he would be one more erased existence. From this vantage point, his desire to be someone whose existence is acknowledged, a public figure and a star, and consequently to be worthy of grief, emerges as logical "within the limits of the possible."[38]

POST MORTEM

Mortem tells the story of Chile as experienced by one of those whom History has forgotten: the third person present at the autopsy of Salvador Allende, a coroner's assistant named Mario Cornejo (Alfredo Castro). This historical but unknown figure was the film's starting point:

> The [autopsy] report [published by the Allende Foundation] is signed by three people. Two of them are very well-known doctors, but the third, a guy called Mario Cornejo, was unknown . . . [we] found out that he was the coroner's assistant. He's dead now, but we got in touch with his family, and I met his son, who actually does the same job as his father.[39]

Set in the weeks shortly before until shortly after the coup, protagonist Mario pursues his plans to win the heart of his neighbor Nancy, when the *coup d'état* interrupts his cocooned little world. An obsessive, occasionally voyeuristic observer of his love object, Mario seems largely uninterested in the political events unfolding around him. The military takeover and Allende's death are psychologically central to the audience, yet visually and dramatically deprioritized. The momentous moment in Chilean history is told through the eyes of "very ordinary people, people who are invisible in society."[40] While history is unfolding in the background and politics are an invisible presence, increasingly threatening to devour the protagonists, the film follows Mario's daily worries.

Mortem opens with an "impossible" view of history. Introducing the film, a long take shot from beneath the undercarriage of a military tank passing over a street littered with debris announces a self-confident camera, and a cinema that offers the audience a point of view that is literally inaccessible to the normal human perception, as the position and perspective of the shot create an image that is out of reach of the human eye. It is a slow-exposure shot, almost completely devoid of human movement. Space seems reduced on the screen and in the frame, as if pressed under a tank, suggestive of "something blind, mechanic, advancing, unstoppable, ready to crush everything in its way."[41] As a result, at the same time that this long take actively renders visible an otherwise inaccessible view, it also, despite its length, shows very little. What is not shown, what is crushed under the tank, emerges into the foreground as visible absence, a metaphor of history. Often associated with "natural" human perception—in avoiding the cut, the viewer remains in the present, free to roam the image, subjected neither to Hollywood's illusionism nor to intellectual montage—the long take also always flaunts its artifice in its intentionality. In *Mortem*, its perspective is unequivocally associated with the machine.

This first long take fractures diegetic time. Where the opening shot seems situated during, or right after, the military takeover, when the narrative trajectory begins, diegetic time is pushed back to before the coup. Mario seeks to conquer his neighbor Nancy, dancer at the Bim Bam Bum (a variety theater famous at the time), and only few corpses arrive at the morgue. Politics take place literally in the background, for instance when Mario cannot continue driving because a *Unidad Popular* demonstration is blocking the road: the camera remains focused on Mario, we barely see the demonstrators. Another time, Mario's employer is heard—not seen—pontificating over lunch.

The chronological trajectory is punctured again fifteen minutes later when the autopsy of a woman is carried out in the morgue. She is identified by an examiner (whose head remains outside the frame) as Nancy Puelma. A seemingly unfazed Mario types up the cause of death, determined as starvation and dehydration, and helps to carry the naked corpse away. This premonitory scene is preceded and followed by scenes of Nancy alive. As she is introduced as an anorexic, the implications of this shot are not immediately clear. Only at the end of the film, where we see Mario effectively incarcerating Nancy, can the audience charge the scene of Nancy's autopsy with political significance. Nancy, a fictional figure, will not be written into official history, yet she is linked to the historical figure of Allende by the repeated motif of the autopsy.

Instead of following an unpredictable, contingent reality as it unfolds, the film therefore breaks temporal unity. There is clearly an organizing agency at work that finds it necessary to structure the narrative differently, to begin with an image that stands for the presence of the coup as already happened, and to present the audience with a scene mid-film that presages Nancy's death. In these instances, the film exits most clearly the selective perception of the protagonist. By dispensing narrative information in this order, the audience cannot immediately attach emotional significance to certain scenes, manipulating our view—and judgment—of Mario.

The coup itself takes place halfway through the film, off-screen, invisible but sonically present and temporally encoded for a knowledgeable audience: the bombardment of the presidential palace took place in the early morning; the image shows the protagonist showering. We hear the sound of low-flying jets, barking dogs, glass smashing, shouting, objects being destroyed, but the camera remains with Mario in the shower. This alerts us again to the presence of an extra-diegetic consciousness. The machine acoustically records the events, and yet the narrative agency chooses to document Mario *missing* the historical moment. Only when he finally steps out into a deserted street full of debris and in eerie silence, is there finally the *visual* evidence of the coup in the form of its aftermath.[42] The morgue is now inundated with corpses, and then there is the pivotal scene of President Allende's autopsy, which is again climactic for the audience but deprioritized in the film in terms of its chronological position mid-film.

The final scene of *Mortem* is another long take during which we see Mario piling up furniture destroyed in the raid in front of a shed in his neighbor's garden. Nancy is hiding in this shed, together with her lover, a member of the *Unidad Popular*. Filmed with a static camera, disconnected from human movement, this last, extremely long take lasts over three minutes. The fixed stare of the machine cuts off Mario's upper body mid-chest, as he exits and re-enters the frame. His movements connect on-screen with off-screen space, or at least draw attention to the existence of off-screen space—metaphorically, the invisible, that which falls through the cracks—through the physical action of disappearing and re-entering. The odd frame makes us aware that it is a *machine's* choice: people tend to focus on human figures, especially the face, and they would not remain entirely static for a long time easily or without support.

The camera's gaze remains fixed on the invisible humans inside the shed, hidden from view. A beheaded (and de-hearted) Mario is imprisoning the bodies of the moribund, those who *will be dying*. In a sense, the entire film is an enacted *futur antérieur*, on a "This will have been" basis, beginning with its title, which anticipates the hauntings of already past events. As the image is being filled with trash, it transforms into a flat, somewhat abstractedly patterned surface, in visual analogy to the scenes of the dead piling up at the morgue, connecting the disappeared and the covering up of the past.

Jonathan Romney ponders the reason for the lack of major tonal change in the film after the coup, and why the cinematography would remain in the palette of pale discolorations: "It is not clear precisely what Larraín is saying about 1973 Chile. The suggestion perhaps is that the nation was already in a state of somnambulistic denial—of the kind depicted in *Tony Manero*—even before the coup."[43] This persistent "aesthetic of death" is one of the reasons why the film was attacked as coming from the ideological right, perhaps adding to the pervasive suspicion of a filmmaker whose parents are associated with Chile's political right. (Ironically, neorealist films, too, were attacked by both the Italian right and left.) And yet, at the end of *Mortem*, we understand that for Mario, life after the coup returned largely to how it was before. We may therefore interpret this figure as representative of an amnesiac and blind—blinded—Chile, a character in denial, a *Mitläufer*. When at the end of the film it becomes clear that Mario has shifted or at least acquiesced to the right, we have also witnessed the moments of danger he finds himself in: at one point, Mario tries to smuggle a survivor in the piles of corpses into the adjacent clinic, only to find him among the pile of dead of the next day, together with the nurse who took him in.

In all of Larraín's dictatorship films, the visual is deprioritized as a means of verification; it is not primarily via vision that we come closer to understanding. We never see clearly in these films; our vision is blocked by objects, cut into odd frames, thrown back as reflections. The final take's brutal framing is only the last in a long line of images that show the characters of *Mortem* trapped, compressed in frames, positioned in stage-like spaces, or with parts of their bodies ruthlessly cut off. For instance, during Nancy's autopsy, the head of her examiner is outside the frame; when Mario searches his neighbor's house, his torso is cut off; and during Mario's and Nancy's brief sexual encounter, the image of Nancy comes from a point of view that cannot be Mario's, a strangely angled close-up on her face and parts of her torso, as if extrapolated from the rest of her body.

As some audiences will clearly recognize, the first long take in *Mortem* is built on the same symbolism as the opening (and closing) shots of the seminal Argentine film *Garage Olimpo* (*Olympic Garage*, Marco Bechis, 1999). *Olimpo* also used classic realist strategies, such as shooting on location and including relatives of disappeared persons. Both *Olimpo* and *Manero* strive to make visible a "militarized gaze," in order to work against its "naturalizing frame of unpunished crimes" (the death flights in *Garage Olimpo*), and to "problematize the afterlife of the dictatorship by showing how it involves a kind of framing that works to imprison the gaze."[44] *Olimpo* begins with an aerial view, shot from a plane, of the Río de la Plata in Argentina. This symbolism links "disappearances, the economy, the political climate [the shot is accompanied by the sound of a weather forecast on the radio and economic climate], and the river [as mass grave]."[45] When discussing which points different audiences may pick up on, we may recall that President Allende's death was also a global event, devastating to a transnational socialist dream that had many people captivated at the time. People remembered where they were when they heard of his death or when they heard the iconic radio speech.[46] The director is clearly aware of the diverging reactions of his transnational audiences: "International audiences laugh at different moments . . . In Chile, nobody laughed at any point in the entire film . . . [in Chile], nobody considered it a black comedy, either."[47]

As in *Olimpo*, the theme is framing itself, making the audience aware of the different actors involved in creating the gaze(s): the camera, the narrative agency, the perspectives adopted by the protagonists, the machine itself. Yet the historical reality is not the historical present, or a past that has only just passed, but a historical reality conveyed through mechanical means. This "mechanical view" of history is clearly limited; it fractures, and leaves most of the human (cost) of history outside the image of history.

Both the corpse of President Allende and the bodies of those killed in the first months after the coup appear in *Mortem*, manifesting the ghostly figures that possess and haunt the country with their traumatic absence. When the morgue team is taken by military men to examine the dead body of former President Allende and to determine the cause of death, a row of soldiers is standing behind them. The setting of the autopsy comes to resemble a stage, with the military men in the background lined up as witnesses, guards, and audience. We watch them watching the morgue team watching Allende. The presence of the military in the background of the image suggests a less than free decision in determining the cause of death and visually implies the unreliability of the emerging account. When the principal doctor concludes that it was suicide, an ominous smile flits over Mario's face.[48] After the autopsy, Mario encounters his colleague Sandra; she insists that Allende has been killed, while a stony-faced Mario repeats, almost pleadingly, that it was suicide. Mario and Sandra embody the two (medical) positions that have historically transpired, as the cause and circumstances of the former president's death have been subject to much debate and long been contested in Chile. The characters not only see but also touch the dead body, surrogates for the Chilean public. Yet despite a literal dissection of Allende's body, the ultimate cause remains unconfirmed. The parallel "small" story, Mario's struggle with the unknown typewriter and his humiliation in being replaced by a more capable—also younger and more handsome—cadet appears to have the same impact on him as the historical event he is witnessing, bringing to mind the strategy used in *Bicycle Thieves* (Vittorio de Sica, 1948) and its "mundane" quest to recover a stolen bike.

The brutal violence of the *golpe* is expressed indirectly, by showing its fallout. In the first part of the film there was the occasional autopsy every other day; after the coup, the morgue is inundated with corpses. The bodies of those killed in the first months, unknown and unnamed, are piling up in corridors, on stairwells; they fill the morgue, and the screen.

Figure 3.2 *Post mortem* (2010).

As with Nancy's autopsy, the juxtaposition of one particular death of a mythical figure and the many anonymous deaths point to a parallel in the uncanniness of the sudden, traumatic disappearances of close loved ones, of a public figure, or even the sudden disappearance of one's world in the form of the previous democratic nation-state, the violently shattered political dream of a socialist Chile. Returning a body to the dead president—even in the form of an image—can also be read as an attempt to humanize this idealized, monumentalized, petrified, and haunting figure. Instead of reanimating Allende, *Mortem* resurrects his corpse, re-embodying the traumatic loss of this singular publicly visible body alongside the bodies of the many disappeared.

These bodies are infused with a symbolic meaning that surpasses their physical reality. Such a referential presence of on-screen bodies counters invisibilities, without erasing the history of their disappearance. For even as we are watching, we lose them yet again, as they are "processed" without finding out their names or cause of death. As the number of victims far exceeds their capacity, the small morgue team is told by the military to resort to a fast-track version of their trade. This fictional reappearance of the first victims of the coup creates a metaphorical, alternate truth, a kind of restorative corporeality for those bodies that went missing, and were perfunctorily quantified and discarded into mass graves. In this context of a violated social body, imaginarily possessing the missing bodies can be considered a powerful gesture.

NO

All films of the trilogy feature bodies that show indexical traces of having lived through the dictatorship period. Larraín explicitly described this technique as a form of re-enacted memory: "It's fascinating to me to see how a person's body says again what it once said, thinks what was once thought, returns to where it once was. It returns, returns, and that's the work of memory."[49]

This strategy also recalls the frequent use of non-professionals in realist films, chosen for a physical fit or for some parallel between the role and their lives. Their presence was supposed to result in an "osmotic" effect on the professional cast as well, creating a "general atmosphere of authenticity."[50]

In *No*, some of the historical players were cast to re-perform their roles, to re-enact themselves, so to speak. Patricio Aylwin, first post-dictatorship president, portrays Patricio Aylwin; Patricio Bañados, presenter of the No campaign, appears as himself; and so does the sociologist Eugenio Tironi. The replication is never meant to be exact, never attempts to suffuse with the original form. An elderly Patricio Aylwin waddles in, shakes the protagonist's hand, and sits in front of the diegetic camera. Then the camera tilts downward to a diegetic television screen that shows Aylwin's younger self announcing the importance of the vote.

These filmic bodies establish the link to the real, precisely *because* they have aged: through their aged bodies, these figures affirm change, or at least, given the historical amnesia diagnosed by Chilean scholars, the passing of time. Bluntly interrupting the suspension of disbelief, these bodies draw our attention to our *perception* of the real. The film seems to ask, what is the value of reality to anchoring authenticity?

Figure 3.3   *No* (2012).

These human bodies of historical players complement what the film does technically: in addition to the casting, the medium itself is turned into an anchor to the real. Footage of the actual ads from the 1988 plebiscite and other archive material, such as Pinochet being embraced by Jimmy Carter, Ronald Reagan, Margaret Thatcher, and Pope John Paul II, amount to 30 percent of the film.[51] These archival scenes are meshed with new ones that are shot using the same material, tools, and style.

In a sense, one may consider this an adaptation of realism's programmatic strategy to let the coincidences of reality unroll: here, the mediated reality, as these lenses create "the deathly pallor of fading wallpaper" in the look of the film all on their own. "People think we spent ages in post-production to get that pale image, but *our whole technique was not to do anything.*"[52]

As Hamid Naficy writes with regards to encounters with the ethos and aesthetics of realism and neorealism in Abbas Kiarostami's *Close-Up* (1990), such "manufactured impressions of casualness and realism [are] hard to produce, not innocent recordings of unfolding reality."[53] But in contrast to what Laura Mulvey calls here a *trompe-l'œil* cinema, which mixes "illusion and reality and create an uncertainty about which is which,"[54] the idea in *No* is never to "trick" the audience. Even though the use of vintage video cameras, lenses, and film stock in the fictionalized parts allows for a softened, often imperceptible suture between archive material and fictional re-enactment, extending the archive look to the whole film, the boundedness of the No campaign clips and the star presence of Gael García Bernal in almost every one of the new scenes clearly delineate which parts are archival and which form part of the diegesis, even for those unfamiliar with Chilean history. The central presence of García Bernal's well-known body enhances the metaleptic possibility, the potential for a transgression of the boundary between diegetic and non-diegetic, pointing to its material existence outside of the film and to García Bernal's popular star persona and his record in acting and producing progressive, politically liberal, and Latin-American-focused productions.

The combination of genuinely old film stock with real archive material effectively sutures two kinds of documentary. The result is an authenticity that acknowledges its artificiality, both evoking and deconstructing the concept of the real, a "double realness" that alerts the viewer to the cultural nature of inherited claims regarding the (transparent) truth of footage material generally. Thus, *No* both authenticates and problematizes our mediated access to history and historical narrative by translating the difficulty of seeing (history) clearly to the material level of their own cinematic "body."

Furthermore, read in the cultural context of Chile's media history, supplementary associations emerge. The collective and social use of video played a role as cultural resistance to the dictatorship, shaping an alternative imaginary of Chilean society, developing an alternative visual language for the No campaign and influencing Chilean documentary style for years.[55]

Poblete suggested that, by re-appropriating formal tools, Latin American hybrid cinema produces a critique of the dominant form. The violence of the economic restructuring of Latin American societies is linked to the violence of hegemonic forms of representation or "regimes of globalized visuality."[56] *No*'s political critique is inscribed precisely in these shifts between original and re-staged registers: they suggest continuity between or the continuation of the past into the present, as if to ask what has really changed. The plebiscite did not end the inequality or the neoliberal system.[57]

CONCLUSION

Rooted in transnational realisms, the trilogy's aesthetic strategies function in a supplementary sense, linking the films to local media history in form and content. As Poblete had argued, supplementarity enables the films "to represent the gaps and contradictions of . . . post-dictatorship memory" and thereby to inscribe political critique.[58] Notwithstanding the limitations on the free selection and presentation of subject matter outlined above, and bearing in mind Schoonover's intervention, I suggest that Larraín's trilogy conjure these preceding realist movements not only in aesthetic terms but also to evoke a sense of their political-ethical drive.

The films' engagement with history *through* the cinematic past speaks to neorealism's approach to eschew "Grand History" in favor of "small" stories, to enable a different kind of emotional engagement, and also to contribute to a distinctively national cinema. Neorealism's notion of the real, argues John Brewer, is about: "larger verities . . . about conflicting temporalities, about the complex dialectic between big history and small everyday lives, and about the way in which the forces of history are constantly led to deviate or change as result of chance."[59]

Larraín's films, too, are telling small stories within big history. They also evoke Chile's social, historical dreams by referencing the aesthetic style of the New Chilean Cinema; and in particular in *No*, the history of national media serves to create an emotional relation to the national past.

At the same time, the films constantly highlight the mediation of history, the intrusive organization of a narrative agency. They therefore clearly destabilize the notion of direct access to historical truth, the idea of a transparent phenomenal world that can be revealed by cinema. Instead, these films point precisely to what is hidden, disappearing or inaccessible about the past, precisely where they diverge from their predecessors in crucial ways.[60] Sometimes, images are peculiarly framed, pointing to what is outside, off-screen, invisible, at other times, visual confirmation is only "present by absence."

According to Elsaesser, this questioning of the old form and the capacity of its techniques to convey reality is typical for world cinema's new realisms. He suggests a "post-epistemological concept of realism," which begins as "perceptual insecurity" and moves on to "a more directly ontological doubt."[61] Following this lead, the engagement with and expansion of neorealist discourse in Chilean cinema can be discussed as a problematization of epistemology through visual means. The neo-neorealist trend can then be framed as a response to the digital turn, its production of seemingly perfect copies, and their infectiously ephemeral, diluting qualities, where the desire for authenticity becomes only stronger "in a universe dominated by simulation and information saturation."[62]

Such epistemological questions are also already dormant in neorealism. According to Schoonover, neorealism's long shots turn the image into a "visual field" that "invites us to watch while telling us that we are just watching," and therefore "confronts the viewer with the profound ambiguity of the real."[63] This is the tendency that Larraín's films pick up on: not the Bazinian relation between cinematic realism and the past reality, the cinematic image as change mummified,[64] but an orientation toward what is ambiguous, self-referential, doubled, perhaps even uncanny: there is trouble, in this kind of realism.[65]

Most remarkable is the central position of the body in these films. In *Manero*, the body translates the schizophrenia of the system, the erosion of social trust and annihilation of a public sphere; in *Post mortem*, bodies are compressed within the frame, persecuted by a cold machine gaze; in *No*, both historical bodies and the body of the medium, in the form of anachronistic film stock, are taken as markers of authenticity, as they exhibit a physically inscribed, lived-in history. The body precisely does not reify a Truth of a Grand History or Theory.

In his analysis of the centrality of corporeality in neorealism, Schoonover suggested that these films used "scenarios of physical suffering to dramatize the political stakes of vision [to an] outside extranational eyewitness ... an imperiled body is offered to a bystander's gaze as an opportunity to exercise ethical judgement."[66] The parallel between a transnational address then and now ends here, where the films emphasize the limitations of vision, where their truths are neither absolute nor relativist, but fragmented and deeply humanist in nature. The bodies presented to the audiences in *Mortem* are not imperiled but already dead, while *No* asks what has really changed, with time passing yet not passing.

Here it is interesting to recall that strategies such as long takes and close-ups also increase the viewers' awareness of their *own* bodies, their physical presence as spectators,[67] and thus, of their *agency*, while the presence of aged bodies—of archive, cinematic medium, and historical players—point to the *distance* between the past and the present, where the viewer feels herself to be. As if incarnating Benjamin's angel of history, these films turn to the past—in form, subject matter, and critical attention to cinema history—while inevitably moving forward.

NOTES

1. A. O. Scott, "Neo-Neo Realism," *The New York Times Online*, March 17, 2009: <https://www.nytimes.com/2009/03/22/magazine/22neorealism-t.html> (accessed February 25, 2020).
2. Recognizing media power, the junta at different points in time either prohibited images completely, in classic anti-pictorial fashion, or used them for spectacular social deceit. The media were involved in public deception and hoaxes, peaking perhaps with the so-called "Operación Colombo," an international, DINA-orchestrated campaign to conceal the disappearance of 119 political prisoners. *El diario de Agustín* (Ignacio Agüero, 2008) shows the level of involvement by the official media in these processes of strategic disinformation, and more importantly, the state of impunity and power that centrally involved authority figures continue to enjoy.
3. Antonella Estévez, "Cine contemporáneo chileno: Joven cine chileno: En la movilización de los márgenes," in *El cine que fue: 100 años de cine chileno*, eds. Claudia Barril and José M. Santa Cruz (Santiago de Chile: Editorial Arcis, 2011), 75–83.
4. Original Spanish: "El cine chileno no aparece cuando quiere, sino cuando puede," qtd. in Jaqueline Mouesca and Carlos Orellana, *Breve historia del cine chileno: Desde sus orígenes hasta nuestros días* (Santiago de Chile: LOM, 2010), 213.
5. María Soledad Montañez and David Martin-Jones, "Uruguay Disappears: Small Cinemas, Control Z Films, and the Aesthetics and Politics of Auto-Erasure," *Cinema Journal* 53, no. 1 (2013): 26–51.
6. Thomas Elsaesser in Montañez and Martin-Jones, "Uruguay Disappears," 29.
7. María Paz Peirano, "Towards a 'cosmopolitan' national film industry: Contemporary Chilean Cinema at International Film Festivals," presentation at Screen, Glasgow, 2013.
8. Mónica Villarroel, *La voz de los cineastas: Cine e identidad chilena en el umbral del milenio* (Santiago de Chile: Cuarto Propio, 2005), 167–88; cf. Peirano, "Towards a 'cosmopolitan' national film industry."
9. There might be a critical tendency to read only films made outside of Hollywood through the paradigm of the national, despite the trend towards transnational audiences and changes in Hollywood film content. Cf. Diana Crane, "Cultural Globalization and the Dominance of the American Film Industry: Cultural Policies, National Film Industries, and Transnational Film," *International Journal of Cultural Policy* 20 (2013): 365.
10. Ann Marie Stock, *Framing Latin American Cinema: Contemporary Critical Perspectives* (Minneapolis: University of Minnesota Press, 1997); Peirano, "Towards a 'cosmopolitan' national film industry."
11. Patrick Blaine, "Representing Absences in the Postdictatorial Documentary Cinema of Patricio Guzmán," *Latin American Perspectives* 40, no. 1 (2013): 114–30. Among the Nuevo Cine Chileno were seminal works such as *Largo viaje* (Patricio Kaulen, 1967), *El chacal de Nahueltoro* (Miguel Littín, 1969), *Valparaíso mi amor* (Aldo Francia, 1969), *Tres tristes tigres* (Raúl Ruiz, 1968). For a critical appraisal of the Chilean scholarship on this period, which situates Chilean cinema in the context of historiography of the continent's cinema, see Verónica Cortínez and Manfred Engelbert, "El cine chileno de los sesenta: Clave para una cultura moderna," in *Arpillera sobre Chile: Cine, teatro y literatura antes y después de 1973*, eds. Annette Paatz and Janett Reinstädler (Berlin: Edition Tranvía-Verlag Walter

Frey, 2013), 13–59; cf. John King, *Magical Reels: A History of Cinema in Latin America* (London: Verso, 1990).
12. Cf. Estévez, "Cine contemporáneo chileno" discusses neorealism's strong influence on contemporary Chilean cinema, cf. Jane M. Gaines, "Political Mimesis," in *Collecting Visible Evidence*, ed. Jane M. Gaines and Michael Renov (Minneapolis: University of Minnesota Press, 1999), 84–102; Barril and Santa Cruz, *El cine que fue*; Pablo Corro, *Retóricas del cine chileno: Ensayos con el realismo* (Santiago de Chile: Cuarto Propio, 2012); Thomas Elsaesser, "Hyper-, Retro- or Counter-Cinema: European Cinema and Third Cinema between Hollywood and Art Cinema," in *Mediating Two Worlds: Cinematic Encounters in the Americas*, eds. John King, Ana M. López, and Manuel Alvarado (London: British Film Institute, 1993), 119–35.
13. Coined by Ascanio Cavallo, the *novísimo cine chileno* has attracted considerable scholarly national and even international attention. Ascanio Cavallo and Gonzalo Maza, *El novísimo cine chileno* (Santiago de Chile: Uqbar Editores, 2010); cf. Andrea López Barraza, *Nuevo cine chileno 2005–2010* (Universidad de Chile, 2011); Cortínez and Engelbert, "El cine chileno de los sesenta."
14. Cf. King, *Magical Reels*; Barril and Santa Cruz, *El cine que fue*; Corro, *Retóricas del cine chileno*.
15. Montañez and Martin-Jones, "Uruguay Disappears."
16. Armida de la Garza, "Realism and National Identity in 'Y Tu Mamá También': An Audience Perspective," in *Realism in the Audiovisual Media*, eds. Lúcia Nagib and Cecília Mello (London and New York: Palgrave Macmillan, 2009), 108–18 (109).
17. Miriam Haddu and Joanna Page, *Visual Synergies in Fiction and Documentary Film from Latin America* (Basingstoke: Palgrave Macmillan, 2009). Alberto Moreiras's "savage hybridity" is cited in Geoffrey Kantaris and Rory O'Bryen, *Latin American Popular Culture: Politics, Media, Affect* (Woodbridge: Tamesis Books, 2013).
18. Qtd. in Juan Poblete, "New National Cinemas in a Transnational Age," 221.
19. Svetlana Boym, *The Future of Nostalgia* (New York: Basic Books, 2001), 42.
20. Poblete, "New National Cinemas in a Transnational Age."
21. Rosalind Galt and Karl Schoonover, *Global Art Cinema: New Theories and Histories* (New York: Oxford University Press, 2010), 17.
22. McGrath in de la Garza, "Realism and National Identity," 109.
23. Galt and Schoonover, *Global Art Cinema*, 15.
24. André Bazin, *What Is Cinema?* (Berkeley: University of California Press, 2005).
25. Richard Allen, "'There Is Not One Realism, but Several Realisms': A Review of Opening Bazin," *October* (2014): 77 (emphasis added).
26. Cesare Zavattini, "Some Ideas on the Cinema," *Sight & Sound* 23, no. 2 (1953): 50–61.
27. Rancière qtd. in Lúcia Nagib, *World Cinema and the Ethics of Realism* (London: Continuum, 2011), 235.
28. Nagib, *World Cinema and the Ethics of Realism*, 10.
29. Tiago de Luca, *Realism of the Senses in Contemporary World Cinema: The Experience of Physical Reality* (London: I. B. Tauris, 2013), 300.
30. Karl Schoonover, *Brutal Vision: The Neorealist Body in Postwar Italian Cinema* (Minneapolis: University of Minnesota Press, 2012), 230.
31. David Bordwell, "The Art Cinema as a Mode of Film Practice," in *Film Theory and Criticism: Introductory Readings*, eds. Leo Braudy and Marshall Cohen (New York: Oxford UP, 1999), 716–24.
32. Qtd. in Jacqueline Mouesca, *Plano secuencia de la memoria de Chile: Veinticinco años de cine chileno (1960–1985)* (Santiago de Chile: Ediciones del Litoral, 1988), 167.
33. Thomas Elsaesser and Warren Buckland, *Studying Contemporary American Film: A Guide to Movie Analysis* (London: Arnold, 2002), 276.

34. Carolina Urrutia, "Hacia una política en tránsito: Ficción en el cine chileno (2008–2010)," *Aisthesis* 47 (2010): 33–44.
35. Urrutia, "Hacia una política en tránsito," 42.
36. Jonathan Romney, "Staying alive," *Sight & Sound* 19, no. 5 (2009).
37. Judith Butler, *Frames of War: When Is Life Grievable?* (London: Verso, 2010).
38. Compare the remarkable phrase by President Patricio Aylwin, who sought "justice within the limits of the possible" ("justicia en la medida de lo posible").
39. Demetrios Matheou, "The Body Politic: Pablo Larraín on *Post Mortem*," *Sight & Sound*, January 29, 2015: <http://www.bfi.org.uk/news-opinion/sight-sound-magazine/interviews/body-politic-pablo-larra-on-post-mortem> (accessed February 25, 2020).
40. Ibid.
41. Original Spanish: "el sentido que reviste para nosotros; algo así como una cosa ciega, mecánica y compacta que avanza . . . imparable . . . irrefrenable, dispuesta a arrasar con todo o destinada a estrellarse." Corro, *Retóricas del cine chileno*, 239–40.
42. Cf. Landy on "conceptual realism" in *Rome, Open City*. She argues that the openness of the films' images "subvert[s] cinematic clichés by making self-conscious its application of image and sound in relation to their past uses." Marcia Landy, "*Rome Open City* (1945), Roberto Rossellini," in *Film Analysis: A Norton Reader*, eds. Jeffrey Geiger and R. L. Rutsky (New York and London: W. W. Norton & Company, 2005), 400–21 (419).
43. Romney, "Staying alive," 46–7.
44. Susana Draper, *Afterlives of Confinement: Spatial Transitions in Postdictatorship Latin America* (Pittsburgh: University of Pittsburgh Press, 2012), 189–90.
45. Draper, *Afterlives*, 189–90.
46. Macarena Gómez-Barris, *Where Memory Dwells: Culture and State Violence in Chile* (Berkeley: University of California Press, 2008), 181.
47. Damon Smith, "Pablo Larraín, *Post Mortem*," *Filmmaker Magazine*, April 11, 2012: <https://filmmakermagazine.com/43874-pablo-larrain-post-mortem/#.Xmy6oxNKgSI> (accessed March 16, 2020).
48. Larraín seems keen to preserve the lack of facial expression in his protagonists' faces. Compare Bazin's interpretation of *Allemania Anno Zero*: "when dealing with the face of the child . . . Rossellini is concerned to preserve its mystery." Bazin, *What is Cinema?*, 37.
49. José Miguel Palacios, "The Problems of Fiction," *The Brooklyn Rail*, November 6, 2012: <http://brooklynrail.org/2012/11/film/the-problems-of-fictionpablo-larran-with-jos-miguel-palacios> (accessed March 16, 2020).
50. Bazin, *What Is Cinema?*, 24.
51. Larry Rohter, "One Prism on the Undoing of Pinochet," *The New York Times*, February 10, 2013: <https://www.nytimes.com/2013/02/10/movies/oscar-nominated-no-stirring-debate-in-chile.html> (accessed February 25, 2020).
52. Matheou, "The Body Politic," emphasis added.
53. Hamid Naficy, "Questioning Reality, Realism, and Neorealism," in *Film Analysis: A Norton Reader*, ed. Jeffrey Geiger (New York & London: W. W. Norton & Company, 2005), 854–8.
54. Ibid., 859.
55. Germán Liñero, *Apuntes para una historia del video en Chile* (Santiago de Chile: Ocho libros, 2010).
56. Poblete, "New National Cinemas in a Transnational Age," 230.
57. Negotiated on the basis of shared fear, and in the continued presence of Pinochet, who had made himself senator for life, the Chilean transition left in place many of the dictatorship's institutions, most notably the constitution and the amnesty laws. This is one of the reasons why the beginning and the end of the transition, as well as the term itself, are heavily contested.

58. Poblete, "New National Cinemas in a Transnational Age," 13.
59. John Brewer, "Reenactment and Neo-Realism," in *Historical Reenactment from Realism to the Affective Turn*, eds. Iain McCalman and Paul A. Pickering (Basingstoke: Palgrave Macmillan, 2010), 79–89.
60. Shared with neorealism is the notable preference for location shooting, employing "historical" bodies and techniques such as the long take. Other characteristics are not shared: realism here does not strive towards a "self-effacement before reality" (de Luca, *Realism of the Senses*, 300), nor is it based on an aesthetic of the contingent, or accidental. Contingency is not a dominant characteristic in the trilogy; there are, however, examples within contemporary Chilean fiction films that use improvised acting and "real time"; for instance, *Sábado, una película en tiempo real* (Matías Bize, 2003) or *La sagrada familia* (Sebastián Lelio, 2005).
61. Thomas Elsaesser, "World Cinema: Realism, Evidence, Presence," in *Realism and the Audiovisual Media*, eds. Lúcia Nagib and Cecília Mello (Basingstoke: Palgrave Macmillan, 2009), 3–19 (10).
62. David Norman Rodowick, *The Virtual Life of Film* (Cambridge, MA: Harvard University Press, 2007), 158. I have elsewhere suggested that contemporary Chilean films also respond to a transnational crisis of faith in an epistemological model that relies predominantly on gaining knowledge through vision. Berenike Jung, *The Invisibilities of Torture*. Edinburgh University Press, forthcoming.
63. Schoonover, *Brutal Vision*, 27.
64. Bazin, *What Is Cinema?*, 15.
65. Margulies argues that the extended duration in new realism produces a "passage from untroubled realism to uncanny hyperrealism." Ivone Margulies, *Nothing Happens: Chantal Akerman's Hyperrealist Everyday* (Durham: Duke University Press, 1996), 46.
66. Schoonover, *Brutal Vision*, xiv–xvi.
67. Cf. Elsaesser, "World Cinema," and de Luca, *Realism of the Senses*.

CHAPTER 4

When Violence Meets Experimentalism: Unraveling Cinematic Suture in Raúl Ruiz's *Tres Tristes Tigres* and Pablo Larraín's *Post Mortem*[1]

Eduardo Ledesma

Since the creation of the Grupo Cine Experimental of the University of Chile in the 1950s, through the New Chilean Cinema of the 1960s, and with the recent explosion of "new" New Chilean Cinema in the 1990s (aka the *novísimo* Chilean film movement), Chilean film has been marked by heterogeneous works ranging anywhere from the experimental to the realist political, as well as those which attempt to combine both representation and formalism.[2] One recurring and unifying tendency in Chilean film—and more broadly, Latin American film—has been the prevalence of violence, whether political, quotidian, or formal. Experimental cinema, in a sense, is itself a form of violence directed against the spectator.[3]

Neither strictly narrative nor documentary, films such as Raúl Ruiz's *Tres tristes tigres* (1968) and Pablo Larraín's *Post mortem* (2010) experiment with a kind of thematic and formal violence that has long characterized Chilean filmmaking. In the 1960s and 1970s Chilean directors such as Miguel Littín, Helvio Soto, Aldo Francia, Sergio Bravo, Pedro Chaskel, Raúl Ruiz, and more recently since the 1990s, Sebastián Silva, Rodrigo Marín, Alicia Scherson, Niles Atallah and Pablo Larraín have negotiated the difficult choice of how much experimentation viewers can tolerate, how much content-based and/or formal violence they might withstand. By exploring the nexus between experimental techniques and violence in Ruiz's *Tres tristes tigres* and Larraín's *Post mortem*, I will argue that not all violence is equal and not all formal experiments serve the same political purpose. Ruiz, for example, deploys violence to protest against social inequality and uses filmic techniques to subvert realism. Larraín, instead, comments on the violence generated by the 1973 coup and undermines narrative form with techniques that have been described as minimalist, detached, and even dehistoricizing. A comparison is useful since these two films could also stand in, respectively, for political films from the 1960s New Chilean Cinema, and post-dictatorship cinema from today's *novísimo* filmmakers. I contend that, ultimately, it is violence itself, perpetrated by the film on the spectator through mechanisms of cinematic suture, that provides the key to understanding both *Tres tristes tigres* and *Post mortem*. This violence concerns slicing open old wounds, and forcing spectators to confront what festers within. As I will show, in one film, that maneuver (undoing the sutures) seeks the possibility of social change, while in the other film, it merely retraumatizes the viewing subject.

SUTURING MECHANISMS AND FILMIC VIOLENCE

Perhaps, since we are speaking of violence, of wounds sliced open (metaphoric and otherwise), the concept of cinematic suture, as developed by Jean-Pierre Oudart and Daniel Dayan in the 1960s and 1970s and further elaborated by Stephen Heath, Kaja Silverman and other theorists, can shed some light on how violence functions within these films; recalling that we are speaking of violence not only in content, but also in editing and formal mechanisms, as long standing cinematic rules are attacked and the viewing subject is exposed to uncomfortable images and realizations. Heath, Silverman, and others derive their understanding of suture from Lacanian psychoanalysis, from its theories of subject formation. For these theorists, the concept of suture defines how subjectivity and meaning are produced through film. The cinematic apparatus—the functioning of the camera, the editing process, and so on—articulates a film language whose basic unit is the shot, and whose grammar relies on the interlocking of subsequent shots through which any given content is rendered. Classical Hollywood style (adopted by most mainstream fiction cinema) typically entails the erasure of the cuts between shots in order to provide a sense of cinematic plenitude, by smoothing over or "suturing" transitions through continuity editing, more specifically through devices like the 180-degree rule, eye line matches, match on action, graphic matches, shot/reverse shot and so on. Filmmakers who oppose the classical style, such as the ones I will examine here, choose to make those shot-to-shot transitions violently visible through a disruption of suturing mechanisms. These formal and stylistic choices are not value-neutral. There is an important ideological function in the eliding of the gap, whether the gap in discourse, the cut in film, the irregularity in history. The erasure of the violent act (the cinematic cut, the economic gap, the historical rupture) serves to manipulate spectators into a kind of passive acquiescence, into a role of uncritical consumerism.

Classical Hollywood style simulates a deceptive window-like transparency into reality that envelops the spectator with its internal filmic logic, purporting a direct relationship to reality. In this logic, signifier and signified become one and the same, and the spectator takes what is before his or her eyes to be a direct capture of the external world. Scars, gaps, fissures, seams, cuts are stitched and smoothed out so they are no longer visible.

Heath draws on the surgical metaphor, recalling wounds that are sewn shut—but that can retain infection, or be torn open again—to effectively describe cinematic suture as:

> a stitching or tying as in the surgical joining of the lips of a wound. In its movements, its framings, its cuts, its intermittences, the [classical Hollywood] film ceaselessly poses an absence, a lack, which is ceaselessly bound up in and into the relation of the subject, is, as it were, ceaselessly recaptured for . . . the film, that process binding the spectator in the realization of the film's space.[4]

Radical filmmakers, rejecting this mechanism, rip the suture and force the wound open to drain its festering contents, compelling spectators to see the artifice, that which had been mystified by the filmic apparatus in its suturing of the Real. The representation of violence itself becomes a violent act, but one whose ultimate purpose is to reveal the film's ideology and facilitate a deeper awareness in the spectator of how he or she is being interpellated through formal and narrative devices. According to Kaja Silverman, this process forces "the viewer into oblique and uncomfortable positions *vis-à-vis* both the cinematic apparatuses and the spectacle which they produce."[5] When classical Hollywood's techniques of cinematic realism that favor suture, such as linear plot structures, narrative closure, continuity editing, synchronous sound, optical realism, or any other method dedicated to simulating the real world are disrupted, suture ceases to work efficiently and the spectator is thrust away from the safely enveloping fiction and into the harsh light exposing ideological manipulation, at least in an ideal scenario.

In the following pages, I will show how the two chosen films have mobilized violence, both formal and content-based, to disrupt the suture-based, naturalized Hollywood cinematic system. It is obvious that historical conditions in Chile were vastly different in the periods in question (the pre-Allende 1960s, and the post-dictatorship era), but it is quite revealing to analyze how these films use formal approaches that undermine narrative suture to take strikingly different political stances. The first film, Ruiz's *Tres tristes tigres*, employs various tactics to undermine what the filmmaker saw as the imperialist filmic apparatus bolstered by Hollywood, including challenging genre-based strategies of melodrama, and employing a rough Third Cinema style characterized by handheld camera and off-kilter framing. After a short analysis of Ruiz's movie, the second and longer film analysis (the main focus of this chapter) is dedicated to Larraín's *Post mortem* (2010). Larraín's film represents a new, postmodern cinema, the product of a very different sociopolitical situation, namely, the post-dictatorship, neoliberal present. It is a present that, as Nelly Richard has cogently demonstrated, is rife with "residues," or "unstable formations of symbolic and cultural deposits and sedimentations," fissures and rough spots that have been smoothed over so they may not betray the flaws of an incomplete democratic transition process.[6] In fact, *Post mortem* disarticulates the operations of cinematic suture by exploring a violent cut in Chilean history that has itself been partially effaced or sewn over: the military coup of 1973, a coup that in addition to its 3,000 disappeared and a litany of human rights abuses, also destroyed Chilean cinematic production and its movie archives, and closed its film schools. This cut represented a gash in the social, political, and cultural history of Chile, and the utter destruction of the utopian project of the Chilean left. Yet despite its recourse to formal and content-based violence, as I will show, Larraín's film is also marked by a troubling ambivalence to political commitment, a stance that the filmmaker posits as neutrality. As such, although both films expose and undermine suture mechanisms, I show that they do so with antithetical intentions.

Undoubtedly, the coup itself represents the ultimate rupture for which there is no possible suture or return, a disruption that pierced into the very fabric of Chilean subjectivity. As Vania Barraza states:

> for those who suffered during the political repression, the military coup erased all resources for expressing reality. Hence, from a Lacanian perspective, it is possible to state that Pinochet's dictatorship destroyed the imaginary dimension of the subject—the mirror identification as the threshold of the visible world—along with the symbolic order for understanding human existence.[7]

The very real violence exerted by the Pinochet regime would have its corollaries at the social and symbolic level, reproduced in official discourse, in state propaganda and in sponsored forms of mass media and artistic representation. It is quite accurate to say, as David Sipprelle does, that after the end of the dictatorship, "in spite of the transition to nominal democracy, trauma [still] haunts Chile."[8] Consequently, violence and trauma have reverberated and resurfaced formally and thematically in the work of contemporary filmmakers.

Larraín, for instance, reopens the lips of the historical wound (unravels the suture) to expose the festering beneath neoliberal erasure; the smoothing over of the past in order to selfishly "move on," a smoothing that neither accounts for the past nor aims for a more just future. As Sipprelle sees it, "Larraín employs cinematographic techniques in order to visually (but symbolically) reproduce violence."[9] However, where Ruiz's film engaged with a sense of collective struggle, Larraín's protagonists display a profound isolation and disconnect from the greater social body, reflecting not only the despair prevalent in 1973, but also today's exacerbated individualism and lack of solidarity.

TRES TRISTES TIGRES: TOWARD A CHILEAN COUNTER-CINEMA

In a 1972 interview, a year before the coup, filmmaker Raúl Ruiz stated his opposition to Hollywood cinema, arguing that "American film aligns itself with imperialist domination [... and uses ...] ideological and cultural mechanisms imposed by the dominant ideology."[10] Ruiz insists that filmmakers on the left have an imperative to disarticulate and expose the mechanisms at work in Hollywood film, adding that "the ideological apparatus that is being analyzed . . . is very easy to dismantle—easier each time."[11]

What Ruiz suggests is that in mainstream American cinema there is a disconnect between form and content, between the seamless continuity of Hollywood filmmaking and the historical cuts and aporias it reinforces or elides. Simply put, classical Hollywood has been instrumental in propagating US ideology and the belief in American exceptionalism. These ideological functions operate through thematic and formal devices, and to some extent, have been inscribed in the cinematic apparatus itself. The workings of ideology in cinema, however, may not be quite as transparent as Ruiz believed. For instance, the ever-present process of suturing, according to Silverman, requires a certain willingness on the part of the spectator:

> The classic cinematic organization depends upon the subject's willingness to become absent to itself by permitting a fictional character to "stand in" for it, or by allowing a particular point of view to define what it sees. The operation of suture is successful at the moment that the viewing subject says, "Yes, that's me," or "That's what I see." Equally important to the cinematic organization are the operations of cutting and excluding. It is not merely that the camera is incapable of showing us everything at once, but that it does not wish to do so. We must be shown only enough to know that there is more, and to want that "more" to be disclosed. A prime agency of disclosure is the cut, which divides one shot from the next. The cut guarantees that both the preceding and the subsequent shots will function as structuring absences to the present shot. These absences make possible a signifying ensemble; convert one shot into a signifier of the next one, and the signified of the preceding

one. Thus cinematic coherence and plentitude emerge through multiple cuts and negations.[12]

Intuitively aware of this ideological process, in *Tigres* Ruiz does his utmost to expose the "negations" and "cuts" that create what Silverman calls the fiction of "cinematic plenitude." No doubt the work Ruiz performs to undo the suture mechanisms has been noted by other critics, even if they have not specifically identified the theoretical underpinnings at stake. John King, for example, claims that, "the very title of the film, a tongue twister in Spanish, points to a work which examines the gaps between signifier and signified, explores genres and poses problems of representation."[13] These gaps between signifier and signified directly point to structuralist and semiotic concerns, which critics of apparatus film theory extensively analyzed in the 1970s (Jean-Louis Baudry, Christian Metz, Stephen Heath, Colin MacCabe, Peter Wollen, Laura Mulvey, to name a few), and are directly related to the Althusserian understanding of the functioning of ideology. Ideology, for Louis Althusser, is a system of representation that coerces the subject's imaginary relationship to the actual, "real" conditions of existence. As such, the spectator does not relate to the actual world that is being represented in the film, but to an "imaginary distortion of the ideological representation of the real world."[14] Now, let us examine how these theoretical observations (rooted in Althusserian Marxism and Lacanian theory) may facilitate our understanding of the oppositional stance taken by Ruiz in his film, and indeed, serve as an impetus for creating a radical counter-cinema.

Based on a 1967 play by the same name from Chilean playwright Alejandro Sieveking, the film has been considered as a cross between a parody of melodrama, social documentary with neorealist tints and experimental cinema. Loosely structured, the plot follows three characters, Tito (Nelson Villagra), Amanda (Shenda Román), and Rudy (Jaime Vadell), in their perambulations through Santiago de Chile. Rudy is a bourgeois businessman (an auto dealer) without scruples, Tito is his undependable and scheming employee, and Amanda—Tito's sister—has been recently fired from her job as a burlesque stripper and is looking for easy money. The film takes place over a weekend during which Rudy is awaiting Tito to arrive with some critical documents to close a sale. While Rudy waits anxiously, Tito goes on a drinking spree with his sister and other questionable characters. Amanda, at Tito's suggestion, sleeps with Rudy with the intent to shake him down for money. Rudy retaliates by firing Tito for being an unreliable drunkard. All the characters display a complete lack of ethics or genuine solidarity. The film ends with a brutal scene during which an angry Tito beats Rudy senseless while Amanda gleefully watches, after which the siblings leave him for dead and flee Santiago. This bleak portrait is, as we shall see, a politically committed call for solidarity that registers and denounces the worst aspects of Chilean society right before the hopeful turn to socialism in 1970. But how is this achieved formally?

In classical Hollywood cinema, cuts are motivated by narrative, and camera position and framing reinforce the main plot by keeping lead characters at the center of the action; the narrative itself is tight and usually there are no loose ends. Thus, in classical realism, there is a seamless interchange "between screen and viewer—that complicated circulation which ensures that I am not only a spectator in the cinema but also, by a process of identification, a character on the screen."[15] Ruiz is antithetical to this closed system, rejecting what he calls the *conflicto central*, that is, the way in which all content and form in classical Hollywood are oriented toward driving the plot forward and seek to reinforce spectator identification with the characters. Instead, he proposes to "invent new techniques so that the submerged component of cinema becomes evident."[16] Describing how he used film form to disarticulate suturing mechanisms, Ruiz explains that:

> the idea [in *Tigres*] was to put the camera not where it would see best, but where it should be, in the normal position. This meant that there is always some obstruction and things are not seen from an ideal standpoint. There was also an antidramatic tendency, working against the narrative, favoring privileged moments; the style was anticompositional, using off-screen space, with everything hand-held . . . There was also an attempt to tackle the embarrassment of Mexican melodrama by a kind of inversion, as if the camera were in the opposite position, showing the secondary characters, extras waiting for the big scene to take place.[17]

By locating the camera in eccentric locations, Ruiz strikes against the accepted Hollywood standards for framing and camera placement. Challenging convention is itself an inherently violent act against established cinematic norms. In that narrow sense, and despite their vastly different styles, Ruiz is following Pino Solanas and Octavio Getino's call for establishing a Latin American Third Cinema as a "cultural weapon" at the "service of class struggle and decolonization."[18] Moreover, according to the critic Carlos Ossa and the filmmaker himself, Ruiz intended to "make visible the subterranean violence that slithers in quotidian relations."[19]

One of the film's more iconic violent scenes illustrates Ruiz's technical methods for exposing and attempting to escape filmic closure. In the scene, we observe how the camera often points away from the main action, avoids expected cutting patterns, and even follows the voices of the actors with a few seconds' delay (the latter is in part due to the dubbing, but this asynchronous element is embraced by Ruiz). The camera also crosses the imaginary 180-degree line that classical continuity editing typically maintains in order to preserve a spatial arrangement subordinate to the narrative action. In addition, unusual camera angles disrupt eyeline matches and Ruiz deliberately disarticulates other devices that help to

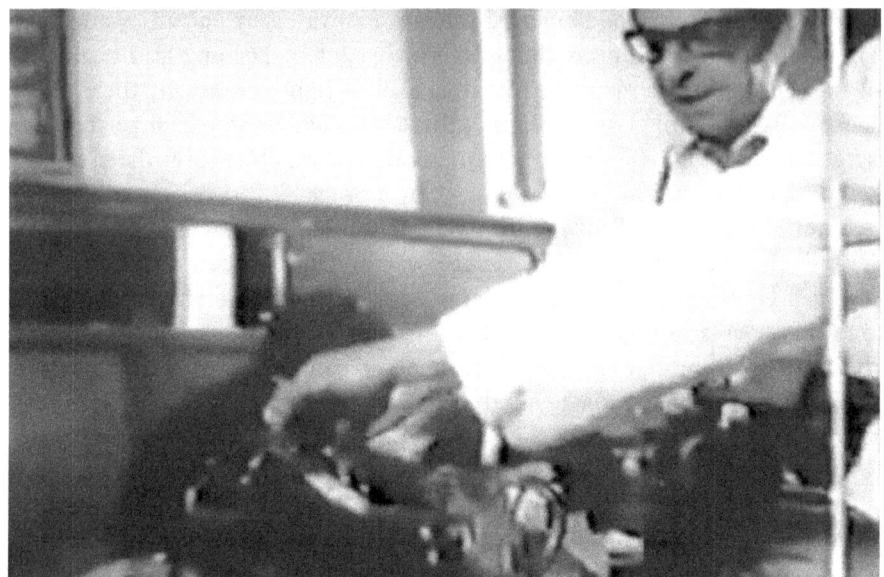

Figure 4.1 Eccentric camera placement and obstruction by the waiter's arm (from *Tres tristes tigres*, 1968).

orient the spectator and respect cause and effect and spatial continuity. Often, objects and body parts obscure our view (see Figure 4.1). These disorienting effects are exacerbated by the dialogue, which at times appears incoherent, as if it were a kind of game of double meanings or as if there were temporal ellipses that render language meaningless. Like the tongue twister that gives the film its name and that Ruiz links to verbal violence, language games and non-sequiturs are frequent throughout the film. These are an attack on the traditional ways of mainstream Hollywood cinema, as well as a challenge to commercial cinema in general.

The scene in question takes place at a bar where Tito is drinking in the company of a friend whose presence is wholly unmotivated by the plot. This tactic—dead end plot turns, inconsequential characters, etc.—occurs throughout the film and also strikes against standard expectations that all plot elements should fit into a pattern. A man at an adjacent table, who is also with a companion, engages Tito in conversation. The man states his dislike of the then centrist president Eduardo Frei, and after Tito indicates his complete distaste for politics, an argument ensues, which will climax as one of the strangers unexpectedly punches Tito's face. While there is obviously a political subtext (the scene reflects mounting political tensions in 1960s Chile), motivations remain unclear. The violence is, on the one hand, puzzling, while on the other it is a realistic portrayal of simmering tensions, since, as Silvia Donoso observes:

we know that during this time period the political was deeply rooted in culture, and therefore, in bar conversations, [since bars were] a second home for many Chileans. This explains the presence in the film of commonplace political dialogue and the exchange of opinions from a non-intellectual perspective. There is also the emergence of the infallible figure of the apolitical individual.[20]

Violence becomes central to the scene, but it is represented as sudden, unexpected, eccentric to the framing (almost off-camera) and somewhat incomprehensible.

Much of this challenge to expectations has to do with the way Ruiz films and edits the scene. He does not rely on establishing shots, nor does he use shot/reverse shot in the fashion of Hollywood narrative style. Instead, Ruiz employs the handheld camera with an unedited style that relies on fairly long takes. The camera circles around Tito's table as if in expectation of the explosion of violence about to occur. There are almost no cuts; the camera circles and at times focuses on objects (such as a wine pitcher), or on faces, although not necessarily of those speaking. The camera, in essence, refuses identification with Tito or the other characters. The camera's chaotic, jerky motion maintains the spectator disoriented, denying any attempt at filmic realism and drawing attention to its own movement. At no point are we allowed an establishing perspective that locates the characters in relation to each other; the space appears to be crowded, fragmented, incomplete. The absurdity of the dialogue and the apparent temporal ellipsis render the scene even more difficult to comprehend. The spectator has to do work to understand the film's logic, and its implicit critique against the structural violence simmering in pre-Allende Chile.

In fact, the viewing subject's position becomes rather uncomfortable in the sequence. The spectator cannot easily surmise any clear message nor does he or she become sutured into the narrative. When the violence unexpectedly arrives, as Tito is punched purportedly for his apolitical stance, it occurs (almost) offscreen. There are scant few frames in which the unannounced punch takes place, too quickly to see (except in slow motion). We are only made fully aware of it once we see Tito holding a handkerchief over his bloody nose. This sudden encounter with a violent act, however, crystallizes what Ruiz calls the simmering "everyday violence" that he argues will be eventually assimilated into "a political context."[21] With its abrupt violence and through its assault on logic, exposed through the formal aggression against the viewer and through its content, the film predisposes us toward an understanding of the urgency for solidarity in pre-Allende Chile. Spectators are not taken in by a film that does not allow them to become immersed in its narrative. It is evident that "the breaking of the imaginary relation between text and viewer [the exposing of suture], is the first prerequisite of political questions."[22] That is to say that the violent formal strategies and the violent content become the mechanism that

Ruiz deploys to force spectators to face ethical dilemmas. The violence must be acknowledged and understood in the context of Chile's political situation prior to the 1973 coup. Accordingly, exposing the simmering aggression in 1968 Chile might have led to greater (working) class solidarity and even furthered the march toward socialism.

POST MORTEM: DISSECTING THE POST-TRANSITION CINEMA OF PABLO LARRAÍN

As in Ruiz's film, Pablo Larraín's *Post mortem* (2010) also relies on scenes of violence, but comes to a very different resolution that demonstrates a certain ambiguity to political concerns. This is not wholly unusual if we consider that the most recent group of young Chilean filmmakers—labeled collectively as the *novísimos* or *Generación 2000*—have departed from the overtly activist and political filmmaking that characterized the previous exile generation (Patricio Guzmán, Miguel Littín, etc.) or even earlier, the filmmakers of the *Unidad Popular* during the Allende years.[23] This current—perhaps apolitical—stance is not surprising given that many of these cineastes are young and did not experience the worst of the dictatorship directly, and many, like Larraín, come from conservative families who did not oppose the coup and may have even benefited from it. The work of the *novísimos* often focuses on personal narratives rather than collective concerns, drifting away from the models of *testimonio* and earlier committed political cinema, best exemplified by Patricio Guzmán's documentaries. Violence and formal experimentalism, however, are still present in these contemporary narratives in which the past is dealt with in increasingly oblique ways. *Post mortem* is captivating and provocative, but also highly controversial in Chile and elsewhere, since many critics felt that the film failed to accurately or fairly deal with the troubled historical past. These criticisms, however, did not establish a clear link between the film's dehistoricizing effects and the ways it upholds or denies the practices of commercial filmmaking. As we shall see, much can be gleaned by investigating this interplay between form and content and relating it to the representation of filmic violence and political ideology.

Post mortem is set in the days immediately preceding and following the 1973 coup. The film's inexpressive protagonist, Mario Cornejo (Alfredo Castro), is a coroner's assistant in the Santiago morgue, in charge of transcribing the medical descriptions offered during autopsies. He is obsessively infatuated with his neighbor Nancy (Antonia Zegers), who, perhaps not coincidentally, like Amanda in *Tigres*, is also a burlesque show dancer (at the Bim Bam Bum theater). Preoccupied with Nancy, Mario seems completely indifferent to the political catastrophe underway. His emotional disconnect becomes evident once the coup takes place and bodies begin to fill the morgue, as he carries on his work like a dutiful *funcionario* and shows little reaction to the horrors around him. Taken broadly, Mario's apolitical stance is presented as symptomatic of alienation between the individual and society. But this alienation does not capture the extremes of political involvement (on both the left and the right) that were present in Chile before, during, and after the coup. Ruiz's film with its sudden outbursts of passionate violence does a better job of capturing that mood of long-simmering conflict than Larraín's portrait of gradual degradation.

Tellingly, the alienation depicted in *Post mortem* reflects a condition more representative of Chile during its troubled post-dictatorial period than in the politically contested *Unidad Popular* years. The result is a strange layering of temporalities, in which the action takes place in 1973, but it simultaneously registers Chile's present moment. This multi-temporality is hardly atypical in Larraín's films, which often use the distant past to comment on the recent past or the present. Overlapping chronologies also point to continuity in the reality of the Chilean experience. For instance, in the years following the end of military rule, the Concertación coalition (firmly in power) "largely continued Pinochet's neoliberal economics, increasing inequality, suppressing union activities, [and] privatizing more of the economy."[24] Indeed, critics have suggested that the apathy and malaise displayed by Larraín's protagonists are directly (if anachronistically) linked to "dissatisfaction resulting from the incomplete task of mourning that took place in the country after the authoritarian regime."[25] Both the unresolved conflicts of the past and the latent violence of the present have seeped into the representation of these characters from the past, whether consciously or unconsciously.

Despite fair criticisms about the film's political ambivalence, *Post mortem* is undeniably original with respect to form and style, bucking mainstream film practices. But whether these formal experiments, visually striking as they are, confer on the film the status of counter-cinema is less evident and worth exploring. Larraín makes his first radical stance against Hollywood cinema with an opening scene that has received considerable critical attention.[26] The film begins with an impossible traveling shot taken from a tank's undercarriage as it rolls through a debris-covered street (see Figure 4.2). The destruction from the coup can be seen even through the small space under the tank: the pavement is littered with rocks, garbage, paper, shrapnel, and other detritus, so that the spectator is claustrophobically trapped by the reduced field of vision and "dragged" (like a corpse) through the streets. As Wolfgang Bongers observes, "it is an impossible point of view, a shot that cannot be assigned to any subject."[27] The unusual camera perspective, rather than mimicking a particular subjective point of view, signals that in this self-reflexive film, framing and screen space will call attention to themselves (as cinematic techniques) and to an ever-increasing undercurrent of violence (in the film's content, but also as part of those same

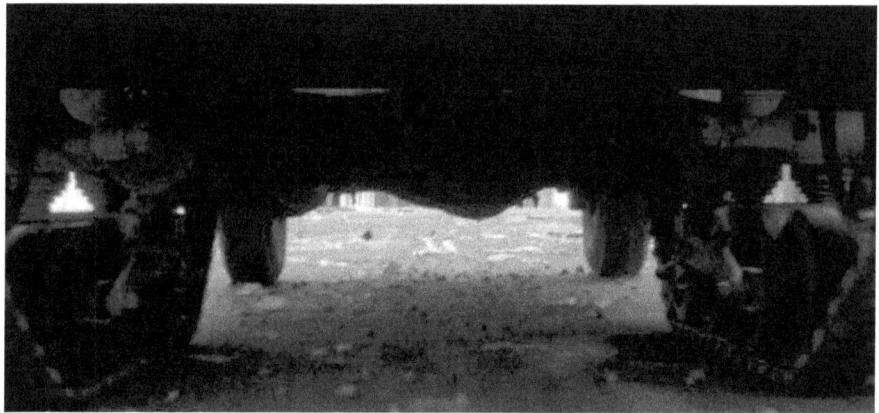

Figure 4.2   Narrow POV from underside of tank (from *Post mortem*, 2010).

cinematic techniques). An undercarriage of violence, we might say, in which the gaze of the subject disappears or is weighed down by events, since, as Bongers indicates "[the subject's gaze] is crushed by the coup d'état that unleashes a universal blindness—a human 'incapacity to see'—and introduces a mechanical and destructive gaze."[28] This mechanical point of view is also quite distant from any human perspective, and therefore, as Carolina Urrutia sees it:

> through the initial sequence with the camera tied to the underside of the tank, which registers a street emptied of any human presence, we can appreciate that from its opening sequence the film presents an ambiguous or even absent point of view.[29]

Political and ethical ambivalence and depersonalization (achieved through framing and POV devices), then, function as a symptom of violence and define the film from its first images.

The film's formal disruption of cinematic continuity and realism will parallel, on a content level, the disruption of normalcy in the Chile of 1973. But it should be noted that Larraín's camera work, despite engaging in counter-suture operations much like Ruiz did in *Tigres*, mobilizes a different set of techniques and yields a very different end result. Whereas Ruiz mostly used a jerky handheld and freely roving camera, Larraín deploys static long takes captured with a Soviet-era wide-angle anamorphic lens and panoramic framing.[30] The Soviet lenses, coupled with filming in 16mm (later transferred to 35), provide a certain ambiance of gray shabbiness to the film, a semblance of historicity that also dovetails perfectly with the morose, pessimistic mood. Although the filmic violence gradually builds to intolerable levels, the plot development and action remain remarkably slow, subdued, and minimalist.

But why does Larraín use a wide-angle lens and letterbox framing (projected at an unusually ultra-long 2.66:1 aspect ratio) with such a limited depth of focus, and what does that have to do with the film's countercinematic possibilities, or lack thereof? I propose that this approach establishes a contrast between wide filmic space and narrow filmic knowledge, between the wide screen's appearance of endless continuity and the spectator's extremely restricted view and knowledge of what is happening inside the character's psyche and outside in the disintegrating world of the diegesis. As the violence mounts, much of it remains outside the scene (obscene, from the Latin *obscaena*, offstage), either audible or presented only in fragments and eccentrically located within the frame; the characters are often awkwardly squeezed into small portions of the screen, and at times only certain body parts are visible, all calling attention to the frame. According to Dayan, Heath, Silverman, and other psychoanalytic film theorists, awareness of the frame by the spectator triggers a desire to know what lies just beyond it, desire that is efficiently sutured by the use of continuity editing techniques such as shot/reverse shot, 180-degree rule, etc. that create an illusion of narrative space (associated with "real" profilmic space). Larraín negates the suture mechanism by not allowing for the continuity techniques to erase the presence of the cinematic frame. The very immensity of the framed space and the way it is used—with eccentrically located characters and objects and an absence of movement within the frame—calls attention to the filmic process. The violence, while not explosive, is pervasive throughout the entire film. In that sense, we could say about *Post mortem* what Silverman had observed about Alfred Hitchcock's *Psycho* (1960), that the film forces spectators into uncomfortable and oblique viewing and subject positions as a product of both its content and style, and as a result of the way the cinematic apparatus itself functions.[31] Moreover, leading characters seem equally obliquely positioned, as well as ignorant, indifferent or passive in relation to the terrible historical events taking place. We might also say that fragmented framing corresponds to ethical disintegration in the plot. Alejandro Gaspar has observed similar issues in framing and composition:

> In *Post mortem* the camera is more stable, the framing is quite elaborate. Within each shot, the wide panoramic screen format strikes a contrast against the isolated figures that are often filmed through doors and windows, or through objects that impede total sight. The result is contradictory and claustrophobic: the horizontality of the screen seems to suggest the possibility of a world with wide and open spaces, but in contrast, space is shown through incomplete fragments, often we can only see a few square meters around the protagonist, while everyone else makes their presence felt through off screen sounds or through shapes that are out of focus.[32]

These framing and editing choices are experimental tactics, aimed at jarring and disorienting the viewing subject and making his or her seamless absorption into the film world difficult. But as I contend, although Larraín aggressively interrupts the suturing mechanisms of conventional cinema, this process does not result in the cathartic revelation of hidden problems or point to potential solutions, as Ruiz does. It leaves the spectator unmoored, neither comfortably ignorant and immersed in the continuity narrative (the fantasy of plenitude), nor hopeful for a more just and equitable democracy. Instead, what remains for the viewing subject is a gray and amorphous empty sensation, a state of driftlessness, all expectation banished. Unable to identify with the narrative's coldly distant characters, or to find a space of his or her own, the spectator is left feeling disempowered.

Speaking about the inscrutable lead characters in *Post mortem* and *Tony Manero* (the earlier film in Larraín's dictatorship trilogy), Barraza makes a case that:

> both men represent subjects expelled—in Lacanian terms—from the Real, becoming automatons or the living dead in a lifeless society. Hence, the anxiety of these individuals can be seen as a crisis of meaning . . . in a hopeless and senseless world.[33]

Mario is presented as an emotionless character, one who stares at horrible wounds and mutilated bodies and records them in grisly detail for his job at the Santiago morgue; however, none of it registers within his consciousness; he remains aloof and shows no empathy toward the pain of others. At the formal level, something similar seems to occur with Larraín's experimental techniques, which record, register, and destabilize the processes of suture, but have a distancing effect on the viewer, suffusing everything with a sense of vacuous banality. Thus the film's violence serves not to awaken or elicit a political response, but to deaden the senses of the viewing subject, to induce a sense of apathetic hopelessness.

Interestingly, critics such as James Harvey have argued for a democratizing potential in the very act of political ambivalence and in the aesthetics of cold minimalism employed by Larraín. According to Harvey:

> ambivalence is made pivotal to [Larraín's] representations of history. If we consider Larraín's strange, distanced representation of the coup in this sense, we can begin to move toward an appreciation for the democratic potential of its aesthetics.[34]

Following that positive appraisal, Harvey insists that:

> where Third Cinema had the intention of staging and slaying inequalities, Larraín presumes the subjective capacities of his spectator, leaving

more to the imagination through an ambivalent approach to history. A shared ambivalent style departs from the committed radicalism of the socialist project.[35]

Furthermore, the critic also argues that the apathy, detachment, and distance displayed by the pared-down formalist styles and the characters in the films of several recent Latin American directors (including Lisandro Alonso, Lucrecia Martel, and Larraín himself), "opens up a space for the involvement of a spectator."[36] In other words, by leaving the political point ambiguously open, the film allows for greater engagement on the part of the viewing subject. The problem is that this flexible position presupposes a spectator already aware of history, of the full context of the events narrated in these films, as if that information had been available and disseminated in Chile for all to see. It neglects the realities of censorship, systemic violence, official propaganda, and historical erasure that have afflicted both the Pinochet years and the democratic period. This is not to say that only films with an overt political message and clear arguments are valid, rather, that ethical ambiguity and an uncertain and shifting narrative lacking in historical grounding, such as *Post mortem*, can easily result in an ambiguous understanding of the past disconnected from the very real suffering of those who opposed Pinochet's rule. A film like that rather easily slips into the neoliberal mechanism for erasing, forgetting, and distorting the past.

While Harvey puts forth a fascinating and highly charitable argument in defense of *Post mortem*'s politics of ambivalence, indeed, an argument that is attuned to both formal and content-based considerations, I remain unconvinced. In my view, the experimental techniques deployed by Larraín—including the characters' emotional detachment, the disturbances to narrative causality, the static framing, the cool colors, the degraded 16mm quality image, the minimalist *mise-en-scène* and editing—become complicit with an avoidance of historical truth, of finding solutions for Chile, in short, with a refusal to acknowledge the past and imagine a better future; instead, past, present, and future are collapsed (flattened) and frozen in a single instant, the moment of the coup on September 11, 1973. Richard has observed a similar phenomenon of "frozen" time in Larraín's *No*, explaining that:

> this is the semiotic device (as decisive as it is semi-invisible) that functions as an operator of anachronism in so far as it immobilizes memory into a "before"—static, arrested, congealed—that makes it impossible for that which is behind (the past) to move forward (toward the present and the future).[37]

Everything is sifted through one of the most terrible episodes of Chilean history, and through the knowledge of its lengthy and brutal aftermath, so that Larraín's trilogy is framed in a profoundly pessimist light. As Christian Ramírez sees this problem, the trilogy's films capture, reflect, and perhaps even perpetuate "the attitude that many a Chilean person had after the coup (to shut their eyes, submerge themselves in the day-to-day, forget the victims and the abuses)."[38] So we can see that Larraín's politics of ambivalence go hand in hand with his experimental style; the two are inextricably connected and function to pessimistically darken past, present, and future.

Echoing some of Harvey's points, Barraza believes that contemporary Chilean films offer "ciphered strategies for criticizing and/or expressing apprehension regarding sociopolitical conditions in today's Chile; so the apparent indifference to depicting the past, in fact, reveals great concern regarding the present."[39] I see no such signs of political concern beneath the streak of indifference or, perhaps more accurately, ambivalence, in Larraín's dictatorship trilogy. No doubt, the present is being addressed by these films, but not through a purposeful and relevant critique. José M. Santa Cruz, instead, presents a credible argument that harshly criticizes *Post mortem*'s dehistoricizing strategies, as evidenced by the fact that:

> the film does not provide any clues about the reasons or causes for the coup. We only see a succession of its effects: the bodies mounting at the morgue, the empty streets, Nancy's destroyed house, and her, hiding in a shed. There is no explanation, only the violent irruption of the event [the military coup], which de-structures everything.[40]

Thus far I have argued that in Larraín's *Post mortem* violence does not serve the purpose sought by Raúl Ruiz in *Tres tristes tigres*, that is, to awaken the spectator to a social condition in desperate need of change, exposing the fissures and inequalities in 1960s Chilean society. Rather than representing a "radical gesture," as Harvey claims, Larraín's work merely retraumatizes the spectator, digging at the same wounds in a recurring autopsy of the national corpse. It is not a productive trauma, which seeks to work through issues. His film's purpose is not truth finding through a (post-mortem) historical analysis, but casting a monochromatic hue onto the past that ultimately muddles and obscures any difference between victims and aggressors; it is, therefore, a reactionary project. Amit Thakkar, channeling Michael Rothberg's concept of the "implicated subject," ascribes this role to Mario (who is neither fully a victim nor strictly a perpetrator), and believes that "by making this film, Larraín is repeating for the nation the initial event, a 'violence that has not yet been fully known,' thus reaffirming its continued relevance."[41] The implicated subject is at once linked and separate from the original historical acts perpetrated (the coup, the repression, etc.). He or she may not be directly involved (or even born in the case of the current generation) but benefits from the acts perpetrated by others. As a new generation of Chileans who did not live through the Allende years reconsider, and in some cases rewrite the past, they may be actively denying their perpetrator legacies by embracing an ambiguous position that refutes and diffuses culpability. This is similar to what Richard refers to as narratives of redemption, in which those who were guilty of crimes are embraced back into society, with ostensibly no punishment.[42] By suggesting the past as an unknowable period, as Larraín's film seems to do, the specificity of guilt and innocence disappears into a haze. In *Post mortem*, all violence is the same, all violence merely accumulates, needlessly and hopelessly, in endless piles of corpses. No one can be blamed, no one is accountable since everyone is implicated.

One key scene of horrifying violence that illustrates this process is the autopsy of a body that is later revealed to be that of Salvador Allende. Setting the somber tone with a dull, blue-gray visual palette, described by Demetrios Matheou as having "the deathly pallor of fading wallpaper,"[43] the scene is endowed with a degree of historical realism as it takes place in the same hospital and room, even on the same dissection table, where Allende's autopsy was performed.[44] The scene begins with a medium shot showing the slow disposition of the instruments for the autopsy, easily transposed by the mind of any spectator into the tools for political torture and interrogation. Then, it cuts to a long take of Mario recording the autopsy with the typewriter as the doctor reads off the details of the grossly mutilated body (see Figure 4.3). The next shot is a static frame of the eerily frozen yet threatening military observers. One of the few camera movements, this is followed by a low downward pan toward the body, which remains at first, slightly off-screen; eventually we can see an unidentifiable mass of bloody encephalic matter. While this could have been an emotional moment, the scene is wholly surreal and the details, despite the attention to historical realism, also seem inauthentic and distant, resulting in a numbing effect for the viewing subject. More shots alternate between a close-up of the body and of Mario's impassive face as he types. When Mario

Figure 4.3 An emotionless Mario transcribes Allende's autopsy (from *Post mortem*, 2010).

becomes unable to type—not because he is overwhelmed by emotion (as one would expect), but because he is unfamiliar with the electric typewriter—a soldier replaces him. The gruesome description continues until Allende's dead body is finally covered with a sheet. What is most notable in the scene from a formal standpoint is the minimal use of editing cuts and the static nature of most shots, including the negligible movement of the characters within the frame. This editing style prompts the question, why, in a scene with so much physical cutting of tissue and body parts is there so little cutting of film?

I would suggest that the autopsy scene actually functions as the reverse of a suture operation, it (literally) represents an opening up of a body rather than a closing down, a ripping apart rather than a healing or joining of the lips of a wound. The wounds of the body politic are exposed and even retraumatized. In this case, the history deliberately repressed for so long is laid out on the film's dissecting table for all to see. Whereas continuity editing, in its constant movements, its centered framings, its smooth cuts and transitions binds the spectator as subject, here continuity is disrupted precisely by painfully extending the length of the takes in order to make the spectator increasingly uncomfortable with the carnage. At the same time no emotional reaction or release is possible, given the surreal and darkly comedic mood. If Mario's impassive attitude recalls the hypocrisy of that historical period, as ideological convictions were overturned in the chaos of the coup, the drab, dark colors and tone of the poorly lit scene likewise betray the opaque morality of the neoliberal present and its market-driven imperatives.[45]

What stance, if any, can we deduce from this scene, one that revisits the coup's primal scene (so to speak), and uncovers Allende's body for all to see? How does this filmic violence relate to Ruiz's work? Larraín himself has marked a clear distance between his films and the work of his 1970s precursors, stating:

> I don't make these movies to change anything or to create a process. The left-wing movies that were made in Latin America during the 1970s expressed a certain ideology. They wanted to change things and create conscience. I'm not after any of that stuff.[46]

Taking no sides by his own admission, Larraín constructs a mood of (apparent) political neutrality in order to offer a voyeuristic observation rather than an involved witnessing or *testimonio*. Larraín associates this apolitical stance with the formal methods he employs:

> I originally thought of using a hand-held camera that could capture the scenes as live testimonies. However, when the filming began, I decided to practically not move the camera and set it up as a "fly on the wall": almost inert, observing the facts cautiously, horizontally, as if the world

extended itself beyond the confines of the frame only on either side, without heaven, without God nor Earth.[47]

The frame's endless horizontality, with its flattening effect, according to the director's words, frees him from judgment from above or below. Without ethical directives, he seems to claim that he is beholden to neither the left nor the right. Although this lack of interest in politics possibly conceals a regressive politics, the quote is otherwise revealing. Larraín's supposed fly-on-the-wall neutrality, the rejection of the proximity of the handheld camera, and his avowal of not presenting a point of view aligned with any sides, goes a long way to validate Santa Cruz's denunciation of the film's depoliticizing and potentially ahistorical stance, when he charges that:

> Larraín's vision does not provoke fissures or cracks in reality's representational weave. The rich audiovisual experimentation he engages in does not generate new cartographies of the visible and the sayable, as it relates to the dictatorship. It is an experimentation that exhausts itself, that forgets its own operations and vanishing points. This self-containment and the construction of the dictatorship into a [kind of] natural history, generates an ahistoricism of low intensity within the image. It looks and functions like a historical discourse, although it does not want to be one.[48]

This is a harsh indictment of a film that, on the one hand, successfully unravels the stale cinematography of Hollywood blockbusters, while on the other, misses an opportunity to align its experimentalism with an ethical stance *vis-à-vis* the representation of history. In sum, in *Post mortem* Larraín disarticulates spectator mechanisms of immersion, but refuses to provide any kind of resolution to historical trauma or engage in discussions of political responsibility, underscoring Thakkar's point that, "Larraín's films are not intended to 'work through' but simply to register."[49] In other words, notwithstanding its many aesthetic qualities, *Post mortem* reinforces the logic of neoliberalism. While credible positive political readings of this movie are possible (as we have seen with Harvey and others), the film's own ambivalent positionality ultimately undermines them.

TAKING STOCK: *TIGRES* AND *POST MORTEM* IN THE BALANCE

What might we conclude from the approach these films take to formal and content-based violence? Both films resist an easy reading and both capture Chile's complex historical reality before and after the coup. While Ruiz's film looks ahead to a violence that is about to occur, a violence located just beyond the reach of the camera, Larraín's looks back, dissecting the irruption of violence that severed Chile's history. But although both films oppose a false cinematic plenitude by reopening the nation's sutured narratives and laying bare mainstream cinema's ideological operations, as we have seen, they arrive at very different results. *Tres tristes tigres* enacted a pre-revolutionary violence aimed at upending class hierarchies and celebrating the rise of the socialism of the *Unidad Popular*. Larraín's film, instead, presents a panoramic landscape of defeat, surveys the trampled collective hopes of the 1960s and 1970s, and offers little (politically) in return; the viewers are left with the mental image of an isolated, lonely figure standing against an immense, gray, empty background in a long, hopeless, interminable take. Nothing redeems Mario Cornejo, or Chile. No identification is possible with Mario, who is at once pitiable, pathetic, and loathsome, a victim who (too) easily becomes a perpetrator. This impossibility of identifying, germane to the violence committed by the character—through both his acts of commission and omission—also undermines the suturing process, since, if we recall, Silverman states that the operation of suture is successful only "at the moment that the viewing subject says, 'Yes, that's me,' or 'That's what I see.'"[50]

It is true that in terms of both aesthetics and content Larraín's film is more layered, more complex with regard to style and cinematography, than Ruiz's. That may be why some critics like Harvey defend *Post mortem* in light of a supposed improvement over the simple directness of 1960s revolutionary films, asserting that "whereas the didacticism of radical cinema in the past sought the reception of a specific social message, *Post mortem* continues a contemporary Latin American cinematic concern for the denial of a master-logic to prevail over the simple-minded spectator."[51] This point rings true, Larraín's film is technically sophisticated and thematically challenging (and granted, aesthetically pleasing), and it avoids the overwhelming logic of both classical Hollywood and some overly didactic 1960s films (*La hora de los hornos* by Pino Solanas and Octavio Getino from 1968 comes to mind). With its eccentric flat framing, its static long takes and other experimental techniques, *Post mortem* impedes the process of suture, which binds the spectator ideologically and psychologically to the filmic narrative, as Heath observed: "images bind the spectator in place, the suturing central position that is the sense of the image, that sets its scene (in place, the spectator completes the image as its subject)."[52] But whereas Larraín liberates the spectator from the violence of the suturing process, he offers no hope or escape from the systemic violence and the trauma, products of the 1973 coup. Scholars such as Robert Wells, who have studied trauma in relation to post-dictatorship cinema, have identified this reinjuring aspect in Larraín's work, explaining that the filmmaker's approach:

rejects the possibility of mastering the traumatic past and, as a result, represents an "indelible" situation—the nature of which he shows to be brutal and absurd, a kind of sick joke. For Chile continues to be overrun by injustice, impunity, and neoliberalism. These are the "disturbing remains" of the dictatorship in postdictatorship and post-traumatic times.[53]

The film retraumatizes the viewing subject, placing him or her at the site of the crime during the coup, but providing no out. The lost sense of an ethical dimension, in which culpability is assigned and responsibility is demanded from the perpetrators, is wholly absent from his work. Impunity reigns: neither the troubled past nor the neoliberal present are held to account. Certainly, the Pinochet years and the transition were/are rife with moral ambiguity, with antiheroes like Mario, and in that sense the claim to realism, to the representation of an existing situation, can be made. But in his rewriting of the past Larraín obscures the crimes of the guilty, and enables the continuity of the moral ambiguity of the present to color the ideology of the younger Chileans who did not experience directly the violence of the coup and its aftermath, and, in some cases, may have even benefited from it. As such, where the experimental cinema of Ruiz used violence to construct the possibility of a (better) future Chile, Larraín's experimental work, technically accomplished as it may be, foments a politically ambivalent and historically ungrounded take on the past, and a barren and hopeless outlook for the future of the nation.

NOTES

1. All translations from the Spanish are my own unless otherwise noted.
2. For a contemporary account of the most recent generation of Chilean filmmakers, see Ascanio Cavallo and Gonzalo Maza, *El novísimo cine chileno* (Santiago de Chile: Uqbar Editores, 2010).
3. As illustrated by Luis Buñuel's famous assault on the eye, on the spectator, and on vision itself, in *Un chien andalou* (1929), or more recently, in the work of filmmakers such as the Mexican Carlos Reygadas, who combine experimental techniques with sex and/or violence creating a blend between extreme cinema and art house. For a detailed study of Reygadas's work in relation to extreme sex and violence in experimental cinema see Chapter 2 in Trent Troy Bordun's *Genre Trouble and Extreme Cinema: Film Theory at the Fringes of Contemporary Art Cinema* (London: Palgrave Macmillan, 2017).
4. Stephen Heath, "Narrative Space," *Screen* 17, no. 3 (October 1976): 98: <https://doi.org/10.1093/screen/17.3.68> (accessed February 25, 2020).
5. Kaja Silverman, *The Subject of Semiotics* (Oxford: Oxford University Press, 1984), 223.
6. Nelly Richard, *Cultural Residues: Chile in Transition* (Minneapolis: University of Minnesota Press, 2004), 3.
7. Vania Barraza Toledo, "Reviewing the Present in Pablo Larraín's Historical Cinema," *Iberoamericana* 13, no. 51 (September 2013): 164.

8. David Sipprelle, "Cinema Remembers: Forming a Collective Memory of Military Dictatorship," *The Trinity Papers (2011–present)* (2014): 51: <http://digitalrepository.trincoll.edu/trinitypapers/34> (accessed February 25, 2020).
9. Sipprelle, "Cinema Remembers," 46.
10. Original Spanish: "El cine norteamericano favorece la dominación imperialista [. . . y trabaja con . . .] mecanismos ideológicos y culturales impuestos por los monopolios de la ideología dominante." Raúl Ruiz, "Prefiero registrar antes que mistificar el proceso chileno," interview by Helvio Soto et al., *Revista Primer Plano* 4 (Spring 1972): <http://cinechile.cl/archivos-de-prensa/entrevista-a-raul-ruiz-prefiero-registrar-antes-que-mistificar-el-proceso-chileno/> (accessed Febuary 25, 2020).
11. Original Spanish: "El aparato ideológico que se analiza . . . es muy fácil de desmontar—cada vez más fácil." Ibid.
12. Silverman, *The Subject of Semiotics*, 222.
13. John King, *Magical Reels: A History of Cinema in Latin America* (London: Verso, 1990), 171–2.
14. Louis Althusser, *Lenin and Philosophy and Other Essays*, trans. Ben Brewster (New York: Monthly Review Press, 1971), 162–5.
15. Colin MacCabe, "Theory and Film: Principles of Realism and Pleasure," *Screen* 17, no. 3 (Autumn 1976): 16.
16. Original Spanish: "Inventar nuevas técnicas para que la parte sumergida [del cine] se haga evidente." Ruiz, "Prefiero."
17. Qtd. in Julianne Burton, *Cinema and Social Change in Latin America: Conversations with Filmmakers* (Austin: University of Texas Press, 1986), 185–6.
18. Zuzana Pick, *The New Latin American Cinema: A Continental Project* (Austin: University of Texas Press, 1993), 101.
19. Original Spanish: "Poner en evidencia la violencia subterránea que se desliza en las relaciones cotidianas." Carlos Ossa, *Historia del cine chileno* (Santiago de Chile: Quimantu limitada, 1971), 78: <http://www.memoriachilena.cl/archivos2/pdfs/mc0014626.pdf> (accessed February 25, 2020).
20. Original Spanish: "Sabemos que lo político en estos tiempos estaba fuertemente enraizado en la cultura y, por ende, en la conversación de los bares, el segundo hogar para muchos integrantes del pueblo chileno. Es por lo que no tardará en aparecer el diálogo común sobre lo político y el intercambio de opiniones desde una perspectiva no necesariamente intelectual en esa película. También surgirá la infalible figura del apolítico." Silvia Donoso Hiriart, "Re-visitando el Cine Chileno Pre-Dictadura: Aldo Francia y Raúl Ruiz," in *Changes, Conflicts and Ideologies in Contemporary Hispanic Culture*, ed. Teresa Fernández-Ulloa (Newcastle: Cambridge Scholars Publishing, 2014, 400–31), 408.
21. Burton, *Cinema and Social Change in Latin America*, 187.
22. MacCabe, "Theory and Film," 21.
23. Chief among these filmmakers working on fiction cinema, we can mention in alphabetical order, Niles Atallah, Matías Bize, Pablo Carrera, Elisa Eliash, Alejandro Fernández Almendras, Pablo Larraín, Fernando Lavanderos, Sebastián Lelio, Rodrigo Marín, Christopher Murray, Alicia Scherson, José Luis Torres Leiva. Barraza Toledo, "Reviewing the Present," 162.
24. Amit Thakkar, "Unclaimed Experience and the Implicated Subject in Pablo Larraín's *Post Mortem*," in *Scars and Wounds: Film and Legacies of Trauma*, eds. Nick Hodgin and Amit Thakkar (London: Palgrave Macmillan, 2017), 262.
25. Barraza Toledo, "Reviewing the Present," 163.
26. See for example, Bongers's and Urrutia's respective analyses of the scene.

27. Original Spanish: "Se trata de un punto de vista imposible, un plano inconferible a un sujeto." Wolfgang Bongers, "La estética del (an)archivo en el cine de Pablo Larraín," *A Contracorriente* 12, no. 1 (Fall 2014): 191.
28. Original Spanish: "[La mirada del sujeto] está aplastada por el propio golpe de estado que provoca una ceguera universal—un 'no ver' humano—e introduce miradas maquínicas, destructivas." Bongers, "La estética del (an)archivo," 192.
29. Original Spanish: "[Mediante] la secuencia inicial con la cámara atada a la parte inferior del tanque, registrando la calle vaciada de presencias humanas, vemos que se establece desde la apertura un punto de vista ambiguo, ausente incluso." Carolina Urrutia, "*Post mortem* y *Tony Manero*: Memoria centrífuga de un pasado político," *Cinemas d'Amérique Latine* 19 (2011): 66.
30. Paul Julian Smith, "Screenings: At the Edge of History," *Film Quarterly* 64, no. 2 (Winter 2010): <https://filmquarterly.org/2010/12/07/screenings-at-the-edge-of-history> (accessed February 25, 2020).
31. Silverman, *The Subject of Semiotics*, 206.
32. Original Spanish: "[En *Post mortem*] la cámara se mantiene más estable, los encuadres están compuestos de una manera elaborada. El formato de pantalla panorámico contrasta con las figuras aisladas que aparecen en el plano, a menudo filmadas a través de puertas, ventanas u objetos que impiden la visión completa. El resultado es contradictoriamente claustrofóbico: la horizontalidad de la pantalla parece sugerir la posibilidad de un mundo de espacios amplios y abiertos; por el contrario, el espacio se nos presenta de manera fragmentada, incompleta, a menudo solamente contemplamos los escasos metros cuadrados que rodean al protagonista mientras el resto del mundo impone su presencia mediante sonidos fuera de campo o formas desenfocadas." Alejandro Gaspar, "La autopsia de Chile: Pablo Larraín disecciona la dictadura de Pinochet en *Toni Manero*, *Post mortem* y *No*," *Visiones* (blog). February 2013: <http://alejandrogaspar.blogspot.com/2013/02/la-autopsia-de-chile-pablo-larrain.html> (accessed February 25, 2020).
33. Barraza, "Reviewing the Present," 160.
34. James Harvey, "Democratic Ambivalence in *Post mortem*," *Journal of Latin American Cultural Studies* 26, no. 4 (November 2017): 543.
35. Ibid., 548.
36. Ibid.
37. Original Spanish: "Este es el recurso semiótico (tan decisivo como semi-invisible) que funciona como operador de anacronía en tanto inmoviliza el recuerdo en un 'antes'—fijo, detenido, congelado—que le impide a lo de atrás (el pasado) avanzar hacia adelante (el presente y el futuro)." Nelly Richard, "Las réplicas del 'NO' a cuarenta años del golpe militar y a veinticinco años del SI y del NO," *Alter/nativas (Online): Revista de estudios culturales latinoamericanos* 5 (Fall 2015): <https://alternativas.osu.edu/es/issues/autumn-5-2015/essays/richard.html> (accessed February 25, 2020).
38. Original Spanish: "La actitud que mucho chileno de a pie tuvo tras el golpe (cerrar los ojos, continuar sumergido en el día a día, olvidar a las victimas y los abusos)." Christian Ramírez, "Pablo Larraín: Una habitación cerrada," in *El novísimo cine chileno*, eds. Cavallo and Maza, 82.
39. Barraza Toledo, "Reviewing the Present," 163.
40. Original Spanish: "La película no da ninguna pista sobre las razones del golpe. Solo vemos la sucesión de sus efectos: cuerpos amontonados en la morgue, las calles vacías, la casa de Nancy destruida, y ella, escondida en un cobertizo. No hay explicación alguna, solo la irrupción violenta del acontecimiento [el golpe militar], que lo desestructura todo." José M. Santa Cruz, "Naturalización de la dictadura: Formas de la historia en la trilogía de Pablo Larraín," *Comunicación y Medios*. Colección Documentos, no. 3 (2014): 77.

41. Thakkar, "Unclaimed Experience," 252.
42. Interestingly, as observed by Jean Franco, Richard is also suspicious of "all that is too neatly sewn together," focusing instead on "residual zones," that is, "deposits and symbolic and cultural sedimentations of torn significations that tended to be omitted or set aside by social reason." Nelly Richard, *Cultural Residues: Chile in Transition* (Minneapolis: University of Minnesota Press, 2004), xi–xii.
43. Pablo Larraín, "The Body Politic: Pablo Larraín on *Post Mortem*," interview by Demetrios Matheou, *Sight & Sound*, January 29, 2015: <http://www.bfi.org.uk/news-opinion/sight-sound-magazine/interviews/body-politic-pablo-larra-on-post-mortem> (accessed February 25, 2020).
44. Larraín, "The Body Politic."
45. In Richard's words, in Chile "the neoliberal model dismantled the solidary links between social organizations and popular movements. It replaced the fervor of historical action with the pragmatism and efficiency of management practices within business culture." ["El modelo neoliberal se preocupó de desarmar el vínculo solidario con las organizaciones sociales y los movimientos populares. Remplazó el fervor de la gesta histórica por el pragmatismo y la eficiencia de la gestión administrativa de la cultura empresarial"]. Richard, "Las réplicas."
46. Violet Lucca, "Projecting and Excavating the Past: An Interview with Pablo Larraín," *Film Comment*, Film Society of Lincoln Center, April 19, 2012: <https://www.filmcomment.com/blog/projecting-the-past-an-interview-with-pablo-larrain> (accessed February 25, 2020).
47. Pablo Larraín, "Interview," interview by John Dhabolt, *Covering Media*, April 2012: <http://www.coveringmedia.com/movie/2012/04/post-mortem.html> (accessed February 27, 2020).
48. Original Spanish: "[La de Larraín] es una mirada que no provoca fisuras o grietas en el tejido representacional de la realidad. La rica experimentación audiovisual que hace Larraín no genera nuevos mapas de lo visible y de lo decible, a propósito de la dictadura. Es una experimentación que se agota en sí misma, que se olvida de sus propias operaciones y puntos de fuga. Esta autocontención, y la construcción de la dictadura es una historia natural, genera una des-historización de baja intensidad en la imagen. Parece y funciona como un discurso histórico, aunque no quiere serlo." Santa Cruz, "Naturalización de la dictadura," 78–9.
49. Thakkar, "Unclaimed Experience," 263.
50. Silverman, *The Subject of Semiotics*, 205.
51. Harvey, "Democratic Ambivalence in *Post mortem*," 548.
52. Heath, "Narrative Space," 99.
53. Robert Wells, "Trauma, Male Fantasies, and Cultural Capital in the Films of Pablo Larraín," *Journal of Latin American Cultural Studies* 26, no. 4 (July 2017), 505: <https://doi.org/10.1080/13569325.2017.1343182> (accessed February 26, 2020).

CHAPTER 5

Gothic Memory and Ghostly Aesthetics: *Post Mortem* as a Horror Film

Rosana Díaz-Zambrana

> *What is a ghost?* A tragedy condemned to repeat itself time and again? An instant of pain, perhaps. Something dead which still seems to be alive.
>
> The Devil's Backbone (2001)

In recent years, the presence in global cinema of ghosts and hauntings has progressively spread as an opportune strategy to address historical injustices and lingering national traumas. This trend is now evident even in countries like Chile, where horror productions were unprecedented or rarities.[1] Chile's cinematic productions of the 1990s—despite the favorable conditions of creative freedom and democracy—shied away from openly tackling the traumatic experience of the military dictatorship years.[2] This more hesitant and dispersed approach to cinematic discourse stands in stark contrast to that of other Latin American countries. The new democratic conditions in Argentina and Brazil, for example, facilitated the arrival of the "torture genre," which dealt symbolically with the remaining anxieties during the post-dictatorship period.[3] In fact, during the 1990s the presence of political cinema in Chile was particularly scarce and only "a limited number of films that depict or take place during the military regime have been produced since 2003."[4] The reason for such a "neutralization of the political discourse" and "serene look to the recent past"[5] is found in the new, post-dictatorship principle of reconciliation that favors national security and economic prosperity at the expense of historic memory and an authentic mourning process.

According to the prominent sociologist Tomás Moulain, the "new Chile" that was promoted by the military regime and its neoliberal ideology created a false notion of transition and democracy, where historical amnesia was implicitly required. As Idelber Avelar establishes in *The Untimely Present*, "the imperative to mourn is the post-dictatorial imperative par excellence," but, by contrast, the rules of the free-market mentality established by the dictatorship required that the "past is to be forgotten because the market demands that the new replace the old without leaving a remainder."[6] Since forgetting was needed to reach national consensus and achieve financial prosperity, one of its negative ramifications at the symbolic and pragmatic level was the "loss of discourse," in which prevailed "the lack of ordinary words to name what has been lived."[7] In fact, the cultural critic Nelly Richard proposes to address the post-dictatorship's fissured experience by considering the allegory of "memory as residue," in order to understand the "dismantled (h)istories," the "broken narratives," and the "disturbed speech."[8]

At the same time, the transition period opened an opportunity for artists, filmmakers, and other intellectuals to address the suppressed past and "speak the trauma" by examining the wounds that unfolded during the previous two decades. Cinematographically, the degrees of political and civil uncertainty—post-dictatorship—are captured through the recurrence of perplexed subjectivities and unhinged conflicts. That is why when referring to the cinema of the 1990s, Ascanio Cavallo identifies loss and disorientation as paramount themes, where the socially and mentally afflicted characters are mainly orphans, nullified and passive, wandering victims.[9]

With the turn of the millennium, a novel wave of directors delivered an unconventional revision of the artificial, sociopolitical pacts that transpired during the Transition. They utilized a plethora of experimental styles, mostly alluding to the past via circumventing narratives. Despite the apparent absence of explicit political discourse on the big screen, Carolina Urrutia notes that, after the year 2000, Chilean cinema proposes a reflection about "being in the world" that presents a saddened space—both private and public—which is a direct effect of the political, economic, and cultural state of affairs.[10] Moreover, this intimate and politically detached cinema—labeled, among other terms, "Newest Chilean Cinema,"[11] "centrifugal cinema,"[12] "cinema of disenchanted intimacies,"[13] and "melancholic cinema"[14]—obliquely relates the sense of quiet hopelessness and quotidian despair of private matters to the unresolved political legacy of the military regime and the erosive impact of the neoliberal experience promoted by the Chilean state during Pinochet.

This analysis focuses on *Post mortem* (2010), an exceptional example of a political film coming from the new national cinema.[15] This second film of an "unintentional trilogy"[16] about Pinochet's dictatorship (1973–90) is directed by Pablo Larraín, one of Chile's most internationally recognized and influential directors, due for the most part to his startling filmic style and caustic undertaking of controversial subject matters. Taking an opposite political stand from his right-wing politician parents, Larraín tackles the Pinochet era by posing questions of institutional distrust, historical violence, and the return of an unpleasant past. The other two installments in the trilogy, *Tony Manero* (2008)[17] and *No* (2012),[18] deal with the same atmosphere of terror that was an undercurrent during the military years and the return to democracy via mediatic strategy, respectively. Of the three films, though, *Post mortem* stands out because it is set at the onset of Chile's darkest years, specifically situated in the days before and after the coup. Altogether, the three filmic proposals are marked by cynical and unforgiving attitudes toward the foundation of the national reconciliation process and the complex politics of remembering. Vania Barraza maintains that the living characters in Larraín's trilogy embody Chile's haunted history, but the films also employ the character of the undead to represent the symbolic debt of Chilean society to its history.[19] Moreover, the narrative economy of ghosts and the (un)dead enrooted in horror cinema finds a propitious vessel through which Larraín creates a representation of the past "as a haunting, rather than a reality immediately accessible to us."[20]

By all means, the tangential components of horror film and political drama are quite effective in dealing with the oblivion of a problematic historical past and its return via ghostly presences. Álvaro Fernández has indicated that, although history-based films depicting graphic cruelty and psychological and physical torment—such as the Argentinian films, *La noche de los lápices* (*Night of the Pencils*, Héctor Olivera, 1987) and *Garage Olimpo* (*Olympic Garage*, Marco Bechis, 1999)—can easily be classified as horror films, their political inscriptions become the focus of interest over horror narrative, and they are thus classified as "political dramas."[21] In Fernández's view this is due to the fact that horror cinema is still perceived as a minor genre; it is not considered a legitimate mechanism with which to address testimonial or historical matters. Nevertheless, the prolific horror film critic Robin Wood has widely established how horror film gives shape to cultural anxieties of a "return of the repressed" and instigates reflection about private and collective fears at any given historical moment.[22]

The cinematic task of approaching grandiose political narratives faces the twin challenge of achieving social engagement while complying with the demands of a market-driven society. Following this logic, Larraín avoids the tendency of filmmakers such as Silvio Caiozzi, Gonzalo Justiniano, and Andrés Wood—among others—to enact traumatic memory using the framework inherited from the New Latin American Cinema of the 1960s, and instead, he aligns his narratives more with genres rooted in the commercial culture industry.[23] In fact, Waleska Pino-Ojeda perceives in Larraín's work an aesthetic of the "macabre baroque," an aesthetic mainly based on liminality and the dislocated positioning of genre, character construction, and narration.[24] It would be safe to say that the experimental adoption of commercial genres or artifices that belong to popular global trends—namely thriller, Gothic, body horror, or macabre baroque for that matter—to dissect political issues plays a cardinal role in Larraín's national and international artistic recognition.

Even if *Post mortem* was traditionally aligned with the genre of political drama, I propose to read it following Sigmund Freud's notion of the uncanny in connection to the cinematic devices and thematic formulas of Gothic horror. In addition, my reading will be informed by Timothy Jones's concept of the "living Gothic," in which the Gothic frame plays a role in conjuring and bringing to the forefront a collective memory of unrest.[25] Since memory is evoked through a suggestive sensory experience, an examination of how the tactical design of spatial, aural, and visual effects in *Post mortem*—within a Gothic aesthetic—contributes to recreating a disquieting portrait of historical trauma and amnesia in the context of post-dictatorial, neoliberal Chile. I argue that *Post mortem* concurs with the horror genre's theme of the return of the repressed. Its Gothic formalistic codes transform and enliven what could have been a dry political drama into a visceral and haunting experience of the past.

GOTHIC MEMORY AND THE RESTLESS PAST

Drawing from the repercussions of an untreated trauma, *Post mortem* relies on the relationship of the Gothic with the uncanny, as defined by Freud. In his essay, "Das Unheimliche" ("The Uncanny," 1919), Freud examines the root of the word, *unheimlich* (unhomely, unfamiliar) and compares it with *heimlich*, its opposite. In one meaning, both words have the same definition. To Freud, then, the uncanny describes an experience that is "in reality nothing new or alien, but something which is familiar and old, established in the mind and which has become alienated from it only through the process of repression."[26] Consequently, the experience of fear arises due to a presumably familiar space becoming foreign because "something which ought to have remained hidden . . . has come to light."[27] By the same token, the uncanny—like the Gothic—is fueled by the exposure of the repressed, an exposure that provides a lens to look, and sometimes expound, upon certain social and cultural unresolved and hidden traumas.

Larraín's cinematography situates the Gothic—and, by extension, the uncanny—at the epicenter of his storytelling and film style. He alludes to a state of ominous unease based on an unsettled relationship with individual and collective "monsters." This Gothic aesthetic and lens—by looking at, for instance, the trajectory of trauma, the mechanism of the unconscious, the instrument of violence, and the symbolism of monsters—provides us with an instrumental tool that can access the human experience and understand historically specific, socio-political crises.[28] In a similar vein, Jeffrey Cohen establishes that monsters are "the embodiment of a cultural moment," and they "must be examined within the intricate matrix of relations (social, cultural, and literary-historical) that generate them."[29] Hence, the emergence of monsters—such as ghosts and other haunted entities—should be scrutinized as a symptom of an unprocessed trauma whose *raison d'être* must be understood within a set of historical coordinates across time.

Although the Gothic is usually restricted to literary and filmic realms, in *The Gothic and the Everyday*, Lorna Piatti-Farnell and Maria Beville suggest the Gothic as a living formulation that "encompass[es] cultural manifestations, lived practices, and its interaction with the narratives of the past."[30] In other words, the Gothic aesthetic lies beyond the restrictions of literary and filmic conventions, existing more as "a perspective on the world that shapes our sense of experience and identity."[31] More specifically, Beville's reading of Gothic commemorative practice in the historical drama is illuminative for our reading of *Post mortem* as a political drama that also uses the Gothic to translate the past into collective memory in the present.

Drawing on Timothy Jones's notion that the Gothic should be read as an "event" or a "lived experience" that does not follow a static set of codes and language, Beville points out that the Gothic can contribute to "the experience of the Gothic remembering" and the "transmission of cultural versions of the past over time."[32] In many aspects, historical past could be triggered by the "Gothic memory," using objects and sensory encounters that revive collective memory and carry the past into the present. By consequence, the Gothic holds a fluctuating quality that goes "across the boundaries that separate art/culture and society."[33] As a fundamental means to evoke collective memory, *Post mortem* reenacts—through a Gothic visual and sensorial narrative—past events from the perspective of a post-conflict society. As we will discuss, from symbolic, thematic, and stylistic perspectives, *Post mortem* employs the Gothic apparatus to consider and express the past and its present legacy.

GHOSTLY VISUAL LANGUAGE: SPECTRAL PRESENCES

Post mortem opens with a traveling shot where the camera lens looks out from beneath a military tank and registers the streets of an apocalyptic "day-after" in Santiago. In the next scene, an unassuming middle-aged man looks thoughtfully outside his front window. His silence is enigmatic, and his corporeal expression is rather puzzling. He sits on the sofa, waits, goes outside, looks at the road, waters the plants, continues to look, and then the object of his curiosity is revealed: a female neighbor. Next, we see him buying tickets for a cabaret show where he meets that neighbor backstage at the precise moment she is being fired because of her gaunt appearance. The man is Mario Cornejo (Alfredo Castro), a taciturn autopsy transcriber who becomes obsessed with the dancehall woman: his neighbor, Nancy Puelma (Antonia Zegers). Right after their first encounter

Mario offers to take Nancy home; on the way they cross paths with a tumultuous march in favor of the left-wing political alliance *Unidad Popular*, headed by the first democratically elected socialist president, Salvador Allende (1970–3). At this point, the film reveals its temporal and historical context: a volatile Chile, days before the *coup d'état* on September 11, 1973. A sudden cut shows the necropsy of an emaciated Nancy with an undaunted Mario transcribing the report dictated by a forensic doctor. Almost immediately, the film takes us back to the morning of September 11 when Mario is searching for Nancy but instead finds an empty house in disarray. In the meantime, Mario submissively follows the military officers' commands at the morgue, which is rapidly becoming congested with murdered bodies piling up in the hallways and stairs. When he finds out that Nancy—now starving and desperate to know the whereabouts of her father and brother—has been hiding in the back shed of his house, he becomes the only link she has with the world until, one day, he discovers that she is sharing the shelter with an activist friend who has also become her lover. Feeling betrayed and having lost the possibility of romantic love with Nancy, Mario decides to block off the shed's only exit, literally transforming their refuge into an imminent tomb.

As established by the film's synopsis, *Post mortem* departs from a precarious love story to frame the military coup's aftermath, where terror and death are the order of the day. Nevertheless, instead of elucidating historical accounts with grand references on screen, Larraín avoids "the political vanguardism, the epic tone and its pedagogical approaches,"[34] letting the ordinary but ineffectual citizen give an intimate version of "history." Since Mario's peripheral view of events is filtered through a Gothic discourse and aesthetic, the spectator can assume a critical position in questioning the role of the collective subject during and long after Chile's repressive years, while creating a sensory experience through which to reassess the past.

For the most part, the Gothic aesthetic is defined by the construction of atmosphere and tone, generated by style, *mise-en-scène*, and narrative techniques.[35] Without a doubt, some of Larraín's visual achievements are indebted to the nuances of Gothic horror: he exploits its visual and aural conventions and theatrical effects. Furthermore, these Gothic stylistic features seamlessly overlap with what Mariana Johnson has observed in Larraín's cinematography; namely, the recurrence of intense proximity to an obsessive male protagonist; the extensive use of close-up; the dim illumination; the claustrophobic interiors; the unusual framings; and the shots that emphasize characters' voyeurism and acts of looking.[36] Larraín's disrupting manipulation of all of these devices and codes leads the viewer to read the return of the past as a ghostly, haunting experience.

The existential and ideological vacuum that prevailed in Chile's past, and especially during the Transition period, is mostly expressed in *Post mortem* through the Gothic characterization of Mario and Nancy. Given their social inadequacy and dislocated affect system, both characters become shadowy shells of their own desires and dreams, and their expressive language follows the same claustrophobic and washed-out style as their own emotional downward spiral. Nancy's physical appearance even has a cadaverous quality that serves as a premonition of the couple's dramatic pathos.

Mario and Nancy both belong to the category of "characters in Larraín's films . . . to whom things just happen,"[37] and this explains why the events that transpire throughout the film—both privately and politically—have a veil of sinister bewilderment that completely escapes the characters' understanding and awareness. Consequently, the pair's anticlimactic romance is visually and symbolically surrounded by shadows and shades. When Mario looks at the vaudeville dancers' poster in front of the cabaret at the beginning of the film, we only see his shadow reflected on the glass. Mario also moves as an invisible entity, walking unnoticed through the halls and rooms of the theater's backstage area, making his way to the basement, where he meets with Nancy for the first time. Ironically, Nancy's "stumble" into Mario, at the moment of her professional demise, appears to be a wan light of hope, but in reality, this is only the beginning of a descent into an abyss for both protagonists, which, coincidentally, will be aggravated by Chile's unexpected but pivotal political turmoil. In a larger sense, Mario epitomizes the antihero during troubled times, an inept and unperceptive citizen who robotically fulfills his deathly duty for a corrupt system to the point that not even his love interest stands a chance.

By embodying minimal gesticulations and unpretentious demeanors, Larraín's characters take on spectral auras; they move by inertia or apathy, as if they were becoming post-mortem rigid. The movie's preference for still shots and the stiffness of the *mise-en-scène* embellish this paralysis in the city that the state has instigated with its new order. As an addition to this somber extension of the private to the public—and vice versa—the cinematic tone has a neutral coloration, a lifeless palette that reproduces the unnerving state of the nation and its citizens.

One symptomatic example of Larraín's mastery of Gothic configuration is a shot of a sleeping Mario, where his silhouette resembles a corpse, just like the ones stacked up at the morgue (Figure 5.1).

Equally poignant is the scene where Mario and Nancy are walking to a restaurant at night and slowly turn into shadowy figures surrounded by zombie-like pedestrians, in what appears to evoke a post-apocalyptic setting. The uncanny impact of this sequence made the film critic Christian Ramírez rank this spectral night stroll as one of the most bizarre encounters of recent Chilean cinema.[38] Besides, this image suggests that the characters' sinister disposition is not only pervasive, but portentous, functioning as a dire premonition of the debacle that is looming for them and for the country.

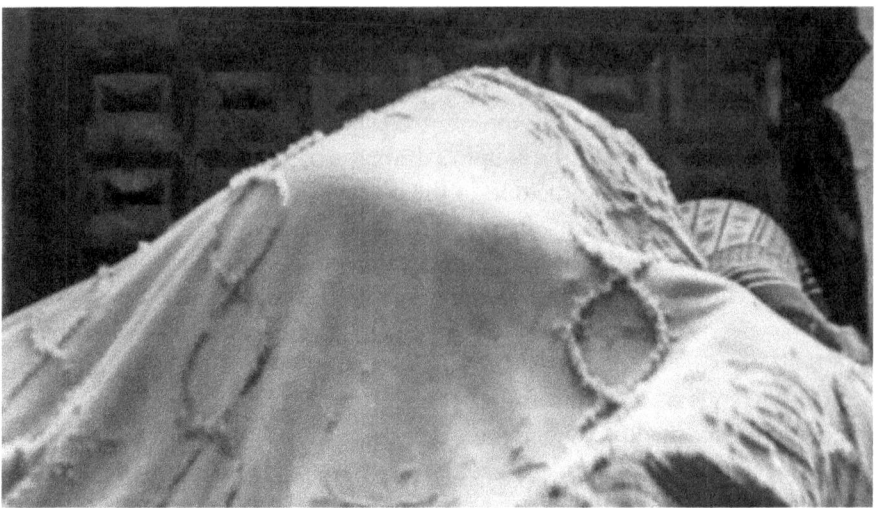

Figure 5.1 Mario's body lying on bed ominously resembles one of the corpses at the morgue (from *Post mortem*, 2010).

As discussed so far, the deliberate composition of Gothic visual imagery in *Post mortem* is partly achieved through the strategic manipulation of the body. This manipulation also borrows certain features from the body horror genre to convey the affective extent of unspeakable memories and their political significance. Also known as biological horror, the genre offers graphic violations and at times clinical representations of the human body. According to Kelly Hurley, body horror is "a hybrid genre that recombines the narrative and cinematic conventions of the science fiction, horror and suspense film in order to stage a spectacle of the human body defamiliarized, rendered other."[39] The graphic exposure and visual excess of the mutilation and destruction of human bodies during the necropsies, especially that of President Allende, forces upon the audience a revisionist view of the historical dead and the fate suffered by undisciplined bodies.[40] As Laura Hubner clarifies, "Gothic can be seen as potentially radical and subversive within specific historical contexts, in the sense it is suggestive of unreason and terror in the light of a rational or ordered society."[41] In this respect, the Gothic questions the validity of rationality by exposing the logic of the state machine, whose political goal is to generate more corpses without properly burying or even naming them. In one revealing scene that confirms the uncanny "return of the dead" and the role of the ghost to call for restitution, Mario is transporting a pile of corpses in a wheelbarrow through the halls of the morgue when he hears a voice coming from the mound of "dead people" asking for help. It is a terrifying, allegorical moment, as a voice from "the other side" forces Mario to unexpectedly face an ethical dilemma and poses a point of resistance from the constraints of the ideological impositions on the social body.

GOTHIC SPATIAL NARRATIVE: CLOSED DOORS AND LIMINAL WINDOWS

The cinematography in Larraín's *oeuvre* places the use of space at the core of his daunting aesthetics and narrative point of view. In the book *The Closed Space*, Manuel Aguirre argues that at the heart of the literature of terror lies the symbol of the closed space, which manifests itself in haunted buildings, in borders and frontiers, in thresholds and walls, in the terror of the shuttered room, and in the promise and dread of the closed door.[42] The use of the closed space in *Post mortem* thus functions as an eloquent metaphor for a city with no sky or horizon, a city that anticipates the beginning of a country "closed" to its history and memory. For instance, there are no orientation or panoramic shots, and the city streets are deserted and eerily quiet. As an unsettling contrast, the morgue is equally quiet but disorderly, loaded with corpses that keep on arriving. This overwhelming, continual traffic of corpses invades the morgue—as the ghostly atmosphere invades the cinematic space—and blurs the boundaries between the living and the dead.

The morgue, a sinister space par excellence, becomes the state apparatus where murdered bodies are legitimized by assigning them a sanitized official cause of death, or just a number, for that matter. Every angle of the morgue, including its bathrooms and dining rooms, shares the same veil of distressing decadence and corruption. There, state employees and doctors follow orders, stacking corpses, both literally and symbolically, washing their hands and teeth while aligning submissively to the new state economy of death. In many ways, this morbid operation impedes any sense of civil solidarity or rebellion; instead it enables the transition of human beings into a sort of living-dead citizenry. The strongest resistance to this state compliance comes from Mario's coworker, Sandra (Amparo Noguera), who screams at the officers and tries to "revive" both the bodies at the morgue and the impassive "living dead" around her: "What happened? I cannot take it anymore! What happened? These people were alive, I saw them! This man was wounded, I saved him, and you killed him again! Why?"[43]

It is no coincidence that a low shot is used in this scene to emphasize Sandra's moral superiority in front of Mario's astonishment and everyone else's indifference. Her frantic rebellion and call for civil action are countered by one of the officers, who mechanically re-shoots the dead bodies, a clear allegory of the double erasure of the dead by the state authority. Even Mario's weedy acts of solidarity, such as asking the military officer about

Nancy's whereabouts or helping to save a dying victim at the morgue, are immediately negated by the military apparatus, and reposition him as a man who loyally "serves the country."

In this regard, *Post mortem* uses space to convey a ubiquitous sense of horror that invades the characters' houses, working places, and ultimately their entire social and personal spheres. In fact, the symbolic use of the door, the window, and the basement are extremely eloquent in constructing domestic settings as uncanny and ambiguous. As pointed out by Aguirre, windows and doors are the most literal manifestations of the concept of liminality, since they are considered the most ambivalent thresholds: they provide opportunities to cross borders but are also signs of imprisonment.[44]

This takes us to another dimension of the horror experience in *Post mortem*: the symbolic crossing to the "other side." In a figurative way, the narrative semiotics of the closed house are twofold: the closed door and the infiltrated door. On the one hand, the military regime "penetrates the door" (Nancy's, the morgue's, and the nation's), allowing urban isolation and the law of terror to take over the country. On the other hand, Mario "closes the door" to any possibility of emotional or human redemption when, without questioning, he joins the cold-blooded terror machine put in motion by the regime. In fact, the ghostly quality of the bodies and the fluidity of the spaces in the movie are equivalent to the way the inside and the outside are depicted. While the interiors are bombarded with dead bodies, the exteriors are taken over by ruins, or what Richard categorizes as "imprints and vestiges of a shattered cultural symbolization, of a landscape torn by a dimension of catastrophe."[45] Ultimately, the triumph of the closed space in the classical horror film is

Figure 5.2   A recurrent cinematic motif of a ghostlike Mario looking through the window (from *Post mortem*, 2010).

distressfully reached in the last scene when the door is barricaded with the ruinous remnants of ordinary living.

Let's return to the opening sequence of the film: an expectant Mario spying from his window on the house across the street (Figure 5.2). This image is not gratuitous, as Mario's body in the window becomes a phantasmagoric cinematic leitmotif. According to Jordi Balló, the window is usually the most privileged opening because it marks the boundary between the interior and the exterior, it is a "reflexive pause" of "inactive action."[46] In *Post mortem*, the dramatic language exploits "the man behind the window" as a suitable image to display the creation of fantasies that help the protagonist cope with his dull existence and civil disengagement. Barraza states that the reason Mario ignores the horror of the political violence is the impossibility of harboring any illusions with the arrival of the coup.[47] As a consequence, Mario is a problematic subject who—in Lacanian terms, having been expelled from the Real—becomes "an automaton or living dead in a lifeless society."[48]

As previously discussed, Larraín's film poetics benefit from the ambiguous and, at times, contradictory nature of the Gothic, given that it problematizes the boundaries between self and other, fantasy and reality, internal and external, familiar and unfamiliar, and rational and irrational, among other oppositions. Pino-Ojeda points out that the standing role of liminality in Larraín's films "focuses on the macabre as well as on liminal spaces that erase distinctions between health and pathology, love and hate, and life and death."[49] In general, Mario's characterization exemplifies the liminality of the Gothic framework. Notably his position between the inside and the "other side," whether fantasy or reality, is purposely reinforced by the glass window: that of his house, his car, the glass cage full of birds at the Chinese restaurant, or the glass he deliberately breaks at the cabaret as an act of defiance on Nancy's behalf. Yet the window is an ambivalent threshold that restricts Mario's possibilities and feeds his inaction and, to some extent, his moral hesitation, since it represents a semi-opening in opposition to the full opening of a door. Similarly, another meaning of the window is the "premonition of lost love,"[50] which for Mario turns his own house into a melancholic space and himself into a spectral figure. In a more political sense, Mario's spying gaze from behind the window serves as a surveillance metaphor for the militarized state. This is evident when Mario's blurred silhouette behind a foggy window appears to be a ghost that Nancy neither sees nor acknowledges. As a liminal character who inhabits the margins of history, Mario, at the decisive moment of Allende's autopsy, is transposed to the periphery because of his inept performance at using the electric typewriter.

The most extreme contrast between the center–periphery or public–private spheres is depicted when Nancy's house is raided. The spectator hears the sound of helicopters and destruction while Mario is viewed from outside the window. He is obliviously taking a shower, unaware of this crucial moment for Chile and, particularly in his case, of the implications for his own sentimental story. Again, Mario is in an in-between space, present and absent, self-absorbed in his own restricted inner window. However, it has been noted the apparent absence of explicit violence throughout the film; an erasure of what is happening outside the walls of the morgue or inside Mario's house, creates a disturbing sense of impunity with no witnesses. Urrutia sustains that this style, based on the "not-seen," relies on a technique that assumes that "if there is nothing to see [it] is because everything has been seen already."[51] She views the piling up of corpses at the morgue as an indication that there is something worse happening, but the characters' limited vision prohibits their access to a global scope of things.[52] This false sense of holistic vision, a spectral reality suggested by the closed door of the morgue, forces the spectator to question what is "beyond the screen," beyond the confinement of official places, or inside supposedly innocuous dwelling spaces.

Coincidentally, the predominance of the sinister space has been identified as another feature of Chilean films of the 1990s.[53] Places are frightening based on the fact that they operate under apparent normalcy (either by ignorance or indifference), but in reality, great sufferings such as torture and death are taking place inside.[54] Moreover, these places reflect a type of social or metaphysical anxiety, acting as metaphors for experiences lived by Chilean society but not registered at a conscious level. Since the Gothic upholds the notion that horror upsurges from within, devastating boundaries between the self and "other" and preconceived concepts of "home,"[55] it is symptomatic that home becomes the place of entrapment and death for Nancy and her family, its façade insinuating an unnerving camouflage of the ordinary. Indeed, *Post mortem*'s sinister use of space acts as a central device to convey how a banal domesticity becomes a place of ghostly hauntings.

GOTHIC AURAL REVERBERATIONS: THE UNSAID AND THE UNNAMABLE

It should be noted that not only off-screen space, but also off-screen sound is fundamental to evoking a Gothic atmosphere. The sound-image experimentation in Larraín's films tends to purposely break the conventions of traditional narrative coherence. He takes the viewer to an imaginary, phantasmal space that is not directly linked to the out-of-field, forcing a conjecture of absent diegetic elements. In a similar fashion, the sound theorist Michel Chion has examined the emotional and filmic impact of acousmatic sound.[56] Remarkably, the use of the off-screen sound, opposed to visualized sound, has a dramatic effect that is frequently explored in suspense and horror cinema. Since there is an expected connection between image and sound, the removal of their seemingly natural relation creates a feeling of uncertainty and ambivalence.

In her reading of *Tony Manero*, Johnson makes a compelling analysis of Larraín's use of off-screen space and off-screen sound as a way to "inscribe the political at the margins of his stories in order to invoke the horror in the everyday."[57] In this sense, Larraín has expressed his preference for using cinematic ellipses in order to awaken the audience's own readings based on their sensibility, imagination, and repressed fears:

> I believe that great cinema sometimes comes from just showing a piece of something . . . There's nothing more dangerous and perverse and sophisticated than human life. If you show images that are completely predigested then you are not using what is interesting in each of us, what we have inside. It's more interesting to let each of us complete the images.[58]

Clearly, Larraín's inclination for the narrative ellipsis allows the Gothic memory to trigger the spectator's active role in reading the negative space and the suggestive implications of the off-screen.

Following that same principle of detachment and ominous ambivalence that rules *Post mortem*'s inner logic, language similarly plays a role in obstructing meaningful communication and affective connection. This narrative language combines meaningful silences and empty words to reinforce the absurdity of human affective bonds and the intermittent irruption of the uncanny. When it does not create unnerving misunderstandings, the linguistic exchanges oscillate between silence and whisper. Silence, as Chion explains, is used for achieving the effects of subjective sound, but it also has a paradoxical anxiety-producing impression when it is followed by a strong sound; or, conversely, sound could also be used as a synonym for silence.[59] In many ways, *Post mortem* invests in the latter, using isolated sounds—sometimes without a source or without a gazing subject—to reinforce the feeling of emptiness or the absurdity of workday tasks in the midst of national catastrophe. Instead, "the silence mirrors the insufficiency of language in truly engaging the trauma of a particular moment in history."[60]

Before September 11, Mario and Nancy's last conversation proves this linguistic defamiliarization, where one is incapable of grasping what is said or what is said is irrelevant. When Mario asks Nancy to marry him, she asks for his name. Mario's marriage proposal is utterly untimely, as is the precise moment he congratulates Nancy when she is being fired. Not only the linguistic but also the social interactions are misleading. At their first meal together, Mario and Nancy abruptly burst into tears without enunciating words. Far from creating a bond of solidarity or complicity, this inexplicable and silent exchange emphasizes their melancholic loneliness before they partake in an unsentimental and rather perturbing sexual encounter. In this encounter, Mario's body is excluded from the frame, and Nancy displays a pathetic grin that evokes pain instead of sexual pleasure, reflecting what Johnson calls "noisy unpleasantness."[61]

The uncanny dynamic between the pair is visually reinforced by camera work. For instance, there is a variety of shots in which they are together, but then one of them seems to "disappear" from the frame, adding to the two-shot sequences and creating a disturbing and ghostly effect. As Urrutia has noticed, various scenes expose "an ambiguous and even absent point of view," an absence of subjectivity that centralizes the body and not the individual within the filmic language.[62] This point of view is subverted by the centrality of the corpses at the morgue, which are reduced to a macabre corporeality. Certainly, the discordant camera shots and angles continually deny the people of their characters and, instead, insist on their artificiality and liminal quality. Even the temporal chronology responds to this liminal pattern. At times it is impossible to place certain events in order, forcing the viewer to ask, does that occur before or after Nancy's death? Before or after the coup? Before or after Sandra's disappearance?

The final sequence of *Post mortem* uses the Gothic image of the closed door as a literal representation of a familiar space that turns into an uncanny burial site and a haunting landscape. During six long minutes, in a static, real-time shot, Mario piles up the odds and ends around his back patio to block Nancy's shelter. Mario's figure, meanwhile, remains mostly off-screen or is shown only from the back. In this way, the camera focuses on the compilation of domestic remnants, which literally and symbolically replace all living presence (Figure 5.3).

Those objects become an allegory of a dilapidated nation, a symbol of a ruinous landscape that alludes to a collective life that no longer exits. The film helps to visualize the ghosts of a historical past, through what Richard calls

Figure 5.3 A disturbing and yet undramatic final shot showing the pile of junk gathered by Mario to fatally block Nancy's exit (from *Post mortem*, 2010).

a "post-dictatorial aesthetics" that "visually imprints an image of a decomposing landscape, reduced to a trash heap of memories, corpses, rubble, vestiges of experience."[63] In many aspects, that visual absence of human presence, replaced by useless commodities and uncanny silence, accords with neoliberal ideology and its obstruction of a proper mourning process.

CONCLUSION: GOTHIC RUINS OF HISTORY

The historical events depicted in *Post mortem* expose private and collective scenarios in true states of ruin, expressed through a dialogue with Gothic narrative and its formulaic traits. Conveniently, the ruin has been studied as a "metaphor for intellectual inquiry" that displays "human inflicted catastrophes created by systemic violence, authoritarian abuses of power, and failed political and economic projects."[64] Furthermore, the focal use of ruins in *Post mortem*—in tandem with liminal spaces and characters—allows an expressive and graphic examination of the dictatorial experience from a post-conflict context.

Clearly, Gothic as a discourse in itself could also be a method of inquiry into our sociocultural conditions.[65] In this sense, *Post mortem* conveys the terror in the prevailing state of things in dictatorial Chile following the Gothic aesthetics of spatial, aural, and visual defamiliarization. To make the familiar strange, the film relies on eloquent silences, symbolic ruins, closed doors, liminal windows, and the spectral use of bodies and shadows. In other words, *Post mortem* exploits the Gothic as a living experience and a mode to recreate historical memory to enact the ghostliness and uncanny aftermaths of Chile's post-dictatorship years through the ruinous images of overflowing cadavers, body dissections, street rubble, and the pile of jumble used to literally exterminate Nancy's life. All of this uncanny sensory imagery in Larraín's filmic narrative profits from the viewer's own imagination, which can relate at a conscious or unconscious level to a historically inaccessible archive.

Overall, *Post mortem* aligns with a critical and historical study of Gothic horror and its concerns with the uncanny, the liminal, and the return of the repressed. Since the film exposes a civil pact of silence and consensus with an authoritarian power, it places an uncanny emphasis on a peripheral vision and silence—signs of symbolic historical blindness and the unspeakable—and, ultimately, it proposes alternative ways in which to access a problematic past via ghostly evocations and Gothic memory.

NOTES

1. As a matter of fact, Chile's late debut within the horror arena took place in the year 2000 with the release of Jorge Olguín's slasher film, *Ángel Negro*. Coincidentally, *Ángel Negro*

presents a ghostly narrative with unresolved aspects of the recent political past; and, as expected, its release spurred a wave of subsequent productions that experiment with horror themes and styles. Other films by Olguín, such as the vampire saga, *Eternal Blood* (2002); the post-apocalyptic zombie tale, *Descendants* (2009); or the mythological ghost story, *Caleuche* (2012), also offer thought-provoking readings of Chile's outlook on the present and past. In 2005, Coke Hidalgo's *El huésped* became Chile's first science-fiction feature film. Another prolific genre cinema producer is Patricio Valladares, known for the fictionalized true story, *Hidden in the Woods* (2012), and the exploitation movie, *Dirty Love* (2009), among others. Productions like *Baby Shower* (Pablo Illanes, 2012), *Green Celery* (Francesc Morales, 2013), and *Madre* (Aaron Burns, 2016), tackle female horror and motherhood as points of departure for more controversial sociocultural commentary. More recently, Lucio Rojas's *Trauma* (2017) used the horror framework to fictionally reproduce a truculent story about the violations and terror of the military dictatorship era.
2. Gastón Lillo, "El cine y el contexto político-cultural en el Chile de la posdictadura," *Revista Canadiense de Estudios Hispánicos* 20, no. 1 (1995): 5.
3. Ascanio Cavallo, Pablo Douzet, and Cecilia Rodríguez, eds., *Huérfanos y perdidos: El cine de la transición 1990–1999* (Santiago: Grijalbo, 1999), 26.
4. Vania Barraza Toledo, "Reviewing the Present in Pablo Larraín's Historical Cinema," *Iberoamericana* 13, no. 51 (2013): 160.
5. Jacqueline Mouesca, *Cine chileno veinte años: 1970–1990* (Santiago de Chile: Ministerio de Educación, Departamento de Planes y Programas Culturales, 1992), 122–3.
6. Idelber Avelar, *The Untimely Present: Postdictatorial Latin American Fiction and the Task of Mourning* (Durham, NC: Duke University Press, 1999), 2–3.
7. Original Spanish: "carencia de palabras comunes para nombrar lo vivido." Tomás Moulian, *Chile actual: Anatomía de un mito* (Santiago: ARCIS-LOM, 1997), 31.
8. Nelly Richard, *Cultural Residues: Chile in Transition* (Minneapolis/London: Minnesota University Press, 2004), 49.
9. Cavallo, *Huérfanos y perdidos: El cine de la transición 1990–1999*, 127.
10. Carolina Urrutia, "Hacia una política en tránsito: Ficción en el cine chileno (2008–2010)," *Aisthesis* 47 (2010): 37.
11. Ascanio Cavallo and Gonzalo Maza, eds., *El novísimo cine chileno* (Santiago de Chile: Uqbar Editores, 2010), 14.
12. Carolina Urrutia, *Un cine centrífugo: ficciones chilenas 2005–2010* (Santiago: Cuarto Propio, 2013), 16.
13. Carlos Saavedra, *Intimidades desencantadas: La poética cinematográfica del dos mil* (Santiago: Cuarto Propio, 2013), 21.
14. Antonella Estévez, "Dolores políticos: reacciones cinematográficas. Resistencias melancólicas en el cine chileno contemporáneo," *Aisthesis* 47 (2010): 16.
15. *Post mortem*, dir. Pablo Larraín (2010; New York: Kino Lorber, Inc., 2012), DVD.
16. Larry Rohter, "Pablo Larraín and His Unintentional Trilogy," *The New York Times*, January 8, 2013: <https://carpetbagger.blogs.nytimes.com/2013/01/08/pablo-larrain-and-his-unintentional-trilogy> (accessed February 25, 2020). When asked about the apparent trilogy about Pinochet, Larraín responded: "Believe me, I never planned it. It just happened to me."
17. *Tony Manero*, dir. Pablo Larraín (2008; New York: Kino Lorber, Inc., 2010), DVD.
18. *No*, dir. Pablo Larraín (2012; Culver City, CA: Sony Pictures Classics, 2013), DVD.
19. Barraza Toledo, "Reviewing the Present in Pablo Larraín's Historical Cinema," 160.
20. Jo Labanyi, "Memory and Modernity in Democratic Spain: The Difficulty in Coming to Terms with the Spanish Civil War," *Poetics Today* 28, no. 2 (2007): 112.

21. Álvaro Fernández, "Horror o Política: El selectivo anclaje de los fantasmas del pasado a ambos lados del Atlántico," in *Horrofílmico: Aproximaciones al cine de terror en Latinoamérica y el Caribe*, eds. Rosana Díaz-Zambrana and Patricia Tomé (San Juan: Isla Negra, 2012), 261.
22. Robin Wood, "An Introduction to the American Horror Film," in *Movies and Methods*. Vol. II, ed. Bill Nichols (Berkeley: University of California Press, 1985), 164–200.
23. Waleska Pino-Ojeda, "Social Cinema in Neoliberal Times: The Macabre Baroque in the Films of Pablo Larraín," in *Contemporary Latin American Cinema: Resisting Neoliberalism?*, eds. Claudia Sandberg and Carolina Rocha (Cham: Palgrave Macmillan, 2018), 198.
24. Ibid., 199.
25. Timothy Jones, "Canniness of the Gothic: Genre as Practice," *Gothic Studies* 11, no. 1 (2009): 124–34.
26. Sigmund Freud, "The Uncanny," in *The Complete Psychological Works*, vol. XVII (London: Hogarth Press, 1955), 224.
27. Ibid., 241.
28. Andrew Hock, *Asian Gothic: Essays on Literature, Film and Anime* (Jefferson: McFarland, 2008), 2–3.
29. Jeffrey Cohen, *Monster Theory* (Minneapolis: University of Pennsylvania Press, 1996), 3.
30. Lorna Piatti-Farnell and Maria Beville, "Introduction: Living Gothic," in *The Gothic and the Everyday*, eds. Lorna Piatti-Farnell and Maria Beville (London: Palgrave Macmillan, 2014), 1.
31. Ibid., 3.
32. Maria Beville, "Gothic Memory and the Contested Past: Framing Terror," in *The Gothic and the Everyday*, eds. Lorna Piatti-Farnell and Maria Beville (London: Palgrave Macmillan, 2014), 54.
33. Ibid., 58.
34. Pino-Ojeda, "Social Cinema in Neoliberal Times," 203.
35. Laura Hubner, *Fairytale and Gothic Horror: Uncanny Transformations in Film* (London: Palgrave Macmillan, 2018), 3.
36. Mariana Johnson, "Political Trauma, Intimacy, and Off-Screen Space in Pablo Larraín's *Tony Manero*," *Letras Hispanas* 12 (2016): 201.
37. Ibid., 200.
38. Christian Ramírez, "Pablo Larraín: Una habitación cerrada," in *El novísimo cine chileno*, eds. Ascanio Cavallo and Gonzalo Maza (Santiago: Uqbar Editores, 2010), 81.
39. Kelly Hurley, "Reading Like an Alien: Posthuman Identity in Alien and Rabid," in *Posthuman Bodies*, eds. Judith M. Halberstam and Ira Livingston (Blomington: Indiana University Press, 1995), 203.
40. President Salvador Allende's remains were exhumed after thirty-eight years in May of 2011 for a criminal investigation related to the human rights offenses that took place during the seventeen-year dictatorship. The results of the autopsy concluded that he had committed suicide, ruling out lingering theories that he was killed by military troops on September 11, 1973. The polemic surrounding Allende's body—two autopsies, two exhumations, and three burials—takes center stage in Larraín's *Post mortem* as a way to symbolically revive the national "dead."
41. Hubner, *Fairytale and Gothic Horror*, 66.
42. Manuel Aguirre, *The Closed Space* (Manchester: Manchester University Press, 1990), 2.
43. *Post mortem*, dir. Pablo Larraín (2010; New York: Kino Lorber, 2012), DVD. Original Spanish: "¿Qué pasó? ¡Yo no puedo más! ¿Qué pasó? ¡Estas personas estaban aquí vivas, porque yo las vi! ¡Este hombre estaba herido! ¡Yo lo salvé y usted me lo volvió a matar!"

44. Manuel Aguirre, "Geometries of Terror: Numinous Spaces in Gothic, Horror and Science Fiction," *Gothic Studies* 10, no. 2 (2008): 15.
45. Nelly Richard, *Cultural Residues: Chile in Transition* (Minneapolis/London: Minnesota University Press, 2004), 49.
46. Jordi Balló, *Imágenes del silencio* (Barcelona: Anagrama, 2000), 21–2.
47. Barraza Toledo, "Reviewing the Present in Pablo Larraín's Historical Cinema," 160.
48. Ibid.
49. Pino-Ojeda, "Social Cinema in Neoliberal Times," 204.
50. Balló, *Imágenes del silencio*, 28–9. In other words, according to Balló, the window can either represent a domestic boundary that encloses the character or allude to a premonition of what will be lost later on in the filmic narrative.
51. Carolina Urrutia, "*Post mortem* y *Tony Manero*: Memoria centrífuga de un pasado político," *Cinemas d'Amerique Latine* 19 (2011): 70.
52. Ibid.
53. Cavallo, *Huérfanos y perdidos: El cine de la transición 1990–1999*, 72.
54. Ibid.
55. Hubner, *Fairytale and Gothic Horror: Uncanny Transformations in Film*, 7.
56. Michel Chion, *Audio-Vision: Sound on Screen*, trans. Claudia Gorbman (New York: Colombia University Press, 1994), 71.
57. Johnson, "Political Trauma, Intimacy, and Off-Screen Space in Pablo Larraín's *Tony Manero*," 200.
58. Benjamin B., "Jackie: Interview with Director Pablo Larrain," *American Cinematographer*, February 12, 2017: <https://ascmag.com/blog/the-film-book/jackie-interview-with-director-pablo-larrain> (accessed February 25, 2020).
59. Chion, *Audio-Vision: Sound on Screen*, 89, 58.
60. Beville, "Gothic Memory and the Contested Past," 61.
61. Johnson, "Political Trauma, Intimacy, and Off-Screen Space in Pablo Larraín's *Tony Manero*," 202.
62. Urrutia, "*Post mortem* y *Tony Manero*: Memoria centrífuga de un pasado político," 70.
63. Richard, *Cultural Residues: Chile in Transition*, 51.
64. Michael J. Lazzara and Vicky Unruh, "Introduction: Telling Ruins," in *Telling Ruins in Latin America* (New York: Palgrave Macmillan, 2009), 2–3.
65. Hock, *Asian Gothic: Essays on Literature, Film and Anime*, 2.

CHAPTER 6

Aestheticization of Politics and the War Machine in *No* by Pablo Larraín

Ignasi Gozalo-Salellas and Xavier Dapena

> The relation between man and machine that characterizes modernity becomes the content and form of the subjective arrangement. Machines, the reality constructed by capitalism, are not phantasms of modernity after which life can run unscathed— they are, on the contrary, the concrete forms according to which life organizes itself, the world transforms itself, and the material connections within which subjectivity is produced.
> Antonio Negri, *On A Thousand Plateaus*

"This does not sell," says the publicist. On the monitor, we see an ad campaign with the slogan "for free elections. Vote No" in front of a large group of the veteran Concertación leaders. It is a dual montage superimposed on the number of tortured, executed, or disappeared citizens: on the one hand, a mix of black and white images of the *coup d'état* and its repression; on the other hand, color images of protesters in the streets listening to the melody of "Vuelvo" by Patricio Manns and Horacio Salinas. The young publicist, newly brought on board as a campaign consultant, asks, "Is this all? Anything else? Something lighter, a little nicer?" To which a young leader replies, "Comrade, do you think that what is happening in Chile is nice?" The publicist responds, "No, no, let's see; this is just as overwhelming to me as it is to all of you. I think this . . . this does not sell."[1]

The debate that arises in the film *No* (2012), by Chilean director Pablo Larraín, is defined by this initial discussion—the pragmatic utilitarianism of the audiovisual rhetoric that characterizes the postmodern advertising of the 1980s and 1990s, very focused on the campaign target, on the emotive force of the speech, and on the modernization of the codes—and represented by the young publicist René Saavedra (Gael García Bernal). It is equally defined by the continuity of the argumentative logic of opposition to Augusto Pinochet's dictatorship, represented by the Concertación de Partidos por el No, the heterogeneous political coalition that ranged from the Christian Democratic Party and the Liberal Party to progressive parties such as the Social Democratic Radical Party, the Democracy Party, and the Socialist Party.

In this chapter, we argue that the film *No* presents a progressive aestheticization of the political through its configuration as a "dispositif" or "war machine."[2] Thus, our argument presents two movements: the first, in which we situate Larraín's film in tension with the "aestheticization of politics" proposed by Walter Benjamin (1931); and Jacques Rancière's (2005) answer in "Politics of Aesthetics," which is embodied in the conflicting positions of the protagonists and the spectacularization of politics versus the representation of history. Also, and as a result of this first movement, we read the film as a "war machine" within the framework of contemporary capitalism. In this sense, we suggest that *No*, as both a technical and a political device, consists of two machinelike effects: at the diegetic level, the advertising language becomes an electoral war machine and television mimics a semiotic apparatus that summons the masses to their ritual of contemplation. At the level of the film's reception itself, the cinematographic machinery also functions as an artifact of political subjectivization.

Larraín tackles the project of *No*, a version by screenwriter Pedro Peirano of Antonio Skármeta's unpublished theater play *El plebiscito*, as the final point in a trilogy about the 1973 coup to overthrow socialist president Salvador Allende and the subsequent military dictatorship. This film reveals the process of creation of the television campaign for No in the framework of the plebiscite held on October 5, 1988 on the continuity of General Augusto Pinochet at the head of the Chilean government. In the end, this plebiscite was an acceleration of the peaceful transition from dictatorship to "consensual democracy," to use Rancière's words, based on the same neoliberal foundations that the Pinochet regime had proposed. This campaign consisted of two fifteen-minute spots per day for each position, Yes or No. On one side, the Concertación, a group of seventeen parties, tries to promote the proposal of No against the pro-government version sponsored by the mesocratic cadres of the dictatorship. Both David Harvey (2007) and Naomi Klein (2008) have pointed to the Pinochet dictatorship as one of the first attempts to form a neoliberal state. The "shock doctrine" combined the coup, torture, and other repressive measures with an economic plan that consisted of progressive privatizations of public resources, natural reserves, and social security, and deregulation that facilitated their exploitation.[3] The "economic miracle," as Milton Friedman, one of its principal ideologues, said, was based not only on a design of the country's economic model but also on the disposition of government technologies, whose objective was the systemic elimination of dissent through disappearances and torture.[4] In this sense, and following the provisions of the 1980 constitution, the law provided for a transitional stage endorsed through a plebiscite of the acceptance or rejection of a proposed candidate.

Hence, the dilemma of the meeting in this first sequence is summarized by a veteran member of the party from the back of the room: "win the plebiscite" or "profoundly transform Chile." To the surprise of René, a young activist speaks up and tries to answer his question: "the comrade asked if you all think we are going to win," to which she herself responds with a blunt "the answer is No." In so doing, she confirms that the objective is not to win but "to create awareness and occupy the spaces that the dictatorship was forced to open."[5] *No* will be the answer to Pinochet but it is also the opposition's conviction about the result of the plebiscite. The meeting ends with a close-up of a reticent René observing the discussion of the leaders, which for the spectator turns into a cacophony of indistinguishable voices.

The list of productions focused on the Chilean dictatorship is limited. *Machuca* (2004) by Andrés Wood, *El baño* (2005) by Gregory Cohen, *Matar a todos* (2007) by Esteban Schroeder, and *Dawson Isla 10* (2009) by Miguel Littín all stand out in this regard. Since the presentation of his debut film *Fuga* (2006), Pablo Larraín has attracted the media spotlight due to his family, class, and ideological origins.[6] Despite some criticisms, the Chilean director has articulated a particular reading of the dictatorship as "a way to reinterpret the stories about dictatorship that I heard from my father."[7] Thus, the trilogy, which includes *Tony Manero* (2008) and *Post mortem* (2010), as well as *No* (2012), consists of a series of films featuring characters who believe that "the political situation is not going to affect them directly"[8] in the context of the Chilean dictatorship. Each film corresponds to a specific moment in national history: the first, *Tony Manero*, was set in the early days of the dictatorship, the 1973 *coup d'état*; *Post mortem* portrays the 1978–9 years; and *No* focuses on the final moments of the dictatorship. The nomination of this last film of Larraín's for an Academy Award as the Best Foreign Language Film of the Year consolidated his position on the international stage, capping an already renowned career, with prizes at the Cannes Film Festival, the Cinema for Peace Award, the Havana Film Festival, and the National Board of Review. *No* definitively opened the doors to him for Hollywood productions.

If the Chilean director's trilogy reveals our fascination for historical processes—as evidenced by the international praise it has received as well as the response from progressive sectors of Chilean society—at the academic level it has had significant repercussions. Critics have generally accused the director of aestheticizing and whitewashing history.[9] Nelly Richard has pointed out the problematic relation between its "conception of historical time" and the participation of the spectator at the moment of incorporating memory, its displacements and "resignifications" entailed by the construction of stories about the past. Also, Richard highlights the lack of interest in, or ignorance about, the role of the social movements and popular protests that surrounded the dictatorship.[10] On the other hand, Robert Wells has read this series of works as "posttraumatic films," in which visualizing the repression of the horrors of the dictatorship results in "unproductive masculine fantasies" relative to the "institutionalization of injustice, impunity and neoliberalism."[11] In a way, Larraín "jumbles together collective and individual memories and rearticulates audiovisual archives in the country."[12]

The main character, René Saavedra, is the creative young man who, due to his past in exile and his father's political commitment, is asked by Urrutia (Luis Gnecco), the director of the Concertación campaign, to advise them. According to the film, René will be one of the architects of the arrival of democracy in Chile, thanks to his work on the campaign. The production, recording, and broadcast of the campaign all face different obstacles, such as the pressures they receive from the official information services, as well as the competition created within the ad agency itself when René's boss "Lucho" Guzmán (Alfredo Castro) accepts the job of running the Yes campaign. Meanwhile, Saavedra's politically engaged ex-wife, Verónica Carvajal (Antonia Zegers), and the threats of the police against René and his son, overlay this film. Above all, the film privileges the unity of the story and advertising language and its forms over the complex historical moment—and its respective antagonisms, hegemonic disputes, and social struggles—thus reducing the political contestation and armed resistance represented by Verónica to a mere aesthetic gesture in a campaign design. Larraín's "dirty imaginary" uses contemporary media technologies themselves—the U-matic video medium—to try to merge it with abundant archival footage, and attempts to bring to life some fictional characters by using the real ones from archival footage, such as in the case of former president Patricio Aylwin Azócar (1990–4) and Patricio Bañados, the television host of the No campaign.[13]

The film has been accused of simplifying a complicated plot, and also of historical inaccuracies and of promoting the prominence of certain individuals instead of the collective action that the plebiscite entailed.[14] The successive characters lack political awareness while they are seen as being questioned by society and are framed in the current social context as is repeated insistently. The ambivalence of the tape "visualizes how traumas were made invisible, and how this was done in order to win, and then construct a pacifying, neutralizing, amnesiac consensus for the future."[15]

Genaro Arriagada, the real campaign coordinator on whom the character of Urrutia is based, has pointed out that in Skármeta's work, "the idea that there was a group of ideologized and outdated politicians and that suddenly a publicist appeared and told them 'this is the right thing to do' is not effective."[16] He notes that the campaign and its strategies must be understood within a broader, collective political process. In this sense, Paula Cronovich specifies that Juan Forch, Ignacio Agüero, and Eduardo Tironi were the three campaign directors and that they divided up the direction of different ads, an aspect on which Teresa Delgado has focused her analysis of the film.[17] An example would be the contrast between the creation of the "No +" slogan by René and the fact that this campaign began with "No +" interventions by the artistic group CADA (Colectivo de Acciones de Arte) in 1983.[18]

NO AS AESTHETIC POLITICIZATION

Although the recent alter-globalist movements have incorporated politicization as a pre-eminent concept of Latin American Marxist thought, and particularly since the *indignados* movement in Spain, its conceptual history is complex.[19] The politicization of aesthetics, as a concept, was proposed by Walter Benjamin in his famous essay *The Work of Art in the Age of Its Technological Reproducibility* by reviving a term that first appeared at the beginning of the century of *Politisierung*, although it would not become popularized until after the end of the First World War in Thomas Mann's antidemocratic pamphlet.[20] Benjamin understood that the accomplishment of *l'art pour l'art* ultimately produces the aestheticization of politics proposed by fascism.[21] That is to say, Benjamin offers as a possibility for confronting specific historical conditions the politicization of art as an antagonistic formula of both the political implications of aesthetic autonomy and the destruction of the aura. When Benjamin points out the dichotomy between aestheticization and the politicization of art, he is supporting the problematics of the position in cultural and political realms of literary works and their producers (or authors):

> Humankind, which once, in Homer, was an object of contemplation for the Olympian gods, has now become one for itself. Its self-alienation has reached the point where it can experience its own annihilation as a supreme aesthetic pleasure. Such is the aestheticizing of politics, as practiced by fascism. Communism replies by politicizing art.[22]

This dichotomy in Benjamin's life cycle consisted of two political systems, fascism and communism. It is within the scope of this conflict that Benjamin points out the notion of the politicization of art. Unlike Bertolt Brecht's approach—taking sides becomes the ultimate goal of taking a position—for Benjamin, taking a position is the goal itself.[23] However, the German thinker did not develop these concepts extensively, merely pointing out some features of a "politicized" author: the lack of autonomy and hence the assumption of class struggle as a driver of history, and taking the side of the proletariat, making visible the relations of production of his time. In other words, the author orients his activity toward what is useful for the proletariat in the class struggle.[24]

On the other hand, Jacques Rancière's proposal transcends *l'art pour l'art* or the politicization of art as proposed by Benjamin. The French author tries to reconstruct the logical aesthetic relationship between art and politics. For Rancière, aesthetics belongs not only to the regime of aesthetic forms but also to the social and political order. Rancière recognizes three main regimes of identification, to wit: the ethical regime of images, the poetic regime, and the aesthetic regime of the arts, the latter of which is distinguished by the "mode of being sensitive that is typical of products of Art."[25] Rancière points to a certain aesthetic regime of democracy characterized by the indeterminacy of identities or by the delegitimization of speech acts. In such an aesthetic regime, the distribution of the sensible would not fit.[26] If the "police," in Rancière's terms, allows us to see and to speak, it also allows seeing and speaking to whomever has the competence to see and the ability to speak, as well as identifying what is common in the discrimination of the management of bodies. On the contrary, "politics" would arise from the forms of visibility on the "part of those who have no part." For Rancière, the aesthetic regime of politics is properly that of democracy. Aesthetics rejects art's pretensions of self-sufficiency as mere dreams of transforming life to art, but it reaffirms an essential idea: art consists of building spaces and relationships to materially and symbolically reconfigure those common territories (or spaces).[27] Thus, according to Rancière, "there is an aesthetic at the base of politics" which has nothing to do with that "aestheticization of politics" that is typical of "the era of the masses."[28] An aesthetics of art has to build spaces and relationships by reconfiguring what belongs to the community, and what makes visible those who have been left on the margins, and who do not take part in representation.

It is in this tension that the debate proposed by Larraín is resolved as a first meeting between the publicist and the politicians of the Concertación. In this meeting the need arises to construct a space that tries to reconfigure the shared imaginary without neglecting representation. There is a need to "create conscience" and "occupy the space" claimed by the politicians of the Concertación because "this is a campaign of silence" that tries to "whitewash an image" and "silence what has really happened," topping it off with "those images are what you are."[29] In this sense, the aestheticization of the film happens on two levels. A first stage promotes the tension pointed out by Benjamin, that is, the confrontation of the creative publicist given over to the "art" of the image and the spectacularization of advertising versus political commitment and its emancipating horizon of representation and of the democratic parties. On another level, or as an extension of this one, the representation of those victims without a voice is always in dispute, as well as its horizon of legitimacy, marked by the ambiguity defined by the tension between testimony and advertising fiction ("I think what we need is more testimonials," to which René responds, "No, more humor").[30]

No, as a technical and political apparatus, profiles at the level of diegesis several sequences that illustrate this confrontation of positions. One of them is the viewing of the spot by the Asociación de Familiares de Detenidos Desaparecidos (Relatives of Disappeared Detainees Association, AFDD), which stokes the tensions between Saavedra and the direction team led by Fernando. In this sequence, the folkloric group of AFDD reinterprets the tune and rhythm of a traditional *cueca* dance, which is part of the national tradition as a popular peasant song. This reinterpretation is called *cueca sola*, and its special feature lies in its members' presentation and their relationship with the disappeared ones. A single woman carrying a portrait of a disappeared loved one and a white flag (or scarf) as a call for justice performs the dance. Their verses refer to the pain of losing the loved one.

In the sequence of the viewing, Fernando hides behind the camera, while Urrutia observes the development with some difficulty. A panoramic shot presents us the film space, empty and dark, barely illuminated by the bodies of a small group of women who sing, play the guitar, and dance. The image suspends the rhythm and style of Saavedra's contributions, featuring older women with a simple, formal presentation, and in sharp contrast to the ideals of the publicist, whose filmic attempt, unlike the video, looks contrastive and expressionist, and therefore generates distance. "I am Alfredo Rodo Castañeda's mother," "I am the sister of . . .," says a succession of arrhythmic voices. The chaining of voices creates an affective, emotional perspective that contrasts with the result of the montage, which is presented from an objective point of view, showing a full shot of half a dozen people who are discussing the material being viewed. "It's good but a little ugly, it's out of tune with what we're doing," remarks René, to which the director replies that the materials will be used because it is something "different, it has content, you have to fill [time]," emphasizing the validity of duration versus rhythm: the "content" versus the "continent."[31] The aesthetic dispute, the political and aesthetic position on the reading of the past that overlays the whole film, the problematic of the occupation of public space, is synthesized in this dialogue, because not only is the whitewashing questioned, but also the final decision-making by the publicist or even the director. René, who insists on the "plaintive, weeping" tone of the images,[32] asks Urrutia about the final decision on the incorporation or not of the AFDD piece. Fernando, the director, puts René in his place and Urrutia ends the discussion with a brusque "it works." This also highlights the documentary stakes of the testimonials by the victims of the dictatorship, as well as the representation of history and its imaginaries in the face of the spectacularization of politics.

NO AS WAR MACHINE

As Gerald Raunig recalls in "Nomadic Lines of Invention" (2008), the war machine "points beyond the discourse of violence and terror, it is the machine that seeks to escape the violence of the state apparatus, the order of representation."[33] In this sense, beyond its politicization, which both perspectives invoke, Saavedra's project proposes an imaginary in the order of representation that seeks to escape from state violence, and at the same time allows the occupation of space, identification of commonalities in the process of differentiating the ordering of bodies, the forms of visibility for those who are not visible.

The debate on politicization does not belong exclusively to the sphere of discourse semantics, understood as documentary versus advertising. While Benjamin seeks an aesthetic solution for two systems of political thought, and Rancière attends to regimes and their order and visibility, the film problematizes the concept of politicization, both in its machinic nature and as a sum of agencies and their aesthetic strategies. The whitewashing and the choice of the advertising code point to the articulation of a war machine. In this sense, the film does not show the referendum process as a struggle between electoral machines in which the war machine of the No is imposed on the state apparatus that represents the Yes. Following the metaphor of the "nomadic war machine" from Félix Guattari and Gilles Deleuze's *Mille Plateaux*, we can argue that the web of agencies that joined forces to achieve the electoral overthrow directed by Urrutia fights with fluidity and flexibility throughout the brief time that the campaign against the "state apparatus" lasts. While for any state "not only is it vital to overcome nomadism, but also to control migration, and, more generally, to claim a zone of rights over an exterior,"[34] say Guattari and Deleuze, the nomadism that characterizes war seeks combat by using conviction and the attraction of an imaginary production with few resources, and avoids a victory by military force.[35]

The war machine that René Saavedra conceives shapes this imaginary, based on his design, of images, music, and innovative slogans of the television and advertising culture of the 1980s. To build this machine, Urrutia brings together several people to his house on the beach in what looks like an advertising brainstorming session in which creative solutions are sought for the No bloc. At one point, Urrutia himself shows his doubts about a certain linguistic drift during their conversation: "I don't like to talk about democracy as a product." René corrects himself, half-heartedly: "No, well, let's call it 'concept,'"[36] a concept that Saavedra quickly associates with "all things happy," concluding, "democracy seems attractive to me. A happy product."[37] Through its design of the joy and democracy to come, the instrumentalization of political concept as aesthetic drift (or simply aesthetics) considers desire as a production of meaning. The publicist's choice of joy as a recurrent leitmotif is diametrically opposed to the meaning of testimony, with which it links not only to the repression of the Chilean dictatorship but also to the victim narrative that defends the final artifact. Thus, the design is defined, because it requires something "without folklore and rock. A jingle,"[38] the primary genre of advertising.

The aesthetic politicization of the film is problematized through the discourse and its machinelike nature. The debate turns on the dilemma of "creativity" versus "norm." Faced with a State that only understands war as an objective in itself, the No bloc's tactics relocate and diversify strategies. Deleuze and Guattari remind us that the war machine is external to the State apparatus thanks to the different strategies offered by the machine ("mythology, epic, drama, and games").[39] Guattari proposed the "machinic" character of the unconscious as a political and material factor by activating collaboration structures and networks through inappropriate works of both individuals and an unbreakable political subject such as the state.[40] For Guattari and Deleuze, the figure of the "artist," which in the film is represented by René Saavedra's creativity, is able to be nomadic and to fight against the subjugation of the state. For this, the "warrior–artist" tries to add desire, an element linked to those agents of aestheticization in the film: advertising, television, the video clip genre, and pop music.

In a Deleuzian sense, this machinery is always activated in the film through antagonism, beginning with the topic of the film: the struggle for victory in the 1988 plebiscite in Chile. This antagonism is marked by the neoliberal context, as a system of norms already deeply inscribed in administrative practices, and in business-like institutional policies. Thus, "it is characterized, in the field of the symbolic, by the imperative of competitiveness, the segmentation of lives and their entrepreneurization."[41] We realize that from the first sequence of the film, where Saavedra presents a video ad to a soda product client, exclaiming, "what you are going to see next is framed in the current social context. The country is ready for a communication of this nature,"[42] in a tone of gravity that makes the clients proud. The spectacularity of the visual presentation is mixed with multiple postmodern kitsch elements, such as clownish characters and high-color saturation. Faced with the antagonism that the final result creates in the client, presented as an expression of national conservatism, the publicist simply insists on the value of rupture: "this is very original; maybe in America there is something similar."[43] Rebellion, the creative director explains, but an orderly one.

With this first sequence, Larraín seeks two antagonisms: first, a social tension between the everyday practices among the circles close to the Pinochet regime and a certain inclination for rupture. Second, an aspirational relationship with the growing influence of the capitalist market is evidenced, through desire, in opposition to the Chilean national socioeconomic structure: "the people have raised a demand for the truth, for what they like. Today Chile thinks about its future,"[44] René repeats both to an interlocutor of the food market and to an electoral coalition committee. The last sentences make explicit the equation between "client" and citizenship, between truth and joy, that is, between modern ideology and postmodern capitalist desire.

NO AS APPARATUS

It is important to distinguish, then, the power of the "machine" from the subjection of the "apparatus," a concept traditionally close to state politics. The subjection of the apparatus acts on the molar; that is, on socially defined categories such as family, school, or work.[45] On the other hand, the "machine" acts on the molecular; that is, on the sphere of emotions such as desire, affection, and the presubjective. To assess the effectiveness of each strategy of our analysis—the strength of the Yes versus the seduction of the No—we must take into account what, according to Jean-Louis Déotte, defines each epoch of contemporary history: the existence of a unique epochal sensibility, based on the conformation of its specific apparatuses, which fight among themselves to achieve consensus, if not hegemony.[46] While Michel Foucault understands the production of hegemony and power as the sums of *énoncés* (statements),[47] Déotte points to the dependence that any statement has on the particular hegemonic technical condition of each era.

In *No*, we see three contemporary apparatuses: television, the images market (advertising), and traditional cinema. The apparatus, as the network of elements that transforms discourse into control, becomes a machine when its effect is to produce a shared sensibility. Rancière calls this formation "aesthetic politicization" when the condition of the device as a prosthesis becomes a newer, more fluid, and delocalized community. This is what Larraín does in the film on a national scale. In this regard, Déotte says, "an apparatus is what articulates sensibility and the law in the form of a call to singularity and togetherness."[48] It has, therefore, an aesthetic component, a sensibility, and a particular context that differentiates it from the instrumental function in Louis Althusser's "apparatus" or in the rhetorical "dispositif" of Foucault and Giorgio Agamben. *No* exhibits the significant impact that technologies of sensibility had within the moment of shift from modernity to postmodernity, which will extol, among other things, the three central elements in the film: television, market, and pop music.

In its material reading, *No* is a sophisticated technical device that would seem to be explicitly planned. Through its technical artifacts within the story, the movie becomes a metalinguistic exercise in "simulacrum." The film is presented at different levels in its narratological process. From the beginning, the movie is narrated from a traditional, objective point of view, but soon two other narrative voices will appear, to complement the first throughout the film. A kind of objective counter point of view is seen in the scenes where René is shown to be in danger. By providing this point of view, the camera displaces the traditional monopoly of objectivism into an antagonism between the parties in dispute. The camera becomes a metaphor for the political body. The camera's point of view is revealed or hidden, depending on its specular relationship to the political ideologies or sides. When we see a stable, solid, even majestic camera, those who speak to us are the No: the tenacity of militant dignity. When the camera trembles and the images appears blurred, it is because it is the Yes, the state, who is watching.

The antagonism of the two sides transcends aesthetic sensibility. While the Yes campaign advocates a more elaborate, orchestrated ad, with choir voices and Pinochet's photos, the No campaign combines testimonials and a more television-like aesthetic based on an advertising jingle: "Chile, happiness is coming" ("Chile, la alegría ya viene"). Both appeal to the emotions; the former, to fear and insecurity based on political technologies and the result of the Chilean neoliberal project; and the latter primarily to happiness, although without moving away from that same project and its own horizons of expectations. However, the formal presentation of the film proposes other modes of imaging. Television as a device takes on a double meaning: as a media "dispositif" (the medium of television) and as a container object (television as a physical device). As Maurizio Lazzarato (2006) points out:

> Television functions through the use of a small number of established, codified statements, statements of the dominant reality; it also uses a series of prefabricated modes of expression. It then claims to transform these statements and expressions into the statements and expressions of individual subjects themselves.[49]

In *No*, this apparatus appears in multiple sequences either as an object or as the driving discourse of everyday life, from images from the national news channel in René's home to archival film material of the battles between the army and the citizens in the *coup d'état*, used for earlier pieces in the plebiscite campaign. The film thus shows us a wide variety of recordings from different periods and media. It makes more evident the antagonism between the jumps to the past (the filmic footage referring to something old and distant) and the jumps to the future (colorful, musical images and infographics). "Chile thinks about its future," René repeats, and a succession of images is triggered, in a frenetic, varied rhythm, into which are inserted two scenes from the popular "We Are the World" campaign, a charity campaign for Africa organized in 1985 by Michael Jackson and Lionel Richie.

René's character is the one who sustains the main antagonisms and contradictions in the film: he is the young publicist but at the same time the partner of a young leftist militant; he is the creative director open to new ideas while his collaborators behave conventionally; he is the "outsider" character, unaffiliated with any stable identity, in opposition to his diverse interlocutors in this political drama. The figure of Urrutia emerges in parallel as a consensus character within the opposition block, but in this chapter, is read as René's opposite. "Make use of all the advertising tricks," Urrutia later demands of René, in an embodiment of the two real opposing paradigms: that of the political "apparatus" of the past (such as militant strategies), and the contemporary war machine (advertising strategies of the 1980s). In doing this, the director is able to exceed the traditional opposition between the paradigm of democracy, represented by opposition leaders and activists, and the dictatorship, depicted by the figure of Pinochet and his team. Both the old militant and the carefree youth are the architects of the victory of the second model of struggle against the state, but also against the old militancy, which is indirectly accused of sharing many codes and a general language with the regime.

In an intimate moment, René and his militant ex-wife Veronica meet with their son. Once again, the television monitor opens the scene. René follows political events through the news on television, accompanied by his son Simón (Pascal Montero), in a position of political conflict mediated by the device of the television. In this regard, Larraín's film proposes a deliberate move to abstract the repressive violence, reducing it to a plot line around this couple, for those who see the tensions between their respective political positions and their family relationship. During their conversation, they never truly face each other; while she looks at the plate, he looks straight ahead. They speak of their son, and also of the repression: "did they hit you a lot?"[50] Then she looks up, her face showing the evidence of the violence she suffered. After a very short interval, she opts for more direct, harder language: "You're going to join the No, right? And for what?"[51] She accuses him of participating in the binary logic of the referendum, of entering Pinochet's game; she calls him a mercenary. He avoids an argument and asks that they all sleep together. They hug. "I love you," she says. "We are going to kick Pinochet out," he says, in direct contradiction of his political inaction.[52]

CONCLUSION

Throughout this chapter, we have attempted to address the problematic politicization in Pablo Larraín's film using a multidisciplinary approach. We proposed three readings of *No* as a technical and political "dispositif": first, as a commodification device that tries to divert the central role of politics into an economic debate on the effectiveness of markets in society, what Jacques Rancière defined as aesthetic politicization. Second, following Guattari and

Deleuze's philosophy, we considered it as a sociopolitical war machine of civil society against the state and its power; and finally, as the expression of a hegemonic formal apparatus, the preeminence in the 1980s of television and advertising. In part, these three readings make more understandable the very different receptions the movie has had in different political and social sectors.

Note, however, that these different readings of *No* happen on two levels. At the diegetic level, advertising language becomes an electoral war machine, where television serves as a semiotic "dispositif" by seducing the masses through contemplation. At the extra-diegetic level (how the audience receives the film, and how they understand the real story behind the plot), the cinematographic machinery behaves as a powerful "dispositive" for political subjectivization. The omnipresence of metalinguistic signs, different levels of montage footages, techniques, and formats, are evidence of semiotic operations throughout the film.

We read the movie as a transformation of sensibilities, subjectivities, and productions of meaning. René's proposal implies a reconfiguration of the political space and its imaginary, since it openly promotes silencing the dictatorship in favor of consensus. However, it is also important to highlight that this reconfiguration is not consummated in the form of cultural and political consumption, due to the perseverance of different political subjects that guarantee testimonies and victims in the movie. In this sense, Larraín's "aesthetics of politics" can be read ambiguously: as a film becoming a spectacle-turned-commodity, or as a metaphor of the political and economic situation of Chile, given over to neoliberal capitalism and the consumer society; either the diegetic time (the 1980s) or the extra-diegetic moment of narration (the 2010s).[53]

NOTES

1. Pablo Larraín, *No* (Culver City, CA: Sony Pictures Home Entertainment, 2013). Original Spanish: "¿Esto es todo? ¿Algo más? ¿Algo más ligero, un poco más simpático?" "Compañero, ¿usted piensa que lo que está pasando en Chile es simpático?" "No, no. A ver, a mí esto me sobrecoge de la misma manera que a todos ustedes. Yo creo que esto . . . Esto no vende."
2. We take the meaning of these two concepts from Michel Foucault's and Félix Guattari and Gilles Deleuze's works. Foucault introduces the concept of "dispositif" as apparatus in "The Confession of the Flesh" in *Power/Knowledge: Selected Interviews and Other Writings* (New York: Pantheon Books, 1980), 194–228. The concept of "war machine" appears in Deleuze and Guattari, *Nomadology: The War Machine* (Los Angeles: Semiotext(e), 1986).
3. David Harvey, *A Brief History of Neoliberalism* (Oxford; New York: Oxford University Press, 2007), 8.
4. Naomi Klein, *The Shock Doctrine: The Rise of Disaster Capitalism* (New York: Metropolitan Books/Henry Holt, 2007); Milton Friedman, "Free Markets and the Generals," *Newsweek*, January 25, 1982, 59.

5. Original Spanish: "crear conciencia y ocupar los espacios que la dictadura se vio obligada a abrir."
6. His father is Hernán Larraín, the Minister of Justice and Human Rights of Chile (since 2018), whose position, in line with that of his own party the Independent Democratic Union party (UDI in Spanish), on the legitimacy of the military coup of 1973 and the case of Colonia Dignidad has been openly controversial. His mother, Magdalena Matte, is a former UDI minister in the cabinet of Sebastián Piñera (during his first term as president of Chile between 2010 and 2014).
7. Pablo Larraín, "Entendiendo a Pablo Larraín," interview by Andrew Chernin, *La Tercera*, January 20, 2013: <http://www2.latercera.com/noticia/entendiendo-a-pablo-larrain> (accessed February 27, 2020).
8. Larry Rohter, "Pablo Larraín and His Unintentional Trilogy," *The New York Times*, January 8, 2013: <https://carpetbagger.blogs.nytimes.com/2013/01/08/pablo-larrain-and-his-unintentional-trilogy> (accessed February 27, 2020).
9. For example, Olga Khazan, "4 Things the Movie 'NO' Left Out About Real-Life Chile," *The Atlantic*, March 29, 2013: <https://www.theatlantic.com/international/archive/2013/03/4-things-the-movie-no-left-out-about-real-life-chile/274491/> (accessed February 27, 2020); and Larry Rohter, "Oscar-Nominated 'No' Stirring Debate in Chile," *The New York Times*, February 8, 2013: <https://www.nytimes.com/2013/02/10/movies/oscar-nominated-no-stirring-debate-in-chile.html> (accessed February 27, 2020).
10. Nelly Richard, "Memoria contemplativa y memoria crítico-transformadora: sobre la película *No* de Pablo Larraín," *laFuga*, 2014: <http://www.lafuga.cl/memoria-contemplativa-y-memoria-critico-transformadora/675> (accessed February 27, 2020).
11. Robert Wells, "Trauma, Male Fantasies, and Cultural Capital in the Films of Pablo Larraín," *Journal of Latin American Cultural Studies* 26, no. 4 (2017), 10: <https://doi.org/10.1080/13569325.2017.1343182> (accessed February 27, 2020).
12. Wolfgang Bongers, "La estética del (an)archivo en el cine de Pablo Larraín," *A Contracorriente: Revista de Historia Social y Literatura en América Latina* 12, no. 1 (2014): 191–212. Original Spanish: "desordena las memorias colectivas e individuales y rearticula los archivos audiovisuales en el país."
13. Pablo Larraín, "Película chilena sobre el plebiscito de 1988 es aclamada en Cannes," interview by AFP, *La Tercera*, May 18, 2012: <http://www2.latercera.com/noticia/pelicula-chilena-sobre-el-plebiscito-de-1988-es-aclamada-en-cannes> (accessed February 27, 2020).
14. Paula T. Cronovich, "'No' and *No*: The Campaign of 1988 and Pablo Larraín's Film," *Radical History Review* 124 (January 1, 2016): 165–76.
15. Wells, "Trauma, Male Fantasies, and Cultural Capital in the Films of Pablo Larraín."
16. Original Spanish: "la idea de que había un grupo de políticos ideologizados y pasados de moda y que de repente apareció un publicista y les dijo 'esto es lo que hay que hacer' no es efectivo." Genaro Arriagada, "El No de Arriagada," interview by Sebastián Rivas, *Qué Pasa*, August 2, 2012: <http://www.quepasa.cl/articulo/politica/2012/08/19-9152-9-el-no-de-arriagada.shtml> (accessed July 12, 2019).
17. Cronovich, "'No' and *No*: The Campaign of 1988 and Pablo Larraín's Film," 169.
18. Teresa Delgado, *NO + Pinochet: Documentación, publicidad y ficción en torno al plebiscito chileno de 1988* (Berlin: Jakob Kirchheim Verlag, 2013), 10: <http://nbn-resolving.de/urn:nbn:de:101:1-201312129087> (accessed February 27, 2020). In Spanish, the symbol "+" after the "NO" can mean both "no plus" and "no more." In the movie, the meaning is the latter.
19. Among other authors, it is worth noting Álvaro García Linera, Juan Carlos Monedero, Colectivo Situaciones, Fernando Fernández-Savater, Marina Garcés, and Salvador López

Petit, and the *Informe sobre desarrollo humano en Chile 2015: los tiempos de la politización* of the United Nations Development Program (UNDP).
20. Kari Palonen, "Reinhart Koselleck on Translation, Anachronism and Conceptual Change," *Why Concepts Matter: Translating Social and Political Thought* 6 (2012): 88.
21. Walter Benjamin, *The Work of Art in the Age of Its Technological Reproducibility, and Other Writings on Media* (Cambridge, MA: Belknap Press of Harvard University Press, 2008), 57.
22. Ibid., 42.
23. Georges Didi-Huberman, *Cuando las imágenes toman posición* (Boadilla del Monte, Madrid: Antonio Machado Libros, 2013), 111.
24. Benjamin, *The Work of Art*, 79.
25. Jacques Rancière, *El reparto de lo sensible* (Buenos Aires: Prometeo Libros, 2014), 35. Original Spanish: "modo de ser sensible propio de los productos del arte."
26. Ibid., 21.
27. Jacques Rancière, *Sobre políticas estéticas* (Barcelona: Museu d'Art Contemporani, Servei de Publicacions de la Universitat Autònoma de Barcelona, 2005), 16–17.
28. Rancière, *El reparto de lo sensible*, 20.
29. *No*. Original Spanish: "crear conciencia," "ocupar el espacio," "ésta es una campaña del silencio," "un lavado de imagen," "silenciar lo que realmente ha ocurrido," "esas imágenes es lo que ustedes son."
30. Original Spanish: "yo creo que lo que necesitamos es más testimonios," "No, más humor."
31. Original Spanish: "Está bueno pero un poco feo, se sale de tono de lo que estamos haciendo," "distinto, tiene contenido, hay que llenar."
32. Original Spanish: "lastimero, llorón."
33. Gerald Raunig, "Nomadic Lines of Invention" (European Institute for Progressive Cultural Policies, April 2008): <http://eipcp.net/transversal/0307/raunig/en> (accessed February 27, 2020).
34. Gilles Deleuze and Félix Guattari, *Mil mesetas: Capitalismo y esquizofrenia* (Valencia: Pre-Textos, 2004), 389. Original Spanish: "no sólo es vital vencer el nomadismo, sino también controlar las migraciones, y, más generalmente, reivindicar una zona de derechos sobre todo un exterior."
35. In the chapter "Tratado de nomadología" of *Mil meseta*s, Deleuze and Guattari propose the state apparatus and the nomadic war machine as two completely opposing concepts. On one hand, the State attempts to "dig furrows in space," marking boundaries, while on the other, the nomadic war machine fights for a "smooth" space, open and without fixed borders.
36. Original Spanish: "no me gusta hablar de la democracia como producto," "No, bueno, llamémosle 'concepto.'"
37. Original Spanish: "todo lo que sea alegre," "a mí la democracia me parece algo atractivo. Un producto alegre."
38. Original Spanish: "sin folclor, sin rock. Un jingle."
39. Deleuze and Guattari, *Mil mesetas: Capitalismo y esquizofrenia*, 359.
40. Félix Guattari, *Psicoanálisis y transversalidad: crítica psicoanalítica de las instituciones* (Buenos Aires: Siglo XXI, 1976), 274–83.
41. Christian Laval and Pierre Dardot, *La nueva razón del mundo: ensayo sobre la sociedad neoliberal* (Barcelona: Gedisa, 2013), 21.
42. Original Spanish: "Lo que van a ver a continuación está enmarcado en el actual contexto social. El país está preparado para una comunicación de esta naturaleza."
43. Original Spanish: "esto es muy original; en América tal vez hay algo parecido."
44. Original Spanish: "la ciudadanía ha subido la exigencia en torno a la verdad, en torno a lo que le gusta. Hoy Chile piensa en su futuro."

45. Deleuze and Guattari, *Mil Mesetas: Capitalismo y esquizofrenia*, 214, 511–23.
46. Jean-Louis Déotte, *La época de los aparatos* (Buenos Aires: Adriana Hidalgo Editora, 2013), 29–43.
47. Michel Foucault, *La arqueología del saber* (Buenos Aires: Siglo XXI, 1970), 131–45.
48. Jean-Louis Déotte, *¿Qué es un aparato estético? Benjamin, Lyotard, Rancière* (Santiago de Chile: Ediciones Metales Pesados, 2012), 72. Original Spanish: "un aparato es lo que articula lo sensible y la ley bajo la forma de un llamado a la singularidad y al ser en común."
49. Maurizio Lazzarato, "The Machine" (European Institute for Progressive Cultural Policies, October 2008): <http://eipcp.net/transversal/1106/lazzarato/en> (accessed February 27, 2020).
50. Original Spanish: "¿te pegaron mucho?"
51. Original Spanish: "¿te vas a meter al No, verdad? Y ¿para qué?"
52. Original Spanish: "Vamos a echar a Pinochet."
53. Rancière, *El reparto de lo sensible*, 14.

CHAPTER 7

Adaptation and the Use of Documentary Material in *No*

Laura Hatry

> Chile, happiness is coming
> Let's stop all the deaths,
> This is the chance to overcome violence
> With weapons of peace
> Because I believe my Motherland needs dignity
> Because Chile is for everyone, we are going to say no.
> Chile, happiness is coming[1]
> *Jaime de Aguirre, composer of the song "No"*

This chapter will analyze Larraín's 2012 adaptation of *No* from the play *El plebiscito* (*The Plebiscite*) by Antonio Skármeta through a close reading and textual analysis of the unpublished play,[2] focusing especially on the ideological shift from one work to the other. Given the vital importance of archival elements in both the play and the film, this chapter also aims to shed light on the way in which Larraín incorporates historic, documentary footage, as well as the real-life participants in the 1988 referendum into his work. I will analyze how Larraín merges the original footage with new shots by means of careful montage and how the construction of this spatiotemporal continuity allows him to visually obscure the boundaries between facts and fiction.

In 1988, international pressure led the Pinochet regime to convene a plebiscite, as projected in the constitution of 1980, with the motive of legitimizing its illicit government. It was the third of its sort since Pinochet had taken power in Chile:

> The first plebiscite was convened by the regime in 1979 as an effort to resist mounting international criticism of its policy of state terror. The

second plebiscite was convened in 1980 to establish "popular ratification" of the new Constitution, and the third plebiscite was intended to provide "popular affirmation" of the legitimation process, conclude the transition to democracy, and confirm a civilian presidency for Chile—albeit preferably by having the old general remain in *La Moneda*, only having to exchange his military uniform for a business suit.[3]

However, the last plebiscite did not turn out the way Pinochet and his allies had anticipated, and this historic event turned into the basis for Skármeta's play. Even though Skármeta's final version is dated 2013, he has stated in interviews that he finished the work in 2008: "That resulted in a theater play called *El plebiscito*, that never premiered, because one attempt to release it failed in 2008 on the occasion of the 20-year-anniversay of the triumph of No."[4] But it was indeed only half a year after the plebiscite, in 1989, when Skármeta first created a version of this play in the form of a fifty-one-minute radio drama, with a title much closer to Larraín's film than to his own play, called "Das Nein" ("The No"), which was broadcast on April 4, 1989 by the German radio station Südwestfunk / Bayerischer Rundfunk / Hessischer Rundfunk.[5] The author also introduced the story in his 2011 novel, *Los días del arcoíris* (*The Rainbow Days*). The novel consists of two plotlines: the first concerns a student at the Instituto Nacional, whose father, a professor, is arrested by agents of the Central Nacional de Informaciones (CNI), and the second focuses on Adrián Bettini, the publicist who created the No campaign; although the second plotline corresponds with the plot of the theater play, it is not recapitulated there in detail.[6] The plotlines intersect with each other, and the publicist's story can be read as a mirroring of the student's on different levels.[7]

The film was very successful at Cannes[8] and was the first Chilean movie to be nominated for an Academy Award for Best Foreign Language Film (2012).[9] The cast includes two stars, one of international stature, Gael García Bernal, and one national, Alfredo Castro. Both the theater play and the adaptation portray the days before October 5, 1988, when the historical vote about whether Pinochet would stay in power for another eight years took place. In the play, the minister calls the protagonist, René Saavedra (Gael García Bernal), a well-known enemy of the regime and likely candidate to head the No campaign, to suggest that he lead the publicity for the Yes campaign. The successful publicist immediately compares it to the 1980 plebiscite, which the minister defends as legitimate. Saavedra replies ironically:

> Since in that plebiscite it was not allowed for the political parties to have delegates at the polling places and the votes were only counted by Pinochet's civil servants, there was no selection board for the election,

and no opposition press was allowed to publish opinions contrary to the government, people were suspicious. But apart from those little details, I'm sure the plebiscite was fair.[10]

History eventually showed that those who mistrusted the results were correct:

Thousands of security agents and civil servants voted multiple times in the plebiscite that Augusto Pinochet had convened in 1980 in support of the constitution that is still in force in Chile, as a former secret police agent has revealed for the first time in a forthcoming book.[11]

The minister vows that this time all complaints will be taken into account, and the whole process will be different from the last plebiscite. They even propose that Saavedra name his own salary, but in spite of their concessions and blandishments, his "answer is *no*,"[12] showing his integrity and utter repudiation of the dictatorship that had imprisoned him after its coup, and on whose blacklist of the unemployable he had subsequently been placed.

The film, however, develops a quite different main character: the son of exiled Chileans, who were forced to seek refuge in Mexico, thereby rendering Gael García Bernal's Mexican accent plausible, although he does insert certain typical Chilean words or phrases into his speech. He could be characterized as a family man who starts out rather apolitical and undergoes a process of politicization. His ex-wife, Verónica (Antonia Zegers),[13] who has been arrested and beaten up for disagreeing and stating openly that she backs the No campaign, represents the brutality of suppression under the dictatorial regime. Her role in *No* partially coincides with that of the publicist's child, Julia, in *El plebiscito*; in the movie, his son is still too young to play an important role and functions only to show how children were used to threaten parents who opposed the regime. The two women, Julia and Verónica, think that there is no point in holding a plebiscite, because they are convinced that "no dictator would hold a plebiscite to lose it, [nor that] by putting slips of paper into an urn one can overthrow a dictator, who seized the power with bullets."[14] At the beginning of the movie, René has similar doubts as to why there should be a campaign at all if the election is already fixed. However, there is an important difference between the two women: while Verónica is more in favor of trying to bring change to the country, even if by clandestine means, Julia has lost all hope for Chile and wants to leave the country as quickly as possible once she has graduated, even though she starts to support her father's position little by little. Their attitudes could be interpreted not only as politically divergent, but also a reflection of their different ages, given that Julia was only five years old at the time of the coup, while Verónica lived through it and the subsequent dictatorship in mature awareness. To include a twenty-year-old in the theater play stresses the fact that what Chile is today has much to do with what happened in the plebiscite, and Larraín concurs: "The pillars, the columns, the basis of Chile today, were established in the way the bloc of the No was set up. The logic that was decisive back then, is still very relevant today in a country like Chile."[15] His interest in the work was also connected to the curious fact that the No bloc used exactly those tools the dictatorship itself had created to overthrow it, which leads to the question: "is it only a defeat for Pinochet, or is it also the victory of Pinochet's model?"[16] What took place is vital in understanding, on the one hand, the difficult time of the transition and, on the other, the current situation in the South American country. Víctor Hugo Ortega says, in this context, that "the end of the dictatorship in Chile is the beginning of an era in which appearances are more important than the truth of a divided country, immersed in inequity, and that is light years away from wanting to find solutions."[17]

Throughout the film we witness the dichotomy between the necessity to condemn the atrocities of the fifteen years of dictatorship and the imperative to do everything possible to make sure that No wins, even if that means using otherwise cynical marketing strategies and the slogan "Chile, happiness is coming," that seem to relegate its brutal history to oblivion. Nevertheless, we should not forget that the fifteen minutes of television presence that the No bloc[18] was granted did not include only pleasant or happy images, but also political content with an optimistic tone to make Chilean voters think beyond their fear. And we should recall that, as soon as the publicists included reports from a judge about instances of regime-sanctioned torture, the broadcast of the No program was immediately censored. Two days after winning the plebiscite, the newspaper *El País* reported the following about Patricio Bañados's presence in the censored program:

> Even though he had been banned from television three years earlier, the leadership of the No campaign invited him as a host for the 15 minutes of their *televised advertisement*. Bañados improvised from notes, which symbolized another milestone in his professional career: when the regime censored a program of the No, because it contained reports of a judge about police torture, for the first time in 15 years a *banging of pots and pans* happened spontaneously and not only after having been previously organized.[19]

It is, of course, merely speculation what might have happened if the campaign had taken a harsher tone, but, to say the least, there was a chance that a primarily aggressive and accusatory attitude would have led to more intensive censorship and therefore could have been less effective in its purpose. The protagonists use all the weapons of advertising to defeat the regime with its own methods, or in Manohla Dargis's words, "the nightmare legacy of the *coup d'état* vanquished by a brilliant coup de théâtre."[20] Pinochet's neoliberal economic program and his zeal for capitalism can be closely associated with the publicity trade that tries to sell a product, no matter what it is or what it might involve, as for example the microwave for which René directs a spot even though he knows it is harmful to people's health. He turns toward the actress and whispers: "you know, be careful, if you get too close, it causes radiation . . . it's not very safe."[21] In the play, the regime has the idea of trying to recruit the best publicist in order to prevent him from working on the opposition's campaign. This highlights the dilemma of an upright character: "When I get offered a job I cannot accept, it is the best salary in the world. When I get offered a job I should accept, there is no salary."[22] In the movie, René is convinced little by little to take a more prominent role in the campaign, and from being an advisor he slowly becomes its brains. He works secretly on the campaign and continues working at his normal job, even accepting favors from his bosses—for example, that the mother of his child be freed from the police station—but in the play he is much more upstanding and never even considers accepting the regime's offer. In addition to this moral predicament there is also the social quandary that the publicists must navigate: a widely varied audience has to be convinced to make the same choice, if not necessarily for reasons that could ever be the same. And Larraín emphasizes the issue, noting:

> some were ladies who were scared of the regime, and others were young people who thought the plebiscite was a scam. There is no commercial that works for both a lady and a young person, and that is what they had to invent and why it was so brilliant.[23]

The prospect of a brighter, happier, less violent, more promising future is what unites both groups in the end.

Although the work is based on a true story, the plotlines around the actual events are fictitious. There was no René Saavedra, but, as screenwriter Pedro Peirano remarks, each character works as a representative of a paradigmatic group.[24] However, Larraín did integrate many archival images in his film, "which he estimated amounts to about 30 percent of the film."[25] In order to avoid abrupt ruptures between the footage from 2012 and the videos from 1988, he chose to record the entire film using three-quarter-inch U-matic tape format—no doubt a surprise for a twenty-first-century spectator who walks into a movie theater—that also produced an ugly, or at least muddy and sometimes fuzzy image, which serves to transport the viewer to a time in the past and recreate the atmosphere of back then: a dirty film for a dirty historical situation. Besides the many takes that are flooded with backlight, the viewer sometimes

Figure 7.1 Patricio Aylwin in *No* (2012).

Figure 7.2 Remediated material from the No campaign video showing Patricio Aylwin (*No*, 2012).

ADAPTATION AND DOCUMENTARY MATERIAL IN *NO* 153

Figure 7.3 Patricio Bañados in *No* (2012).

Figure 7.4 Patricio Bañados in the original No campaign video (*No*, 2012).

has the sensation of watching a 3D movie without the 3D glasses. Defending this decision wasn't easy,[26] and indeed many critics disagreed with it, because it would be "commercially damaging. Theatrical distributors will likely be hesitant to present a film that by today's hi-def standards looks murky and flat."[27] The director, however, preferred the more daring and artistically committed option over the commercial one. Another ingenuity of the film is the inclusion of the historical figures who were part of the 1988 plebiscite, such as Patricio Bañados or Patricio Aylwin. They appear in the movie without any changes to their current age and wearing the same clothing as in the recording that was used for the original publicity campaign (Figures 7.1–7.4). Through montage, Larraín achieves a clear transition that gives the impression of being a single recording. And that is how he makes the line between fiction and fact disappear: the archival material seems to be part of the fiction and the fiction becomes visually part of the documentary material, creating "a strange spatial-temporary continuity between past and present, documentary and fiction, archive and recreation, over a span of 25 years."[28]

The inclusion of real images of the campaign had also been planned for the theater play, which contains stage directions such as "the following are nine minutes of real images from the authentic No campaign from 1988 which form an essential part of the dramaturgy of this play and can be found attached to the text in a DVD-format."[29] The movie adds a view of the intriguing process of how the campaign came to life and was filmed, while this aspect is missing from the play, in which the viewer is directly confronted with the result, rather than the development. It also does not mention that Pinochet initially made a public declaration that the Yes had won, even though he already knew the real results. In any event, Peirano concluded, in my opinion, rather unfairly, that the original format:

> was much more imaginative, the work did not narrate how the campaign had been designed, the attitude of the work was more about how poetry can put an end to a dictatorship. More poetic. And we immediately knew that that was not the story.[30]

There is surely much journalistic work behind *No*,[31] but *El plebiscito* never suggests that it was poetry alone that defeated the dictatorship. It is also the convictions of its characters, their courage in defending them, and their profound desire for change that ended it. And Skármeta's own ambition to make public how the dictatorship ended is every bit as human and political and practical, because while the story of how Pinochet seized power is well known, the way Chile found its way back to democracy is not.

Even though it is its central topic, neither of the two works claims that the only reason that No won was the publicity campaign, as some have reproached it for doing, because, in Skármeta's words, "there is no movie or song or campaign that can change history," but "the No was that spark at the right time. It was the straw that broke the camel's back, that enabled a bigger change, but it came from a very deep current within the people, an enormous force against the dictatorship."[32]

There is an important difference in how the two works conclude: *El plebiscito* maintains that justice should be served, which means that Pinochet must be jailed and that the parties that united in the No campaign must continue working toward that goal. The minister who cannot stop laughing over such a statement, because it seems impossible to him that that will ever happen, is, unfortunately, right: Pinochet is never put on trial, or put in jail—if we do not count his brief detention in London in 1998—and dies a free man and a millionaire. The ending of the film is less encouraging, and the victory it portrays might be seen as bitter: René resumes his job as a publicist and is shown using the same sentence he had already used for both a drink advertisement and then for the first video of the No campaign, this time for a television show. In all three cases, he begins by saying: "what you are about to see is framed within the current social context . . . Today, Chile is thinking of its future."[33] With this repetition reappearing at the end, the film suggests that even though the No has won, there are still—too—many things that remain the same, given that the dictatorship was not eliminated at the root, but has actually been accorded a sort of legitimacy in simply having lost a political referendum. One of the attendees during a meeting of the No bloc points out that the campaign precisely silences what really happened. Pinochet loses, but Pinochet also wins, he receives impunity and, indeed, he stays on as head of the armed forces. In 2012, Bañados would report that once the No had won, to his surprise, he never again heard from the Concertación. His assessment of the aftermath is rather gloomy, since he had expected:

> A shift towards a more civilized society. It is not about destroying everything that had been done, but the constitution that governs us now was imposed under military occupation at the command of "Daniel López" (Pinochet) and was not a product of the popular will. I expected a gradual and rational shift, I thought there was a plan to change the society behind it intelligently, and that has been completely frustrating.[34]

Larraín offers similar thoughts about the winners of October 5, 1988, the legacy of the dictatorship, and the current state of Chile in an interview with Rob White:

> Who won on that day in 1988? The "No" campaign was triumphant,[35] but how much from the "Yes" stayed? A lot. Pinochet remained as

commander-in-chief of the army for another four years and then he became a lifetime senator with immunity from prosecution. Meanwhile the state sector continued to shrink. My country became a company. Today the state is tiny. Chile is owned by eight guys, and one of them happens to be the president, who's a billionaire.[36]

Irina Dzero, in her article about the film as a simulacrum,[37] points out that while Skármeta's play is structured like a *Bildungsroman*, in which the young in Chile become a generation of politically committed people, the film refutes this coming-of-age transformation and shows no meaningful impact among the young. She further argues that it is this philosophical disagreement, rather than the medium they used, that led to the narrative and aesthetic choices Skármeta and Larraín made:

> The novelist shows the profound and irreversible impact of the referendum on the society, especially on the Chilean youth who will ensure the country's resolutely democratic development. In contrast, the filmmakers created an anti-coming-of-age story that contrasts with the writer's optimism about the democratic transition. They represent that transition as a simulacrum—an empty shell, both visually and verbally, created by a professional adman who does not have to believe in the product in order to sell it to the audience.[38]

Works like these explain the predicament in which Chilean society has been immersed since the plebiscite and why it is still divided in two. That both *El plebiscito* and *No* succeed in communicating the violence of the era without having to actually depict it explicitly, suggests that they represent separate but necessary aspects of an "accurate metaphor for a fractured country."[39]

NOTES

1. All translations are mine. Original Spanish: "Chile, la alegría ya viene . . . / Terminemos con la muerte, es la oportunidad / De vencer a la violencia con las armas de la paz / Porque creo que mi patria necesita dignidad / Por un Chile para todos, vamos a decir que No . . . / Chile, la alegría ya viene."
2. I would like to thank Antonio Skármeta for providing me with the text to be able to cite and comment on it.
3. Harry L. Simón Salazar, *Television, Democracy, and the Mediatization of Chilean Politics* (London: Lexington Books), 2018, 15.
4. Antonio Skármeta, qtd. in Marcelo Soto, "Antonio Skármeta y la chispa del *No*," *Capital Online*, January 28, 2013: <http://www.capital.cl/poder/2013/01/28/45003/antonio-skarmeta-y-la-chispa-del-no. Original Spanish: "Eso desembocó en una obra de teatro que

se llama *El plebiscito*, que no ha sido estrenada porque se frustró un intento de presentarla en 2008, con motivo de los 20 años del triunfo del NO."
5. See "Das Nein" in the ARD-database: <http://hoerspiele.dra.de/vollinfo.php?dukey=1374518&vi=1&SID> (accessed February 27, 2020).
6. The correspondence of the scenes from the play and the chapters and pages of the book (according to the first edition: Antonio Skármeta, *Los días del arcoíris*, Barcelona: Planeta, 2011) are the following: scene 1 – chapter 2 (pp. 13–14); scene 2 – chapter 4 (pp. 20–4 and 29–31); scene 3 – chapters 8 and 10 (pp. 37–9 and 45–50); scene 4 – chapter 12 (pp. 57–9); scene 5 – chapters 12 and 14 (pp. 59 and 65–6); scene 6 – chapter 16 (pp. 71–4); scene 7 – chapter 18 (pp. 80–5); scene 8 – chapter 20 (pp. 91–3); scene 9 – chapter 22 (pp. 104–6); scene 10 – no correspondence, since in the play only historic images are projected during this scene; scene 11 – chapters 38 and 39 (pp. 196–8 and 199–201).
7. "While for Bettini it is his career and his physical integrity that is in play, for the boy, his father's life is in play, and therefore his family; while Adrián is detained in a police station for running into a patrol car, Nico is taken to the school's director because he questions the school's authority; while one says the prayer for his dead professor, the other presents—against his will—the 'No' jingle to his adversaries. That is how the life of one of the characters finds its echo in the other's." Arone Ru Gumas, "Plebiscito del 88 y ¿retorno a la democracia? Algunos aspectos en *Los días del arcoíris* de Antonio Skármeta," *Mapocho: Revista de Humanidades* 75 (2014): 120. Original Spanish: "Mientras que en la historia de Bettini lo que está en juego es su carrera y su integridad física, en la del muchacho es la vida de su padre y, con ello, la de su familia, aquello que corre peligro; mientras que Adrián es detenido en una comisaría por chocar contra una patrulla de carabineros, Nico es llevado a la rectoría del colegio por interpelar a una autoridad escolar; mientras que uno pronuncia un responso por su profesor asesinado, el otro presenta—sin quererlo—la composición del jingle del 'no' ante sus adversarios. De esta manera, la vida de uno de los personajes encuentra eco en la del otro."
8. See EFE, "Pablo Larraín-Cannes: Película *NO* es una historia que 'merecía contarse,'" *La Nación*, May 18, 2012: <http://www.lanacion.cl/pablo-larrain-cannes-pelicula-no-es-una-historia-que-merecia-contarse/noticias/2012-05-18/114922.html> (accessed April 1, 2014).
9. In 2017, Sebastián Lelio's *A Fantastic Woman* was the second Chilean film nominated in that category and was proclaimed the winner.
10. All quotes of Skármeta's play come from the copy he provided me with. Original Spanish: "Como en ese plebiscito no estaba permitido que los partidos políticos tuvieran delegados en las mesas receptoras de votos y los votos los podían contar sólo funcionarios de Pinochet, y no había tribunal calificador de elecciones, y no se permitía una prensa de oposición que publicara la opción contraria al gobierno, la gente se puso desconfiada. Pero aparte de estos detallitos, el plebiscito debe haber sido limpio."
11. EFE, "Revelan fraude en plebiscito que aprobó Constitución de 1980," *La Nación*, June 11, 2012: <https://mqh02.wordpress.com/2012/06/12/constitucion-de-1980-fue-aprobada-con-fraude (accessed March 16, 2020). Original Spanish: "Miles de agentes de seguridad y funcionarios votaron varias veces en el plebiscito convocado por Augusto Pinochet en 1980 para refrendar la Constitución aún vigente en Chile, según revela por primera vez un ex agente de la policía secreta en un libro de próxima aparición."
12. The emphasis is in the original. Skármeta, e-mail. Original Spanish: "la respuesta es *no*."
13. In fact, it is not really clear what kind of relationship they have or had, other than that René suffers from the lack of a romantic relationship with her and that they have a child together.

14. Ibid. Original Spanish: "ningún dictador organiza un plebiscito para perderlo [ni que] poniendo papelitos en una urna se derroque a un dictador que tomó el poder disparando balazos."
15. Larraín qtd. in EFE, "Revelan fraude." Original Spanish: "Los pilares, las columnas, las bases del Chile de hoy, se mapeó en la manera en la que se constituyó la franja del NO. La lógica que hay ahí sigue siendo hoy día muy relevante en un país como Chile."
16. Ibid. Original Spanish: "¿es solo la derrota de Pinochet o es también la victoria del modelo de Pinochet?"
17. Víctor Hugo Ortega, "*No* y la alegría que no llegó," *Cinechile*, 2012: < <http://cinechile.cl/criticas-y-estudios/no-y-la-alegria-que-no-llego>. Original Spanish: "el fin de la dictadura en Chile es el comienzo de una era en donde las apariencias son más importantes que la verdad de un país dividido, sumido en la inequidad, y que está a años luz de querer buscar soluciones."
18. In the play, Julia quotes the headline of the *El País* newspaper from October 7, 1988: "Fifteen minutes were enough to finish off fifteen years." Manuel Délano, "Patricio Bañados: Quince minutos bastaron para acabar con quince años," *El País*, October 7, 1988: <htttp://elpais.com/diario/1988/10/07/ultima/592182007_850215.html> (accessed February 27, 2020). Original Spanish: "Quince años bastaron para acabar con quince años."
19. Délano, "Patricio Bañados: Quince minutos." Original Spanish: "A pesar de que estaba casi proscrito en televisión desde hace tres años, el Comando del No le invitó como presentador de los 15 minutos de su *franja publicitaria*. Bañados improvisaba sobre la base de apuntes. Ya puede anotar otro jalón en su carrera profesional: cuando el régimen censuró un programa del *no* por contener denuncias de un juez sobre torturas de la policía, por primera vez en 15 años hubo un *caceroleo* espontáneo, no convocado."
20. Manohla Dargis, "Cannes Film Festival: From Chile, Pablo Larraín's *No*," *The New York Times: ArtsBeat*, May 22, 2012: <http://artsbeat.blogs.nytimes.com/2012/05/22/cannes-film-festival-from-chile-pablo-larrains-no/?_r=0> (accessed Febuary 25, 2020).
21. *No*, dir. Pablo Larraín (2012; Culver City, CA: Sony Pictures Classics, 2013), DVD. Original Spanish: "sabes, cuidado, si te acercas demasiado, causa radiación [. . .], no está muy seguro."
22. Peirano qtd. in Yenny Cáceres, "Peirano en la mira," *Qué pasa*. Cultura, July 12, 2012: <http://www.quepasa.cl/articulo/cultura/2012/07/6-9016-9-peirano-en-la-mira.shtml> (accessed January 31, 2016). Original Spanish: "Cuando me ofrecen un trabajo que no puedo aceptar es el mejor sueldo del mundo. Cuando me ofrecen un trabajo que debería aceptar el sueldo es *ad honorem*."
23. Larraín qtd. in Vivian Murcia González, "El 'No' que silenció a Pinochet va por el Óscar," *La Hora*, February 1, 2013, 4. Original Spanish: "uno eran las señoras que estaban asustadas con el régimen, y el otro eran los jóvenes que creían que el plebiscito era una estafa. No existe un comercial de un producto que sirva para una señora y para un joven al mismo tiempo, y eso es lo que tenían que inventar y por eso son tan geniales."
24. Peirano explains those archetypes as follows: "Luis Gnecco plays a political operator, a cross of Genaro Arriagada and Juan Gabriel Valdés, while Alfredo Castro is the head of the Yes campaign. On the other side, Néstor Cantillana represents the most radical left wing, and Gael García, son of exiled Chileans (in order to justify his accent without having to speak with a Chilean accent), is the practical guy who wants the campaign to work as a strategy. He prefers to speak of 'persons,' rather than 'the people.'" Peirano qtd. in Cáceres, "Peirano en la mira." Original Spanish: "Luis Gnecco interpreta a un operador político, una cruza entre Genaro Arriagada y Juan Gabriel Valdés, mientras que Alfredo Castro es el jefe de la campaña del Sí. Del otro bando, Néstor Cantillana representa a la izquierda más dura, y Gael García, hijo de exiliados (para justificar su acento y no forzarlo a hablar como chileno), es el tipo práctico

que quiere que la campaña funcione como una estrategia. El que prefiere hablar de 'gente' en vez de 'pueblo.'" For the real life people who inspired many of the characters, see Rodrigo González, "Mapa con los personajes y hechos que inspiraron la cinta *No*," *La Tercera*, 2012: <diario.latercera.com/2012/08/05/01/contenido/culturaentretencion/30-115421-9-mapa-con-los-personajes-y-hechos-que-inspiraron-lacinta-no.shtml> (accessed April 7, 2014).
25. Larry Rohter, "One Prism on the Undoing of Pinochet," *The New York Times*, February 10, 2013: <https://www.nytimes.com/2013/02/10/movies/oscar-nominated-no-stirring-debate-in-chile.html> (accessed February 25, 2020).
26. Larraín explained that he studio-tested various cameras before the shooting began: "Super 35, Super 16, the latest HD cameras, VHS, regular video beta, DigiBeta and, finally, an analogue three-tube camera from 1983. When we went to the editing room, there was just no doubt that we needed to shoot in the old format. This initially created concern on the part of the backers. You can't just say: 'Hey, I'm going to shoot this Gael García Bernal movie with 600 extras in a period setting needing elaborate production design and costume—and, by the way, I'm going to use this camera that has less resolution than an iPhone camera.' The case needed to be made persuasively, but of course everyone finally agreed." Larraín qtd. in Rob White, "Truth & Dare," *Frieze*, June 20, 2013: frieze.com/article/truth-dare (accessed February 27, 2020).
27. David Rooney, "*No*: Cannes Review," *The Hollywood Reporter*, May 18, 2012: <http://www.hollywoodreporter.com/review/no-cannes-review-326644> (accessed February 27, 2020).
28. Gonzalo de Pedro, "Pablo Larraín: 'Los chilenos no fuimos capaces de juzgar a Pinochet,'" *El Cultural*, February 8, 2013: <http://www.elcultural.com/articulo_imp.aspx?id=32284> (accessed February 27, 2020). Original Spanish: "una extraña continuidad espacio-temporal entre el pasado y el presente, entre el documental y la ficción, entre el archivo y la recreación, con un salto de veinticinco años."
29. Skármeta, e-mail. Original Spanish: "lo que sigue son nueve minutos de imágenes reales de la auténtica campaña del NO en 1988 que pertenecen esencialmente a la dramaturgia de esta obra y que va adjunta como DVD al texto."
30. Peirano qtd. in Cáceres, "Peirano en la mira." Original Spanish: "era mucho más fantasiosa, la obra no contaba cómo había sido hecha la campaña, la actitud de la obra era cómo la poesía puede acabar con una dictadura. Más poética. Y muy al principio nos dimos cuenta de que la historia no era ésa."
31. For that, Peirano had the help of Lorena Penjean, who "interviewed around 20 people who had participated in the publicity campaign." Cáceres, "Peirano en la mira." Original Spanish: "hizo entrevistas a cerca de 20 personas que participaron en la campaña publicitaria."
32. Skármeta qtd. in Marcelo Soto, "Antonio Skármeta y la chispa del *No*." Original Spanish: "no existe una película o una canción o una campaña que cambien la historia, [sino que] el No fue esa chispita del momento oportuno. Es una gotita de agua que rebalsó el vaso, que hizo posible un cambio mayor, pero era algo que ya venía de una corriente muy profunda en el pueblo, una fuerza enorme contraria a la dictadura."
33. *No*, dir. Larraín. Original Spanish: "que lo que van a ver a continuación está enmarcado dentro del actual contexto social . . . Hoy Chile piensa en su futuro."
34. Patricio Bañados (interview), "Patricio Bañados y la franja del *NO*: después del '06 de octubre de 1988 nadie me llamó por teléfono de la Concertación, nunca más,'" *The Clinic*, January 10, 2012: <https://www.theclinic.cl/2012/01/10/patricio-banados-y-la-franja-del-no-el-06-de-octubre-de-1988-nadie-me-llamo-por-telefono-de-la-concertacion-ni-nunca-mas> (accessed March 16, 2020). Original Spanish: "un cambio hacia una sociedad más humanizada. No se trata de destruir todo lo que se había hecho, pero la Constitución que nos rige ahora fue impuesta bajo ocupación militar a gusto de 'Daniel López'

(Pinochet), y eso no fue un producto del deseo popular. Yo esperaba un cambio paulatino y racional, creí que había un plan para cambiar inteligentemente la sociedad detrás, y eso ha sido totalmente frustrante."

35. According to Urrutia, in the movie, "the triumph is not the people's triumph, but that of a protagonist who 1. only wants to live peacefully (his struggle is not epic, but more anecdotal, or even mundane), and 2. there is not a moment in which Saavedra thinks that the happiness his slogan anticipates will come, although he does sense that the No will win the plebiscite. Just like René Saavedra, *No* is a cynical film, a film that does not believe that change or a bright future is possible; and that's probably the respect in which it is most lucid." Carolina Urrutia, "*No*. Más alegre que la alegría," *laFuga*, 2005: <http://www.lafuga.cl/no/571. Original Spanish: "el triunfo [. . .] no es el triunfo de un pueblo, es el del protagonista que, 1. Sólo quiere vivir tranquilo (su lucha no es épica, es más bien anecdótica, curricular, incluso), y 2. Saavedra en ningún momento cree que va a llegar la alegría que reza su slogan, aunque sí intuya que el No va a ganar el plebiscito. Tal como René Saavedra, *NO* es una película cínica, una película que no cree en un cambio posible o en futuro colorido; y ahí, probablemente, está su principal lucidez."

36. Larraín qtd. in White, "Truth & Dare."

37. See Irina Dzero, "Larraín's Film *No* and Its Inspiration, *El plebiscito*: Chile's Transition to Democracy as Simulacrum," *Confluencia* 31, no. 1 (Fall 2015): 120–32.

38. Dzero, "Larraín's Film *No*," 130.

39. Víctor Hugo Ortega, "*No* y la alegría que no llegó." Original Spanish: "certera[s] metáfora[s] de un país fracturado."

CHAPTER 8

The Blurred Image: The Aesthetics of Impunity in Pablo Larraín's *No* and *El Club*

Susana Domingo Amestoy

This chapter analyzes two works by the Chilean filmmaker Pablo Larraín, *No* (2012) and *El club* (2015), in relation to his desire to find not only a script and appropriate dramatic structure, but also the means to achieve what he describes as a certain tone or texture. To this end, Larraín employs filters that simulate old anamorphic lenses and natural lighting. The director's desire for an image that captivates the senses has everything to do with the subject matter of his films, particularly as these relate to the legacy of Augusto Pinochet's military dictatorship and the theme of impunity. His approach to digital film, his conscious effort to overcome what he calls a lack of "geopolitical texture" produced by the standardization of the digital image, are symptomatic of his aim not just to narrate atrocities but to employ cinematic tools to create an aesthetic of impunity.[1] For instance, in *El club*, a film about the Catholic Church's efforts to silence and cover up cases of child abuse in Chile, Larraín draws on this aesthetic by making use of a fogged lens to mark the eerie remnants of the past in the present. Similarly, his earlier film *No* makes use of a vintage U-matic video system and a shallow focus with an eye to underscoring the very machinations that cause history to disappear in the wake of the market's triumph. In both *No* and *El club*, Larraín explores a certain inability to bring forth justice in Chile by deploying a specific tone and texture of the image that have come to define his own signature style—his aesthetics of impunity—thereby making present the un-present. In both films, ethics and aesthetics are interwoven, for, as Larraín explains, "The word aesthetics or the concept of aesthetics is linked with the concept of ethics, that in this case is a film that is about impunity and its consequences."[2]

This chapter attempts to understand how Larraín's cinematic techniques produce and extend what Jacques Rancière calls the politics of aesthetics, a "distribution of the sensible" that determines "the system of self-evident facts of sense perception," or, in other words, the relationship between the "sensible" or that which is given to sense perception.[3] However, the authority to perceive also determines what is perceived, and so, for Rancière, a work of art is political only if it disrupts the "relationship between the visible, the sayable, and the thinkable."[4] For this reason, Rancière is not interested in a didactic cinema, but in a cinema that is aware of its own limitations while at the same time able to recast new aesthetic configurations.

I argue that Larraín's aesthetics of impunity is political due to his deployment of cinematic techniques that disrupt the conventional relationship between the viewer and the image, creating a propitious distance for questioning the visible or the pretension of the visible to become all there is to see. More specifically, I examine how the blurred images and shallow focus in Larraín's films expose the texture of the unseen. These images haunt the narrative as an uncanny presence. Rancière calls a suitable political art one that "would ensure, at one and at the same time, the production of a double effect: the readability of political signification and a sensible perceptual shock caused, conversely, by the uncanny, by that which resists signification."[5] I argue that this happens in Larraín's films by way of the director's decision to place certain aspects of Chilean history outside the frame, creating a sense of unresolved trauma in *No* and an element of mystery in *El club*. If, for James Harvey, Larraín creates in *Post mortem* (2010) a "thesis on the politics and ethics of cinematic representations of traumatic history" by breaching "conventional representational tendencies,"[6] I claim that in *No* and *El club* Larraín breaches conventional aesthetics by using a cinematography that insists on a meaningful presence of an atmosphere, a tone, and a texture.[7] This atmosphere goes together with a community or society in stasis, unable to evolve to a new state, a stasis derived from a legacy of impunity, presented in both films: the neoliberal legacy of Pinochet and the unpunished crimes of the Catholic Church. In the last section of this chapter, I will consider Larraín's aesthetics in relation to the national and international reception and signature style of these films.

In his account of Larraín's second film *Post mortem*—which deals with the events following the coup of La Moneda Palace and the death of Salvador Allende—James Harvey also draws on Rancière's theory of politics, aesthetics, and historiography. In particular, Harvey focuses on the "ambivalence" of *Post mortem*'s main character in terms of political ideology and how "he does not suffer persecution nor is he a persecutor."[8] Harvey argues that this ambivalence prevents the film from presenting "clear-cut classifications of character" and denies the spectator the "ability to align herself with his experience." In doing so, Larraín's work locates the spectator "on the peripheries," thus "obstructing the possibility of clarity."[9] I maintain that Larraín disturbs the "distribution of the sensible" in *No* and *El club* by preventing the viewer from enjoying the image as a consumer artifact, thereby disrupting any kind of identification with the films' protagonists.[10]

NO: THE BLURRED VICTORY OF A TRANSITION

No is the last film in what has been called Larraín's "Chilean dictatorship trilogy" alongside *Tony Manero* (2008) and *Post mortem* (2010). The critical reception of this trilogy helps us understand the problematic representation of a traumatic past from Pinochet's coup on September 11, 1973, followed by seventeen years of dictatorship and, beginning in 1990, by the transition to democracy. As Vania Barraza Toledo explains, even though Larraín, son of right-wing politicians, "did not inherit a disturbing memory . . . nevertheless, in his movies, the director has assimilated a traumatized collective memory."[11] That being the case, despite making fiction films instead of documentaries, Larraín has been criticized for whitewashing the work of the resistance efforts to counteract Pinochet's dictatorship. In particular, this lack of historical accuracy or whitewashing has been pointed out in relation to Larraín's focus on the perpetrators of the coup and dictatorship rather than on its victims, and as such on the exploration of the effects of the politics on those who were left unpunished for their crimes.[12] Indeed, this can be understood as part of an interest in provoking the viewer. Far from an Aristotelian pathos generating a favorable emotional response, Larraín tries to create uneasiness in his works. This uneasiness creates a space for viewers to think about the image of a bleak past of the dictatorship and the representation of its cynical contradictions that are projected into the present.

In his film *No*, Larraín focuses on the historical events surrounding the 1988 *plebiscito* and the televised *franja de propaganda electoral*. Shown over the course of a month, the campaign consisted of fifteen-minute electoral television ads. The Yes campaign supported Pinochet's bid to remain in power for eight more years, and the No campaign, which aligned the seventeen political parties of the Concertación, was against Pinochet's re-election.[13] The film contains 30 percent archival footage together with a recreation of film archives using actors who were themselves part of the historic political events. For example, in the film, Patricio Aylwin, the first president after Pinochet's dictatorship, plays a younger version of himself more than two decades later. Accuracy between historical facts and fiction is not a central concern in the film, since Alfredo Castro, who in real life supported the No campaign, occupies the opposite political spectrum in the film, playing the role of Lucho Guzmán. Larraín's choice to cast Castro as Guzmán could be interpreted as a tactic to underscore the challenge of knowing the truth about the past, so that they do not forget that what they are watching is a fiction that needs to be viewed critically. In the film, Guzmán has ties to Pinochet and works for the Yes campaign. Guzmán is also the boss of the film's main character, René Saavedra (Gael García Bernal), who is the architect of the No campaign.

No presents democracy as a thing bought and sold, as the campaign drew heavily on the language of advertising as if it were a consumer product. This fact, along with Larraín's decision to use the same type of U-matic camera commonly used throughout the 1980s in Chile for making commercials, has divided critics. In broad terms, on one hand there are those who believe that *No* is a reductionist caricature of the plebliscite and on the other hand those who understand that Larraín, by leaving out of the frame almost all the resistance efforts, demonstrates the continuity of the economic legacy of Pinochet's dictatorship. According to James Cisneros, the transition to democracy was defined by stasis and a "presentism induced by consumerism." He adds: "the neoliberal policies that remain in place from the dictatorship through the referendum and into the government of the Concertación—a coalition of political parties that would hold power from 1990 to 2010—are a measure of a stationary history."[14] By making explicit the continuity of neoliberalism in democracy, Larraín underscores the invisibility of the resistance efforts to change the economic-political system.[15] While for Cisneros Larraín's aesthetic mannerism obscures "the signifying processes and the cultural practices, as well as the politics of the trace, elaborated through analog media,"[16] I argue that the film's aesthetics of impunity in *No* goes beyond the use of analog media and underlies and problematizes the presentism by displacing the trace of the old archive into the blurred image.

It is by paying attention to the film's form itself that we can see that a critique of neoliberalism is shown through different filmic techniques.[17] This critique is expressed through a number of blurred images, but the film's opening shot introduces the viewer to a clear presentation of a commercial campaign in tune with a market-oriented society. In the opening close-up shot, the main character's speech is established:

> Well, first of all I must tell you that what you are about to see is framed within the current social context ... We must keep in mind that the public has raised expectations around what it considers the truth about what the public enjoys.[18]

This speech is a key element in the film in relation to a democracy that will not abandon the neoliberal strategy implemented during the dictatorship. Saavedra is a Chilean exile who has recently returned from Mexico and who works as an ad executive. Saavedra has family connections with Allende politics through his father and the left resistance in Chile through his ex-wife and the mother of his child, Verónica (Antonia Zegers). She is, at first, adamant about Saavedra's campaign, which seems to portray an unreal image of Chile, and only at the end accepts the possibility of the No campaign's winning strategy of using advertising techniques. Saavedra's words come to act as the film's leitmotiv, punctuating its beginning, middle, and end. The sentence metaphorically foreshadows and encapsulates the selling of democracy and the end of the Pinochet dictatorship. In this first scene, Saavedra is trying to sell a commercial pitch created for the soft drink "Free" (a Chilean version of Pepsi). In the director's comments of the DVD, Larraín acknowledges how this created an analogy between selling the product and democracy as a process of "cocacolization" of the No campaign. In this scene, as in the other two instances—the *No* "franja publicitaria" and a James Bond pastiche of a Chilean soap opera at the end of the film—Saavedra describes the readiness of the country for the products that he is helping to sell. Saavedra's pitch frames these expectations about what the public enjoys and a national truth around a present that is projected not in the country's past, but in a future framed in the television screen. This present alluded to in the pitch of the soft drink is recycled into the No campaign. It is portrayed in tension with opposing voices and with filmic techniques that underline the erasure of history.

The main slogan of the *No* campaign points to a democratic future announced by the lyrics of the happy campaign jingle with people singing, dancing, having picnics, smiling. This is contrasted with the account of the human rights violations perpetrated during the dictatorship as selling points to end the dictatorship. Some members of the No campaign insist on the need to allow the victims of the dictatorship to take center stage in the campaign to prevent these crimes from remaining unpunished. In one of the scenes containing the screening of the No campaign, its member Ricardo (Alejandro Goic) voices the need for a systemic change, and rejects the idea of a pragmatic attitude without ethical limits. Ricardo is against the idea of subscribing to the neoliberal system installed by the dictatorship. Saavedra does not recognize the dictatorship killings and disappearances as a selling point, and requests something lighter and nicer to convince the voters. Ricardo sees this strategy as endorsing impunity and refuses to be part of it. Ultimately, with the exception of Ricardo, the voices against the No campaign envisioned by Saavedra grow weaker as the film unfolds.

José Tomás Urrutia (Luis Gnecco) appears in the scene when Saavedra is showing the pitch as the others are listening to someone who talks about the idea of rebellion and rock. Paradoxically, following Saavedra's explanation about the pitch, Guzmán, opening the same soda drink as in the commercial, frames the idea of youth rebellion in Chile promoted by North America, between the words of "order" and "respect" that were imagined as necessary under Pinochet's dictatorship. The interference in the scene by Urrutia, who is described pejoratively by Lucho as "the communist," is the first time viewers may realize that Saavedra will end up working for the No. He is present in four more scenes in which the image gets blurred. The director of photography, Sergio Armstrong, achieves this effect thanks to the tube camera system of the U-matic 3:4 used in the 1980s that works with heat. When sun hits the frame, it blurs the image.[19] For Larraín, this creates the idea of a spectral haunting. The idea of the spectral emerges encapsulated in images that can be understood to disturb any conventional distribution of the sensible and as such to unsettle the realistic logic of the narrative. Larraín sees this blurring as a way of blending the narrative with archival footage but the viewer can still distinguish these images from those of the archival footage. The film uses blurriness in very precise scenes, for example, when the traditional Chilean left appears in the frame on the *mise-en-scène*. They are often portrayed in a spectral, dissident, and precarious present. This goes together with the questioning of the word "communism." By doing this, the blurred image points toward the failure of definitions of a past political project disrupted by the *coup d'état*. The blurred image happens as an effect of the sun in the camera: first, on the street with Urrutia talking to Saavedra; later, when the supporters of the No campaign question Saavedra about his attempt to erase from the campaign any trace of trauma; and again, when they are brainstorming at the Chilean seaside, in a house belonging to a Chilean exiled dissident.

Figure 8.1   A blurred image with Fernando and Urrutia's heads missing (from *No*, 2012).

As argued above, Larraín is invested in avoiding the pristine image and lack of texture created by the digital camera, as his peculiar cinematography attempts to leave a mark. In his study on the Derridean concept of the archive, Wolfgang Bongers also sees Larraín's filmic techniques as a way to counteract the ahistorical associated with digital technologies. Bongers explains how by referring to a historical event and using an outdated camera Larraín creates a double attempt to leave a mark. Bongers, drawing on Jacques Derrida, explains how any attempt to recreate the past is a performative act that always leaves a remnant, a trace behind.[20] This haunting past and its impunity is invoked by a shallow focus that blurs the background, but also by the use of the tube cameras to create and recreate the archive and its moments of blurriness.

The precariousness of the blurred image can also be extrapolated to the precariousness of the Chilean transition to democracy. In *No*, the political transition implies a reconfiguration that presents the insidious persistence of neoliberalism. In fact, as one of the characters of the No campaign states, the economic triumph of the dictatorship and its legacy entailed that 40 percent of the Chilean population lives below the poverty line. Or as the Italian philosopher Roberto Esposito observes, "modern democracy speaks a language that is opposed to that of community insofar as it always has introjected into it an immunitary imperative."[21] In the Chilean case, we can also consider the immunity of Pinochet himself.[22] Pinochet accepted the plebiscite results knowing that the constitution ensured him diplomatic impunity.

In the film's aesthetics, while scenes with characters on the left spectrum of politics are blurred, the right-wing conservative Yes campaign never gets this treatment and instead the image acquires a more defined presence. It is also presented with more normative conventions. There are two scenes in which this defined presence recreates the Janus-faced aesthetic of impunity. If the trauma remnants and ambivalent victory of the No campaign are shown together backstage with the blurred image, the scenes of the Yes campaign are shown defined by an insistence on covering up the mark of the unseen. This unseen is defined by economic inequality, torture, and political repression. This becomes explicit when one of Pinochet's ministers explains to Guzmán that the plebiscite is a way to legitimatize Pinochet abroad and requests he keep his eyes shut when entering the office where the Yes campaign will be discussed. In the previous scene, in the orange garden of Santiago Palace, the minister tells Guzmán that his paranoia comes from allowing communists and homosexuals into his office, reinforcing the representation of the Pinochet regime as a normative accepted discourse and that of homosexuality and communism as deviant.

Even more symbolic is the fact that in this scene a minister is using a cannon as a dustbin to throw his orange peels away—as the dustbin of history for an army minister, which in itself becomes a visual metaphor for covering up history. Later, inside the office where they discuss the Yes campaign, Guzmán listens to an Argentine executive hired to defend Pinochet's image and economic achievements against the No campaign. Guzmán explains that Pinochet's image and economic achievements are not enough to counteract universal values, such as "happiness," used by Saavedra. Guzmán's criticism of the Yes campaign up to this moment makes him the new mastermind behind the efforts to turn it into a successful campaign. Nevertheless, it ends up failing against the upbeat energy created by Saavedra, selling democracy as a happy product. Paradoxically, the thrill of defending the happiness of ending the Pinochet dictatorship as a product that you can consume does not seem too far from the preliminary speech by the Argentinian executive hired by Pinochet politicians and supporters to defend the initial Yes campaign through the idea of prosperity. The Argentinian believes that the correct strategy to hold out the country's votes is the promise that under Pinochet anyone can achieve wealth: "mind you," he adds, "anyone; not everyone."[23] As Dierdra Reber explains, Larraín's scriptwriter Pedro Peirano brilliantly represents the hidden verticality within the concept of equal opportunity, which Reber equates to the myth of the American dream: "the rhetorical sleight of hand of equal opportunity is that democracy and fair distribution of resources exists only in the hypothetical; in reality, only a lucky few achieve this prosperity."[24] This approach to a democracy linked to neoliberalism entails the idea that in order to become possible, a new post-Pinochet Chilean ideal of a nation has to exclude, and as such be immune to, a past and a present of those more affected by social inequality. In his study of the etymological origin of the word *community*, Esposito states that the idea of community corresponds with its opposite "immunization" in a kind of originary co-belonging. He explains: "if the members of the communitas are bound by the same law, by same duty, or gift to give (the meanings of *munus*), immunis is he or she who is exempt or exonerated from these."[25] Esposito adds that "Immunis is he or she who has no obligations towards the other and can therefore conserve his or her own essence intact as subject and owner of himself or herself."[26] The trace of the blurred image in *No* points toward those who are left inside the community, but who are not immune to the awareness of the implications brought forward by the No campaign, as the transition to democracy in Chile through the plebiscite is presented as a continuation of Pinochet's neoliberal policies.

North American celebrities and philanthropists supported the No campaign financially to help put an end to Pinochet's human rights violations. Larraín incorporates archival footage with Jane Fonda, Richard Dreyfuss, and Christopher Reeve. Nevertheless, this support did not enable the No campaign to imagine a system that would eliminate the socioeconomic asymmetries created by neoliberalism. As Reber underlines, "Free-market capitalism is not just about economics" since this also engenders "a way of 'thinking' as a way of feeling; a way of organizing what Jacques Rancière calls the 'distribution of the sensible' in the world."[27] However, Larraín turns the spectator into a witness of an unclear reality with the sequence of the victory through his aesthetics of impunity. As viewers, through a point-of-view shot, we see what Saavedra sees. The camera is placed just behind him, and with a shallow focus we see a blurred victory in the background, the blurred victory of the end of Pinochet as president but not the end of neoliberalism as a legacy of his government.

EL CLUB: A BLURRED IMPUNITY

While *No* is about the creation of images that will compete in a democratic election for votes, *El club* is about uncovering the truth in history and fiction. Both expose how the covering up works: the immunity of those unpunished as well as the exertion of power over vulnerable victims. As in *No*, the concept of "immunization" relative to impunity is also prevalent in *El club*. The title itself refers to a type of exclusive community protected from outside judgment. In *El club*, the priests' community inside the house knows itself to be under threat and is aware that what keeps it together and immune to punishment is what it is able to hide, the unseen. Larraín connects his trilogy with the chamber piece *El club*. For him, "The trilogy is basically a different text on the logic of impunity. With *El club* it's another sort of impunity. Every structure of power has impunity."[28] In this case, Larraín sees a paradox because the church in Chile also helped the victims of violence and torture while the dictatorship was active. As the documentary *Habeas Corpus* (2015) by Claudia Barril and Sebastián Moreno examines, the Vicariate of Solidarity, an agency of the Catholic Church, helped to halt abuses of the Pinochet government. *El club* explores the culture of silence inherited from the dictatorship in the story of a group of priests isolated in a retirement home, a Vatican safe-house, in a secluded Chilean coastal town. The stasis, or aimless motion, in this film occurs through silent long shots that give form to the idea that remorse for the crimes committed never takes place; it appears as an invisible cold violence in the "distribution of the sensible." This goes together with filmic techniques such as shallow-focus Soviet LOMO anamorphic lenses and blue filters, alternated talking head shots, and ellipsis of scenes of violence that try to increase the sense of impunity with a contrast between close-ups inside the house and long shots outside.

Most of the action happens inside or around the house, which takes on the role of a character, where its dwellers live in apparent harmony. A dramatic event disrupts their sense of community, threatening the impunity and immunity that church protection provided. The Church ends up restoring this immunity but not without a certain ambiguity. The event is the arrival and suicide of a new priest, after he hears his crime spoken aloud outside the house by the victim of sexual abuse who follows him there. The sense of uneasiness is also prevalent in the film, establishing the suspense of a detective narrative, where the camera and the characters' points of view do not often coincide. In the first opening sequence a chain of four long shots creates this sensation of stillness or senseless motion that ends with a blurred horizon or blue whiteness of shallow focus seen through the windows from the inside of the house. In these shots we see the priests in their daily routines. Lenses with a blue filter were used to create a strange sense of time. It is never clear during what part of the day the narrative develops. There is a blurring of time in the image between day/sunset and night/sunrise: the outside light seeps into the house and further accentuates a sense of stasis and mystery. The specific use of light is an element not just of the film's form but also of its content, marked at the beginning of the film with the sentence from Genesis 1:4: "God saw the light was good, and he separated the light from the darkness."[29] Sarah Wright, who further explains the cinematographic effects used by the director of photography, states that this use of specific lenses creates a "shadowy pre-hell limbo." For Wright, an ambiguity pervades the film that is "made palpable through the murky, gloomy light, symbolic in turn perhaps of the moral turpitude of the film's protagonists, whom the film refuses to condemn outright."[30]

The static sense of time is accentuated by the fact that the inhabitants of the house are allowed to leave it only in the early hours of the morning and late afternoon. The opening shot is of Father Vidal (Alfredo Castro) with a flirt pole moving in circles training a greyhound by the seaside shore in what appears to be the early, still dark moments of the morning. This circular repetitive movement seems to foreshadow the inherent habitus of the house's inhabitants, the routine they adopt of caring for each other silently, and also highlights the centrality of the dog in the narrative. The dog later becomes a metaphor for the silenced victims of the priests' crimes.[31] This initial shot is followed by a shot of caretaker Sister Mónica (Antonia Zegers), who is portrayed first as nurturing but turns coldhearted later. She is sweeping the outside stairs in a compulsive, obsessive fashion (from right to left and back again), symbolically foreshadowing the cleaning of the sin and the blood of a priest who dies later. Then, inside the house, we see Father Ortega (Alejandro Goic) looking after a frailer priest with dementia, Father Ramírez (Alejandro Sieveking), while another priest is tending to the garden. Afterwards, the viewer sees them together, congregating by the seashore, training Rayo, the greyhound. After a still, long shot of the house, they are again inside eating together in silence before going to the village to make Rayo compete in a race. But the routine of the house is disrupted by the arrival of Father Lazcano (José Soza). After hearing the house rules from Sister Mónica, the priests hear the voice of Sandokan (Roberto Farías) from outside singing and screaming the sexual abuses committed against him by the newly arrived priest. Lazcano's turmoil when hearing Sandokan's screaming testimony of sexual violence ends suddenly when he commits suicide. The other priests try to cover up the reason for the suicide, because they want to keep their sense of community, and their impunity, intact. This only lasts until Father García (Marcelo Alonso), a member of a new church that wants reformation, arrives in the house as a priest in charge of dismantling the retirement/penitence home. He uncovers the house secret thanks to the speech of the priest with dementia who repeats Sandokan's testimony of abuse. The cover-up of Lazcano's death also presents itself as a symbol of the priests' insistence on immunity for the sins with which the house might be identified, as well as for each of the inhabitants' disturbing past: Father Vidal is guilty of the sexual abuse of minors; Father Ortega, of child abduction and trafficking; Sister Mónica, of mistreating a child she brought back from a mission to Africa; the army priest Father Silva (Jaime Vadell), reportedly of keeping secrets about cases of torture. According to Wright, the fact that the actors were given the scripts the night before filming gives an "immediacy to their performances, but the cuts between talking heads sequences is bewildering, distancing."[32] Also, the sense of community is created by their implicit understanding that everything must look as normal as possible, nothing must change their daily routine, no secrets must be unveiled to the public, otherwise they would not be able to preserve their immunity within the house.

While the character of Sandokan is presented as a victim, his insistence on voicing his past does not give him the total blurred treatment. In *El club*, it is the dog Rayo that gets this spectral image as allegorizing the silenced victims. The use of Soviet LOMO lenses, as Wright points out, "embeds a blur into the film's fabric in the sequence where Rayo is captured in movement while training . . . Thus the dog is here materially bound up in spectral projection, creating phantom alliances and divisions."[33] In one of the scenes we also have the bleached texture next to the dog and his trainer Father Vidal, who is most attached to him. Again, in one of the scenes by the seashore we see Sandokan and the dog as recurring and ambivalent victims around the priest. The initial shot of Father Vidal training Rayo reappears, this time, with Sandokan looking at them from above. The image triangulates the dog, the priest, and Sandokan in a threatening posture. Sandokan is looking down from above a high wall and is portrayed as a menacing figure. He circles the priests until he gets to the heart of the house. The repetition of scenes with variations on Sandokan circling/closing up on the priests is suggestive of a movement from the past to the present, and from the outside to the inside of the house.

Figure 8.2   Sandokan's gaze, a long take, impunity in jeopardy (*El club*, 2015).

The film could be divided into three sections. The first entails the setting of the house members' routines until Lazcano's suicide; the second, García's interviews with the house members; and the third, the various plots to get rid of the body of the priest who committed suicide and whose haunting presence is jeopardizing the impunity of the other members of the household. In this last part, the inhabitants of the house, with the exception of Father Vidal, kill all the grayhounds in the village, including Rayo. The killings are done in order to discredit Sandokan and eliminate his presence. Even though the villagers beat Sandokan, he remains alive and ends up being looked after by Father García, who decides to let him stay in the house with the priests so as to keep the threat he poses to their immunity inside.

The character of Sandokan reminds the priests (and nun) that they are as fragile as the victim's power to punish them. Described by Father Vidal as lower class "roto" ("broken"), he follows them around and camps just outside the house screaming for attention, loudly revealing his past. Even though these members of the club were not the ones who committed the crimes against him, they feel frightened that others in the village might identify them for being guilty of similar crimes. Sandokan, because of the crimes committed against him in the past, feels entitled to stay in the house. He wants the religious institution that pretended to care for, but in reality traumatized him, to take him in. He is presented as sexually frustrated and an outcast. Larraín's reference to the character of Sandokan and the film in general acknowledges that no explicit violence is shown even though the words and the atmosphere are violent.

The lack of emotional empathy in the film is suggestive of a cinematographic convention—sadomodernism—associated with the works of directors like Lars von Trier, Michael Haneke and predated by Fritz Lang, as a style that wants to shock the viewer. In her article on the cinema of Haneke, Moira Weigel explains what she understands by this type of modernism in relation to spectatorship: "Sadomodernism expresses its suspicion toward conventional cinematic storytelling by denying audiences the pleasure of conventional narrative and/or subjecting them to pain."[34] In almost all Haneke films, an animal dies on screen, but in Larraín's film, even though we see how the dogs are going to be killed, we do not have the explicit image of these killings. Larraín may be said to gesture toward the convention of sadomodernism with this film; however, for him what is not made explicit, but rather left for the spectator to imagine, helps create a sense of mystery. While "the sadomodernist uses cruelty perpetrated on-screen to terrorize his audience,"[35] in Larraín's film we are asked to imagine the terror of what is not there, the indeterminacy of the blurred, that which is marked by impunity. The stasis in the film is created through cinematic techniques such as long takes, and especially the use of the blue filter and lenses, which create a consistent blurred/misty atmosphere where the time of day is hard to discern. This aesthetics also expresses the idea that the members of the club never evolve toward any type of remorse.[36]

Beyond the theme of impunity, the film style is created with a texture that blurs defined lines and allegorizes a new commitment to the politics of cinema in what Harvey calls "the ambivalent style of contemporary Latin American filmmakers."[37] But Larraín's use of the blurred image also reminds us of what Rancière calls the mental image: "the image that has escaped from the directed frame of the moving image, evaded the formula of response to a received change with an executed change."[38] The time or mental image in Latin American cinema derives from a cinephilic wave of directors, but also perhaps in a collateral way to a concern in getting funding from international film festivals.

NATIONAL VERSUS INTERNATIONAL RECEPTION

Juan Poblete ascribes Larraín's cinema to a type of festival cinema, which is to say, the kind of cinema that is shown first in festivals abroad, and then locally, while addressing national themes; in this case, the themes related to Chilean history.[39] Both *No* and *El club* were selected as the Chilean entry for the Academy Award of Best Foreign Language Film, but while Haneke won the prize with *Amour* (2012) against Larraín's *No*, Larraín won the Jury Grand Prix for the Berlin International Film Festival for *El club*. Previously, his film *Tony Manero* (2008) had won the Hubert Bals fund at the Rotterdam

Film Festival, which privileges a type of cinema related to national realities but with a concern for specific cinematographic aesthetics and artistic value.

No was one of the first fictional films about the end of the dictatorship and it provoked a strong public media reaction in Chile. Internationally acclaimed, acquired by Sony Pictures Classics, premiered in Cannes, *No* nationally screened in cinemas for eleven weeks. In the same year, the Chilean comedy *Stefan v/s Kramer* was an unprecedented box office success and together with *No* broke attendance records in Chile. Larraín's filmic techniques might explain why his work has been so acclaimed internationally, but his national filmic subject allows him to also have an audience in Chile. The film *No* motivated unprecedented public debate because it was accused of being "both reactionary and a piece of left-wing propaganda."[40] In her account of the national and international reception of the film, María Paz Peirano explains how this public debate unfolded like no debate about a film has done before, the persistent wounds of the unresolved conflicts of the Pinochet dictatorship, bringing out the cultural fractures of Chile's political and neoliberal economical legacy.

Within fifteen weeks, *El club* sold 45,118 tickets at the box office and was screened in twenty-three Chilean cinemas, competing with the film *El bosque de Karadima* (2015), which sold 307,695 tickets and was screened in fifty-five cinemas.[41] Yet the fact that Larraín's cinema explores national events by means of an aesthetic that problematizes the relationship between the viewer and the image moves it away from popular cinema. Moreover, Larraín's cinephilic interest is more in tune with the history of an earlier cinema, both national and foreign. His use of Soviet lenses already suggests as much, and Larraín himself indicates why in his director's comments to both films. One of the reasons why Larraín's cinema is hard to categorize, in other words, is that it constructs a dialogue between the national and international histories of cinema, blurring the line between them. With this ambiguity, Larraín presents his cinema as the product of a form of auteur cinema that aims to dialogue with art house cinema to create an aesthetic of impunity that not only disturbs the distribution of the sensible of what can be seen as popular cinema, but also questions the role politics plays in cinema. Impervious to the cinematographic conventions of popular cinema, Larraín's filmmaking occupies a unique place in contemporary Chilean cinema that Carolina Urrutia calls "centrífugo," which is akin to the aesthetics of transnational film festivals that allow him a certain aesthetic autonomy.[42] In films like *El club* and *No*, this aesthetic contributes to the ambivalence of the image that complicates not just Larraín's place in Chilean cinema, but also the aesthetics of politics itself.

NOTES

1. Maria M. Delgado, "The Capacity to Create Mystery: An Interview with Pablo Larraín," in *A Companion to Latin American Cinema*, eds. Maria M. Delgado, Stephen

M. Hart, and Randal Johnson (Chichester: John Wiley & Sons, 2017), 461. Even though Larraín does not explicitly coin the term in this interview, he refers to his films' aesthetics in very similar terms, as I will explain later.
2. Pablo Larraín, "La estética de la impunidad," interview by María Muñoz, *Berlin Amateurs*, September 28, 2015: <http://www.berlinamateurs.com/pablo-larrain-club-la-estetica-la-impunidad> (accessed February 27, 2020). In this interview about *El club* and its reception at the Berlinale, Larraín refers to impunity in relation to ethics and aesthetics: "La palabra estética o el concepto estético se vincula con el concepto ético, transformándose en una sola cosa, que en este caso es una película que trata de la impunidad y sus consecuencias." (The English version is my own translation.)
3. Jacques Rancière, *The Politics of Aesthetics: The Distribution of the Sensible* (London: Continuum, 2007), 12.
4. Ibid., 63.
5. Ibid.
6. James Harvey, "Democratic Ambivalence in *Post mortem*," *Journal of Latin American Cultural Studies* 26, no. 4 (November 2017): 539.
7. Pablo Corro Penjean, "La dictadura y las enfermedades de la luz," *Literatura y Lingüística* 28 (2013): 89. In his article on the rhetoric use of light in Chilean art, Corro Penjean points out that Larraín's use of the conscience of light as tone and atmosphere can be read as a tribute to a previous generation of Chilean filmmakers (1973–90), and especially to the cinema of Cristián Sánchez.
8. Harvey, "Democratic Ambivalence in *Post mortem*," 539.
9. Ibid.
10. Eugenio Di Stefano, *The Vanishing Frame: Latin American Culture and Theory in the Posdicatorial Era* (Austin: University of Texas Press, 2018), 18. Di Stefano frames *No* in relation to a break in human rights discourse, because he sees Larraín's aesthetic frame as a "critique of capitalism primary and morality secondary."
11. Vania Barraza Toledo, "Reviewing the Present in Pablo Larraín's Historical Cinema," *Iberoamericana* 13, no. 51 (September 2013): 163.
12. See Robert Wells, "Trauma, Male Fantasies, and Cultural Capital in the Films of Pablo Larraín," *Journal of Latin American Cultural Studies* 26, no. 4 (July 2017): 504.
13. The film was inspired by Antonio Skármeta's play *El plebiscito*.
14. James Cisneros, "Precarious Images: Media and Historicity in Pablo's Larraín's *No*," in *The Precarious in the Cinemas of the Americas*, eds. Constanza Burucúa and Carolina Sitnisky (Cham: Palgrave Macmillan, 2018), 42.
15. Wells argues that *No* "visualizes how traumas were made invisible." See Wells, "Trauma, Male Fantasies, and Cultural Capital," 515.
16. Cisneros, "Precarious Images," 54.
17. Nelly Richard, "Memoria contemplativa y memoria crítico-transformadora," *laFuga* 16, 2014: <http://2016.lafuga.cl/memoria-contemplativa-y-memoria-critico-transformadora/675> (accessed February 27, 2020). For Nelly Richard, Larraín's *No* erases the marks between the historical and the present by mixing real footage with footage created using the U-matic camera.
18. Original Spanish: "Lo que van a ver a continuación está enmarcado dentro del actual contexto social. Nosotros creemos que el país está preparado para una comunicación de esta naturaleza. No hay que olvidar que la ciudadanía ha subido sus exigencias, en torno a la verdad, en torno a lo que le gusta. Seamos honestos, hoy Chile piensa en su futuro."
19. James Cisneros explains the relevancy of the U-matic in Chile not only during the 1980s, but more recently, as mainstream Chilean television has recycled the images made by the semi-clandestine video group *Teleanálisis* as excerpts in the fictional television series *Los 80* (2008–14, Canal 13), 45.

20. Wolfgang Bongers, "La estética del (an)archivo en el cine de Pablo Larraín," *A Contracorriente* 12, no. 1 (Fall 2014): 194.
21. Roberto Esposito, *Terms of the Political: Community, Immunity, Biopolitics*, trans. Timothy Campbell (New York: Fordham University Press, 2013), 39.
22. See Luis Martín Cabrera, *Radical Justice: Spain and the Southern Cone beyond the Market and the State* (Lanham: Bucknell University Press, 2011), 169. The Chilean government of the Concertación argued in 1998 that as a former head of state, Pinochet had diplomatic immunity.
23. Original Spanish: "Ojo," he adds, "cualquiera, no todos."
24. Dierdra Reber, *Coming to Our Senses: Affect and an Order of Things for Global Culture* (New York: Columbia University Press, 2016), 244.
25. Esposito, *Terms of the Political*, 39.
26. Ibid.
27. Reber, *Coming to Our Senses*, 246.
28. Larraín, "The Capacity to Create Mystery," 461.
29. Original Spanish: "Y vio Dios que la luz era buena y separó la luz de las tinieblas."
30. Sarah Wright, "The Muteness of Dogs: Pablo Larraín's *El Club* (2015)," *Bulletin of Spanish Visual Studies* 1, no. 1 (March 2017): 101. In this article Wright explains in detail the use of light in the film: "Cinematographer Sergio Armstrong's experimentalism led him to use a blue 'Day For Night' filter, normally used to film night-time scenes, but here employed for the scenes during the day, combined with an 'Enhancing' filter. The former diluted the colours; the latter brought them out. The combination of filters, with a palette of blues, greys and browns which give texture to the light, functioned in such a way as to blur the edges, breaking down boundaries and confusing the markers of time so that one is neither sure what time of day the scenes take place nor whether this is a story set in the past or the present."
31. Sarah Wright focuses on how the death of a dog articulates biopolitical regimes, human rights abuses, and child abuse.
32. Wright, "The Muteness of Dogs," 109.
33. Ibid., 103.
34. Moira Weigel, "Sadomodernism. Haneke in Furs," *n+1*, no. 16 (2013): <https://nplusonemag.com/issue-16/essays/sadomodernism> (accessed February 27, 2020).
35. Ibid.
36. No doubt the music in this film is consistent as well with the misty atmosphere created by lenses and filters. The use of sound and music is indeed important in Larraín's cinema but due to space constrains it will not be developed here.
37. Harvey, "Democratic Ambivalence in *Post mortem*," 549.
38. Jacques Rancière, *The Intervals of Cinema* (London: Verso, 2014), 21.
39. Juan Poblete, "National Cinema," in *The Routledge Companion to Latin American Cinema*, eds. Marvin D'Lugo, Ana M. López, and Laura Podalsky (New York: Routledge, 2018), 26.
40. María Paz Peirano, "Larraín's *No*: A Tale of Neoliberalism," in *Contemporary Latin American Cinema: Resisting Neoliberalism?*, eds. Claudia Sandberg and Carolina Rocha (Cham: Palgrave Macmillan, 2018), 136.
41. *El bosque de Karadima* by Matías Lira, released the same year as *El club* and *Habeas Corpus*, is based on real events involving powerful Catholic priest Fernando Karadima, who committed crimes of child abuse and pedophilia between the 1980s and the 2000s.
42. Carolina Urrutia, *Un cine centrífugo: ficciones chilenas 2005–2010* (Santiago: Cuarto Propio, 2013), Kindle. Urrutia, like Corro Penjean, places Larraín in relation to Cristián Sánchez's cinema. For them, Larraín's cinema refers to the effects of the dictatorship with aesthetic concerns in mind.

CHAPTER 9

Reimagining the Left in *Neruda*: Inclusivity and Encounters with Secondary Characters

Rachel VanWieren and Victoria L. Garrett

Neruda (2016), the latest release by Pablo Larraín at the time of writing, centers on the political persecution and escape of renowned Chilean poet, Pablo Neruda (Luis Gnecco), during the government of Gabriel González Videla (1946–52). González Videla, who was elected with the support of the Chilean Communist Party, turned his back on his leftist supporters once in office, making the Communist Party illegal in 1948 and initiating a campaign of intense persecution against known party members, including then-Senator Neruda.[1] At the same time, however, the Communist Party was gaining ground: it earned 16.5 percent of the vote in the 1947 municipal elections, garnered the support of more than half of Chilean miners, and had a number of elected senators, including Neruda, and three cabinet ministers.[2] While the main antagonism driving the film's plot is González Videla's government's pursuit of Neruda, the Chilean Communist Party is a central part of the film, with interactions between key secondary characters in the film and Neruda highlighting spaces of internal conflict on the left. Through their words, tone, and body language, these characters express frustrations with the Communist Party and with cultural icon Pablo Neruda, both of whom they choose to support but challenge to be more inclusive.

Larraín has said in interviews that in portraying the past, he has no interest in hiding that he is doing so from the perspective of the present.[3] Indeed, the explicit portrayal of tensions on the left seems to be informed by the importance that contemporary leftist political movements and parties in Chile place on fully incorporating a diverse constituency in their agendas, which would not have been central concerns of the Communist Party or leftist politics in general in the late 1940s. Present-day images of women, students, gay rights activists, and indigenous leaders marching together in Chile for myriad causes and flying flags of diversity are a far cry from a mid-century Communist Party that treated homosexuals as deviants and kept women in subservient roles.[4] And yet, *Neruda*'s representation of the Chilean Communist Party through key secondary characters gives visibility to characters who represent such diverse concerns. This chapter analyzes these characters as spectral figures that evoke groups historically marginalized within the Communist Party, whose appearance makes an affective demand on the viewer for inclusion. We argue that the performances by these secondary characters cast a critical light on the party's past while also reminding the viewer of the inclusivity that will be possible in its future.

LARRAÍN'S IMAGINED NERUDA: GENRE AND METACINEMA

Set in the late 1940s, Larraín's film is a fictionalized rendition of the historical police chase of Pablo Neruda. But rather than a history lesson attempting to faithfully document this episode in Neruda's life, Larraín draws on many of the ideas—often contradictory—that circulate about who Neruda was and places them within metacinematic framing devices to create "a riff on the legends that attach themselves to great artists."[5] As Ella Taylor aptly notes in her review of the film:

> [the character Neruda's] treatment of women, to say nothing of the workers and leftist politicians and intellectuals who faithfully abet his efforts to escape the authorities, careens between loving, evasive, and downright cruel. The son of a railwayman and a dedicated champagne Communist who hangs out with bohemians and intellectuals, Neruda is a political animal who fairly bursts with contradictions that Larraín delights in playing off one another ... Larraín's *Neruda* engages in iconoclastic play with clichés that have clung to a national legend.[6]

First and foremost, this is a film created for viewing pleasure and commercial success that capitalizes on the controversies surrounding Neruda's legacy. More than a picture about the man himself, *Neruda* artfully toys with different genres to blend elements of the biopic, chase film, cat-and-mouse, and road movie with classical film *noir* style, to create what Larraín has called "a Nerudian cocktail."[7]

Most notably, *Neruda* employs a neo-*noir* style—the Hollywood style in vogue at the time of the film's setting—in a metacinematic play that repeatedly draws the viewer's attention to the artifice involved in making a film about the past. Through liberal use of *noir*'s characteristic chiaroscuro and contre-jour lighting, eerie, dramatic, and suspenseful non-diegetic music, and a hard-boiled detective character, this film insistently draws the viewer's attention to its fictional—cinematic as well as literary—nature.[8] As Thomas Schatz explains in his tome on classical Hollywood film genres, the *noir* style and hard-boiled detective genre express anxiety about the arbitrariness of how the past is constructed, particularly through the detective who attempts to piece together a life and a story from material fragments and subjective memories, but also because of historic developments in filmmaking:

> As the style became increasingly familiar to both filmmakers and audiences, the tenets of American Expressionism became evident: style determines substance, mood overwhelms plot, narrativity (the *process* of storytelling) emerges as narrative, emphasis is shifted from the *what* to the *how*, form becomes inseparable from content.[9]

In parallel fashion, the return to this iconic Hollywood style allows Larraín to make a film about *how* one *might* tell Neruda's story.

Particularly through the fictional Neruda's apparent need to always be at the center of attention and action, the film emphasizes the importance of staging and performing over historical evidence. Pablo poses for several photo shoots, recites his poetry to captive audiences at lascivious gatherings, wears a variety of make-up and costumes to adopt different personae, and reflects on whether the events of his pursuit are unfolding as he had scripted them in his imagination. To the dismay of some critics and to the delight of others, rather than aspiring to historical accuracy, this film emphasizes that it is constructing the past by suturing together fragments, rumors, and clichés that may have happened one way or another.

Three key devices maintain an unresolvable tension between Neruda's legacy and his intentional de-monumentalization: voiceover, scene sequence, and jump cuts. In ironic contrast to the attention that Neruda commands in the opening scenes—whether in the Senate or a gathering of artists in his home—the police agent in pursuit of Neruda provides the voiceover, thus introducing us to the protagonist as a hypocritical and repulsive egomaniac who wreaks of seaweed. The voiceover conditions the viewer to loathe Neruda's lascivious lifestyle, commenting that Neruda and his privileged friends "don't know what it's like to sleep on the floor. But they're all from the left . . . It is said Neruda is the most important Communist in the world."[10] At the same time, we are always reminded that the detective is working with gossip ("it is said") and biased perspectives that insufficiently account for the poet's undeniable appeal. Likewise, the sequencing of the scenes intentionally juxtaposes multiple perspectives that both validate and exceed this negative characterization, refusing to assert a unified vision of the historic figure. This is especially clear when several shots of massive round-ups of working-class communists immediately follow scenes suggesting that Neruda is enjoying the cat-and-mouse chase that only confirms his importance. The individualized special treatment that Pablo receives from the party and his fans simultaneously portrays him as privileged and hypocritical while reinforcing the aura of respect and awe that he commands. Finally, several tense dialogues that constitute power struggles between Neruda and other characters have seamless audio but are disrupted visually with jump shots.[11] This style—made famous by Jean-Luc Godard in his nouvelle vague film *Breathless* (1960)[12]—can be employed for different purposes, but the effect in the context of this historical film is to cast doubt on the veracity of these tense exchanges, suggesting that they may have happened as one person or another remembered them, creating a sort of garden of forking paths in the past, or as Larraín deems it, "a Nerudean story overlapping with a Borgesian process."[13]

Thus, rather than a historic biopic that affirms or refutes any particular vision of Neruda, what we have is an anti-biopic that plays with the way a great story is told, the way a renowned writer's legend overshadows real life, and the inaccessibility of the historical referent, which is always just out of reach. The emphasis on artifice notwithstanding, it is important to note, as we mentioned above and develop below, that there are "moments of abrupt realism, serving as a reminder that the Communist Party's struggles in Chile had very real meaning for the mistreated working class."[14]

Before moving to our analysis of the realist representation of the Communist Party through secondary characters, it is important to pay attention to how the perspective and voice of policeman Óscar Peluchonneau (Gael García Bernal) frame the narrative. Although he takes the name of a historical detective who pursued Neruda for a time, Peluchonneau is a fictionalized character developed to frame the story through liberal use of voiceover and his developing attraction to the poet, who will gradually pull him into his orbit. While he fancies himself the author and protagonist of the story, commenting on the plot, characters, and settings as if the film were actually a hard-boiled detective novel,[15] his authorship competes with that of Neruda, who also attempts to write this story in such a way that he is the protagonist. In fact, Peluchonneau himself and other characters comment explicitly on the former's fictional status, playing with the possibility that he is a character invented by the fictional Neruda for self-aggrandizement. As Neruda's wife Delia del Carril (Mercedes Morán) will eventually insist to the detective:

> He wrote all of this long ago . . . In his mind, he's writing a fabulous novel. He has written about you. The tragic officer. He wrote about me, the absurd woman. He wrote about himself, the addict fugitive . . . He wrote about you, thinking about himself.[16]

Although he initially rejects Delia's claims, Peluchonneau later recognizes that "I also wrote about myself. And I sucked at it. I invented myself having no life. Alone. Loveless. The poet wrote about me as furious, instead . . . He even wrote an awesome death for me. A police death."[17] This artful use of metafiction allows the film to play with historic material, rumors, and clichés about Neruda (and communists in general) as expressed by Peluchonneau while also emptying them of any claim to narrative authority or truthfulness.

Over the course of the film, the detective will shift from aspiring to continue the legacy of the fictional Olivier Peluchonneau—described in the film as the legendary founder of the Chilean Police whom Óscar claims as his father—to accepting his status as a secondary character enamoured with Neruda: as one made "eternal" only because of his role in the poet's story.[18] Rather than a source of truth, authority, or insight, Peluchonneau comes to revel in his own failure as author, protagonist, and police officer/detective. Like Neruda's, Peluchonneau's character is explicitly de-monumentalized in a way that makes clear that this is a central theme of the film. His ever-changing story about his lineage is a prime example. While he introduces himself as son of the legendary police officer whose statue is in one of the government buildings he is shown admiring early in the film, his introduction includes a Freudian slip that belies the illegitimacy of his claim: he will later admit that as a son of a courtesan, he has no idea who his father actually was. In a parallel manner, his claim to live up to his father's fame proves false, as he will fail in his pursuit in increasingly humiliating moments, with Neruda taunting him by leaving notes in police novels, brazenly leaving his hideouts unprotected, and even averting the detective's gaze by disguising himself as a courtesan and a self-portrait in a frame shop. Peluchonneau's changing modes of transportation throughout the pursuit also reflect his de-monumentalization. When he exchanges his car for a motorcycle in pursuit of Neruda to the south in the film's climax and denouement, the shots of García Bernal in riding gear comically recreate the well-known motorcycle journey of Ernesto "Che" Guevara and Alberto Granado as portrayed in Walter Salles's iconic road movie *The Motorcycle Diaries* (2004).[19] Through the visual citation of el Che and Granado's historic/cinematic journey in reverse (north to south)—first in a motorcycle sidecar and later on a single motorcycle that, like Guevara's, will also break down—*Neruda* blends the prototypical Latin American road movie genre with a hard-boiled detective story. But in Larraín's twist on genres, the hard-boiled police officer does not emerge as a hero, nor does the traveler emerge as a revolutionary hero-in-the-making, as in *The Motorcycle Diaries*. Rather, he is someone completely outwitted, seduced, and overcome by the author of *Twenty Love Poems and a Song of Despair*, whom he initially despises. If the detective is a surrogate for the audience's consciousness, this shift in his character places us alongside the ineffective pursuer in this cat-and-mouse story: Neruda's always-elusive figure never ceases to seduce us, even in his least attractive moments.

The ambivalent representations of these male stars of the film—Neruda and Peluchonneau—positions the viewer among two fallible, flawed characters who are full of contradictions. The "venereal infection's son," as Peluchonneau eventually calls himself, is joined by desire with the "railway worker's son" and his "squid sweat," as he notes in his voiceover of his romantic encounter with Neruda's first wife.[20] In spite of his initial claims to the contrary, Peluchonneau is just like Neruda's fans (in addition to literally being his "follower" in the sense of pursuer, he refers to himself as "another half-breed in a history of millions of half-breeds" to position himself alongside the communist workers who adore Neruda).[21] Thus, with the police just as with the fawning crowds who gather to hear his famous poetry recited, "[w]e are shown Neruda's huge influence, as a Communist poet, over his natural constituency: the ordinary working man."[22] The ambivalent representations of these two stars of the film open the space in which to criticize Neruda as well as his politics, and to recognize both the lasting appeal and the significant shortcomings—i.e. its verticalism, machismo, and hetero-sexism—in the historic Communist Party. The inclusion of key secondary characters, whose representations we analyze below, reflects such critiques, thus reverse-haunting the film (i.e. present realities haunt the portrayal of the past, instead of the past haunting the present, as is more typical) with the kinds of greater inclusion that are occurring in contemporary politics in reality.

REIMAGINING THE CHILEAN COMMUNIST PARTY

As Juan José Beteta notes in his in-depth review of the film, the distance between Neruda and the secondary communist characters stems from their marked class differences.[23] Additionally, issues of identity are at play in the poet's interactions with certain key secondary characters which cannot be reduced only to class: the concerns of youth, sexual minorities, and women are portrayed as important. Diversity, which the Chilean left currently champions, was not a part of the party's agenda at that time. In reality, while the party historically sought to support all workers and improve their socioeconomic conditions, the Chilean Communist Party was socially conservative in many regards in the late 1940s. As Carolina Fernández explains, the ideal was for members to be hardworking, sacrificial, come from humble origins, and lead upstanding lives, according to the moral standards of the day.[24] They were celebrated by party leadership if they were exemplary partners and parents, in addition to their lives as active party members. In theory, there were some more progressive attitudes within the party: men and women were considered equals and marital separation was an accepted practice.[25] However, the interactions between Neruda and Communist youth, women, and sexual minorities that we analyze below appear as anachronistic insertions designed to question from a present-day point of view the party's prior (in)ability to absorb such a broad range of social concerns.

COMMUNIST YOUTH

At the time in which the film is set, youth organizations had only recently begun to gain traction in Chilean leftist politics. Nicolás Acevedo Arriaza argues that in the Chilean context "the second half of the decade of the '30s was a period of relative consolidation of the Communist Youth."[26] He points out that in the 1930s Chilean young people were migrating to cities in massive numbers in search of work, and the concept of youth begins to have greater relevance in Chile around this time. A youth organization known as the Juventudes Comunistas (JJCC) was created, and their goals were related to the "right to education, to improving working conditions, and the right to sports and healthy recreation among youth."[27] However, the party's greater goals often superseded these youth-related issues.[28]

The character in charge of hiding Neruda in the film is based on real life Álvaro Jara Hantke, a twenty-four-year-old history student whom Neruda biographer Adam Feinstein credits as the "main organiser" and "chief mastermind" of Neruda's hiding, with the Communist Party providing just cars and other services.[29] Jara had been part of the JJCC but was not formally a member of the party when he organized Neruda's escape. The tense relationship between the characters of Jara (Michael Silva) and Neruda depicted in the film—with Jara overseeing and planning Neruda's hiding places and travel arrangements with utmost care and Neruda often not respecting the restrictions on his movement and the delicate nature of his clandestine status—seems to be historically accurate in this regard. According to Feinstein,

> Jara handled the arrangements with almost military precision—too military and too precise for Neruda's liking. The poet did not enjoy being bossed around by a man twenty years younger than he. And Jara, it seems, did not have a much better opinion of Neruda.[30]

Like what takes place in the film, Feinstein recounts that Jara ended up tiring of Neruda's fickle demands and lack of respect for the effort put into protecting him, and quit his role before the escape to southern Chile.[31]

Jara's depiction as wise beyond his years—orderly and serious, with great burdens on his shoulders—resembles that of the party leadership, who interact with Neruda at different points in the film. Jara's poise and readiness to accept responsibility within the party seem to foreshadow the importance that youth will have in future generations of the Chilean Communist Party. Neruda, in contrast, is characterized as temperamental and childish. In a scene in which Jara challenges Neruda about his clandestine outing to a brothel and chides him over what could happen to him if he gets caught, Neruda responds angrily, attacking him for being young, rejecting his advice, and telling him to grow up. Paradoxically, Jara seems like the adult in the scene, remaining calm while Neruda loses his temper and goes on the attack when confronted. Their final encounter has a similar tone. In this scene Jara announces that he is leaving and not coming back because Neruda does not follow instructions. He wants to give the poet input about his escape through southern Chile, and once again Neruda refuses to listen. He accuses the poet of desiring a "great escape."[32] Rather than deny this, Neruda says that he needs this type of heroic escape in order to be "a popular giant."[33] Jara asks him to be more humble and, quietly seething, reminds him that "they're actually killing us."[34] He provides Neruda and the viewer with a sobering reminder that being a communist pursued by González Videla's government is not a game, a fact reinforced by short scenes in the Pisagua prisoner camp in the Atacama Desert run by none other than Augusto Pinochet.[35] In Jara's attitude toward Neruda we can feel the tension that arises from the sharp contrast between all of the individual, intimate attention and delicate handling that Neruda receives both from those who protect him and pursue him, and the *en masse*, violent persecution of the other anonymous communists shown in the film. Having these reminders of the dangers of the greater political context come from a young man, who is portrayed as someone whom Neruda should be taking more seriously, previews the leadership that youth will have in the party in future generations.

SEXUAL MINORITIES

During Neruda's aforementioned outing to a brothel, he has a brief, intense encounter with a male-to-female singer in drag who is performing there. When the man recognizes Neruda he stands, smiles, and opens his arms, markedly showing more enthusiasm as he continues singing. Then suddenly one of the sex workers, seemingly drunk, comes up and dumps a drink on the singer's head. A fight breaks out and the singer is very upset that she has broken his concentration and interrupted his performance for Neruda. The poet saves the situation and the man's dignity by going up and engaging with him. He agrees to recite yet again "Tonight I [can] write (the saddest lines)" from *Twenty Love Poems and a Song of Despair*. The singer holds Neruda's face, enraptured while he recites the poem, and then interrupts the recital by kissing the poet. Neruda himself then dresses in drag, in a prostitute's nightgown and robe, to disguise himself when the police suddenly show up looking for him.

Figure 9.1   A man in drag kisses Neruda inside a brothel (from *Neruda*, 2016).

Although the film would suggest that he was quite comfortable with the kiss and the man who gives it, Neruda's respectful engagement with this man would not have been typical in the Chilean Communist Party of the late 1940s. Alfonso Salgado points out that negative attitudes among the Chilean left toward homosexuality persisted into the early 1970s, even among young people, stating, "The tendency to link homosexuality with pornography, vice, and depravation was strong within the left."[36] When the singer is taken to the police station for questioning in a later scene he seems very nervous and worried, which was a justified attitude. Gay men in Chile suffered violence at the hands of police at that time and for decades after that, especially those who were sex workers, since sodomy was illegal until the 1990s.[37] However, in an anachronistic portrayal of this time period, the questioning is done with no signs of violence. When Peluchonneau interviews him, at first he seemingly lies when he claims that he did not know that Neruda was a communist. However, after that he changes to a more sincere tone and tells him candidly about how valued Neruda made him feel. He talks about the moment they shared and the respect he felt from the poet and the dignity that can come from art and being respected as an artist, recalling that Neruda called him "an art worker" and talked to him as a peer, "from one artist to another," "from one man to another," and "with human respect."[38] At the end of the police interview he lowers his voice to a more typical male register and tells Peluchonneau sternly that he will never be able to understand his special encounter with the poet. Unlike the scenes of conflict with Jara, Neruda's positive attitude toward sexual diversity and the singer's meaningful experience with him feel much more at home in contemporary leftist Chilean politics than in the context of the 1940s.[39]

COMMUNIST WOMEN

Even more prominently than youth or sexual minorities, *Neruda* shows women positioning themselves as central to this (hi)story. Most notably, Delia emerges as an anti-femme fatale: rather than taking a secondary or sexually objectifying role, this strong, self-assured woman effectively rebuffs any attempt to relegate her to a supporting role. Delia poses in the first political photo shoot with Pablo, engages in debates with party representatives as an equal partner, and reminds Pablo when needed that "the artist is me."[40] Even when he attempts to cast her as a hysteric when they definitively separate, Delia resists his false narrative when she later tells Peluchonneau that although Pablo wrote her as "the absurd woman," she—unlike the policeman—is not a fiction but rather is real and eternal. In their encounter, which is also filmed with disorienting jump cuts, Delia's version of the events destabilizes and essentially replaces Peluchonneau's voice, which allows her to emerge as a voice of narrative authority.[41] Even though his voiceover continues until the film's end, his last words confirm Delia's assertion that he can only hope to become eternal through proximity to the poet: "Neruda made me eternal. His art made me come alive."[42] The way that Delia challenges Neruda, Peluchonneau, and other characters can be interpreted as a reference to strong, prominent communist women in contemporary Chilean politics.

Working-class communist women are also important agents throughout the film, with party business and other important work being performed by women. However, although the role of women in the historic party was beginning to change at this time, there were still many challenges that would not be addressed until later decades. Starting in the 1940s there were some members who started to question the status quo, which led to "an incipient communist discourse of feminine inclusion and solidarity with sectoral demands, that is, the idea of a feminine front."[43] However, this did not greatly increase the numbers of women as members or leaders in the party, and as Fedora Rojas Mira explains, traditionally the Chilean Communist Party viewed feminism as a bourgeois distraction because they believed that the triumph of the working class would bring with it women's liberation.[44] In fact, upper-class women like Delia were looked at disdainfully for being frivolous,[45] an attitude that can be felt in the film when the party leadership look in at Neruda's and Delia's lives: they observe them enjoying a lavish costume party at the beginning of the film and later notice that Delia does not do housework, such as washing dishes or clothes. Another factor that contributed to women not being a political priority in Chile at this time is that they were not given the right to vote until 1949.

Fedora Rojas Mira points out that women who did become involved in the party sought out a new role and voice for themselves outside the home, even though they did not explicitly acknowledge this and their political work was

Figure 9.2 Working-class communist woman Silvia challenges Neruda, who is seated with his wife Delia del Carril and party detail at an upscale gathering (from *Neruda*, 2016).

often subordinated to issues related to domestic life.[46] For working-class women who worked outside the home, being involved in the party meant yet another responsibility on top of their domestic life and work.[47] The weariness and resentment that could come from this type of overwork is felt when Silvia (Amparo Noguera), a working-class female communist, confronts Neruda when he and Delia are sitting at the table at a dinner party. In one of the longest and most weighty interactions that Neruda sustains with a secondary communist character, Silvia drunkenly approaches the table to greet Neruda.

We learn that she has "cleaned shit for the bourgeoisie" as a domestic worker since she was eleven years old and been a member of the Communist Party since she was fourteen.[48] She asks Neruda for a kiss, which he agrees to, and then starts to become more confrontational with the poet about a number of topics. She makes fun of the characteristic tone in which he always recites his poems and then brings up the idea that the government wants to keep Neruda on the run, but not actually catch him. She asks him if, when communism becomes a reality, everyone will be like her—a maid—or like him, to which he flippantly replies that they will all be like him: "We'll eat in bed and fornicate in the kitchen."[49] The comment feels intentionally unsatisfactory, like an empty promise that fails to really engage with this woman's day-to-day struggles. We do not learn anything about her personal family obligations, but her frustration with her job is clear and she probably has responsibilities in the party as well. With her initial kiss we can see that she feels attracted to and fascinated by Neruda, but at the same time she criticizes the distance between his communist world and hers in a cynical and caustic tone. This direct questioning of a communist icon by a maid brings to the forefront issues of gender inequality, questioning the past from a present-day perspective in which women and their concerns are more fully incorporated into leftist political discourse.

These secondary characters show diverse socioeconomic, age, and gender identities coexisting in tenuous ways within the Chilean Communist Party at the time that the film takes place. Their intense encounters with the poet seem to criticize the past from the present, as Larraín openly recognizes about the film. Even if Neruda was always perfectly *pro-pueblo*, as some of the Chilean critics of the film want to claim, or whether he was a "champagne communist" as many of the reviewers argue, presenting the reminder of the issues that these people face, and the real work of the party focusing on them rather than on iconic figures like Neruda, is an important role that the secondary characters play in the film. Although the specific needs of youth, sexual minorities, and women would not be fully addressed for decades to come, they are highlighted in scenes that feature them as a future debt to be fulfilled by the party.

CONCLUSION

The Chilean Communist Youth Organization (JJCC) became very important in the 1960s, when youth culture gained importance in Chile and worldwide. Gladys Marín became its president, exemplifying the traditional characteristics that were celebrated in communist women—she was of humble origins, a young wife and mother, and educated in the Chilean teacher's college system (Escuela Normal)—while also representing the youth culture of the 1960s with her mini-skirts and taste in music. She became a party member as a young teen and, as she recalls in a radio interview with her dear friend Pedro Lemebel, an openly gay performance artist and writer, the "euphoria" and "chaos" of her era of the JJCC contrasted markedly with the more somber period portrayed in *Neruda*, which was characterized by gray and brown clothing and having already survived González Videla's persecution.[50] She states:

> I believe that my entry into the Communist Youth in the early sixties signified the meeting of two worlds, of two attitudes. The people of the Communist Youth Party of that time bore the burden of very hard years and previous clandestinities in their bodies. Pisagua had already happened for a part of the militancy of the Communist Youth.[51]

The JJCC continued to grow in membership and importance during Salvador Allende's *Unidad Popular* government.[52] However, this would quickly be followed with a new generation of Chilean Communists experiencing intense persecution and being forced into hiding after the military coup that ended Allende's government in September 1973. In the case of Gladys Marín, her husband was "disappeared" and she had to go into exile. When the party resumed its activities openly in the 1990s Marín became a Party leader and eventually its presidential candidate.

Today Camila Vallejo is a potent example of women and youth continuing to have central roles in the Chilean Communist party. She has been a student movement leader, JJCC central committee member, and Chilean congresswoman elected as a member of the Communist Party. As one of the key leaders of the student protest movement beginning in 2011 and president of the University of Chile's student union (FECh) at that time, she fought for educational reform, with the movement's signature achievement being that Chilean public elementary and high school education is now free. Both Marín and Vallejo are examples of women and youth leading the party in key moments in Chilean politics. The possibility of this future shift is foreshadowed with the frustrations expressed by the secondary characters Jara and Silvia in their encounters with Neruda in the film.

However, according to Chilean gay rights activist Carlos Sánchez, it would take until the end of the 1990s for the Communist Party to become the first group in the Chilean left to be interested in and involved with the fight for gay rights.[53] He explains that for this to take place the gay community had to prove that they were serious about participating in the party's other protests and movements alongside workers and other marginalized groups, such as indigenous people and religious minorities.[54] He recalls that the Chilean Communist Party formed "a working group on sexual diversity within their ranks" in the year 2000, and he attributes this in large part to Pedro Lemebel participating in Gladys Marín's presidential campaign in 1998.[55] In his aforementioned radio interview with her, Lemebel asks Marín about those who felt that they had to hide their sexual orientation to belong to the party in previous decades.[56] She acknowledges that this happened and that "within the party there was an attitude of tremendous distrust and rejection,"[57] and Lemebel tells of his own failed attempts to be accepted as an openly homosexual man within the party before the 1990s. However, Marín points out that by the time of the interview the party had declared "absolutely and with all of its letters, acceptance and respect for sexual diversity."[58] This more closely resembles the attitude expressed in the treatment of sexual diversity in the film: women and youth are powerful actors with voices that are heard, (male) political and cultural icons like Neruda are humanized and can be challenged, and a spectrum of gender and sexual expressions are possible without any kind of stigma or repression. In this way, *Neruda*'s secondary characters embody a retrospective desire for this change, which was decades away from happening at the time the film was set, but is very much underway today.

NOTES

1. From the beginning of his presidency, González Videla alienated the left and pursued instead favorable status with the US (Chile's largest copper buyer at the time) and the economically powerful in Chile, which left no room for Communists in his government. Enrico Mario Santí, "Prologue," in *Canto General* (Madrid: Cátedra, 1990), 48–50.

2. Officially a member of the Chilean Communist Party since 1945, Neruda subsequently won the Senate seat for a northern mining zone, far from where he was born in southern Chile and later lived in central Chile, where the Communist Party was very strong. Neruda had known González Videla for many years, and as part of a political alliance that included both Communists and Liberals, was Jefe Nacional de Propaganda in his presidential campaign. Ibid., 45–6.
3. Larraín has been quite forthcoming that his intention was to bring to life a certain spirit of the past, not the historical facts about the life of Neruda: "I'm a storyteller. I don't want to relay facts. I want to play. And to create a problem." José Teodoro, "The State That I Am In" *Film Comment* (November/December 2016): <https://www.filmcomment.com/article/pablo-larrain-jackie-neruda-interview> (accessed February 27, 2020). In another filmed interview, he and star actor Gael García Bernal speak of wanting to recapture through Neruda's character the purportedly lost role of the artist as a public figure with a huge impact on society, such as Pablo Picasso or the Mexican muralists. Anne Thompson, "Pablo Larraín and Gael García Bernal Discuss the Poetic World of 'Neruda'—Watch," *IndieWire*, December 16, 2016: <http://www.indiewire.com/2016/12/pablo-larrain-gael-garcia-interview-neruda-1201759041> (accessed February 27, 2020). See also Carlos Aguilar, "Omnipresent Poet: How Pablo Larraín Captured the Essence of Neruda Without Simplifying His Humanity," *Filmmaker Magazine*, December 28, 2016: <https://filmmakermagazine.com/100792-omnipresent-poet-how-pablo-larrain-captured-the-essence-of-neruda-without-simplifying-his-humanity/> (accessed February 27, 2020) and Manuel Betancourt, "Pablo Larraín on His 'Anti-Biopic' About Pablo Neruda & Gael García Bernal's Mysterious Face," *Remezcla*, November 23, 2016: <http://remezcla.com/features/film/interview-neruda-pablo-larrain-gael-garcia-bernal-new-york-film-festival> (accessed February 27, 2020).
4. On May 17, 2018, the Chilean Communist Party and its youth organization Juventudes Comunistas (JJCC) reaffirmed their commitment to supporting sexual diversity by hanging rainbow flags on the front of their office building in Santiago. At the event the current president of the JJCC, Camilo Sánchez, clearly stated the party's goals for societal transformation for all minority groups: "we must build a different society from the current one, which has been naturalized through various methods, and our role as Communists is to eradicate any type of domination, be it based on class, race, gender, or anything else." (Original Spanish: "debemos construir una sociedad distinta a la actual, la cual se ha buscado naturalizar a través de diversas formas, y nuestro rol como Comunistas es erradicar cualquier tipo de dominación, sea de clase, racial, de género u otro tipo.") Manuel Da Corte, "PC y JJCC izan banderas de la diversidad en el día contra la homolesbobitransfobia," Partido Comunista de Chile, May 18, 2018: <http://www.pcchile.cl/2018/05/18/pc-y-jjcc-izan-banderas-de-la-diversidad-en-el-dia-contra-la-homolesbobitransfobia> (accessed February 27, 2020).
5. Ryan Gibley, "Lives of the Poets: New Films Explore the Stories of Pablo Neruda and James Baldwin," *New Statesman Magazine*, April 6, 2017, 78: <https://www.newstatesman.com/culture/film/2017/04/lives-poets-new-films-explore-stories-pablo-neruda-and-james-baldwin> (accessed February 27, 2020). This film frustrates the desire for historicity of reviewers who, like Maximiliano Salinas, find Larraín's inventiveness "fastidioso" (tiresome). Maximiliano Salinas, "El fastidioso y poco creíble Neruda de Pablo Larraín" *El Mostrador*, August 16, 2016: <http://www.elmostrador.cl/cultura/2016/08/16/el-fastidioso-y-poco-creible-neruda-de-pablo-larrain>. For those interested in the line between historical fact and fiction, however, see Beatriz Díez, "5 cosas que son reales y 3 que no tanto en '*Neruda*,' la película sobre el poeta chileno nominada a los Globos de Oro," *BBC Mundo*, January 5, 2017: <http://www.bbc.com/mundo/noticias-38374598>

(accessed February 27, 2020). For an excellent contextualization of the modes of production and reception of Larraín's earlier work, see Leah Kemp, "La amoralidad del individualismo en *Tony Manero* y sus antecesores," in *El estado de las cosas: cine latinoamericano en el nuevo milenio*, eds. Gabriela Copertari and Carolina Sitnisky (Madrid: Iberoamericana; Frankfurt am Main: Vervuert, 2015), 205–28.
6. Ella Taylor, "'Neruda' Affectionately Dismantles the Myth Surrounding the Chilean Poet," *NPR.org*, December 29, 2016: <https://www.npr.org/2016/12/29/507376652/neruda-affectionately-dismantles-the-myth-surrounding-the-chilean-poet> (accessed February 27, 2020).
7. Betancourt, "Pablo Larraín on His 'Anti-Biopic.'"
8. Larraín has described his filming technique to create this effect: "We shot on digital, and we used anamorphic lenses, but we filtered it a lot. With the help of production designer Estefania Larrain and Sergio Armstrong, the DP, we built this aesthetic that is in motion, not just because we are moving the camera, but also because we had 70 locations. We never spent more than two days in one place, so we were always moving and finding different light conditions, and try to capture them with a color palette, speed and rhythm that would ideally just belong to Neruda." Aguilar, "Omnipresent Poet." It should be noted that like other directors from Latin America working within transnational contexts of production, Larraín works with elements from recognizable Hollywood genres but repurposes them with local histories and cultural codes to create hybrid representations. See Luisela Alvaray, "Hybridity and Genre in Transnational Latin American Cinemas," *Transnational Cinemas* 4, no. 1 (January 2013): 67–87: <https://doi.org/10.1386/trac.4.1.67_1> (accessed February 27, 2020).
9. Thomas Schatz, *Hollywood Genres: Formulas, Filmmaking, and the Studio System* (New York: McGraw-Hill, 1981), 115.
10. Original Spanish: "no saben lo que es dormir en el suelo, pero son todos rojos . . . Dicen que Neruda es el comunista más famoso del mundo." Pablo Larraín, *Neruda*. DVD (The Orchard, 2016).
11. Jump shots are employed when Neruda verbally spars with Senate president Alessandri, his then-wife Delia del Carril, his minder Álvaro Jara, and the landowner who facilitates his final escape through the southern Andes; they also disrupt the extended (approximately five-minute) showdown between Delia and Óscar Peluchonneau, when she informs him that Neruda authored this story and reserved the role of protagonist for himself and when she emerges as the voice of truth in the film.
12. Interviewer Anne Thompson notes this, with Larraín acknowledging his inspiration taken from Godard. Thompson, "Pablo Larraín and Gael García Bernal Discuss the Poetic World of 'Neruda'—Watch."
13. Ibid. Various reviewers have also deemed the film Borgesian. See Sarah Lyall, "Pablo Larraín on His Latest Films, 'Jackie' and 'Neruda,'" *The New York Times*, May 9, 2018: <https://www.nytimes.com/2016/12/15/movies/pablo-larrain-interview-jackie-neruda.html> (accessed February 27, 2020); Christian Ramírez, "Pablo Según Pablo," *Revista Capital*, August 4, 2016: <http://www.capital.cl/pablo-segun-pablo/> (accessed February 27, 2020); and Adam Feinstein, "Fast, Loose and Lyrical: Pablo Larraín's Neruda Anti-Biopic," *The Guardian*, April 6, 2017: <http://www.theguardian.com/film/2017/apr/06/neruda-pablo-larrain-biopic> (accessed Febuary 25, 2020).
14. Jay Weissberg, "Film Review: 'Neruda,'" *Variety*, May 13, 2016: <http://variety.com/2016/film/festivals/cannes-film-review-neruda-1201773713> (accessed Febuary 25, 2020).
15. For example, when he first appears on screen in shots whose lighting and soundtrack evoke classical Hollywood detective films, Peluchonneau comments, "This is where I

come in. I must enter. I'm coming from the blank page. I'm coming to find my black ink. This is the cop's entrance." (Original Spanish: "Aquí entro yo. Tengo que entrar. Vengo de la página en blanco. Vengo a buscar mi tinta negra. Aquí entra el policía.") He proceeds to comment in this fashion on various recognizable cliché elements of the genre, such as introducing the confession scene, "This is a good example of a whispered confession" (original Spanish: "Este es un buen ejemplo de una confesión a susurros"); commenting on the moment when he kisses Neruda's ex-wife Maria Haagenaar, "The scavenger wolf's kiss" (El beso del lobo carroñero); and signaling when the chase intensifies, "This hunt is lacking terror." (Original Spanish: "a esta persecución le falta terror.") Larraín, *Neruda*.

16. Original Spanish: "Él tiene escrito esto desde antes . . . En su cabeza está escribiendo una novela fascinante. Él te escribió a ti. Policía trágico. Me escribió a mí, una mujer absurda, y se escribió a él, el fugitivo vicioso . . . Él te escribió a ti, pensando en él." In fact, Delia fearlessly "schools" the naive detective, condescendingly pointing out: "You don't get it, do you? You don't get a thing . . . In this fiction, we're all around the main character . . . Books, for example. This one. You have been reading it. It's got a hunter, a runaway, a starring role, and a supporting role. Why do you think he did not kill you, then? . . . Because he wants you to chase him down to the south." (Original Spanish: "Usted no entiende, no? No entendés nada . . . En esta ficción todos giramos alrededor del protagonista. Los libros, por ejemplo. Este. Que usted ha estado leyendo. Tiene un perseguidor, un fugitivo, un principal, y un secundario . . . Por qué crees que no te mató entonces? . . . Él quiere que lo sigas hasta el sur.") She proceeds to retell the whole movie, complete with a montage of previous events, this time with Neruda gleefully watching Peluchonneau in his "impotent" (*impotente*) pursuit. She concludes with an explicit reference to Peluchonneau's sexual desire for Neruda: "All detectives are in love. And all detective novels have beds" (Original Spanish: "Todos los detectives están enamorados. Y en todas las novelas policiales hay camas.") Ibid.

17. Original Spanish: "Yo también me escribí, y lo hice pésimo. Me inventé sin vida, solo, sin amor. En cambio, el poeta me inventó furioso . . . Me escribió una muerte fabulosa, una muerte policial." Ibid.

18. As he lies dying in the snow, Peluchonneau's voiced-over monologue suggests that he is at peace with Delia's account: "I was after the eagle, but I can't fly . . . I lived my life believing that I was a Peluchonneau . . . Yet, now, now I think I might have been a Neruda. A son to the people . . . But I die white. Because no one else persecuted the poet . . . I don't care that he wrote about me. That he made me a supporting character." (Original Spanish: "Perseguí el águila, pero no sé volar . . . Viví creyendo que yo era un Peluchonneau . . . Sin embargo, ahora, pienso que tal vez fui un Neruda, un hijo del pueblo . . . Pero me muero blanco. Porque nadie más siguió al poeta . . . No me importa que me haya escrito, que me haya hecho secundario.") Ibid.

19. The connection is not lost on the actor/director pair, as Larraín acknowledges: "So it's funny, Gael keeps saying this and it's true, that when he did *The Motorcycle Diaries*, which is this trip all over South America that Che Guevara did with his friend, it's the same years. So that's the moment. These were people who wanted to change the world." Betancourt, "Pablo Larraín on His 'Anti-Biopic.'"

20. Original Spanish: "hijo de infección venérea; hijo de obrero ferroviario; sudor de calamar." Larraín, *Neruda*.

21. Original Spanish: "otra cabeza negra en la historia de cabezas negras." Ibid.

22. Feinstein, "Fast, Loose and Lyrical." There are multiple instances in the film in which adoring fans show the poet's broad appeal when they beg Neruda to recite his famous love poetry, and we hear the familiar first line of the last poem from *Twenty Love Poems and A Song of Despair* (*Veinte poemas de amor y una canción desesperada*)—"Tonight I [can]

write the saddest lines" (Puedo escribir los versos más tristes esta noche)—in Neruda's characteristic intonation. We are also reminded of the power of his poetry to denounce political injustice when his poetic rendering of González Videla as a traitor (later published in *Canto general*) is composed, circulated, and then read collectively with call-and-response in scenes set in prisoner camps. At the film's end, Peluchonneau more closely resembles Neruda's fans when he engages with both kinds of poetry, first asserting that his love poems are forgotten and replaced by "the rage poems . . . of an imaginary future" (poemas de furia . . . de un futuro imaginario) and then reciting Neruda's aforementioned famous line. Larraín, *Neruda*. All of these readings remind the viewer of the wide range of Neruda's poetry and the poet's role as a voice of the people in twentieth-century Chile.
23. Beteta's position is the following: "Larraín once again questions the Chilean left, showing the class differences between Neruda's world and that of communist-based workers. This contradiction is not expressed in ideological or political terms, since both the PC and its illustrious senator defend the same program, but in terms of social behavior and marked cultural differences, which the base does not refrain from openly exposing to Neruda, leaving him quiet on some occasions" (Original Spanish: "Larraín vuelve a cuestionar a la izquierda chilena mostrando las diferencias de clase entre el entorno de Neruda y los trabajadores de base comunistas. Esta contradicción no se expresa en términos ideológicos ni políticos, ya que tanto el PC como su ilustre senador defienden un mismo programa, sino en términos de comportamientos sociales y marcadas diferencias culturales, que los militantes de base no se ahorran en evidenciar abiertamente ante Neruda, dejándolo callado en alguna oportunidad.") Juan José Beteta, "'Neruda,' de Pablo Larraín: una extraordinaria película, exigente y provocadora," *Cinencuentro*, January 24, 2017: <https://www.cinencuentro.com/2017/01/24/neruda-de-pablo-larrain-una-extraordinaria-pelicula-exigente-y-provocadora> (accessed February 27, 2020).
24. Carolina Fernández-Niño, "La muchacha se incorpora a la lucha popular: la militancia femenina comunista. Una aproximación a la cultura política del Partido Comunista de Chile, 1965–1973" (Universidad Austral de Chile, 2008), 42.
25. Fernández-Niño, "La muchacha se incorpora a la lucha popular," 42.
26. Original Spanish: "la segunda mitad de los años '30 fue un período de consolidación relativa de la Juventud Comunista." Nicolás Acevedo Arriaza, "Un mundo nuevo contra el fascismo: las juventudes comunistas en tiempos del frente popular (1937–1942)," in *Un trébol de cuatro hojas: las juventudes comunistas de Chile en el siglo XX*, eds. Rolando Álvarez and Manuel Loyola (Santiago: Ariadna, 2014), 59.
27. Original Spanish: "derecho a la educación, al mejoramiento de las condiciones laborales y al derecho al deporte y la recreación sana entre los jóvenes." Ibid., 71.
28. Arriaza, "Un mundo nuevo contra el fascismo," 60–8.
29. Adam Feinstein, *Pablo Neruda* (New York: Bloomsbury, 2008), 204.
30. Ibid., 204–5.
31. Ibid., 222.
32. Original Spanish: "escape grandioso." Larraín, *Neruda*.
33. Original Spanish: "un gigante popular." Ibid.
34. Original Spanish: "nos están matando de verdad." Ibid.
35. Pisagua was a notorious military detention center used early in the Pinochet dictatorship and where one of the first mass graves of his regime was discovered. The site in Chile's northern Atacama Desert had been a place of sexual and political persecution for generations, serving as a prison for gay men under the military dictatorship of Carlos Ibáñez del Campo (1927–31), an internment camp for citizens of enemy nations during World War II, and a concentration camp for Chilean Socialists, Communists, and anarchists under González Videla, as we see in the film. See Lessie Jo Frazier, *Salt in the*

Sand: Memory, Violence, and the Nation-State in Chile, 1890 to the Present (Durham: Duke University Press, 2007), 161–88; Mary Helen Spooner, *The General's Slow Retreat: Chile after Pinochet* (Berkeley, Los Angeles: University of California Press, 2011), 57–8.

36. Original Spanish: "La tendencia a vincular la homosexualidad con la pornografía, el vicio y la depravación era poderosa en la izquierda." Alfonso Salgado, "Una pequeña revolución: las juventudes comunistas ante el sexo y el matrimonio durante la Unidad Popular," in *Un trébol de cuatro hojas: las juventudes comunistas de Chile en el siglo XX*, eds. Rolando Álvarez and Manuel Loyola (Santiago: Ariadna, 2014), 154.

37. Carlos Sánchez, "Obstáculos y alternativas políticas del movimiento homosexual en Chile," in *Varones: entre lo público y la intimidad: IV Encuentro de Estudios de Masculinidades*, eds. José Olavarría and Arturo Márquez (Red de Masculinidad/es, Chile, 2004), 45.

38. Original Spanish: "un obrero del arte; de tú a tú; de artista a artista; de hombre a hombre; con respeto humano." Larraín, *Neruda*.

39. As alluded to above, the anachronistic treatment of homosexual desire in the film extends beyond these scenes to interactions between Neruda and Peluchonneau. Whereas the classical police genre is known for latent homoerotic desire between detective and criminal that threatens to destabilize a strong heterosexist construction of masculinity, here the sexual attraction is overt and presented unproblematically, as illustrated in these lines by Peluchonneau: "I have him attached to me. And I'll take him to prison that way. I'll put him to sleep. I'll watch him dream. And I'll end up sitting on his chest." (Original Spanish: "Yo lo tengo abrazado. Y abrazado lo voy a llevar a la cárcel. Y lo voy a hacer dormir. Y lo voy a ver soñar. Y voy a terminar sentado en su pecho.") Ibid.

40. Original Spanish: "el artista soy yo." Ibid.

41. Original Spanish: "la mujer absurda." Ibid.

42. Original Spanish: "Neruda me hizo eterno, su arte me dio vida." Ibid.

43. Original Spanish: "un incipiente discurso comunista de inclusión femenina y solidaridad con las demandas sectoriales, es decir, la idea de un frente femenino." Fernández-Niño, "La muchacha se incorpora a la lucha popular," 45.

44. Claudia Fedora Rojas Mira, "¿Mujeres comunistas o comunistas mujeres? (segunda mitad siglo XX)," in *1912–2012 El siglo de los comunistas chilenos*, eds. Olga Ulianova, Manuel Loyola, and Rolando Álvarez (Instituto de Estudios Avanzados de la Universidad de Santiago de Chile, 2012), 356: <https://books.openedition.org/ariadnaediciones/143> (accessed February 27, 2020).

45. Fernández-Niño, "La muchacha se incorpora a la lucha popular," 58.

46. Rojas Mira, "¿Mujeres comunistas o comunistas mujeres? (segunda mitad siglo XX)," 345.

47. Ibid., 348. It may also have exposed them to sexual assault, as suggested when Neruda demonstrates everyday, normalized misogyny with working women, such as his typist whom he fondles in passing while she is working. There are several scenes in which he is shown reveling in being surrounded by topless women, both prostitutes in a brothel and party goers at his home. While the film seems to include these scenes in order to highlight Neruda's flaws, it should be noted that they visually reinforce classical sexist representations of female bodies, existing as narrative devices to advance the male protagonist's story or character development but not speaking, having stories, or otherwise appearing as fully human.

48. Original Spanish: "limpiando la mierda de los burgueses." Larraín, *Neruda*.

49. Original Spanish: "comiendo en la cama y fornicando en la cocina." Ibid.

50. Original Spanish: "alegría; desorden." Ibid.

51. Original Spanish: "creo que mi ingreso a la Juventud Comunista a comienzos de los años sesenta significó como el encuentro de dos mundos, de dos actitudes. La gente de

la Juventud del Partido Comunista de ese tiempo venía arrastrando también años muy duros y ya clandestinidades en sus cuerpos. Ya había existido Pisagua para una parte de la militancia de la Juventud Comunista." Pedro Lemebel, *Mi amiga Gladys* (Buenos Aires: Planeta, 2017), 79.
52. Carolina Fernández-Niño, "Revista Ramona (1971–1973): 'Una revista lola que tomará los temas políticos tangencialmente,'" in *Un trébol de cuatro hojas: las juventudes comunistas de Chile en el siglo XX*, eds. Rolando Álvarez and Manuel Loyola (Santiago: Ariadna, 2014), 128.
53. Sánchez, "Obstáculos y alternativas políticas del movimiento homosexual en Chile," 55.
54. Ibid., 54.
55. Original Spanish: "un área de trabajo sobre diversidad sexual al interior de sus filas." Ibid., 53.
56. Lemebel, *Mi amiga Gladys*, 81.
57. Original Spanish: "en el partido había una actitud de un tremendo recelo y rechazo." Ibid., 82.
58. Original Spanish: "absolutamente y con todas sus letras, la aceptación y respeto por la diversidad sexual." Ibid., 84.

CHAPTER 10

Surfaces in *Jackie*: Representing Crisis and the Crisis of Representation

James Harvey

Pablo Larraín broke new ground with his trilogy of films that engaged directly with events surrounding the Pinochet dictatorship. These films proved controversial in Chile due to the ongoing contestation around the official histories, from the events leading up to the election of Salvador Allende to the contemporary Chilean social landscape. *No* proved especially controversial, since it chose to revolve its story of the 1988 plebiscite around the director of the advertising campaign (in many ways, a cog in the neoliberal experiment that placed Pinochet in the first place). Like *Tony Manero*, and *Post mortem* before it, *No* presents events from "an ambivalent perspective."[1] This fraught position gives the impression that these films side no more with the traumatized mourners of past atrocities than they do with those that remain loyal to the dictatorship. As Nike Jung has termed it, this shift away from "evidential documentation to imaginative represents a shift away from empirical veracity"[2] and toward "emotional states that can be aligned with historical experience."[3] The ethical debates surrounding historical representation[4] and postmemory narratives[5] thus become crystallized. In these films, attention regularly turns away from *what* happens to *how*; from *when* to *how long*; from mimetic truth-seeking to phenomenological historical fictions that foreground "the structures of direct experience."[6]

As I have argued elsewhere,[7] Larraín's approach to historical fiction is concerned above all with what Jacques Rancière termed "the poetics of knowledge,"[8] which recognizes a negotiation that occurs between testimony and empiricism in historical narratives. Larraín's fictions are especially provocative versions of this, due to their preoccupation with matters of national identity and collective trauma. These films provide a way of intervening in ongoing public conversations, in ways that challenge the consensus narrative. This narrative is largely determined by a universalized discourse of dictatorship; detached from emotional insight; limited to restrictive testimonies within the narrow framework of bipartisanship; and ultimately lacking interrogation of more contradictory histories. With *Tony Manero*, *Post mortem*, and *No*, Larraín has utilized the ambivalence at the heart of history in order to mobilize the poetic potential of fictions, thus reorienting the constituent actors and timelines of historical events. This chapter explores the historical poetics of *Jackie*: a unique fictionalization of Jackie Kennedy's response to the murder of her husband, President John F. Kennedy.

THE KENNEDYS AND THE CRISES OF REPRESENTATION

The American governmental landscape changed in the 1960s. This change was rooted in the departure of conservative leader Dwight Eisenhower and the subsequent appointment of the liberal poster boy, JFK. Mirroring societal, cultural, and technological changes, the American public's fascination with Kennedy was—as is well documented by many cultural historians[9]—indicative of a new order of governmental personality. In hindsight, the success of Western leaders since Kennedy (especially noticeable at a time of high populism) can be rooted, in many ways, in the cult of personality surrounding his campaign for candidacy.[10]

Gregory Frame has drawn attention to the fundamental role played by film and television in the myth-making surrounding JFK, particularly to the role played by Jackie in the formation of their brand's iconographic imagery. Focusing on the *Life* magazine interview around which Larraín's film revolves, Frame argues that Jackie played a pivotal role in securing Kennedy's legacy through the invocation of "fictional, fantastical, and filmic metaphor."[11] Such was the success of this myth, Kennedy has since become the "idealised reflection of American leadership . . . built on a simple vision of utopian promise."[12]

The image politics of the Kennedy campaign fuses profoundly with a politics of the image in D. A. Pennebaker's pioneering documentary, *Primary* (1960).[13] The film's formal style is rooted in the direct cinema tradition, "predicated as much on a philosophical reawakening as on the portability of equipment."[14] This observational style sometimes clashes with the new form of governmental personality. Stephen Mamber argued that *Primary* was an "agonizingly artificial"[15] rendition of the *cinema vérité* aesthetic, confusing the receptive camera of Albert Maysles with artistic naiveté. We might instead note—with Jeanne Hall—Pennebaker and Maysles's visionary ability to capture the "planned political drama on stage,"[16] exemplified with Jackie's fidgeting, white-gloved hands, showing the "spontaneous mini-dramas"[17] that take place away from the larger picture of things. This intimate detail, critiqued by documentary theorists, is emblematic of the wider mediatization of Jackie. Both self-possessed to engrossing extents and stylized from outside by external sources, her public image echoes the ambivalent figuration of American pop cultural icons of the era, such as Marilyn Monroe.

The authenticity of Jackie's character is a question that Larraín mobilizes throughout. This is crucial in both a thematic and formal sense, since superficiality is emblematized through a conceptual preoccupation with surfaces. Insofar as surfaces govern the strategies of Brand Kennedy, Larraín is concerned throughout with foregrounding the scarcity of depth in Jackie's persona and the bubble she inhabits, thus mapping the surfacing of the political in textual, textural, and gestural dimensions across the diegesis. The film achieves this, as I will demonstrate, through a complex combination of visual textures that draw from diverse formal, historiographical, and technological choices. Echoing *No*'s use of diverse textures, Larraín creates a distinctive visual style by combining technologies of the past and the present, thus recognizing the ideological rootedness of representational images. Mediated content, fictional narratives, and the technologies themselves all exist as products of specific times and places, bound in a "dispositif" of politics aestheticized.

While consistent with Larraín's body of work, *Jackie* also needs to be understood in relation to the debates around the visual culture of Kennedy and his murder. Images of the event can be cited alongside the most iconic of the twentieth century. Yet for all their apparent signification (the shocking murder of a Western leader in the open and, with it, the death of a liberal dream), good semioticians know to distrust images and to attend to their more intensely coded signifiers. For Roland Barthes,[18] images are regularly rooted in cultural myths, reifying meaning and regularly detaching the text from wider historical contexts. In postmodern image culture, this has changed through the relentless recycling and repurposing of iconic images that "replaced history and virtually abolished historicity."[19] The contextlessness of said images renders them empty signifiers. In the contemporary digital media landscape, the meaning of images is always under threat through now-commonplace practices of appropriation. Where before, then, the image of the Kennedys in the motorcade might have signified the end of a great liberal myth,[20] its meaning today can vary wildly.

WARHOL'S *JACKIE* AND THE SURFACE

Jackie begins with an image of the protagonist in mourning, which might invoke immediately the film's context as a site of empathic engagement between spectator and image.[21] However, there is something unconventional about this particular image of grief, something that does not fit codified images of grieving widows. Take for instance the coupling of Mica Levi's strained strings with Jackie's vacant gaze as she walks toward the frame.[22] She is shell-shocked and overwrought, but also pristinely manicured, invoking immediately the tension between sincerity and performance that seems to define her public image. Ambivalently holding Jackie between states, this is a jarring representation that foregrounds a chaotic psychological crisis. Crucial to the film's innovation, too, this offers a more diverse experience of grief than the usual melancholic inertia typically associated with images of grieving women. Marta Zarzycka has contested the widespread embrace of empathic readings, in ways especially relevant to Natalie Portman's performance of grief. The grieving mothers of war veterans, for instance, are regularly:

> appropriated by the public sphere and framed within a larger, national context, effectively undermin[ing] the woman in her function as an individual and a lover, turning her into the fantasy of the weeping widow who has honorably sacrificed her lover to the nation.[23]

The reification of such images short-circuits any response other than a melancholic one, which restricts the grieving woman to the role of the widow. This is especially problematic with Jackie Kennedy. As a public figure routinely marked by notions of cosmeticism, there is a danger of simply reinforcing cultural myths.[24] This is not to say that Larraín recuperates Jackie's image. *Jackie* is by no means a straightforwardly sympathetic treatment of its subject. Rather, by challenging the popular conception of the grieving First Lady, *Jackie* attends to the broader social and cultural dynamic that founds and debunks popular cultural myths.

By staging this dynamic, the film implicitly creates a dialogue with Andy Warhol's series of works on Jackie's grief. Warhol produced over 300 silkscreens, focusing on eight images shortly before and after her husband's death. Lifted from their original context, reproduced, recolored, placed side by side, the series aggravates the conception that images of mourning can account for authentic experience. Cécile Whiting has argued that Warhol's images show how Jackie's private grief became public ritual; that her sorrow was not hers, but belonged to the nation.[25] Echoing Zarzycka's argument, Whiting stresses that the public image of Jackie is not her private self but a contrived image that Warhol exposes for its superficiality. Keith Tester makes a similar claim, arguing that these portraits display "the amorality of technologically reproduced images"[26] and ultimately shows up news media's "surface representation of the state and place of the individual."[27] Warhol's Jackie, then, is a harsh evocation of soulless celebrity, detached from human emotion and defined instead by surfaces. This theme carries over into Larraín's film.

The film centers on the interview Jackie gave to *Life*[28] after John's death and is structured around a series of flashbacks. The first flashback shows the filming of the famous White House tour, broadcast on CBS and NBC in February 1962. In one of several intimate discussions with Nancy Tuckerman (the White House Social Secretary, played by Greta Gerwig), Jackie faces her, practicing her introduction with her trademark husky whisper. Nancy tells her to refer to the White House as "The People's House" (now a common nickname) in order to "make it seem more personal." This is an early example of Jackie's manufactured public image. However, it does not show the staged performance as a deceptive act by a spin artist, but as though honed through training: she is working. From this angle, carefully designed self-presentation is the labor of a First Lady, in ways that do not mark the Kennedys' term out very much from that of the Eisenhowers' or Roosevelts' before them. This changes in the flashback that follows shortly after, though, when we first return to the day of the murder. Twenty-one months pass between the two events. The shift in Jackie's persona—from labored amateur to trained professional—is clear.

Jackie is shown, back to the frame, facing a three-way mirror, the two wings revealing two sides of her face, the middle blocked by the back of her head (and a famous arch of dark brown hair). The same husky whisper is heard rehearsing a speech in Spanish, which she will deliver to voters in Massachusetts, juggling her visit to Dallas with the next scheduled appearance. The cut shows her striding through Air Force One to accompany the president as they exit the plane. The sound of the crowd outside is audible as the pair are shown, side by

Figure 10.1   Jackie prepares for a campaign event (from *Jackie*, 2016).

side, in close-up. He asks if she is ready and Jackie's reply has the air of a sultry, seasoned performer. In this tone, the husky whisper brings about an erotically charged quality usually reserved for her diametrical opposite in popular culture mythology ("are you a Jackie or a Marilyn?"). If the earlier scene appeared to show Jackie's manufactured image as the product of duty and labor, this scene gives the impression of mastery, revising, in hindsight, the damsel-like image displayed there. And as she descends the stairs from the plane and arrives in the mass of bodies, the camera captures her flicking her fringe sideways, gazing out awkwardly, aloof, and overcome by the atmosphere. Therefore, the rapid transition between these two states gives the sense that Jackie's public image is no more than a surface that she can remove and replace at will.

The arrival scene also utilizes a formal language of feminine performance from diverse sources. With its use of mirrors, *Jackie* draws parallels with the melodramas of Douglas Sirk and Rainer Werner Fassbinder, as well as more recent revisionist melodramas by the likes of Todd Haynes and Darren Aronofsky. Frequently utilized in order to "embody social critique or a self-reflexive awareness of the conditions of representation,"[29] the mirror is used in *Jackie*—as in other melodramas—to seek "confirmation of her sense of self by habitually studying her appearance."[30] Yet as a reflective surface, the mirror allows for an immanent questioning of the image presented beyond the subject-centered notion of selfhood. By presenting a literal *mirror image*, the spectator is encouraged to view the image of Jackie as a construct, be that an ideological one interpellated from without, or a theatrical one performed as though from within.

This utilization of the mirror image along more or less Lacanian lines relies also upon its coupling with another familiar visual technique: the close-up. Mary Ann Doane detects a similar inclination to resolve the meaning of facial close-ups in binary terms, claiming that "theories of the face come to terms in some way with this opposition between surface and depth, exteriority and interiority . . . The close-up in the cinema classically exploits the cultural and epistemological susceptibility to this binary opposition."[31] Drawing on early film theory and silent films, Doane argues that the facial close-up usually regards the spectator as much as the image, assuring us that "we can indeed see and grasp the whole."[32] Visibility and intimacy hereby apparently lead to an authoritative image of the bigger picture. The facial close-up "acts as a nodal point linking the ideologies of intimacy and interiority to public space,"[33] echoing Zarzycka and Whiting's comments on the blurring of public and private self. Larraín's Jackie is constantly urging us to engage with the surface of the image so as to attend to its aesthetic design and never simply its emotional force.

Evident initially in Warhol's series, Larraín utilizes the binary logic of inner and outer depth in Jackie Kennedy's iconic image. *Jackie* demands we remain with the surface in order to appreciate its sociocultural design, regularly problematizing the view of Jackie as authentic or inauthentic. Instead, the surface provides an imperative aesthetic concept for the deconstruction of representational crises, originally explored in Warhol, but reformulated here in twenty-first-century visual culture.

REMEDIATION

In *Zaprudered: The Kennedy Assassination Film in Visual Culture*,[34] Øyvind Vågnes argues that the remediation of images throughout the twentieth and twenty-first centuries has complicated the public imaginary of historical events, even those witnessed by hundreds at the time, millions on television, and millions more since the event. Vågnes contrasts the reified emotional schema of *In the Line of Fire* (Wolfgang Petersen, 1993) with Christopher Brown's painting, *Elm Street* (1995), which foregrounds the potential for distortion in documentary images. Far from becoming reified and folded back into the larger myth of JFK then, the appropriation and restaging of Kennedy's death and the events surrounding it can have more contingent aesthetic effects.

The same subversive potential might be found in *Jackie*'s generic domain. Biopics are regularly guilty of contributing to the mythological tendency of reification. This is produced primarily, as Belén Vidal explains, through the "delivery of consensual pleasures related to formal conservatism."[35] As box office figures and middling critical responses suggest, the biopic represents a routine exercise in film spectatorship, frequently presenting the life and times of a hero in the orderly spatiotemporal domain of a clear narrative. Rather than departing from the present in order to seek shelter in the past, Larraín utilizes contemporary digital cinema's ability to bring together many different media forms, mixing old with new in order to refine and revise the archival images of representational media. In this sense, what Jussi Parikka would call media archaeology occurs: "new media remediates old media."[36]

The aim of this remediation of the technologies used at the time of the diegetic narrative is to achieve greater historicity (than that typically afforded by historical fictions). It recognizes the specificity of the media form as central to the effects of that signified. For example, while the historical fiction of the American Civil War has changed its narrative radically from D. W. Griffith to John Ford to Nate Parker, the technologies of each film's production are themselves imbued with questions of ideology. And insofar as the media product is itself, as Marshall McLuhan teaches us, emblematic of the technology, a semiotics of the 16mm, 35mm, and digital cinematic image reveals a historical dimension to be unpacked alongside the mimetic fiction that unfolds on-screen. By using technologies contemporaneous with the events depicted on-screen, *Jackie* broaches contemporary debates on the nostalgia of representational media.

SURFACES IN *JACKIE* 203

Figure 10.2   Remediating archive footage in the camera operator's screen (from *Jackie*, 2016).

The starkest use of this technique is the reconstruction of the White House tour. Jackie is shown in deep conversation with Nancy Tuckerman about how to best impress the public. She receives some words of reassurance before walking away from the foreground, deeper into the image. She greets the camera operator, and the introductory montage of the (real-life) televised program can be glimpsed momentarily on the screen of his monitor (Figure 10.2).

A cut then blows up these images and switches the aspect ratio from *Jackie*'s 16:9 to early television's academy ratio. We see the grand exterior of the White House and an authoritative voiceover reminds the spectator of the historical context. This mimics the images and sounds of the original. The cut to interior shows Portman's Jackie walking toward the frame, again impersonating precisely the pace and gait of her source. Her opening dialogue is lifted verbatim from the response provided in the original. Where slight details change, this seems to be an attempt to convey economically the characteristics portrayed in an hour-long program in the much shorter sequence afforded it in this film. For example, where the presence of a quiver in Portman's voice was not originally present in one statement, it can be located in later answers in the original.

One subtle difference regards the adjustment to the framing of Portman's initial entrance. Where in the original, the camera is situated at a greater height and at an angle (providing a stylized presentation of the depth of the hallways and splendor of the arched ceilings), *Jackie* utilizes symmetry, flattening the image and using the frames of doorways as decorative frames

Figure 10.3 Remediating archival photography on the surface of the windshield (from *Jackie*, 2016).

for the subject (again reminiscent of Sirkean melodrama). The stasis and positioning of the camera provides a disconcertingly staged quotation of the original film's spatial configuration. This repositioning of the subject at the center of the image is an unsettling reintroduction of quattrocento vision. It pre-empts other uses of symmetry in the film, such as the tableau reconstruction of Jackie's return from Texas, positioned too centrally alongside Bobby Kennedy, in a way both evoking and troubling the spatial arrangement of archival images.

Archival images are utilized even more daringly later in the film, as Jackie is shown in a limousine departing for the funeral procession. Visually quoting Clint Eastwood's moment of crisis in *In the Line of Fire*, archival still-imagery of assembled mourners is superimposed on the windshield and atop the face of Jackie. The window acts as a screen for the masses to be projected upon. And it is a projection, not a reflection, for those bodies in (Figure 10.3) the world outside the diegetic car are not the ones we see in this image, thus producing yet another fusion of old and new forms of image making, in ways evoking both the repressed in historical accounts and the ethics of historical reconstruction. Layering one image atop another—through montage and superimposition—the diversity of sources and histories is foregrounded through the clash and conjunction of the surface.

CORPOREAL SURFACES

Doane's take on the facial close-up regards the sense of physical proximity as much as it does interior meaning. She claims that critics' and theorists' preoccupation with the technique is emblematic of "an attempt to reassert the corporeality of the classically disembodied spectator."[37] Insofar as *Jackie* invites an interrogation of the surfaces of Jackie's expressive façade, then, its close-ups are also significant for the affective dialogue initiated with the spectator. This seems like the opposite to Warhol's approach. Where his series of works aggravates the common patterns of grief and tragedy, this view of *Jackie*'s close-ups would appear to favor more conventional notions of empathic reception and "emotional contagion."[38] However, rather than offering an antithetical alternative, I would like to argue that there is a corporeal intensity in *Jackie* that does not rely (solely) on a "semiotic phenomenology" reflective of "the universality of specific scopes of experience."[39] Rather, the corporeality of *Jackie* continues Warhol's concern with surfaces, beneath the epidermal layer. At its moments of graphic violence, the corporeal intensity of the film does not limit the potential spectatorial responses to the restrictive terms of empathy; it multiplies them. This promotes an affective response, apart from the immediacy of the narrative present and thus "disengaged from the customary constraints of spatial coherence and temporal chronology."[40] The material remnants of her husband's death force us to engage with the image in ways undetermined by what Davide Panagia terms the "narratocracy"[41] of diegetic or extra-diegetic accounts. Story, as the "prevailing regime of perception in the theoretical analysis of political phenomena,"[42] prioritizes seamlessly intelligible accounts in the historical archive. It thereby "commits vision to readerly sight while partitioning the body into specific areas of sensory competency."[43] *Jackie* foregrounds the materiality of flesh and blood in ways that attend to the historical value of bodily surfaces.

Analyzing representations of dying in mainstream cinema, Michelle Aaron writes of "a cinematic lexicon of dying" consisting of "self-sacrifice, saintliness, triumph, self-discovery, painlessness, stoicism, futurism, beauty and the good death."[44] *Jackie*'s presentation of JFK's death is very far from "good." His life is taken; the mythical saintliness—routinely expounded in popular histories—is mocked; disorder is preferred to triumph; a fraught crisis of selfhood is favored over self-discovery (of the dead and the grieving). There is nothing painless, stoic or beautiful about John's brutal murder in *Jackie*. Despite Jackie's attempts to describe her husband's broken skull, mass of blood and pieces of flesh as "beautiful," one cannot avoid the gruesome nature of the event. The corporeal effects of a bullet's entry into a head cannot be questioned and, as one of the few facts taken for granted in the film, flesh and blood offers a source of empirical evidence as it navigates "the poetics of knowledge."

Figure 10.4 Restaging the swearing-in of Johnson, with the bloodstains in view (from *Jackie*, 2016).

Reports from the events following the murder tell of Jackie's refusal to change her bloodstained dress. Images of Lyndon B. Johnson's swearing-in to office show Jackie in a daze. JFK's blood is hidden from frame, but its scent must be present, imaginable one assumes in the awkward expressions of the onlookers, the new President included. Larraín's foregrounding of the soiled dress throughout the film is a form of historical excavation, bringing to light something that has been suppressed in the testimonial archive (Figure 10.4).

Hiding the violence from reportage is a form of sanitization, which Larraín hereby interrogates. It is a continuation of the "restorative corporeality"[45] of *Tony Manero* and *Post mortem*, but in the very different context of the American liberal political landscape and celebrity culture.[46] One gets a sense of this in the reconstruction of the moments immediately following the assassination.

By setting the film during the aftermath of JFK's murder, *Jackie* promises to enliven its narrative with a spectacular explosion of flesh and blood, of the sort usually associated with horror films. For a long time, this does not arrive. Most of the film is more concerned with the bureaucratic dialogues that arise in response to the death of a president (in ways again highly reminiscent of *Post mortem*). We are deprived of the event itself; the spectator is left only with the aftermath. With no visualization of the moment of bodily penetration, nor sonic representation (of rupturing flesh and bone, gunfire, or horrified vocal reaction), the body of the deceased is privileged over the murder of the president. When Jackie is asked to describe the sensation of the event, we are shown the motorcade departing from the scene of the crime with the corpse of

John sprawled out over her lap. One can make out specks of red on the back of the car, but John's body is mostly hidden from view due to the angle.

This is subverted late in the film when, in counsel with a priest, Jackie confesses to having lied about her lack of memory of the event. Immediately a cut takes us back to the murder. A two-shot shows the aftermath of the first gunshot, with John holding his throat, but with no blood visible. A cut takes us, momentarily, to a side-on view of the couple with John in the foreground. This allows for a view of the bullet's impact rather than its flight and, as such, a more explicit rendering. John's head flies immediately back then forth; the blur of its movement covers Jackie's face. Its falling back is accompanied by a splattering of red across the frame. As it falls forward, the effects on his head (the amassing of blood; the exposure of the cranial cavity; the red-pink of the brain) are shown long enough for the spectator to note the meticulous detail afforded its depiction. His head hangs forward, revealing the horrified expression of Jackie, herself now caped in her husband's blood. This is the moment that is too distant in the Zapruder video and hidden altogether from the Johnson inauguration images. Blood—this blood—haunts the film, and it is in this moment that this becomes most apparent. As Xavier Aldana Reyes has argued, the common attribution of spectacle to violent images tends to conflate the affective with the appreciative/cognitive, delimiting the possibility for thought beyond the instrumentalization of diegetic horror.[47] Similarly, rather than criticizing the exploitation of harm for the purposes of spectacle, the gruesome portrayal of bodily harm contains the potential for something invisible to enter the image.

Yet this is not to claim that these images have a coded signification akin to allegory, either. Leveling the narrativized signification and the cold materiality of the body, the spectator is instead confronted with the bodily event of death in ways similar to the "body horror" of David Cronenberg's films, as analyzed by Steven Shaviro, who argues that they "display the body in its crude, primordial materiality."[48] For Shaviro, corporeal trauma depicts "new arrangements of the flesh [that] break down traditional binary oppositions between mind and matter, image and object, self and other, inside and outside, male and female, nature and culture, human and inhuman, organic and mechanical."[49] Such a new arrangement of the flesh exists in this image, which foregrounds the surfaces of John's insides atop the external surfaces of Jackie.

The spectator is thus invited into the reactivation of history, using a technique that subverts narratocracy through corporeal surfaces. It does this not through a "semiotic phenomenology" bound up in the mainstream "cinematic lexicon of dying." Rather, the "restorative corporeality" of these images "short-circuit the social logic of information and representation by collapsing this logic back into its physiological and affective conditions."[50] The crisis of representing reality is thus bound not only to bodies *representative* of crisis, but in and of themselves, thus exceeding "the limits of social control to the extent that they locate power and desire directly in an immanent experience of the body."[51]

TEMPORAL DISRUPTION

While using remediation to historicize the visuality of surface meanings, Larraín simultaneously engages in the reconfiguration of historical narratives through challenges to chronology and temporal experience. As Eleftheria Thanouli has explained, challenging models of linearity is a common tendency in contemporary cinema, as significant changes in the systems of causality, time, and space alter "the way the narrative controls the transmission and flow of story information."[52] A similar argument has been made by Jan Simons, who brings together poststructuralist theories of history and narrative with contemporary takes, in order to define a model for "complex narratives."[53] Citing Paul Ricoeur, Simons claims that narrative "configures" what would otherwise be a simple succession of events into a "meaningful whole."[54] In defense of complex narratives, Simons argues such narratives "remind us that we need to make our languages more complex to grasp the ways contemporary films cope with increasingly complex social and cultural environments."[55] *Jackie* draws upon this heterogeneous narrative form in ways contemporary with the time of the film's release; but also, divergently, contemporaneous with the crisis point from which the complexity of social and cultural environments (or at least the mediatization of that complexity) might have originated. In other words, disrupting the causal, chronological logic of classical narrative is not a mere puzzling affectation that can be located across Larraín's films; it is the formal structure that is most socially adept to historicizing this particular fiction.

Like the elliptical timelines reflecting the allegorical psychological crises of Raúl Peralta in *Tony Manero* and Mario Cornejo (both played by Alfredo Castro) in *Post mortem*, *Jackie* plunges its spectator into different times and spaces in order to reflect the effects of social and psychological crises that spawn from the event of JFK's murder. In order to get beyond the tendency for narratives that take place "within an uncriticized temporal framework, within a time that corresponds to the ordinary representation of time as a linear succession of instants,"[56] Larraín employs a narrative that disrupts linearity. The diegetic present appears to be the interview. From here, flashbacks take us to (among other events) the assassination, the funeral, the many bureaucratic discussions, intimate moments between Jackie and John, her discussion with John Hurt's priest. Sometimes these events are introduced more or less explicitly, through the *Life* journalist's related question. But there are other, more nuanced formal techniques used to redirect the narrative, such as the use of sound bridges fusing together past and present.

Visually, slow motion is also employed, as though bringing to the surface time itself, in ways reminiscent of Gilles Deleuze's "time image."[57] As with Deleuze's notion of the crystal image of time in cinema, "the past is constituted not after the present that it was but at the same time . . . it has to split the present in two heterogeneous directions, one of which is launched toward the future while the other falls into the past."[58] Collapsing both the present moment of the interview and the virtual past, *Jackie*'s narrative evokes the fraught sensation of a present enraptured by legacy and doubt. This might account for the unsettlingly overbearing presence of the White House, stressed through framing techniques and Levi's eerie score. Taking Jackie's lead in the White House tour, the film hopes to reinstall a sense of historical memory of the events that have emanated from this house. From national campaigns of enslavement and settlement (from Columbus to Washington to Kennedy, Johnson, Nixon, and so on) to a newfound regard for public image, the crystallization of time brought about by Jackie's remembering is an exemplary version of Larraín's founding of the present in the past. Two invisible entities—Jackie's personal and America's public memory—are brought to the fore, then, through the employment of disruptive timelines and the unsettling *tableaux vivants* of American colonial history. Jackie's testimony thus becomes a site of temporal coexistence between past and future.

CONCLUSION

Jackie Kennedy's personal crisis becomes a stage for the elaboration of social and cultural crises emanating from 1960s America. The film interrogates the surfaces of expressive performance, of the divergent textures of different media forms, and of trauma inflicted on the body. The surface becomes a fruitful aesthetic device for Larraín in ways conceptually similar to Warhol, but formally far more diverse. Like Warhol, Larraín is attentive to the superficial tendency of Jackie's image, formed for and through public expectations; but these multiple aesthetic techniques result in a subject more developed and complex in character.

Jackie's status as a cinematic work is crucial in this sense. Unlike the moralizing of Warhol's factory-line (as explained by Tester), Larraín broaches the historical development of technological reproducibility (now in its conclusive stage of immanent reproduction through the digital) in order to unpack a history of Western image culture, refiguring the event through a disruption to chronology and crystal images, objects, and tableaux. That *Jackie* is Larraín's first Hollywood film is significant in this sense, too. It brings to bear aesthetic techniques utilized across his Pinochet trilogy on the industry whose "reactionary cultural fanaticism wholeheartedly serves [the] methodical idolization of individuality."[59] Max Horkheimer and Theodor Adorno's observation on the cult of personality in popular culture is mapped on to the new governmental images initiated by Brand Kennedy. The moment of the protagonist's personal crisis brings to light a dual consciousness, which is itself the product of a contemporaneous crisis: that of representation in twentieth-century global media.

In *Jackie*, then, Larraín's ability to correlate actors in world history picks up from where he left off with earlier work. Another link is made in Larraín's broader historiographical project: from *Jackie*'s historical focus on its site of origin in the US, to the neoliberal coup of Pinochet and the absolutism of global capitalism in *No*. In order to arrive at the leadership of Ronald Reagan, and Pinochet, the US had to have the myth of JFK and the institutionalization of mediatized political coverage, incentivizing the public around a simplistic social narrative.[60]

NOTES

1. James Harvey, "Democratic Ambivalence in *Post mortem*," *Journal of Latin American Cultural Studies* 26, no. 4 (2017): 539–51.
2. Nike Jung, "History, Fiction and the Politics of Corporeality in the Dictatorship Trilogy of Pablo Larraín," in *History, Memory and Film*, eds. Jennie Carlsten and Fearghal McGarry (Basingstoke: Palgrave, 2015), 121.
3. Ibid., 129.
4. See Theodor Adorno, "Cultural Criticism and Society," in *Prisms* (Cambridge, MA: MIT Press, 1983), 17–34; Jean-François Lyotard, *Le Différend* (Minneapolis, MA: University of Minnesota, 1988).
5. Marianne Hirsch, *Family Frames: Photography, Narrative, and Postmemory* (Cambridge, MA and London: Harvard University Press, 1997).
6. Vivian Sobchack, *The Address of the Eye: A Phenomenology of Film Experience* (Princeton, NJ: Princeton University Press, 1992), 5.
7. Harvey, "Democratic Ambivalence in *Post mortem*," and James Harvey, *Jacques Rancière and the Politics of Art Cinema* (Edinburgh: Edinburgh University Press, 2018).
8. Jacques Rancière, *The Names of History* (Minneapolis, MA: University of Minnesota Press, 1994), 23.
9. Including Thomas Brown, *JFK: History of an Image* (London: I. B. Tauris, 1988); John Hellmann, *The Kennedy Obsession: The American Myth of JFK* (New York: Columbia University Press, 1997); Paul R. Henggeler, *The Kennedy Persuasion* (Chicago: Ivan R. Dee, 1995).
10. This point is central to Robert C. Smith's argument in *John F. Kennedy, Barack Obama, and the Politics of Ethnic Incorporation and Avoidance* (Albany, NY: State University of New York Press, 2013).
11. Gregory Frame, "The Myth of John F. Kennedy in Film and Television," *Film & History: An Interdisciplinary Journal* 46, no. 2 (Winter 2016): 25.
12. Ibid.
13. Indeed, Larraín seamlessly refers to this by revolving the narrative around the interview Jackie gives to *Life* magazine. Robert Drew produced *Primary* whilst editor at *Life*, thus

foregrounding the close ties the Kennedy had to the magazine. This subtly adjoins the tailored account given by Jackie to the preferential image documented in Pennebaker's observational film.
14. Dave Saunders, *Direct Cinema: Observational Documentary and the Politics of the Sixties* (New York: Wallflower Press, 2007), 189.
15. Stephen Mamber, *Cinema Verite in America: Studies in Uncontrolled Documentary* (Cambridge, MA: MIT Press), 32.
16. Jeanne Hall, "Realism as a Style in Cinema Verite: A Critical Analysis of 'Primary,'" *Cinema Journal* 30, no. 4 (Summer, 1991): 31.
17. Ibid.
18. Roland Barthes, *Mythologies* (London: Jonathan Cape, 1972).
19. William Wees, *Recycled Images: The Art and Politics of Found Footage Films* (New York: Anthology Film Archives, 1993), 45.
20. In ways very similar to those identified by Jean-Luc Comolli and Paul Narboni in their analysis of *Young Mr. Lincoln*: Cahiers du Cinéma, "John Ford's *Young Mr. Lincoln*: A Collective Text by the Editors of Cahiers du Cinéma," trans. Helene Lackner and Diana Matias, *Screen* 13, no. 3 (1972): 5–44.
21. As explored by Susan Sontag in *Regarding the Pain of Others* (London: Penguin, 2013).
22. Played by Natalie Portman, whose previous melodramatic work includes Executive Producer Darren Aronofsky's *Black Swan* (2010). Portman carries some of that performance's expressive tendencies over here, too. For a closer engagement with the expressive performance of Portman, see Lucy Bolton's *Contemporary Cinema and the Philosophy of Iris Murdoch* (Edinburgh: Edinburgh University Press, 2019).
23. Marta Zarzycka, "Outside the Frame: Reexamining Photographic Representations of Mourning," *Photography and Culture* 7 (2014): 71.
24. Karen Dunak has argued that even some of the cosmetic features of Jackie's persona need to be understood as contributing to "the shaping of broader expectations and transformations of womanhood." Karen Dunak, "Jackie Reconsidered, again: Jacqueline Kennedy and 1960s-era American womanhood," *The Sixties: A Journal of History, Politics and Culture* 11, no. 1 (2018): 62.
25. Cécile Whiting, "Andy Warhol, the Public Star and the Private Self," *Oxford Art Journal* 10, no. 2, "The 60s" (1987): 66.
26. Keith Tester, "Moral solidarity and the technological reproduction of images," *Media, Culture and Society* 17, no. 3 (1995): 478.
27. Ibid., 479.
28. Theodore White, "For President Kennedy: An Epilogue," *Life*, December 6, 1963.
29. Barbara Klinger, *Melodrama and Meaning: History, Culture, and the Films of Douglas Sirk* (Bloomington, IN: Indiana University Press, 1994), 9.
30. Tarja Laine, *Bodies in Pain: Emotion and the Cinema of Darren Aronofsky* (New York and Oxford: Berghahn Books, 2015), 137. Again, it is interesting to note that Tarja Laine is writing, here, in relation to Portman's performance in *Black Swan*.
31. Mary Ann Doane, "The Close-Up: Scale and Detail in the Cinema," *differences: A Journal of Feminist Cultural Studies* 14, no. 3 (Fall 2003): 96.
32. Ibid., 109.
33. Ibid.
34. Øyvind Vågnes, *Zaprudered: The Kennedy Assassination Film in Visual Culture* (Austin, TX: University of Texas Press, 2012).
35. Belén Vidal, "Introduction: The Biopic and its Critical Contexts," in *The Biopic in Contemporary Film Culture*, eds. Tom Brown and Belén Vidal (New York and Abingdon: Routledge, 2014), 20.

36. Jussi Parikka, *What is Media Archaeology?* (London and Malden, MA: Polity Press, 2012), 3.
37. Ibid., 108.
38. Carl Plantinga, *Moving Viewers: American Film and the Spectator's Experience* (Berkeley and Los Angeles, CA: University of California Press, 2009), 126.
39. Sobchack, *The Address of the Eye*, 6.
40. Matilda Mroz, *Temporality and Film Analysis* (Edinburgh: Edinburgh University Press, 2012), 30.
41. Davide Panagia, *The Political Life of Sensation* (Durham, NC: Duke University Press, 2009), 11.
42. Ibid.
43. Ibid., 13.
44. Michele Aaron, *Death and the Moving Image: Ideology, Iconography and I* (Edinburgh: Edinburgh University Press, 2014), 104.
45. Jung, "History, Fiction and the Politics of Corporeality in the Dictatorship Trilogy of Pablo Larraín," 125.
46. Although it might be argued that a much closer analogy can be made here, whereby Cold War American policy folds into the mapping out of Latin American governance as portrayed in his earlier films.
47. Xavier Aldana Reyes, *Horror Film and Affect: Towards a Corporeal Model of Viewership* (New York and Abingdon: Routledge, 2018), 90.
48. Steven Shaviro, *The Cinematic Body* (Minneapolis, MN: University of Minnesota Press, 1993), 114.
49. Ibid., 115.
50. Ibid., 114.
51. Ibid., 125.
52. Eleftheria Thanouli, "Post-Classical Narration: A New Paradigm in Contemporary Cinema," *New Review of Film and Television Studies* 4, no. 3 (2006): 192.
53. Jan Simons, "Complex Narratives," *New Review of Film and Television Studies* 6, no. 2 (2008): 111–26.
54. Ibid., 122.
55. Ibid., 123.
56. Paul Ricoeur, "Narrative Time," *Critical Inquiry* 7, no. 1, "On Narrative" (Autumn, 1980): 170.
57. Gilles Deleuze, *Cinema 2: The Time Image* (Minneapolis, MN: University of Minnesota Press, 1983).
58. Ibid., 81.
59. Max Horkheimer and Theodor Adorno, "The Culture Industry: Enlightenment as Mass Deception," in *Dialectic of Enlightment*, trans. Edmund Jephcott (Stanford, CA: Stanford University Press, 2002), 112.
60. With thanks to Tina Kendall, Claudia Sandberg, Tom Watson, Matilda Mroz, and Lucy Bolton.

CHAPTER 11

"When on Stage, I Am Not There, I Am Not That One"

An interview with Alfredo Castro, conducted and translated from Spanish by Arturo Márquez-Gómez

Over the last ten years, Alfredo Castro, a Chilean actor, director, and playwright, has played various roles, from a madman to a president, in Pablo Larraín's movies. Beginning with *Fuga* in 2006 and most recently *Neruda* in 2016, Castro and Larraín have built a cinematic and professional collaborative relationship exploring and bringing Chilean dramatic imagination to the forefront of critical interpretation.

Castro is a recognized international actor as well as an important figure in Chilean dramatic art, theater, and public television. As an actor in soap operas, Castro has created a tight connection with local Chilean- and Spanish-speaking audiences in diverse and mostly funny characters, for example in productions like *La fiera / The Beast* (1999), *Romané* (2000), and *Los Pincheira* (2004).

He is the founder of the theater company La Memoria (The Memory), known particularly for its innovations in theater at the start of Chile's democracy in 1989. The theater's productions of *La trilogía testimonial de Chile* (*Chile's Testimonial Trilogy*): *La manzana de Adán* (*Adam's Apple*, 1990), *Historia de la sangre* (*Blood's History*, 1991), and *Los días tuertos* (*The One-eyed Days*, 1993–4) exposed a new artistic approach to testimonies, re-elaborating narratives via dramatic theater language and live performance.

La Memoria worked with the notion of "testimony" and "non-performances," two innovative aspects that reshaped theatrical production at the end of the dictatorship in Chile. Crucial to these innovations was the theatrical adaptation by Castro of *La manzana de Adán*, a book of testimonies and photographs of transvestites, published in 1990 by photographer Paz Errázuriz and writer Claudia Donoso. According to Castro, the dramaturgy built on the idea of the testimony allowed him to reconfigure his theatrical work and recover a more quotidian language. Testimonies, therefore, permeate the scenes, actors, and spectators, transcending the scenic space. Actors are not seen as *performing* the words as much as words are seen to be performing their own worlds of meaning through the actors. These elements are crucial in *La trilogía* and they are also transferred to some of Castro's masterly performances as Raúl Peralta in *Tony Manero* from 2008, Mario Cornejo in *Post mortem* from 2012, and father Vidal in *El club* from 2015.

Castro is currently working on a performance of *Los arrepentidos* (*The Regretters*), a play by the Swedish playwright Marcus Lindeen, at the Cultural Center Gabriela Mistral (GAM) in Santiago de Chile. We thank him for sitting down with us to talk about his career in theater and cinema, and his professional relationship with Pablo Larraín, particularly his work as an actor in Larraín's films, the theatrical innovations of La Memoria, and how his notions of acting have permeated Larraín's films.

I. CONTEXTS

Arturo Márquez-Gómez: You are a recognized and respected actor and a renowned theater performer in Chile and Latin America. How did you start to work with Pablo Larraín, a rising filmmaker at the time?

Alfredo Castro: When Pablo Larraín invited me to participate in his first film, *Fuga*, I did not know him. He left the script at my place while I was working on a television program, and I recall asking an actress friend if she knew him. She told me he had worked with Mateo Iribarren, actor and playwright, and that he was a reliable person to work with.

AM: Has the medium of cinema modified or altered your acting style?

AC: In *Fuga*, I played a small character, a delirious homosexual in a psychiatric institution, a character that was based on Pedro Lemebel's text *Manifiesto*. If you watch *Fuga*, the character of Claudio is much exaggerated, overacted. A year ago, I saw it again and I told myself, "how horrible, to act that much!"

AM: But it was not that bad, it actually became a prototype for the character in *Tony Manero*, did it not?

AC: It did, but after that experience, Pablo Larraín prohibited his actors and actresses from acting. In *Tony Manero*, I found myself working with a completely different director, another person. During the first scenes we shot, he had the camera right next to my face for weeks. A very subjective camera, very close to me, a constant lurking eye on me. Pablo told me: "do not gesticulate, do not raise your voice, do not move your eyebrows, do not move your mouth, do not frown." So, after a few days, I intuited what he wanted from me, and we got the tone, the atmosphere, you know. Pablo taught me to do cinema. I have always been interested in how *Tony Manero* morphed from a photograph. As a portrait, the photo was beautiful; a guy sitting on a sofa in boxer shorts close to a window. We reproduced that photo and the atmosphere in the movie, right before the old woman is assaulted, when Raúl first helps her and then kills her.

AM: So, cinema has imposed on you a different way of acting than theater.

AC: Absolutely, of course. I think it is very interesting that after working with Pablo, different foreign productions have called me to work with them precisely because of that particular way of acting. And by that, I mean, an actor who does not speak, who physically has been associated with certain roles, and who manifests his emotions implicitly. For example, for the Venezuelan movie *From Afar* (2015), the director Lorenzo Vigas looked for actors in Argentina, Mexico, Venezuela. When he finally contacted me, he told me: "I reached out to you because you are an actor who works in silence. For this role, I need an actor who works the silence, what is not said, the subtext." The same happened with the Italian movie *È stato il figlio* (*It Was the Son*, 2012) by Daniele Ciprì, a very interesting film director. After we finished filming, he told me that when he bought *Tony Manero* he watched it many times, and that at home he edited some scenes that he liked a lot using Mozart's *Lacrimosa* as a soundtrack. Then, when he had been called to direct *È stato il figlio*, he had not directed in a long time and said that he would only do it if I was in the film as the character of the narrator. So, I went to Italy, precisely because of the performing style that I had developed with Larraín. Ciprì liked the silent work, very emotional, mysterious.

AM: It is still interesting how, for an actor of your stature, you agreed to work with an emerging director.

AC: Our relationship is mutual. I mean it. Pablo is very talented; he has an entirely idiosyncratic and poetic approach to cinema, a unique aptitude. Someone like me, who has experience working with new artists, can see the creative capability in young people. It is their eye, their sensibility, they are in charge. And as an actor, you are inclined to believe in that vision. Pablo arrived at a very important moment in my own life as an actor. I had stopped doing theater for a while; I was afraid of doing theater, because I felt that it was a very painful jail. I was not feeling comfortable, and I understood that my acting was settling into a recurring cycle: acquire a role, believe in it, etc. But in the middle of that disenchantment, I met Pablo and got to know his new, poetic vision. He just asked me to be there, in a very profound sense of the word.

II. PERFORMING AND THE THEATER OF LA MEMORIA

AM: During the transition to democracy, framed by a new cultural institutionalism, what was the intervention of La Memoria for Chilean dramatic imagination? What has been its legacy?

AC: The first play we did was *La manzana de Adán*, a text by Claudia Donoso and the photography of Paz Errázuriz. How things come together . . . It was a play that expressed my discomfort with how theater was developing during that time in Chile. Back then, I could not find a place to express my own sensibility, my own poetics as an actor and director. In *La manzana de Adán*, there is no acting because it is a testimonial text; the company—Amparo Noguera, Paulina Urrutia, Rodrigo Pérez, Verónica García Huidobro, Luis Gnecco, Maritza Estrada and I—worked for many months researching the notion by Tadeusz Kantor (1915–90) of "Zero Theater" or the "Degree Zero." I saw Kantor's *The Dead Class* (1975) in London while studying there and did not understand what he was referring to with the "zero degree of acting," but I appreciated being on scene, *in silence* (Figure II.1).

Figure II.1 Theater company La Memoria performing *La manzana de Adán* (1990). Directed by Alfredo Castro, texts by Claudia Donoso and Paz Errázuriz. From left to right: Rodrigo Pérez (Keko-Pilar), Alfredo Castro (Leo-Evelyn), and Amparo Noguera (Leyla). The original also included Paulina Urrutia (Mercedes, La Madre) and Luis Gnecco (Sr. Padilla). Courtesy of Alfredo Castro.

In *La manzana*, we were on the stage without acting. We whispered the testimonies transcribed in the book of *La manzana*. The audience was entranced. I clearly remember the reaction to the spectacle by very young journalists from the newspapers *El Mercurio* and *La Segunda*; they said that they were very touched by the *mise-en-scène*. To be honest, at that time I did not understand what they meant, but later I realized that when we were fully in scene, there was no concept of character or "other" to interpret it. Later, when I talked to Francesca Lombardo about acting and not acting, she said that in theater the actor "metabolizes" a text, one does not memorize or study it, but the text becomes part of one's blood. I have been using this idea now, in Rodrigo's and my performance of *Los arrepentidos* (2006), another testimonial work. And this is similar to what we mentioned regarding the photo that inspired *Tony Manero*. For Larraín, there is something testimonial, something about the photo that transpired in the film. It is no coincidence that Pablo and I found each other on the same path regarding creativity. The question seems to be: how do we push on from those testimonies in cinema, in theater, from the uncanny?

AM: Where can we find the testimonies in Larraín? In the case of *La manzana* the testimonies are real, they exist, they are there in the book. But in Larraín's films there is no testimony, there are fictional characters: Claudio from *Fuga*, Raúl from *Tony*, and Mario from *Post mortem*.

AC: The gay character from *Fuga*, I think, is in another place, in another order. I do not think that he belongs to the same order of characters as Raúl from *Tony* or Mario from *Post*. There is no affiliation. For those who study the cinema of Pablo, it is important to understand that after *Fuga* there is a rupture. Pablo enters a new space, the space of testimony in the wide sense of the word. What Pablo wants from me is that I testify as an actor, and the camera to testify for him, for his eye. The text and the story testify about a place, about an era. In *Post*, for example, the *coup d'état* is portrayed, from the beginning, from the lower part of a tank that drives over the trash in the city. It is brutal, but also subtle. There is no text about that testimony. In *Post* the only textual testimony is Allende's autopsy. Pablo turned it into a dramaturgy and simultaneously allowed the actors to testify about themselves, too.

AM: Has La Memoria's legacy of testimonial dramaturgy influenced Larraín?

AC: Perhaps. I prefer to talk about transmission rather than teaching. I remember Pablo's remarkable exercises in the seminars that we taught at the Center for Theater Research La Memoria. He studied with people that ended up being very creative and productive. Most of those students experimented with the concepts discussed during our seminars; in one way or another they saw themselves in those concepts. For example, the idea of the scene proposed by Lacan, the unconscious, uncanny scene. We worked on how the uncanny could be staged or acted. In the seminars, we would first go through some theory and then the students were asked to present a biographical exercise in which they had to speak about themselves. Not telling the story of their lives, but working with a biographical element, camouflaging that biographical story so that it could acquire a political dimension. We wanted them to say, "I lived these specific scenes, and I am going to stage them, in a way that one cannot perceive they are *my scenes* translated into something more political, that ultimately will connect to all our lives." I think that Pablo got the uncanny scenes spot on; he discovered something about himself. I remember one of Pablo's exercises: it was a scene about Jaime Guzmán, who Pablo met when he was a kid. He staged a memory he had of Guzmán coming over for a New Year's party during which Guzmán invites him to play chess. Pablo chose an actor who looked very similar to Guzmán. Francesca and I were very shocked. Staging that episode, Pablo could express something about himself, but at the same time he was doing something political; he was experimenting with the persona of someone who played a crucial role in installing the Constitution during the dictatorship in Chile. Pablo's strong arm was the *mise-en-scène*.

AM: So, students were asked to experiment responding to what was real, lived through drama?

AC: They wrote texts and worked with actors. They could bring along people they knew, sexual workers, grandparents, neighbors, anybody. We were persistently working with the notion of the "Real" in Lacan. We asked them to start with a reality and allow that to be turned into an "acting out" and open up to the "other scene." Think about the endings of Pablo's films, they are devastating. The endings of *El club*, *Tony Manero*, and *Post mortem* were endings that were made while filming. Pablo used to ask out loud: "How do I work this scene?" They are all his immediate, live occurrences. I am not going to attribute anything to myself, but for example that disgusting scene when Raúl shits on Goyo's suit in *Tony Manero*, Pablo did it right there, he thought of it and he did it. Sometimes, I feel like I function as a father figure in the way that I say to him: "Hey dude, do it. Just do it now." And he would answer: "but it is too much." "Just do it, it does not matter." It is always a creative dialogue, we have gotten close enough, like he and Sergio Armstrong (the cinematographer in most of Larraín's films). For *El club* we filmed three endings. In one of them, I leave the community with Sandokan to go to Santiago and we set up a sort of mafia. In another one, Sandokan is left by himself, and suddenly Pablo says to all of us, "No, I think that hell is here. They must remain here."

AM: In Larraín's work, there are different manifestations of the uncanny and the practice of the testimonial. How is this represented in Larraín's trilogy?

AC: *El club* has a different anchorage; it is based on another experience. If we consider what we have said about testimony and the very work developed by La Memoria in *La trilogía*, we could think about how that experience structured Pablo's own trilogy. I, however, think that the trilogy is not the one mentioned by his critics, but one composed by *Tony Manero*, *Post mortem*, and *El club*. Those three films define another corpus, a very powerful one, an aesthetic and political trilogy. *No*, for example, deviates toward another way of filming production, is another language, another thing. In *No*, an international superstar—Gael García Bernal—enters, and there is more money. It took six weeks to shoot. Everything changed with that movie, it is a "normal movie." If you watch the three films that I mentioned together, you will realize that there is a guiding thread, there is a recurrent aesthetic, a dramaturgy, a cinematography, a more similar language. *Tony* and *Post* worked with big production teams, but for *El club* it was a very small one. There was no make-up, no continuity; we had the basics: a camera, sound, and the actors. And that was it. We shot *El club* in three weeks. So, I see that these productions are different in the way they were born. They are the result of Pablo's elaboration of the "Real," like "let's do this right now." That is why I think that the testimonial is crucial here, because in these movies Pablo testifies about himself as an artist. On the contrary, *No* required an investigation, deeper research in history, interviews with people. The trilogy that I am speaking about emerged from Pablo, there was not a single interview. I feel as if, in the moment that the research apparatus enters, there is another kind of project, another type of cinematography. In the trilogy (*Tony*, *Post*, *El club*), one can see Pablo's *jouissance*. There is no imposing story: he shoots and that's it. It reminds me of Raúl Ruiz, because he did not give a damn about the interior or the exterior. And none of the protocols of shooting mattered to him. I see Pablo having a lot of fun filming, having laughing fits like a kid—the whole team laughs a lot—in part because of the irreverence of what we are doing.

AM: It seems then, that La Memoria has supplied not only to Larraín, but to Chilean cinema as a whole, a "theater capital." I am referring to how you and your colleagues at La Memoria created a school of acting.

AC: Yes, I think so. I think that La Memoria opened different scenarios in Chilean theater at the end of the dictatorship. At that point, when we started it, I was not fully aware of that. I was experiencing a lot of frustrations at that time. I staged *The Diary of Christopher Columbus* (1933) by Paul Claudel and the French institute supported me. But it was a total disaster. We had very few spectators, almost no audience; maybe five, ten people? A complete failure. It was during those days that I was invited by Claudia Donoso and Paz Errázuriz to see, clandestinely, the exhibition *La manzana de Adán*. When I entered the main room, on the walls were large photocopies with texts of the testimonies and photographs. I spent hours reading and looking at the portraits. I was deeply moved by them, I cried, and I said to myself: "this is our language. This is what we speak. I recognize myself in those bodies, places, origins, roots, belongings, an ideology, a poetic, and a very precarious aesthetic." After seeing the exhibition, I talked to the photographer, Paz Errázuriz, and I begged her to see if we could adapt it to theater. And when we did, after two days we staged a play. La Memoria emerged from that experience and burst with new actors. It opened a space where artists could find their own poetics. As a school of acting, it revised certain relevant concepts for people who were already professionals. It created a space where professionals could connect to new trends, and allow them to testify their own origins, social class, loves, sadness, their own biographies.

AM: So, psychoanalysis has always been present in your work.

AC: Out of respect for my friend Francesca Lombardo, I would say not exactly psychoanalysis. She always got so mad when I spoke about theater and psychoanalysis. She used to say, "Alfredo, please, I do not do psychoanalysis in the theater. I am a psychoanalyst formed in La Sorbonne, but what I do here is culture. I draw from certain ideas of psychoanalysis, philosophers, and thinkers that allow me to have a specific structure that enables me to discuss culture."

III. THE ACTOR AND THE CHARACTERS

AM: As a professional actor, which aspects of your performance technique have been tested by the work with Pablo Larraín?

AC: I would like to mention two aspects. One is the fracture of the self, and the other is the testimonial work. Regarding the first, in my work with Francesca and my own psychoanalyst, I discovered that I have worked and thought in fragments and scenes my whole life. And, that I have transformed those pieces and fragments into my own poetics. I like to believe that if one works with fragments, at some point, suddenly the uncanny, the monster, will break through.

I also think that La Memoria introduced the idea of testimony to Chilean theater. Some artists did it before us, but that was more an imitation of reality. We used testimony as the reconstruction of a scene. When I do this, I move as far away from reality as I can, and I elaborate on it as if that testimony was my own. That is the case with *Historia de la sangre*: the mapuche man, who I interviewed in jail for the play and who killed his brother, told me that he had

Figure 11.2 Theater company La Memoria performing *Historia de la sangre* (1991). Directed by Alfredo Castro, texts by Francesca Lombardo, Rodrigo Pérez, and Alfredo Castro. From left to right: Paulina Urrutia (La chica del peral); in the back, Maritza Estrada (Isabel, la Mapuche); Francisco Reyes (Papito Taca-Taca, La Gran Bestia); kneeling, Rodrigo Pérez (Cachito, El Chilenito Bueno); Pablo Schwarz (El Boxeador, Peso Hoja, Mosca, Junior); on the far right, Amparo Noguera (Rosa, la descuartizadora); above, Gaby Hernández (La Madre, Laika, La Perra). Courtesy of Alfredo Castro.

had sex with a cow, an ox, when he was eight years old. Then at eleven he did it to a hen, to a dog, whatever . . . I take that testimony home, I listen to it again, I transcribe it and I start to work on the dramaturgy of other episodes, like when he watched the stars. That is, I elaborate someone else's testimony and make it my own.

The participants of La Memoria appropriated this idea and then used it in their own works. Their work, therefore, is a testimony of other testimonies, but it is always personal and unique. Biography deeply informs that elaboration. It is like the reconstruction of a crime scene: I know where the crime happened, I can outline the body with chalk, I can describe the trajectories of the bullets, but it will never fit the real scene. Throughout my career as an actor, I have never used models, someone else's way of dress, way of speaking, or another actor's imaginary. This is a dramaturgy. Pablo, also, has never been interested in the real object. In *Post mortem*, for example, we interviewed the guy who does the autopsies in the morgue, but the interview is not related to the character at all. The same happened with the photo of the serial killer that inspired *Tony Manero*: the original guy is skinny and old like me, but the energy of the character that I performed is not in the photo, it is different.

AM: In that sense, of all the characters you have played in Larraín's work, which one has challenged you the most as an actor?

AC: I deeply love *Tony Manero*. I believe that the film, the character, everything, installed a very powerful poetic that also helped me discover who Pablo was. Discover that the main theme in all his films is impunity, that all his characters break with some kind of law and enter a realm of absolute impunity. Manero is a transgressor, a pariah, a predator who must have thought "if the dictator can kill more than 3,000 people, why can I not kill an old woman for a television, and then make a glass floor to dance in my own room?" Raúl Peralta is deprived of any ideology, moral belonging, ethics; he dances and hides from soldiers; he does not understand any of the reality he sees, shits on Goyo's suit, and he is not punished for that. In *Post mortem*, Mario Cornejo asks, "Why can't I confine these people?" For me, Raúl and Father Vidal are two roles that I like, because they live outside the law. I am interested in these characters because of the idea of an absolute transgression of all moral and ethical precepts. These are Pablo's poetics, even in *Jackie* and *Neruda*. However, I think Pablo pinpoints this idea with the characters of *Tony Manero*, *Post mortem*, and *El club*. He signals in these three characters something very intimate. Is it up to him to say what he is transgressing, the father's name? I do not know. I think it is class; he belongs to a certain class and he wants to transgress using the criminal action, the impunity, the death. Freud said it in *Oedipus*: "every society rests on a crime."

As a creator, I am very pleased to start from the idea of impunity and a transgression of the law. In spite of their madness, these characters are wonderful for what they express. Think of the character of *El club* vis-à-vis the movie *El bosque de Karadima* (Matías Lira, 2015), which premiered around the same time. There were some arguments with the other director about the premieres coinciding. And Pablo said to me, "What is the problem? They are two completely different films!" Here you see how he creates his own gaze; rather than presenting a real story about a pedophile in the Catholic Church, he represents a story of transgression, and the characters that are condemned to live there. Pablo liked it a lot, when in La Memoria we told him something that I learned from the writer Diamela Eltit, worth mentioning here. She has been a very important person in my career. Very obliquely, because I have never taken classes with her, but what she did was crucial for me. Once, she invited me to her house and showed me all the videos of the *acciones de arte* (performances) that she did with Lotty Rosenfeld in the 1980s. She showed them all to me and then said goodbye. And I thought: "What does she mean by this? Why this invitation?" Later, I understood that she was telling me that if I thought that I was modern and a transgressor, I should know about that previous artistic material, and think about how I was making changes in art at the time that I had to live in. With Pablo, perhaps, the same thing happens... One thing that I find fascinating is that the word *testimony* means "to pass on," as the stick that you pass in a relay race. Look how beautiful it is when you transfer this idea to theater: one runs with everything, gives everything—his biography, basically—all to another person who grabs it and runs off to another destination with his own biography, and he passes it to yet another. This relay race is precious to Pablo. What Francesca and Diamela gave me, I gave to Pablo, and he, surely, gave it to many young directors whose minds he has opened. So, it seems to me that the subject of testimony is what weaves us together as creators.

AM: How did you study and prepare for these transgressing characters like Claudio, Raúl Peralta, and Mario Cornejo?

AC: We did not do anything! I remember that for *Tony Manero* we read, we wrote, and then we started shooting. From one day to the next, we tried costumes, we talked, we read together, deleted some material, and then went back to shooting. It was the same with *Post mortem* and with *El club*. Our scripts and dialogue arrived the night before, and I spent a full night studying. But there is no such thing as memorizing.

AM: And what about *Fuga* and the reference to Pedro Lemebel?

AC: In Larraín's films—in the ones in which I have participated—there was no thorough pre-production. Of course, there was a wardrobe, locations, lens tests, color, camera, sound. But other than that, there was nothing, and I have gotten used to that. In other projects that I have participated in, I have had to rehearse. I have been asked to rehearse. I recently filmed a movie in Mexico with Gael García Bernal called *Museo* (Alonso Ruiz Palacios, 2018), and we had to rehearse for three days every morning with all the actors, children, families. But I could not open my mouth. I told the director, "do not worry. I can do it without rehearsing. I have gotten used to it. I work with a different methodology." From my own experience as an actor, from my readings, I am very inspired by Artaud's idea of transfiguration: the transformation of one thing into another without it ceasing to be what it is. Years ago, I wrote a text in which I spoke about the "third body" which is a theory that I use to explain the poetics of acting. It says that while acting, I need to raise a third body, a mediator between the madness of the actor and character. Both my madness and the character's require the creation of a third body to exist, to live. When I was a young actor, I often went crazy, a bit psychotic with the characters that I was working on because I was not able to leave them behind. I suffered a lot because of that, but now, as an old man, I understand that what happened was that a third body had emerged. A body that is dressed, that speaks, moves, gesticulates... I see myself in *Tony Manero*, but I am not there. I am not that person in *El club* or *Post mortem*. That person is another, it is Raúl. To me these ideas have allowed me to set a point of sanity in my own madness. For that reason, I do not believe that fiction exists, Raúl is there.

AM: Recently, in an interview for the radio of the University of Chile you spoke about acting as "lending the body." Can you comment on that idea, please?

AC: I use that idea in my classes to emphasize that whoever is on stage is not the actor. I do not like to settle in places of certainty, I prefer uncertainty. Lending the body is an artistic procedure, an operation. When on stage, I am not there, I am not that one.

Santiago de Chile, May 28, 2018

Index

A Fantastic Woman (2017), 3–4, 33, 157n
Aaron, Michelle, 205
Academy Award, 3–4, 33, 133, 148, 173
Acevedo Arriaza, Nicolás, 183
adaptation (cinematic), 8–9, 12n, 24–5, 36n, 61, 94, 147–56, 214
adaptation (theatrical), 17, 21, 24, 30, 37n, 213, 220
Adorno, Theodor, 210
aestheticization of politics, 8, 132, 135–7, 139, 140, 142; *see also* Benjamin, Rancière
Adriazola, Carolina, 2
Agamben, Giorgio, 140
Agüero, Ignacio, 85, 135
Aguirre, Manuel, 121, 122
AIDS, 16, 24, 25–6
Air Force One, 61, 200
Alberdi, Maite, 15–16
Aldana Reyes, Xavier, 207
Alessandri, Arturo, 44, 64n, 191n
Allende, Salvador, 40, 41, 76, 79–80, 118, 132, 196
  autopsy, 6, 33, 75, 76, 77, 105, 120, 123, 129n, 217
  corpse, 79–80, 106
  death, 75, 78, 162
  era, 98, 105, 118, 188
  exhumation, 129n
  pre-Allende era, 91, 97
  supporters, 46, 164
  see also Unidad Popular
Alonso, Lisandro, 103
Alonso, Marcelo, 45, 46, 49, 56, 171
Althusser, Louis, 94, 140; *see also* Althusserian Marxism
Althusserian Marxism 94; *see also* Althusser
American Civil War, 202
Amour (2012), 173
anamorphic lenses, 10, 82, 100–1, 161, 169, 170–1, 173, 174, 191n
Ángel Negro (2000), 127–8n
anti-biopic, 10, 180; *see also* biopic
archival images, 7, 9, 12, 82, 84, 134, 141, 147, 151–4, 163, 164, 166, 167, 168, 202–4, 205, 206
archive *see* archival images
Argento, Darío, 15
Armstrong, Sergio, 166, 176n, 191n, 218
Aronofsky, Darren, 201, 211n
Arrate, Jorge, 41
Arriagada, Genaro, 134–5, 158n
Artaud, Antonin, 30, 223
Asociación de Familiares de Detenidos Desaparecidos (AFDD), 137

Atallah, Niles, 89, 110n
audience, 5, 7, 28, 32, 64n, 69–73, 79, 85n, 173–4, 213; *see also* festival circuit
Aurora (2014), 32, 36n
Avelar, Idelber, 114
Aylwin, Patricio, 9, 54–5, 81, 87n, 134, 154, 163

Baby Shower (2012), 128n
Badham, John, 6, 26, 38, 73
Balló, Jordi, 123, 130n
Bañados, Patricio, 9, 81, 134, 150, 153, 154, 155
Barraza Toledo, Vania, 8, 16, 18, 92, 102, 104, 115, 123, 163
Barril, Claudia, 169
Barthes, Roland, 198; *see also* Barthian
Barthian, 21; *see also* Barthes
Baudry, Jean-Louis, 94
Bazin, André, 69, 72–3, 84, 87n
Bechis, Marco, 78, 115
Benjamin, Walter, 8, 84, 132, 135–6, 138; *see also* aestheticization of politics, Rancière
Beteta, Juan José, 182, 193n
Bettini, Adrián, 148, 157n
Beville, Maria, 117
Bicycle Thieves (1948), 79
Bildungsroman, 156
biopic, 11, 12, 178, 180, 202; *see also* anti-biopic
Bize, Matías, 2, 88n, 110n
Bleu (*Blue*, 1993), 15
Blocks (2010), 25
body horror, 8, 115–16, 120, 207; *see also* Gothic horror
body politic, 8, 39, 40, 58, 61–2, 106
Bongers, Wolfgang, 48, 99–100, 167
Bordwell, David, 73
Borges, Jorge Luis, 11; *see also* Borgesian
Borgesian, 180; *see also* Borges
Bravo, Sergio, 2, 89
Breathless (1960), 180
Brecht, Bertolt, 135

Brewer, John, 83
Brown, Christopher, 202
Buckland, Warren, 74
Burns, Aaron, 128n
Butler, Judith, 74–5

Caetano, Adrián, 50
Caiozzi, Silvio, 115
Caleuche (2012), 128n
Camiruaga, Gloria, 19
capitalism, 6, 12, 45, 48, 49, 56, 63n, 74, 131, 132, 139–40, 143, 151, 168–9, 175n, 210
  disaster capitalism, 40, 42, 46–8, 49, 51, 52, 56, 58–61
  high-density capitalism, 5, 39, 49–50, 52, 54, 55–8, 60
  see also Klein, neoliberalism
capitalist *see* capitalism
Carandiru massacre, 9
Carrera, Pablo, 110n
Carter, Jimmy, 82
Casa Particular (*Brothel*, 1990), 19
Casas, Francisco, 20
Castro, Alfredo, 4, 5, 6, 10, 16–18, 19, 21, 24–5, 27–33, 38–9, 41–3, 45, 48, 51–2, 53, 55, 56, 57, 59, 61, 62n, 65n, 73, 75, 98, 117, 134, 148, 163, 170, 208, 213–14
  interview with, 214–21
Catholic Church, 10, 56, 161–2, 169, 222
Cavallo, Ascenio, 2, 86n, 114
Central Nacional de Informaciones (CNI), 148
Chaskel, Pedro, 2, 89
chiaroscuro, 11, 178
Chicago boys, 6, 40; *see also* Chicago School, Klein, Milton, neoliberalism
Chicago School 6, 40–1, 52, 56; *see also* Chicago boys, Klein, Milton, neoliberalism
"Chile, la alegría ya viene" ("Chile, happiness is coming"), 51, 66, 139, 141, 147, 150, 157n, 165

Chilean Communist Party, 10–11, 12, 24, 43–4, 177–8, 180, 182–9, 190n
Chilean Communist Youth Organization *see* Juventudes Comunistas
Chion, Michel, 124–5
CIA, 40
Cinema Law No. 19.981, 1
cinema vérité, 197
Ciprì, Daniele, 215
Cisneros, James, 164, 175n
Claudel, Paul, 219
Close-Up (1990), 82
close-up (technique), 26, 73, 78, 105, 118, 133, 164, 169, 201, 205
Cohen, Gregory, 133
Cohen, Jeffrey, 116
Colectivo de Acciones de Arte (CADA), 135
communist women, 186–8
communist youth, 183–4, 188; *see also* Juventudes Comunistas
Concertación, 53, 99, 131–2, 134, 136, 155, 163–4, 176n
consensual democracy, 132
consumerism, 52, 90, 164
contre-jour lighting, 179
Cortínez, Verónica, 71
Costa-Gavras, 6
counter-cinema, 93–4, 99
coup d'état, 3, 5, 6, 12, 20, 40, 42, 45–7, 60, 61, 63n, 75–8, 79, 80, 89, 92, 98–100, 102, 103–4, 106, 107, 108–9, 115, 118, 123, 125–6, 129n, 131, 132, 133, 141, 144n, 149, 151, 162, 163, 166, 188, 210, 217; *see also* dictatorship, Pinochet
Cronenberg, David, 207; *see also* Cronenbergian
Cronenbergian, 28; *see also* Cronenberg
Cronovich, Paula, 135
crosscutting *see* editing
cueca, 24, 30, 137
Cultural Center Gabriela Mistral (GAM), 214
cutting *see* editing

Dardenne, Jean-Pierre and Luc, 2
Dargis, Manohla, 151
"Das Unheimliche" ("The Uncanny," 1919), 116
Dávila, Juan, 19
Dawson Isla 10 (2009), 133
Dayan, Daniel, 90, 101
de Aguirre, Jaime, 147
de Dios Larraín, Juan, 3
de Luca, Tiago, 72–3
de Sica, Vittorio, 79
Deleuze, Gilles, 8, 138–9, 142–3, 145n, 209; *see also* Guattari, war machine
Delgado, Teresa, 135
Déotte, Jean-Louis, 140
Derrida, Jacques, 167; *see also* Derridean
Derridean, 167; *see also* Derrida
Descendants (2009), 128n
dictatorship, 1, 2–3, 4, 5–8, 10, 15, 16, 19, 21, 24, 25, 27–8, 30, 31, 33, 36n, 39, 40–2, 44, 45, 47–8, 51–3, 55, 56, 59, 69, 74, 78, 80, 82, 85n, 92, 98, 103, 107, 109, 113–14, 127, 128n, 132–4, 137, 139, 142, 143, 147–50, 154–6, 161, 163–8, 169, 174, 193n, 196–7, 213, 218, 219; *see also coup d'état*, Pinochet, post-dictatorship
dictatorship trilogy, 1, 3, 5, 6, 7, 8, 15, 18, 28, 31–2, 38–9, 62n, 64n, 69–70, 72, 73–85, 88n, 102, 104, 114–15, 132, 133–4, 163, 169, 196, 209, 219
Castro's alternative trilogy, 32, 219
see also synecdochic series
diegesis, 47, 53–4, 82, 101, 124, 132, 137, 143, 198, 202, 204, 205, 207
diegetic camera, 81
diegetic time, 76, 143, 208
extra-diegetic, 6, 77, 143, 205
non-diegetic music, 11, 179
non-diegetic sound, 46
diegetic *see* diegesis
Dirección de Instituto Nacional (DINA), 50, 75, 85n, 149
Dirty Love (2009), 128n
dispositif, 132, 140–3, 198

Doane, Mary Ann, 201, 205
Donoso, Claudia, 20, 30–1, 213, 216, 220
Donoso, Silvia, 96
Drew, Robert, 210n
Dreyfuss, Richard, 168
Dzero, Irina, 156

È stato il figlio (*It Was the Son*, 2012), 215
economic miracle, 19, 132
editing, 7, 44, 53–5, 76, 82, 90–5, 97, 100–3, 105–6, 108, 126, 147, 169, 171, 179, 202–4
   180-degree rule, 90, 95, 101
   continuity editing, 9, 91, 95–6, 100–2, 106, 147, 154
   crosscutting, 12, 58
   extreme jump cuts, 5, 12, 44, 53–4, 56
   eyeline matches, 90, 95
   graphic match, 90
   jump cuts, 179, 180, 186, 191n
   match on action, 54–5, 90
   see also montage, remediation
Eisenhower, Dwight D., 197
El baño (2005), 133
El bosque de Karadima (2015), 32, 174, 176n, 222
El chacal de Nahueltoro (1969), 85n
El cielo, la tierra y la lluvia (2008), 64n
El club (*The Club*, 2015), 1, 5, 10, 28–9, 32, 33, 38, 43, 44, 55–8, 60, 161–2, 169–74, 214, 218, 219, 222, 223
El diario de Agustín (2008), 85
El happening de las gallinas (*The Happening of the Hens*, 1974), 19
El huésped (2005), 128n
El infarto del alma (*Soul's Infarct*, 1994), 4, 16, 19, 21–3
El pejesapo (*The Goosefish*, 2007), 2
El plebiscito (play), 8–9, 132, 147–9, 151, 154–6
Eliash, Elisa, 110n
Elm Street (1995), 202
Elsaesser, Thomas, 74, 83
Eltit, Diamela, 4, 21–3, 35n, 222–3
Ema (2019), 12n

Engelbert, Manfred, 71
Errázuriz, Paz, 4, 16–19, 21–3, 25, 28, 30–1, 33, 34n, 213, 216, 220
Escuela de Cine de Chile (Film School of Chile), 2
Esposito, Roberto, 167, 168
Estrada, Maritza, 216, 221
Eternal Blood (2002), 128n

Fabula, 3
Farías, Roberto, 10, 33, 57, 171
Fassbinder, Rainer Werner, 201
Faúndez, Rosa, 31
Feinstein, Adam, 11, 183, 192n
Fénix Film Award, 29, 37n
Fernández Almendras, Alejandro 2, 110n
Fernández, Álvaro, 115
Fernández, Carolina, 182
festival circuit, 7, 33, 64n, 70–1; *see also* film festivals, audience
film festivals, 70–2, 173–4
   Berlin International Film Festival, 173, 175n
   Cannes Film Festival, 133, 148, 174
   Cartagena Film Festival, 4, 15
   Cinema for Peace Award, 133
   Havana Film Festival, 133
   International Film Festival of Viña del Mar, 1
   National Board of Review 133
   Rotterdam Film Festival, 173
   see also festival circuit, audience
filters, 10, 161, 176n
   blue, 169, 170, 173, 176n
   day-for-night, 55, 56
Flores, Carlos, 73
Fonda, Jane, 168
Forch, Juan, 135
Ford, John, 202
Foucault, Michel, 140
Frame, Gregory, 197
Francia, Aldo, 16, 85n, 89
Frecuencia Mod, 30, 36n
free market *see* neoliberalism
Frei, Eduardo, 96

Freud, Sigmund, 116, 222; *see also* Freudian slip
Freudian slip, 181; *see also* Freud
Friedman, Milton, 6, 40, 61, 132; *see also* Chicago boys, Chicago School, neoliberalism
Friedmanian, 46, 61; *see also* Friedman
From Afar (2015), 215
Fuga (2006), 1, 4, 5, 12, 15–17, 19, 21–5, 28, 33, 34n, 38, 40, 42, 43, 55, 58–60, 133, 213, 214, 217, 223
Fuguet, Alberto, 2
funding, 70–1, 173

galgo (grayhound), 10, 33, 56, 170–1, 172, 176n
Garage Olimpo (*Olympic Garage*, 1999), 78, 115
García Bernal, Gael, 10, 42, 43, 52, 54, 82, 132, 148, 149, 164, 180, 181, 219, 223
García Canclini, Néstor, 71
García Huidobro, Verónica, 216
García Martín, Joseba, 56
Gaspar, Alejandro, 101
Gaviria, Víctor, 55
Generación 2000 see novísimos
Gerwig, Greta, 200
Getino, Octavio, 95, 108
Gilliam, Terry, 15, 36n
Giridharadas, Anand, 12n, 61
Gloria (2013), 3
Gnecco, Luis, 10, 32, 43, 45, 54, 134, 158n, 165, 177, 216
Godard, Jean-Luc, 180, 191n
Goic, Alejandro, 56, 165, 170
González Videla, Gabriel, 10, 42–5, 51, 59, 177, 184, 188, 189n, 190n, 193n
Gothic horror, 116, 118, 127; *see also* body horror
Granado, Alberto, 181
grayhound *see galgo*
Green Celery (2013), 128n
Griffith, D. W., 202
Grupo Cine Experimental, 7, 89

Guattari, Félix, 8, 138–9, 142–3, 145n; *see also* Deleuze, war machine
Guevara, Ernesto "Che," 181, 192n
Gundermann, Christian, 50
Guzmán, Jaime, 218
Guzmán, Patricio, 2, 98

Habeas Corpus (2015), 169, 176n
Haneke, Michael, 173
Harvey, David, 132
Harvey, James, 102, 103, 104, 107, 108, 162, 173
Haynes, Todd, 201
Heath, Stephen, 90, 91, 94, 101, 108
Hechos consumados (*Accomplished Facts*, 1981), 16
Hernández, Gaby, 221
Hidalgo, Coke, 128n
Hidden in the Woods (2012), 128n
Hirsch, Marianne, 18
Historia de la sangre (*Blood's History*, 1992), 17, 31, 213, 220–1
Hitchcock, Alfred, 101
Hollywood
  cinema, 12, 21, 26, 28, 30, 64n, 76, 90–1, 93, 95–6, 97, 99, 107, 108, 133, 178–9, 191n, 209
  icon, 42, 73
  non-Hollywood cinema, 70, 85n
homosexual *see* homosexuality
homosexuality, 16, 24, 27–8, 34n, 167, 178, 185, 189, 194n, 214; *see also loca*, sexual diversity, transvestitism
Horkheimer, Max, 210
horror film, 8, 113–27, 127–8n, 206
Huacho (2009), 2
Hubner, Laura, 120
Hurley, Kelly, 120
Hurt, John, 208

Ibáñez del Campo, Carlos, 193n
Illanes, Pablo, 128n
impunity, 10, 41–2, 74, 85n, 109, 124, 134, 155, 161–2, 164, 165, 167, 169, 171–3, 174, 175n, 222

In the Line of Fire (1993), 202, 204
indignados movement, 135
Iribarren, Mateo, 214

Jackie (2016), 1, 10, 11–12, 33, 60–1, 197, 198–210, 222
Jackson, Michael, 141
Janáček, Leoš, 9
Jara Hantke, Álvaro, 183
Jarmusch, Jim, 2
JFK (1991), 9
JFK *see* Kennedy, John F.
jingle *see* "Chile, la alegría ya viene"
Jofré, Cristián, 9
Johnson, Lyndon B., 206, 207, 209
Johnson, Mariana, 8, 118, 125, 126
Jones, Timothy, 116, 117
Jung, Berenike, 196
Justiniano, Gonzalo, 115
Juventudes Comunistas (JJCC), 183, 188–9, 190n

Kantaris, Geoffrey, 50
Kantor, Tadeusz, 216
Katia Kabanova, 9
Kaulen, Patricio, 85n
Kaurismäki, Aki, 2
Kennedy, Bobby, 204
Kennedy, Jacqueline, 11, 12, 60, 197–8, 199–201, 203, 204, 206, 209, 210–11n
Kennedy, John F., 11, 197–8, 200, 202, 205–6, 208, 210
Kiarostami, Abbas, 82
Kieślowski, Krzysztof, 15
King, John, 94
Klein, Naomi, 40, 49, 56, 61, 132; *see also* Kleinian, shock doctrine
Kleinian, 43; *see also* Klein, shock doctrine
Kubrick, Stanley, 15

l'art pour l'art, 135–6
La conquista de América (*The Conquest of America*, 1989), 20
La esquina es mi corazón: Crónica urbana (*The Corner Is My Heart: Urban Chronicles*, 1995), 25

La fiera (*The Beast*, 1999), 213
La frontera (1991), 2
La hora de los hornos (1968), 108
La manzana de Adán (Adam's Apple, 1990), 16, 17, 19–21, 22, 24–5, 27, 30–1, 213, 216–17, 220
La Memoria (research center), 17–18, 29, 31–2, 217–19, 221–2
La Memoria (theater company), 4, 5, 16, 17–18, 28–32, 34n, 213–14, 216–22
La Moneda, 43, 77, 148, 162, 167
La nana (*The Maid*, 2009), 2
La noche de los lápices (*Night of the Pencils*, 1987), 115
La pasión de Michelangelo (*The Passion of Michelangelo*, 2013), 25
La sagrada familia (*The Sacred Family*, 2007), 2, 88n
Lacan, Jacques, 218; *see also* Lacanian
Lacanian, 19, 90, 92, 94, 102, 123, 201; *see also* Lacan
Lacrimosa, 215
Lang, Fritz, 173
Largo viaje (1967), 85n
Larraín, Esteban, 25
Larrain, Estefania, 191n
Larraín, Hernán, 13n, 144n
Larraín, Ricardo, 2
Las Yeguas del Apocalipsis, 19, 36n
Lavanderos, Fernando, 110n
Lazzarato, Maurizio, 141
Leiva, Gonzalo, 19
Lelio, Sebastián, 2, 3, 33, 88n, 110n, 157n
Lemebel (2019), 25
Lemebel, Pedro, 4, 16, 18, 19, 20, 23–5, 27–8, 33, 34n, 35n, 36n, 188–9, 214, 223
lenses *see* anamorphic lenses
Leppe, Carlos, 19
Levi, Mica, 11, 199, 209
Libertador Simón Bolívar (*The Liberator Simón Bolívar*, 1994), 19
Life (magazine), 11, 197, 200, 208, 210n
Lindeen, Marcus, 214
Lira, Matías, 32, 176n, 222

Littín, Miguel, 2, 85n, 89, 98, 133
loca, 16, 24, 25, 27, 28, 34n; see also homosexuality, sexual diversity, transvestitism
Loco afán: Crónicas de sidario (*Wild Urge: Chronicles from the AIDS Asylum*, 1996), 25
Lombardo, Francesca, 30, 32, 217, 218, 220, 221, 223
LOMO Soviet lenses *see* anamorphic lenses
Los arrepentidos (*The Regretters*), 214, 217
Los días del arcoíris (*The Rainbow Days*), 148, 157n
Los días tuertos (*The One-Eyed Days*, 1993), 17, 31, 213
Los Pincheira (2004), 213
Luttwak, Edward, 54

MacCabe, Colin, 94
Machuca (2004), 2, 133
McLuhan, Marshall, 202
Madre (2016), 128n
Mamber, Stephen, 197
Manifiesto. Hablo por mi diferencia (*Manifesto. I Speak from My Difference*), 4, 23–5, 35n, 214
Mann, Thomas, 135
Manns, Patricio, 131
Marín, Gladys, 188–9
Marín, Rodrigo, 89, 110n
Martel, Lucrecia, 103
Martin-Jones, David, 71
Matar a todos (2007), 133
Matheou, Demetrios, 105
Matte, Magdalena, 13n, 144n
Maysles, Albert, 197
Maza, Gonzalo, 2
Metz, Christian, 94
military coup *see* coup d'état
Mille Plateaux, 138
minimalism, 7, 90, 100, 102–3
minimalist *see* minimalism
Missing (1982), 6
Monroe, Marilyn, 21, 198

montage, 9, 47, 76, 131, 137, 143, 147, 154, 203, 204; *see also* editing, remediation
Montañez, María Soledad, 71
Montero, Pascal, 142
monumental temporality, 5, 39, 43, 45, 51–6, 58, 60
Morales, Francesc, 128n
Morales, Héctor, 6, 50
Morán, Mercedes, 180
Moreno, Sebastián, 169
morgue, 6, 76–7, 79–80, 98–9, 102, 104, 118, 119–22, 124, 126, 221
Moulain, Tomás, 113
Mozart, Wolfgang Amadeus, 215
Mulvey, Laura, 82, 94
Murray, Christopher, 110n
Museo (2018), 223

Naficy, Hamid, 82
Nagib, Lúcia, 72–3
narratocracy, 205, 207
neoliberal *see* neoliberalism
neoliberalism, 5, 6, 7, 9, 10, 12, 16, 39–62, 63n, 74, 83, 92, 99, 103, 106, 107, 109, 112n, 113–14, 116, 127, 132, 134, 139, 141, 143, 151, 162, 164–5, 167–9, 174, 196, 210; *see also* capitalism, Chicago School, Klein, shock doctrine
neorealism, 7, 71, 72–3, 78, 82, 83–4, 86n, 88n, 94
neo-neorealism, 84
see also realism
Neruda (2016), 1, 5, 10, 11, 12, 33, 38, 42–5, 51, 53, 177–89, 191n, 192n, 194n, 213, 222
Neruda, Pablo, 10, 11, 42, 43, 60, 177, 178–9, 180, 181, 183, 188, 189, 190n, 193n
New Chilean Cinema *see* Nuevo Cine Chileno
New Latin American Cinema, 8, 115
Newest Chilean cinema *see novísimo cine chileno*

No (2012), 1, 5, 6, 7, 8–9, 10, 11, 12, 15, 32, 33, 38, 42, 44, 48, 51–5, 58, 60, 64n, 65–6n, 69, 80–4, 103, 115, 131–43, 147–56, 157n, 160n, 161–9, 173–4, 175n, 196, 197, 210, 219
   adaptation, 147–56
   as aesthetic politicization, 135–7
   as apparatus, 140–3
   as war machine, 138–40
Noguera, Amparo, 26, 32, 49, 121, 187, 216, 221
noir, 11, 178–9
   neo-*noir*, 11, 178
non-diegetic *see* diegesis
North America *see* United States of America
Northern Empire *see* United States of America
novísimo cine chileno, 2, 15, 33, 71, 86n, 89, 90, 98, 114
novísimos see novísimo cine chileno
Nuevo Cine Chileno, 2, 71, 85n

Olguín, Jorge, 127–8n
Olivera, Héctor, 115
ollas comunes, 6
Ortega, Víctor Hugo, 150
Ossa, Carlos, 95
Oudart, Jean-Pierre, 90

Palacio Cousiño, 44, 64n
Panagia, Davide, 205
Parikka, Jussi, 202
Parker, Nate, 202
Pauls, Gastón, 58
Pedro Lemebel: Corazón en Fuga (*Pedro Lemebel: Fleeting Heart*, 2008), 25
Peirano, María Paz, 70, 174
Peirano, Pedro, 132, 151, 158n, 159n, 168
Pennebaker, D. A., 197, 210–11n
Pérez, Rodrigo, 30, 216, 221
Petersen, Wolfgang, 202
Piatti-Farnell, Lorna, 117
Piñera, Sebastián, 13n, 45, 51–2, 59, 144n

Pino-Ojeda, Waleska, 115, 123
Pinochet coup *see* coup d'état
Pinochet dictatorship *see* dictatorship
Pinochet, Augusto, 1, 6, 26, 30, 40, 41, 45, 58, 60, 62–3n, 67n, 82, 87n, 132, 141, 142, 147–50, 154, 155–6, 163–4, 167–9, 176n, 184, 196, 210, 222
Pisagua (prisoner camp), 184, 188, 193n
Pizza, birra, faso (1997), 50
Plana, Cristián, 32
plebiscite, 6, 7, 9, 15, 51, 53, 82, 83, 132–3, 134, 138, 139, 142, 147–54, 155–6, 160n, 164, 167, 168, 196
Poblete, Elsa, 26
Poblete, Juan, 48, 51, 72, 83, 173
Politisierung, 135
Pope Francis, 56
Pope John Paul II, 82
Portman, Natalie, 11, 61, 199, 203–4, 211n
Post mortem (*Post Mortem*, 2010), 1, 3, 4, 6, 7, 8, 12, 15, 19, 38, 42, 45–8, 64n, 69, 75–80, 84, 89–90, 92–3, 98–109, 114–15, 116–27, 129n, 133, 162, 163, 196, 197, 206, 208, 214, 217, 218, 219, 221, 222, 223
post-dictatorship cinema *see* post-dictatorship
post-dictatorship, 4, 16, 19, 29, 51–2, 54–5, 81, 83, 87n, 90, 91–2, 99, 108, 109, 113–14, 116, 118, 127, 132–3, 148, 150, 156, 162, 163, 164, 167, 168, 216; *see also* dictatorship, Pinochet
postmemory, 16, 18, 28, 29, 30, 196
presidential palace *see* La Moneda
Primary (1960), 197, 210–11n
Profondo Rosso (*Deep Red*, 1975), 15
Prófugos (*Fugitives*, 2011–13), 9, 32
Psycho (1960), 101

Qüense, Verónica, 25

Radrigán, Juan, 16
Ramírez, Christian, 104, 119

Rancière, Jacques, 8, 10, 72, 132, 136, 138, 140, 142, 161–2, 169, 173, 196
  distribution of the sensible, 10, 136, 162, 166, 169, 174
  mental image, 173
  poetics of knowledge, 196, 205
  "Politics of Aesthetics," 9, 132, 161
  see also aestheticization of politics, Benjamin
Raunig, Gerald, 138
Reagan, Ronald, 82, 210
realism, 7, 69, 71–3, 78, 81–2, 83–4, 87n, 88n, 89, 91, 95, 97, 100, 105, 109, 180; see also neorealism
Reber, Dierdra, 168
reception see audience
Reeve, Christopher, 168
referendum see plebiscite
remediation, 152, 202–4, 208; see also editing, montage
Reposi, Joanna, 25
Reyes, Francisco, 221
Richard, Nelly, 4, 20, 92, 103, 105, 112n, 114, 122, 126, 133–4, 175n
Richie, Lionel, 141
Ricoeur, Paul, 208
Rivas, Marialy, 25
Rojas Mira, Fedora, 186
Rojas, Lucio, 128n
Román, Shenda, 94
Romané (2000), 213
Romney, Jonathan, 77
Rosenfeld, Lotty, 222
Rothberg, Michael, 104
Ruiz Palacios, Alonso, 223
Ruiz, Raúl, 2, 7, 85n, 89, 91–2, 93–8, 99, 100, 102, 104, 106, 107–9, 219

Saavedra González, María Lorena, 57
Sábado (*Saturday*, 2003), 2, 88n
sadomodernism, 173
Salgado, Alfonso, 185
Salinas, Horacio, 131
Salles, Walter, 181
San Miguel prison, 9

Sánchez, Carlos, 189
Santa Cruz, José M., 104, 107
Saturday Night Fever (1977), 6, 26, 30, 38, 42, 49, 65n, 73, 74
Schatz, Thomas, 179
Scherson, Alicia, 2, 89, 110n
Schoonover, Karl, 73, 83, 84
Schroeder, Esteban, 133
Schwarz, Pablo, 221
Scott, A. O., 69
Se arrienda (*For Rent*, 2005), 2
secret police see Dirección de Instituto Nacional
Semler, Willy, 59
September 11, 1973 see coup d'état
Sepúlveda, José Luis, 2
Sepúlveda, Rodrigo, 32, 36n
sexual abuse, 57, 170–1, 194n
sexual dissidence see sexual diversity
sexual diversity, 11, 16, 20, 24–5, 27–8, 30, 34n, 182–3, 184–5, 188, 189, 190n, 193n, 194n; see also homosexuality, *loca*, transvestitism
sexual minorities see sexual diversity
sexual violence see sexual abuse
Shaviro, Steven, 207
shock doctrine, 40, 43, 46, 59, 61, 132; see also capitalism, Klein, neoliberalism
Sieveking, Alejandro, 94, 170
signifier/signified, 91, 93–4, 198
silence see soundtrack
Silva, Michael, 183
Silva, Sebastián, 2, 89
Silverman, Kaja, 90, 91, 93–4, 101, 108
Simons, Jan, 208
simulacrum, 8, 52, 140, 156
Sipprelle, David, 92
Sirk, Douglas, 201; see also Sirkean
Sirkean, 204; see also Sirk
Skármeta, Antonio, 9, 132, 134, 147–8, 154–6, 157n, 175n
Solanas, Pino, 95, 108
Soto, Helvio, 89
sound see soundtrack

soundtrack, 11, 30, 36–7n, 46–7, 77, 78, 91, 123, 124–5, 127, 176n, 191n, 200, 202, 208, 209, 215–6
   off-screen sound, 101, 124–5
   see also diegesis
Soviet lenses see anamorphic lenses
Soza, José, 57, 171
Stagnaro, Bruno, 50
Stefan v/s Kramer, 173
Stone, Oliver, 9
suture see editing
synecdochic series, 5, 38–43, 61; see also dictatorship trilogy

Tagle, Marcial, 47, 49
Tarr, Béla, 2
Taylor, Elizabeth, 20, 21, 25
Taylor, Ella, 178
Tester, Keith, 199, 209
testimonio see testimony
testimony, 17, 20–1, 30–2, 98, 106, 115, 137, 139, 141, 143, 171, 196–7, 206, 209, 213–14, 216–21, 223
Thakkar, Amit, 46, 104, 107
Thanouli, Eleftheria, 208
Thatcher, Margaret, 82
The Adventures of Baron Munchausen (1988), 36
The Dead Class (1975), 216
The Diary of Christopher Columbus, 219
The Motorcycle Diaries (2004), 181, 192n
The Shining (1980), 15
The Shock Doctrine see shock doctrine
The Theater and Its Double, 30
The True American (forthcoming), 12n
The Work of Art in the Age of Its Technological Reproducibility, 135
third body, 30, 223
Third Cinema, 91–2, 95, 102
Tironi, Eugenio, 81, 135
Tony Manero (2008), 1, 3, 4, 5, 6, 7, 8, 15, 16, 19, 21, 23, 25–30, 37n, 38–40, 42, 48–51, 64n, 65n, 69, 73–5, 78, 84, 102, 115, 125, 133, 163, 173, 196, 197, 206, 208, 214–15, 217, 218, 219, 221, 222, 223–4

Torres Leiva, José Luis, 64n, 110n
transition see post-dictatorship
transvestite see transvestitism
transvestitism, 19–21, 25, 30, 213; see also *loca*, sexual diversity
Trauma (2017), 128n
Travolta, John, 6, 25, 26–8, 42, 73
Tres tristes tigres (1968), 7, 85n, 89–90, 91, 93–8, 104, 106, 107–9
Trilogía testimonial de Chile (*Chile's Testimonial Trilogy*), 17, 30, 31, 213, 219
Truman, Harry, 43–4
Tuckerman, Nancy, 200, 203
Twelve Monkeys (1995), 15
Twenty Love Poems and a Song of Despair, 181, 184, 192n
tyranny of velocity, 50, 54, 56

uncanny, the, 8, 116, 119, 125, 127, 162, 217, 218, 219, 220; see also "Das Unheimliche"
Unidad Popular, 76, 77, 98, 108, 118; see also Allende
United States of America, 5–6, 9, 12, 38, 39–46, 48–50, 52, 58–9, 60–2, 64n, 65n, 70, 93, 165, 168, 179, 189n, 197–8, 202, 206, 209, 210
   US interventionism, 5, 40, 44, 45, 58
Urrutia, Carolina, 3, 74, 100, 114, 124, 126, 160n, 174
Urrutia, Paulina, 216, 221
US see United States of America

Vadell, Jaime, 44, 46, 56, 94, 171
Vågnes, Øyvind, 202
Valladares, Patricio, 128n
Vallejo, Camila, 189
Valparaíso mi amor (*Valparaiso My Love*, 1969), 16, 85n
Vega, Daniela, 4
Venezia 70 Future Reloaded (2013), 12n
Vicuña, Benjamín, 4, 23, 58
Vigas, Lorenzo, 215
Village People, 27
Villagra, Nelson, 94

Virilio, Paul, 50
voiceover, 43, 45, 179, 180, 182, 186, 203
von Hummel, Alexandra, 32
von Trier, Lars, 173

war machine, 8, 132, 138–40, 142, 143, 145n; *see also* Deleuze, Guattari
Warhol, Andy, 11, 12, 198–9, 201–2, 205, 209
"We Are the World" (campaign), 141
Weerasethakul, Apichatpong, 2
Weigel, Moira, 173
Wells, Robert, 47, 67n, 108, 134
Welsh, Brian, 44
White House, 60–1, 200, 203, 209
  tour, 200, 203, 209
White, Rob, 155
White, Theodore H., 11
Whiting, Cécile, 199, 201
Wollen, Peter, 94
Wood, Andrés, 2, 133
Wood, Robin, 115
Wright, Sarah, 170, 171, 176n

Young and Wild (2012), 25

Zapruder video, 207
Zaprudered: The Kennedy Assassination Film in Visual Culture, 202
Zarzycka, Marta, 199, 201
Zavattini, Cesare, 72
Zegers, Antonia, 10, 46, 53, 56, 98, 117, 134, 149, 164, 170
Zero Theater, 216

EU representative:
Easy Access System Europe
Mustamäe tee 50, 10621 Tallinn, Estonia
Gpsr.requests@easproject.com

www.ingramcontent.com/pod-product-compliance
Lightning Source LLC
Chambersburg PA
CBHW070345240426
43671CB00013BA/2413